Studies in the Dead Sea Scrolls and Related Literature

Peter W. Flint and Martin G. Abegg Jr., General Editors

The Dead Sea Scrolls have been the object of intense interest in recent years, not least because of the release of previously unpublished texts from Qumran Cave 4 since the fall of 1991. With the wealth of new documents that have come to light, the field of Qumran studies has undergone a renaissance. Scholars have begun to question the established conclusions of the last generation; some widely held beliefs have withstood scrutiny, but others have required revision or even dismissal. New proposals and competing hypotheses, many of them of an uncritical and sensational nature, vie for attention. Idiosyncratic and misleading views of the Scrolls still abound, especially in the popular press, while the results of solid scholarship have yet to make their full impact. At the same time, the scholarly task of establishing reliable critical editions of the texts is nearing completion. The opportunity is ripe, therefore, for directing renewed attention to the task of analysis and interpretation.

Studies in the Dead Sea Scrolls and Related Literature is a new series designed to address this need. In particular, the series aims to make the latest and best Dead Sea Scrolls scholarship accessible to scholars, students, and the thinking public. The volumes that are projected — both monographs and collected essays — will seek to clarify how the Scrolls revise and help shape our understanding of the formation of the Bible and the historical development of Judaism and Christianity. Various offerings in the series will explore the reciprocally illuminating relationships of several disciplines related to the Scrolls, including the canon and text of the Hebrew Bible, the richly varied forms of Second Temple Judaism, and the New Testament. While the Dead Sea Scrolls constitute the main focus, several of these studies will also include perspectives on the Old and New Testaments and other ancient writings — hence the title of the series. It is hoped that these volumes will contribute to a deeper appreciation of the world of early Judaism and Christianity and of their continuing legacy today.

Peter W. Flint
Martin G. Abegg Jr.

The
DEAD SEA SCROLLS
and the
ORIGINS OF THE BIBLE

EUGENE ULRICH

William B. Eerdmans Publishing Company
Grand Rapids, Michigan / Cambridge, U.K.

Brill Academic Publishers
Leiden, Boston, Köln

Published jointly 1999 by Wm. B. Eerdmans Publishing Co.
255 Jefferson Ave. S.E., Grand Rapids, Michigan 49503 /
P.O. Box 163, Cambridge CB3 9PU U.K. and by
Brill Academic Publishers
P.O. Box 9000, 2300 PA Leiden, The Netherlands

Printed in the United States of America

04 03 02 01 00 7 6 5 4 3 2

Library of Congress Cataloging-in-Publication Data

Ulrich, Eugene Charles, 1938-
The Dead Sea scrolls and the origins of the Bible / Eugene Ulrich.
p. cm. — (Studies in the Dead Sea scrolls and related literature)
Includes bibliographical references and indexes.
ISBN 0-8028-4611-4 (pbk.: alk. paper)
1. Dead Sea scrolls. 2. Bible. O.T. — Criticism, interpretation, etc.
3. Bible. O.T. Greek — Versions — Septuagint.
4. Bible. O.T. Latin — Versions — Old Latin.
I. Title. II. Series.
BM487.U47 1999
296.1′55 — dc21 99-20790
CIP

To my friends and colleagues in the Department of Theology
and the Graduate Research Office at
the University of Notre Dame

Contents

Preface ix

Abbreviations and Sigla xiv

PART 1
THE SCROLLS AND THE HEBREW BIBLE

1. The Community of Israel and the Composition of the Scriptures 3
2. The Bible in the Making: The Scriptures at Qumran 17
3. Double Literary Editions of Biblical Narratives and Reflections on Determining the Form to Be Translated 34
4. The Canonical Process, Textual Criticism, and Latter Stages in the Composition of the Bible 51
5. Pluriformity in the Biblical Text, Text Groups, and Questions of Canon 79
6. Multiple Literary Editions: Reflections Toward a Theory of the History of the Biblical Text 99

7. The Palaeo-Hebrew Biblical Manuscripts from Qumran Cave 4 — 121

8. Orthography and Text in 4QDan[a] and 4QDan[b] and in the Received Masoretic Text — 148

PART 2

THE SCROLLS, THE SEPTUAGINT, AND THE OLD LATIN

9. The Septuagint Manuscripts from Qumran: A Reappraisal of Their Value — 165

10. Josephus's Biblical Text for the Books of Samuel — 184

11. Origen's Old Testament Text: The Transmission History of the Septuagint to the Third Century C.E. — 202

12. The Relevance of the Dead Sea Scrolls for Hexaplaric Studies — 224

13. The Old Latin Translation of the LXX and the Hebrew Scrolls from Qumran — 233

14. Characteristics and Limitations of the Old Latin Translation of the Septuagint — 275

Acknowledgments — 290

Index of Modern Authors — 292

Index of Ancient Literature — 298

Preface

For the past two decades, my primary publishing task has been the editing of the Qumran biblical scrolls. The present volume contains a series of essays articulating the lessons I have learned along the way. I was invited by friends and colleagues to write each of them for various conferences and collections, mostly honoring leading figures in the textual study of the Bible.

The essays form a unified picture, each focusing on and attempting to develop particular aspects of the history of the biblical text. They deal first with the Hebrew texts and then with the Greek and Old Latin texts, which help us understand the development of the Hebrew texts. The order of the essays on the Hebrew text moves from the more general to the more specific in scope, although Chapters 3–6 progress in chronological order, following the development of my thought concerning multiple variant editions of the books of Scripture.

The essays on the Greek text follow the ancient chronological progression from the Septuagint as it appears at Qumran, through Josephus's use of it, its transmission up to Origen, and finally the Hexapla. The Old Latin articles are out of print or virtually inaccessible, and since there is so little research on this highly valuable version, it seemed good to include them here.

I have over the past two decades considered it an academic and collegial obligation — something approaching a vocation — to produce the critical editions of the Qumran biblical scrolls as expeditiously and responsibly as possible. As is evident from my work on 4QSam^{a} and 4QSam^{c}, there is a great deal more that can and should be done on each of the scrolls beyond what routinely appears in the editions in Discoveries in the Judaean Desert. But for the full collection of the biblical scrolls to be edited within a reasonable period, the task had to be done by a small, manageable team who could work together smoothly, trustingly, and with a shared approach, and the editions had to strike a compromise between a sufficiently thorough treatment and a frustratingly lean one. The DJD editions are, in fact, *editiones principes;* fuller and more thorough analyses can always be — and hopefully will be — undertaken.

The result of this marathon of producing editions, however, is that I have not had the time to write a comprehensive study of the text of the Hebrew Bible so richly illumined by the biblical scrolls. My long-term colleague and friend Emanuel Tov has helped by writing *Textual Criticism of the Hebrew Bible.* In most areas I agree with him, and where I do not, my arguments are developed in these essays. Eventually, I will probably synthesize the contents of this collection and the work behind it into a full-scale monograph, but in the meantime it seems good to make these essays conveniently available.

There is a certain amount of repetition in this volume. But each chapter usually offers a somewhat different presentation of the larger picture in order to focus on a specific aspect treated in closer detail.

Chapter 1, "The Community of Israel and the Composition of the Scriptures," focuses on the very composition of the Scriptures, recalling the long tradition of literary analysis of each of the biblical books, and emphasizing that they all passed through successive literary editions. It places the patterns of variation documented in the Qumran biblical scrolls within the much larger history of the origins and development of the biblical books. It also poses the question, right from the beginning, of variant literary editions of the books of the Bible as the key to understanding the history of the biblical text.

Chapter 2, "The Bible in the Making: The Scriptures at Qumran," focuses on the shape near the end of the Second Temple period, the time of Hillel and Jesus, of what came to be called "The Bible." It treats the external shape and internal shape of the books then considered as Scripture. That is, it first considers matters later termed "canon": which books would have been included in "the Law and the Prophets," and whether and which of "the other books of our ancestors" (Prologue to Ben Sira) would have been considered Scripture. It secondly considers the nature of the text of the individual scriptural books.

Chapter 3, "Double Literary Editions of Biblical Narratives," represents the first of these efforts; it was written as I was thinking out the principles for the translation committee of the New Revised Standard Version. I laid out a series of examples of double literary editions, showing that the phenomenon was not isolated but occurred in many of the books of the Torah, the Prophets, and the Writings.

In Chapter 4, "The Canonical Process, Textual Criticism, and Latter Stages in the Composition of the Bible," I try to clarify the often confused terminology related to canon. I then show that the literary growth of successive editions of a biblical book was closely linked to the religious phenomenon of the canonical process that eventuated in the canon of the Hebrew Bible.

Chapter 5, "Pluriformity in the Biblical Text, Text Groups, and Questions of Canon," building on the tri-level separation in the "Orthography and Text" essay, begins with a critique of theories by Cross, Talmon, and Tov concerning the history of the biblical text, and attempts to advance a theory that explains the new evidence for textual pluriformity of the developing biblical books.

Chapter 6, "Multiple Literary Editions: Toward a Theory of the History of the Biblical Text," articulates my developing theory more fully and sets out to correct two positions that this new viewpoint illuminates. I argue that "Qumran practice" is a misleading concept and term for the newly relearned styles of Hebrew orthography and morphology found in the scrolls, and that the celebrated Psalms scroll from Cave 11 (11QPs[a]) is properly classified as a biblical manuscript, once it is understood what biblical manuscripts were like at the time of Hillel and Jesus.

In Chapter 7, "The Palaeo-Hebrew Biblical Manuscripts from Qumran Cave 4," I analyze the six texts of the Pentateuch and Job written in the Palaeo-Hebrew script in terms of their physical features, palaeography and date, orthography, and textual character. In none of these categories are those texts distinguishable from the other biblical manuscripts, nor does there appear any distinction between scrolls copied outside Qumran and those possibly copied at Qumran.

Chapter 8, "Orthography and Text in 4QDan[a] and 4QDan[b] and in the Received Masoretic Text," distinguishes the three levels of orthographic differences, individual textual variants, and variant editions, demonstrating their independence of each other.

I wrote Chapter 9, "The Septuagint Manuscripts from Qumran: A Reappraisal of Their Value," after completing the editions of the Cave 4 Septuagint scrolls. Patrick Skehan had completed editions of all four and published two of them. He and I had shared the developing editions with John Wevers, who was preparing the Göttingen critical editions of the Pentateuch and who in turn shared his developing work with us. Skehan originally thought that 4QLXXNum represented a form of the Septuagint version of the book of Numbers that was earlier than the text generally preserved in the Septuagint manuscript tradition; Wevers thought that it was "an early revision of the Septuagint of Numbers," and Skehan later adopted this view. But upon analysis of the fifteen variants of 4QLXXLev^a and the four most salient variants of 4QLXXNum, I concluded that the Septuagint manuscripts at Qumran — four centuries older — were, not surprisingly but also not necessarily, textually earlier than and at times superior to Vaticanus and the rest of the manuscript tradition. Wevers subsequently adopted this view, at least partially.

In Chapter 10, "Josephus's Biblical Text for the Books of Samuel," I compare Josephus's recasting of the Samuel narrative in his *Jewish Antiquities* with 4QSam^a and with the Masoretic and Septuagint texts of Samuel and Chronicles. My study demonstrates (a) that Josephus used a biblical text with contents documented only in 4QSam^a, not in any other extant biblical text; (b) that he used a Greek, not Hebrew, form of the biblical text; and (c) that he thus used an early form of the Septuagint version of Samuel which, though no longer extant, more faithfully reflected a text like 4QSam^a.

With Chapter 11, "Origen's Old Testament Text: The Transmission History of the Septuagint to the Third Century C.E.," I present a review of the origins and character of the Old Greek, the transmission of the Greek text tradition and recensions up to Origen's time, and some aspects of Origen's Hexapla. Included in the last are discussions about how much Hebrew Origen may have known and against Pierre Nautin's view that the Hexapla did not contain a Hebrew column.

Chapter 12, "The Relevance of the Dead Sea Scrolls for Hexaplaric Studies," attempts to offer students of the Hexapla an understanding of the history of the biblical text that had been lost by Origen's time and that he himself most likely would have wished to have known. In contrast to the single Masoretic tradition, there existed variant Hebrew editions of most biblical books, and the Old Greek translation of many books probably faithfully translated one or another of those Hebrew editions. Thus, Origen's "revision" toward the Masoretic text unwittingly and unfortunately moved his fifth, "Septuaginta," column further away from the Old Greek, not closer.

Chapter 13, "The Old Latin Translation of the LXX and the Hebrew Scrolls from Qumran," is a long and highly detailed study of the Old Latin of Samuel in comparison with 4QSam^a and 4QSam^c, the Masoretic text, and the Septuagint. Hopefully, it will spur some to study the Old Latin, which, as my friend Julio Trebolle Barrera notes, can sometimes be used where it alone preserves original text to get to a lost Old Greek, which in turn reflected, in contrast to the Masoretic text, a now lost Old Hebrew.

Chapter 14, "Characteristics and Limitations of the Old Latin Translation of the Septuagint," represents my contribution to a panel analyzing grammatically what different translations of the biblical text could or could not adequately reflect in textual comparisons and critical apparatuses.

I wish to thank Professors Frank Moore Cross, the late Patrick W. Skehan, and John Strugnell for teaching me to ask the questions that gave rise to these essays, and to thank other teachers and mentors, especially Professors Joseph A. Fitzmyer, S.J., Shemaryahu Talmon, and James A. Sanders.

I am grateful to Drs. Peter Flint and Martin Abegg, the series editors, and especially Dr. Daniel Harlow, the academic editor at Wm. B. Eerdmans, for initiating this volume and for carefully processing it. Both Drs. Flint and Harlow had to endure the theories contained in this volume during Ph.D. studies at the University of Notre Dame, and I am all the more grateful that they are nonetheless eager to publish them. I also thank those who have been my graduate assistants at Notre Dame: Robert Kugler, Leslie Walck, Katherine Murphy, Richard Bautch, and Kelli O'Brien. Thanks also go to Andrea Alvarez for her resolve in facing the numbing task of preparing the indexes.

No one writes in isolation, and I warmly express my appreciation to family, dear friends, and dialogue partners who have enhanced my life and thought and have contributed indirectly to this volume: Sarianna Metso, Sabrina Odessa, Ivan and Amy Hall and Quinn, Meg and Laura Colleton, Evelyn and Jim Whitehead, Emanuel Tov, James VanderKam, Julio Trebolle, Émile Puech, Florentino García Martínez, Lawrence Schiffman, and Peter Flint.

Abbreviations and Sigla

Periodicals, Reference Works, and Serials

ALGHJ	Arbeiten zur Literatur und Geschichte des hellenistischen Judentums
ANRW	*Aufstieg und Niedergang der römischen Welt*
Ant.	Flavius Josephus, *Jewish Antiquities*
ASOR	American Schools of Oriental Research
BA	*Biblical Archaeologist*
BASOR	*Bulletin of the American Schools of Oriental Research*
BETL	Bibliotheca ephemeridum theologicarum lovaniensium
BibOr	Biblica et orientalia
BIOSCS	*Bulletin of the International Organization for Septuagint and Cognate Studies*
CBQ	*Catholic Biblical Quarterly*
CBQMS	Catholic Biblical Quarterly Monograph Series
DBSup	*Dictionnaire de la Bible,* Supplément
DJD	Discoveries in the Judaean Desert
DSD	*Dead Sea Discoveries*
EncJud	*Encyclopaedia Judaica*
HSM	Harvard Semitic Monographs
HSS	Harvard Semitic Studies
HTR	*Harvard Theological Review*
HUCA	*Hebrew Union College Annual*
IDBSup	*Interpreter's Dictionary of the Bible,* Supplementary Volume
ICC	International Critical Commentary

Int	*Interpretation*
IEJ	*Israel Exploration Journal*
JBL	*Journal of Biblical Literature*
JJS	*Journal of Jewish Studies*
JNES	*Journal of Near Eastern Studies*
JQR	*Jewish Quarterly Review*
JSOT	*Journal for the Study of the Old Testament*
JSOTSup	Journal for the Study of the Old Testament Supplement Series
JTS	*Journal of Theological Studies*
McCQ	*McCormick Quarterly*
NRSV	New Revised Standard Version
NTS	*New Testament Studies*
OBO	Orbis biblica et orientalis
OTS	*Oudtestamentische Studiën*
QTSJ	Eugene Ulrich, *The Qumran Text of Samuel and Josephus*
RB	*Revue biblique*
RevQ	*Revue de Qumrân*
SBLDS	Society of Biblical Literature Dissertation Series
SBLRBS	Society of Biblical Literature Resources for Biblical Study
SBLSCS	Society of Biblical Literature Septuagint and Cognate Studies
STDJ	Studies on the Texts of the Desert of Judah
TDNT	*Theological Dictionary of the New Testament*
VTSup	Vetus Testamentum Supplements
WTJ	*Westminster Theological Journal*
ZAW	*Zeitschrift für die alttestamentliche Wissenschaft*
ZNW	*Zeitschrift für die neutestamentliche Wissenschaft*

Ancient Texts and Versions

α′	Aquila's recension of the Septuagint (the third column of the Hexapla)
A	Codex Alexandrinus
Aeth	Ethiopic Version
Ambr	Ambrose's citation of the Latin
Arab	Arabic Version
Arm	Armenian Version
Arm^{te}	Armenian Version, text
b.	Babylonian Talmud (followed by name of tractate)
B	Codex Vaticanus
Bo	Bohairic Version

C	Chronicles
$C^{MT,G}$	Masoretic and Greek texts of Chronicles
Co	Coptic Version
Dtr_2	The second, exilic edition of the Deuteronomistic History (Joshua–2 Kings)
$\mathfrak{G}$	Septuagint
$\mathfrak{G}^{A}$	Codex Alexandrinus
$\mathfrak{G}^{B}$	Codex Vaticanus
$\mathfrak{G}^{ed}$	Septuagint, John Wevers's edition
$\mathfrak{G}^{O}$	Origen's (Hexaplaric) recension of the Septuagint
G	Septuagint
G^{B}	Codex Vaticanus
G^{L}	(Proto-)Lucianic Greek text
G^{R}	"Palestinian" or *kaige* recension of the Greek text
J	Josephus; Niese's text of *Jewish Antiquities*
La	Latin
LXX	Septuagint
$\mathfrak{M}$	Masoretic Text
$\mathfrak{M}^{q}$	Masoretic Text, *qerê* reading
m.	Mishnah (followed by name of tractate)
MT	Masoretic Text
o′	Origen's Hexaplaric recension of the Septuagint
OG	Old Greek
Philo	Syriac Version of Philoxenus
Q	Qumran
$\mathfrak{S}$	Syriac Version
σ′	Symmachus's recension of the Septuagint (fourth column of the Hexapla)
S	Syriac Version
SP	Samaritan Pentateuch
$\mathfrak{m}$	Samaritan Pentateuch
$\mathfrak{m}^{ed}$	Samaritan Pentateuch, A. von Gall's edition
$\mathfrak{m}^{Ken}$	Samaritan Pentateuch, B. Kennicott's edition
$\mathfrak{m}^{mss}$	Samaritan Pentateuch manuscripts in A. von Gall's critical apparatus
Syh	Syro-Hexaplar version
$\mathfrak{T}$	Targum
$\mathfrak{T}^{J}$	Targum Pseudo-Jonathan
$\mathfrak{T}^{O}$	Targum Onkelos
$\mathfrak{T}^{P}$	Palestinian Targum

T	Targum
θ′	Theodotion's recension of the Septuagint (sixth column of the Hexapla)
𝔙	Latin Vulgate
V	Latin Vulgate

Qumran Literature

CD	Cairo Genizah copy of the *Damascus Document*
8ḤevXII gr	The Greek Minor Prophets Scroll from Naḥal Ḥever
MasPs[b]	The second in a series of Psalms scrolls from Masada
pap4QLXXLev[b]	The papyrus scroll that is the second in a series of scrolls of Greek Leviticus from Qumran Cave 4
pap4QparaExod gr	A papyrus fragment of a Greek paraphrase of Exodus from Qumran Cave 4
1QS	*Serek ha-Yaḥad* or *Rule of the Community* from Qumran Cave 1
4QMMT	*Miqṣat Maʿaseh ha-Torah* or Halakic Document from Qumran Cave 4
4QpaleoExod[m]	A palaeo-Hebrew scroll of Exodus from Qumran Cave 4
4QSam[a]	The first of a series of Samuel manuscripts from Qumran Cave 4
4Qunid gr	An unidentified Greek text from Qumran Cave 4
4Q171	Document number 171 in a series of fragmentary scrolls from Qumran Cave 4

Text-Critical Sigla and Signa

א̇	A Hebrew letter whose identification is probable (denoted by a dot)
א̊	A Hebrew letter whose identification is possible (denoted by a circlet)
1°, 2°, etc.	the first, second, etc. occurrence of a word in a verse or section of text
1°⁀2°	haplography by parablepsis from the first to the second occurrence of a word
*	the original reading of the manuscript
=	the manuscripts cited agree
≠	the manuscripts cited do not agree

>	becomes, changes into
<	is derived from, develops from
]	separates the reading of the manuscript from variant readings
[ ]	indicates restored text
< >	indicates the original reading of an earlier text
ad fin	to the end (of the verse)
fin	end (of the verse)
mg	in the margin of the manuscript
MS(s)	manuscript(s)
om	omit
sub ÷	indicates text marked with Origen's obelus symbol as present in the Septuagint but lacking in the Hebrew
tr	transposes
vid	*ut videtur:* so it seems from the evidence

PART 1

THE SCROLLS AND THE HEBREW BIBLE

CHAPTER 1

The Community of Israel and the Composition of the Scriptures

James Sanders has been one of the leading voices in the last third of this century reflecting on the relationship between the text and canon of the First Testament, and I thank him for being a catalyst, teacher, and conversation partner for my own thinking.[1] The purpose of this study is to reflect further on the interrelationships between a number of topics for which he has made contributions. Can we gain further focus on the interrelationships between customary questions such as: How did the Scriptures come to be, how were they composed? What is the text of Scripture, what form of the text do we seek in the text-critical endeavor or when translating "The Holy Bible"? What do the Qumran scrolls teach us about the nature of the scriptural text at the time of Hillel the Elder and Jesus Christ? And a question I do not think I have ever heard asked: does the way that the Scriptures were *composed* have a bearing on the text form we present as Scripture?

The Community That Composed the Scriptures and Its Method of Composition

The community of Israel (בני ישראל) composed the Scriptures over the course of approximately a millennium, from the time of the early monarchy

1. See esp. J. A. Sanders, *Torah and Canon* (Philadelphia: Fortress, 1972); idem, *Canon and Community: A Guide to Canonical Criticism* (Philadelphia: Fortress, 1984); idem, *From Sacred Story to Sacred Text* (Philadelphia: Fortress, 1987).

to within a generation or so of the fall of the Second Temple. The name בני ישראל, originally probably a sociopolitical designation, eventually became a religious designation, as the people became identified as a political unit and the political unit became identified with its established religion and its God. Even after the united monarchy split into Israel and Judah, and after the Assyrian imperial greed and cruelty put an end to Israel as a state, the citizens of Judah continued to be called Israel with respect to their religious identity. In this study I will be dealing explicitly with the Hebrew Scriptures, but much will be true and transferable to the traditions and writings of that part of the בני ישראל that eventually came to be called Christians. As continuing Christian tradition attests, Israel remained a spiritual designation for the Christian community as well as it did for the Rabbinic community.

The Torah

During the monarchy and, according to the classical Documentary Hypothesis, even during the early monarchy, authors or tradents produced something of a national epic — much like Rome's *Aeneid* and Finland's *Kalevala*[2] — that was a blend of historical, tribal, folk, religious, and national-identity literature. The theory that dominated the first three quarters of this century was that four main "authors/compilers," each from four different periods in Israel's life before God and life in the volatile Near East, used partly the same, partly different sources to teach the Israelites how God's word needed to be heard in their own generation. These were four different messages, each in their drastically changed historical situations. Each, using a selection of mostly familiar sources, sought to help the Israelites remember the ancient story of their ancestors with their God. They offered "model stories" that portrayed the character of the people, instilled national pride and traditional values, and served indirectly as instruction concerning how to act and how not to act.[3]

For our purposes, it does not matter whether the medium of the literature was oral or written, for the dynamics and function are identical.[4] Our fo-

2. *The Kalevala; or, Poems of the Kaleva District* (compiled by Elias Lonnrot; trans. F. P. Magoun, Jr.; Cambridge: Harvard University Press, 1963).

3. The origins and growth of the Pentateuch, of course, are bewilderingly more complicated than this brief description can indicate, even as the Kalevala had not one but three "finished" versions of the collection of adapted sources: the first in 1833, a second in 1835, and a third, the "New Kalevala," in 1849.

4. The cultural traditions of some modern peoples still remain oral. Cambodia, for example, almost lost its age-old music and dance traditions — which had been transmit-

cus is on the *method* by which the literature was produced. The authors took national or folk traditions, individual stories told and remembered for certain purposes — sometimes recoverable now, sometimes not — and wove a series of such stories together with many other components into a narrative that can be viewed as a national epic. Whether we imagine authors or tradents or schools, such as J and P, along the lines of the Documentary Hypothesis, or whether we attempt revised hypotheses,[5] we are most likely left with this conclusion: the narratives and the law codes that now constitute the Torah were composed through a repeated process of older traditions being retold in a new context and in a new form, with the resulting composition on the one hand faithful to the spirit of the old traditions and their intent, and on the other creatively revised to teach the people and help guide their future destiny.

The Deuteronomistic History

In the late monarchy, probably during the reign of King Josiah (640-609 B.C.E.), one or more Deuteronomistic authors/tradents (Dtr) produced the largest complex that has come down to us as a biblical unit: the Deuteronomistic History (the books from Deuteronomy through Kings). The analysis and description of this composition is as fascinating as that of the Torah.[6] But again, the method by which Dtr composed this opus was one of largely faithful recital of numerous older traditions creatively and richly imbued with a theological perspective. The History[7] selected myriad sources, arranged them in a framework that is both chronological and at least partly theological,[8] and presented the new composition as a theological reflection

---

ted and were alive only in the memories of the trained performers — due to the purges of Pol Pot.

5. Cf., e.g., J. Blenkinsopp, *The Pentateuch* (New York: Doubleday, 1992); R. Rendtorff, *The Problem of the Process of Transmission in the Pentateuch* (Sheffield: JSOT Press, 1990); J. Van Seters, *Abraham in History and Tradition* (New Haven: Yale University Press, 1975); idem, *Prologue to History: The Yahwist as Historian in Genesis* (Louisville: Westminster/John Knox, 1992).

6. Cf. esp. M. Noth, *Überlieferungsgeschichtliche Studien* (Tübingen: Niemeyer, 1943); F. M. Cross, *Canaanite Myth and Hebrew Epic* (Cambridge: Harvard University Press, 1973) 274-90; G. Knoppers, *Two Nations under God: The Deuteronomistic History of Solomon and the Dual Monarchies* (2 vols.; HSM 52-53; Atlanta: Scholars Press, 1993).

7. "History" is perhaps an apt term if viewed in its own era, although perhaps today it is better styled a theological interpretation of the people's history.

8. One example of theological arrangement is the recurrent prophecy-fulfillment

on the people's history that is at once simple to characterize and rich as an example of ancient religious instruction. The major edition of this large opus was probably composed in the reign of Josiah, but after the failure of Josiah's dreams and the destruction of Jerusalem and exile of Judah's leadership, the work underwent a revised edition during the exile for a double purpose. It was important both to bring the history up to date by including the subsequent events and to offer a rationale for the destruction and exile by underscoring at numerous loci throughout the narrative the "curse" dimension that characteristically accompanied the "blessing" attendant upon Israel's choice of fidelity or infidelity. Again, the Deuteronomistic History is a vast repository of diverse national literature composed by scores of anonymous creative "authors."

The Latter Prophets

Also during the monarchy and continuing through the post-exilic period, the words of certain prophets were remembered and transmitted, probably already in adapted and rearranged form by the time they were first committed to writing. These collected sayings also encountered a series of new editions as they traversed the centuries. For example, the collected "Words of Amos" were eventually reedited by the Deuteronomists, probably after the destruction of the altar of Bethel by Josiah in 622, to serve — a century after the fall of the Northern Kingdom, which Amos had excoriated — as a warning against a similar possibility for the Southern Kingdom. Yet a third major new edition was produced after the exile, seen principally in the oracles of salvation placed at the end (Amos 9:11-15). The purpose of this new edition was to impart much-needed hope to the despairing people in the gloom of the fallen monarchy and temple, but at the same time it dramatically changed the overall perception of "the book of Amos."

The books of Isaiah, Jeremiah, and indeed virtually all the prophets evolved through a similar process into the editions that we encounter. The process entailed both faithful repetition of older text and creative reshaping for new historical and theological contexts. That creative reshaping was achieved through augmentation with additional material, rearrangement, rewording, and contemporizing the theological viewpoint dependent upon the new situation in which the בני ישראל now found themselves. Although the

motif. It is uncertain how much of the arrangement of sources was done by Dtr and how much may already have been found in the sources taken up by Dtr.

process may not have been frequent for major new forms or editions of a book in general, the frequency of the process in smaller additions, for example, for the book of Isaiah, was beyond counting.

Considerable editorial activity can be seen in the book of Daniel as well, which is being treated in this section because it was considered a prophetic book by both Jews and Christians in the first century.[9] It has been transmitted in one edition in the Masoretic Text (MT or 𝔐), and in an expanded edition (with "the Additions") in the Septuagint (LXX or 𝔊). So far, the Daniel manuscripts from Caves 1, 4, and 6 at Qumran all attest to the edition as in 𝔐, although the possibility must remain open that the reason no fragments of the expanded edition have been identified is that there is no Hebrew/Aramaic version of the expansions extant, and thus no Semitic text for easy comparison in the identification process. But prior to the form of the edition as found in 𝔐, there was a lengthy history of composition. At the earliest stages, even prior to any *collection* of stories, individual stories probably circulated, as suggested at Qumran by 4QPrayer of Nabonidus (4Q242). It is difficult, however, to know whether it and texts such as 4Qpseudo-Daniel ar^{a-c} (4Q243-245) were isolated texts or already part of a cycle.[10] Subsequently, to form the book as we now know it there was probably an early collection of the Aramaic chapters 2–6 in the Ptolemaic period, then augmented by chapter 7 and expanded with chapters 8–12 at the time of Antiochus IV Epiphanes.[11]

The Writings

It has also long since been recognized that the books of Psalms and Proverbs are the results of long and multi-staged editing processes. We will return later to look more closely at the variant editions of the Psalms.

Another example of a book in which the editing process has produced dramatically altered views is the book of Job. It is notoriously perilous, especially in short compass, to present views on the composition of Job. But it is

9. See E. Ulrich, "The Bible in the Making: The Scriptures at Qumran," in *The Community of the Renewed Covenant: The Notre Dame Symposium on the Dead Sea Scrolls* (ed. E. Ulrich and J. VanderKam; Notre Dame: University of Notre Dame Press, 1994) 77-93, esp. 81-82. This paper is now reprinted as Chapter 2 of the present volume.

10. See J. J. Collins, "*Pseudo-Daniel* Revisited," in F. García Martínez and É. Puech, eds., *Hommage à Józef T. Milik* = *RevQ* 17 (1996) 111-35; and P. W. Flint, "4Qpseudo-Daniel ar^{c} (4Q245) and the Restoration of the Priesthood," in *Hommage à Józef T. Milik*, 137-50.

11. See J. J. Collins, *Daniel* (Hermeneia; Minneapolis: Fortress, 1993).

clear at a minimum for our purposes that two different traditions, the tale in the Prologue-Epilogue and the Dialogue with the YHWH Speeches, have been juxtaposed in marvelous tension in the final edition of the book as transmitted. Each breathes an easily discernible theology regarding suffering, wisdom, and the divine-human relationship, and the two theologies stand defiantly opposed to each other.

In sum, the various books of the Bible were produced through a complicated series of editorial stages by a process that included two major thrusts: the faithful repetition or retelling of important traditions, and the creative reshaping of those traditions in new theological directions often as a response to the pastoral needs of the people of Israel as perceived by major editors or tradents whom we call the biblical authors. The composition of the Scriptures was dynamic, organic. It was in a sense evolutionary, insofar as the traditions remained static for a period and then in a burst of creativity leaped to a new form, a new literary edition, due to the creative adaptation effected by some religious leaders, usually in response to a new situation.

The Qumran Biblical Manuscripts: Continuation of the Same Process

Direct evidence for the biblical text begins to appear in the latter half of the Second Temple period. The manuscript evidence shows that the same process that characterized the composition of the Scriptures from the earliest times was still continuing through the Hellenistic, Hasmonaean, and Herodian periods.

Our earliest evidence for biblical manuscripts was found at Qumran. The Great Isaiah Scroll (1QIsa^{a}) was the first and most dramatic biblical manuscript to gain widespread fame, and especially because the text displayed multifaceted disagreement with the Masoretic *textus receptus,* an assumption was made that it was a (specifically) Qumran text of Isaiah. When the biblical texts continued to surface and continued to show pluriformity of textual character, the view continued to prevail that those texts were "sectarian" or "vulgar." The assumption apparently was that the biblical text as preserved in the Masoretic *textus receptus* had already become standard in the Hasmonaean period, and insofar as any text in the late Second Temple period varied from it, that text was aberrant or substandard.

But the biblical texts from Qumran, just as most of the nonbiblical, are general Jewish texts, representative of the shape of the Scriptures elsewhere. There are certain nonbiblical works which do reflect the theology of a specific group within Judaism which probably had one of its centers at Khirbet Qumran, but a number of the works are clearly a part of the general Jewish literature of the day, and it is arguable that the majority of them were probably representative of general Jewish literature.[12] Similarly, the biblical texts from Qumran are representative of the shape of the Scriptures elsewhere in Judaism. There is nothing in the biblical texts to suggest that they are specific to Qumran or to any particular group within Judaism. In fact, everything we know about the biblical text prior to the end of the first century C.E. — for example, the Samaritan Pentateuch (SP), the Septuagint, Philo, Josephus, the New Testament, Rabbinic quotations, as well as in 𝔐 — indicates that the text was pluriform.

The Samaritan Pentateuch,[13] the Septuagint,[14] and Josephus[15] demon-

12. The fact that the texts are representative of the broad spectrum of Second Temple Judaism is probably one of the factors that led Norman Golb to leap to the opposite extreme, claiming that the texts were brought from Jerusalem (presumably all on a single occasion) and were simply hidden at the (uninhabited?) site. Golb's position is developed most fully now in his book *Who Wrote the Dead Sea Scrolls? The Search for the Secret of Qumran* (New York: Scribner, 1995).

13. Contrast the text of SP and that of MT especially for Exodus and Numbers; see also 4QpaleoExod^{m} in P. W. Skehan, E. Ulrich, and J. E. Sanderson, *Qumran Cave 4, IV: Palaeo-Hebrew and Greek Biblical Manuscripts* (DJD 9; Oxford: Clarendon, 1992) 53-130; and 4QNum^{b} in E. Ulrich and F. M. Cross, with J. R. Davila, N. Jastram, J. E. Sanderson, and E. Tov, *Qumran Cave 4, VII: Genesis to Numbers* (DJD 12; Oxford: Clarendon, 1994) 205-67.

14. The books of Jeremiah and Daniel are two of the most dramatic examples of variant literary editions documented in the Septuagint; see Tov, "Some Aspects of the Textual and Literary History of the Book of Jeremiah," in *Le livre de Jérémie: Le prophète et son milieu, les oracles et leur transmission* (ed. P.-M. Bogaert; BETL 54; Leuven: Leuven University Press, 1981) 145-67; and E. Ulrich, "The Canonical Process, Textual Criticism, and Latter Stages in the Composition of the Bible," in *Sha'arei Talmon: Studies in the Bible, Qumran, and the Ancient Near East Presented to Shemaryahu Talmon* (ed. M. Fishbane and E. Tov with W. W. Fields; Winona Lake, Ind.: Eisenbrauns, 1992) 283-87 (reprinted as Chapter 4 in this volume). But the phenomenon is more widespread, including sections or passages of books, e.g., the David-Goliath narrative in 1 Samuel 17–18. For the detailed characteristics of those two variant editions, see D. Barthélemy, D. W. Gooding, J. Lust, and E. Tov, *The Story of David and Goliath: Textual and Literary Criticism: Papers of a Joint Research Venture* (OBO 73; Fribourg: Éditions Universitaires; Göttingen: Vandenhoeck & Ruprecht, 1986).

15. The priest Josephus (*Vita* 418) had books from the Temple allowed to him by Titus. His text for Joshua–2 Samuel was a developed form of the Old Greek (OG), not the MT; see A. Mez, *Die Bibel des Josephus untersucht für Buch V-VII der Archäologie* (Basel: Jaeger und Kober, 1895), and E. Ulrich, *The Qumran Text of Samuel and Josephus* (HSM 19; Missoula, Mont.: Scholars Press, 1978). The latter demonstrates that Josephus was us-

strate bountifully that there were variant literary editions of the books of Scripture in the late Second Temple period. The evidence for a series of variant literary editions of the biblical books now documented in the manuscripts found at Qumran has been described in a long list of publications. Some of the firsthand evidence confirms the parallel literary editions already known from the SP (4QpaleoExod^{m}, 4QNum^{b}),[16] the LXX (4QJer^{b,d}),[17] and Josephus (4QSam^{a}).[18] Yet more manuscripts supply the evidence of the same phenomenon for other books, such as Joshua,[19] Judges,[20] Psalms,[21] Canticles, etc.[22]

From a historical point of view, the text of each book as in the MT was

---

ing a text type represented in Hebrew by 4QSam^{a} and in Greek by a slightly developed form of the OG, in contrast to the text transmitted in the MT.

16. See P. W. Skehan, "Exodus in the Samaritan Recension from Qumran," *JBL* 74 (1955) 182-87; J. E. Sanderson, *An Exodus Scroll from Qumran: 4QpaleoExod^{m} and the Samaritan Tradition* (HSS 30; Atlanta: Scholars Press, 1986); Skehan, Ulrich, and Sanderson, *Qumran Cave 4, IV: Palaeo-Hebrew and Greek Biblical Manuscripts,* 53-130; N. Jastram, in Ulrich and Cross, et al., *Qumran Cave 4, VII: Genesis to Numbers,* 205-67.

17. See the contribution of E. Tov in E. Ulrich, F. M. Cross, R. E. Fuller, et al., *Qumran Cave 4, X: The Prophets* (DJD 15; Oxford: Clarendon, 1997) 172.

18. See F. M. Cross, "The History of the Biblical Text in the Light of Discoveries in the Judaean Desert," *HTR* 57 (1964) 281-99; and Ulrich, *The Qumran Text of Samuel.*

19. E. Ulrich, "4QJoshua^{a} and Joshua's First Altar in the Promised Land," in *New Qumran Texts and Studies: Proceedings of the First Meeting of the International Organization for Qumran Studies, Paris 1992* (ed. G. J. Brooke with F. García Martínez; STDJ 15; Leiden: Brill, 1994) 89-104 and plates 4-6. See also L. Mazor, "The Septuagint Translation of the Book of Joshua," *BIOSCS* 27 (1994) 29-38.

20. J. Trebolle Barrera, "49. 4QJudg^{a}," in E. Ulrich and F. M. Cross, with S. W. Crawford, J. A. Duncan, P. W. Skehan, E. Tov, and J. Trebolle Barrera, *Qumran Cave 4, IX: Deuteronomy, Joshua, Judges, Kings* (DJD 14; Oxford: Clarendon, 1995) 161-64; and idem, "Textual Variants in 4QJudg^{a} and the Textual and Editorial History of the Book of Judges," in F. García Martínez, ed., *The Texts of Qumran and the History of the Community: Proceedings of the Groningen Congress on the Dead Sea Scrolls (20-23 August 1989),* 1. *Biblical Texts* = *RevQ* 14 (1989) 229-45.

21. J. A. Sanders, *The Psalms Scroll of Qumrân Cave 11 (11QPs^{a})* (DJD 4; Oxford: Clarendon, 1965); idem, *The Dead Sea Psalms Scroll* (Ithaca, N.Y.: Cornell University Press, 1967); idem, "Variorum in the Psalms Scroll (11QPs^{a})," *HTR* 59 (1966) 83-94; idem, "Cave 11 Surprises and the Question of Canon," *McCormick Quarterly* 21 (1968) 1-15 (reprinted in S. Leiman, ed., *The Canon and Masorah of the Hebrew Bible: An Introductory Reader* [New York: Ktav, 1974] 37-51); idem, "The Qumran Psalms Scroll (11QPs^{a}) Reviewed," in *On Language, Culture, and Religion: In Honor of Eugene A. Nida* (ed. M. Black and W. A. Smalley; The Hague and Paris: Mouton, 1974) 79-99; and P. W. Flint, *The Dead Sea Psalms Scrolls and the Book of Psalms* (STDJ 17; Leiden: Brill, 1997).

22. E. Tov, "Three Manuscripts (Abbreviated Texts?) of Canticles from Qumran Cave 4," *JJS* 46 (1995) 88-111.

simply one form of that book as it existed in antiquity. In fact, the principal evidence we have for confirming that the texts of the books as found in the medieval manuscripts of the Masoretic Bible are closely faithful to ancient texts is the evidence from Qumran. And that evidence from Qumran, when seen in perspective, demonstrates that there were multiple editions of the biblical books in antiquity — one form of which survives in each of the books of the MT collection, while other forms may or may not have had the good fortune to survive in the SP, the LXX, at Qumran, or elsewhere.

Thus, we can see at Qumran, but it is evidence for Judaism in general, that the scribes and their predecessors were at work along two lines. First, they often simply copied the individual books of the Scriptures as exactly as humanly possible. But secondly, sometimes the scribes intentionally inserted new material that helped interpret or highlight for their contemporary congregation in a new situation the relevance of the traditional text. These creative biblical scribes were actively handing on the tradition, but they were adding to it, enriching it, and attempting to make it adaptable and relevant. They knew explicitly what they were doing, just as the redactors of the JEDP material, the exilic Dtr^2, and the compilers of the prophetic material, the psalmic and proverbial literature, etc., knew what they were doing.

Insofar as the scribes were handing on the tradition, they became part of the canonical process. Handing on the tradition is a constitutive factor of that process, and Sanders labels it the "repetition" factor.[23] Each repetition confirms that this material is important to the scribe and to the congregation, with importance from the past, importance in the current situation, and importance for the future. The texts were authoritative texts, and through the repetition they were being rendered more authoritative.

Insofar as the scribes were also updating the tradition and making it relevant to the current situation, they were also contributing to the canonical process. They were giving it another constitutive canonical characteristic, a complementary factor that Sanders terms "resignification."[24] The tradition now proves itself adaptable, capable of having new significance in this new particular situation. The word, heard in earlier times with significance in that situation, is now heard with revived significance in this new situation.

Thus, the same process that characterized the composition of the Scriptures from their beginnings was still continuing all the way through the Second Temple period. The process becomes visible and documented through the Qumran manuscripts starting around the middle and late third

23. Sanders, *Canon and Community*, 22.
24. Sanders, *Canon and Community*, 22.

century B.C.E. When and why the period of pluriformity in the biblical text ended is still uncertain, although the first half of the second century C.E. is a plausible suggestion. Though the Greek Minor Prophets Scroll[25] shows that there were efforts toward bringing the Old Greek translation back to closer agreement with the Hebrew text, or at least with *a* Hebrew text, made apparently in the latter part of the first century B.C.E., most of the evidence points toward pluriformity at the time when both Christianity and Rabbinic Judaism were in their formative stages. It appears that the organic or developmental process of the composition of the Scriptures was brought to a halt only due to two factors: (1) the fact that Rome posed such a threat to the continued life of Judaism, and (2) the growing tension between those Jews on the one hand who looked principally to the Torah, minimized apocalyptic and eschatological themes, and used the Scriptures in Hebrew, and those Jews on the other hand who followed Jesus, looked to the larger Gentile world, and used the Scriptures in Greek. The second century more than the first — that is, closer to the Second Revolt than to the First Revolt — appears to be a more likely setting for the crystallization of the view that a single form of the text was a necessity.

The "Original Text" of Scripture and an Alternate View

If the text of the Scriptures was pluriform and organic at the time when both Christianity and Rabbinic Judaism were in their formative stages, then the question must be raised: What form of the text should be the object of our search? At the start one might think that this question may well be answered in one way by Jewish scholars and in another way by Christians, and perhaps in different ways by Catholic and Protestant scholars. On the contrary, however, are we not all eventually drawn to base our denominational views on the clearest and best historical evidence we can attain? Thus, theoretically we would all come to a uniform conclusion based on the evidence, if the evidence is reasonably clear.

What form of the text, then, should be the object of our search? "The original text" is commonly listed as the object of textual research, the object of text criticism, and the object of those who produce translations of the Holy Bible for religious, literary, and historical purposes. But when one presses in detail to find out what precisely "the original text" is for the sum of all the

25. E. Tov with R. A. Kraft, *The Greek Minor Prophets Scroll from Naḥal Ḥever (8ḤevXIIgr)* (The Seiyâl Collection 1; DJD 8; Oxford: Clarendon, 1990).

passages of a biblical book, there is a bewildering array of meanings, differing phrase by phrase through the text. Possibilities are:[26]

1. The "original text" of the *source* incorporated by an early author or tradent (e.g., the Canaanite or Aramean stories incorporated by J).
2. The "original text" of the work produced by an early author or tradent (J, Dtr, P).
3. The "original text" of the *complete book,* recognizable as a form of our biblical book, as it left the hand of the last major author or redactor (e.g., the book of Exodus or Jeremiah).
4. The "original text" as it was (in developed form) at the stage of development when a community accepted it as an authoritative book.
5. The "original text" as the consonantal text of the Rabbinic Bible (the consonantal text that was later used by the Masoretes).
6. The "original text" as the original or superior form of the MT as interpreted, vocalized, and punctuated by the Masoretes.
7. The "original text" as fully attested in extant manuscript witnesses.
8. The "original text" as reconstructed from the extant testimony insofar as possible but with the most plausible conjectural emendations when it is generally agreed that no extant witness preserves a sound reading.

Our imagination is a powerful tool in our learning and specifically in our reconstruction of history. But our imagination, when not properly disciplined, can also mislead us, or at least paint the details of a historical reconstruction quite differently from the way those details actually were. One thinks of the artistically great, but historically inaccurate, settings of Italian or Dutch renaissance paintings of biblical or classical scenes, or of Albert Edelfelt's powerful painting of Christ and the Magdalene; Christ is clearly Scandinavian, and the scenery quintessential Finland. So, when we move from art to history, it is important to discipline our imaginations.

Emanuel Tov has recently discussed "The Original Shape of the Biblical Text" and made a proposal concerning the form of the text that is the goal of textual criticism.[27] His argument rests on such a comprehensive set of data and such a nuanced discussion that I fear I cannot do it justice in a small sec-

26. For further discussion, see Ulrich, "Jewish, Christian, and Empirical Perspectives on the Text of Our Scriptures," in *Hebrew Bible or Old Testament? Studying the Bible in Judaism and Christianity* (ed. R. Brooks and J. J. Collins; Christianity and Judaism in Antiquity 5; Notre Dame: University of Notre Dame Press, 1990) 69-85, esp. 73-77.

27. E. Tov, *Textual Criticism of the Hebrew Bible* (Assen: Van Gorcum; Philadelphia: Fortress Press, 1992) 164-80.

tion of a short study. But I think that it may be a useful step in the ongoing discussion to present briefly an alternative idea here. Tov makes a preliminary conclusion that

> At the end of the process of the composition of a biblical book stood one textual entity (a single copy or tradition) which was considered finished at the literary level, even if only by a limited group of people, and which at the same time stood at the beginning of a process of copying and textual transmission.[28]

He then proposes a conclusion based on the previous one:

> Since only one finished literary composition is in our mind when we deal with textual issues, textual criticism aims at that literary composition which has been accepted as binding (authoritative) by Jewish tradition, since textual criticism is concerned with the literary compositions contained in the traditional Hebrew Bible. This implies that the textual criticism of the Hebrew Bible aims at the literary compositions contained in 𝔐, to the exclusion of later (midrashic) literary compilations such as the Hebrew text behind several sections in 𝔊, viz., sections in 1-2 Kings, Esther, and Daniel . . . , and earlier and possibly parallel compositions, such as 𝔊 of Jeremiah, Joshua, Ezekiel, and sections of Samuel. . . .[29]

No one in our generation has contributed more than Emanuel Tov to our understanding of the textual criticism of the Hebrew Bible, especially in light of the scrolls. But I am sure he would agree that it will take time for us to assimilate all this new evidence and achieve a fully balanced perspective. I think that a check on the scene imagined here may help move the discussion forward, and so I suggest that we revise our imaginative scene to include the diachronic complexity of the text, and then test both formulations. First, insofar as the argument of this paper has validity, there would normally have been, at any one time, not one but two or possibly more editions of many of the biblical books in circulation. Was there really an "end of the process of the composition of a biblical book" that was anything more than the abrupt interruption of the composition process for external, hostile reasons (the Roman threat or the Rabbinic-Christian debates)? And clearly, for some books two variant editions "stood at the beginning of a process of copying and textual transmission."

Secondly, I think the time has come to question the traditional as-

28. Tov, *Textual Criticism,* 177.
29. Tov, *Textual Criticism,* 177.

sumption that "only one finished literary composition is in our mind when we deal with textual issues." That has, of course, been the assumption, but it derives from the period when we had only a single witness to each book of the Hebrew Bible (since the Samaritan Pentateuch was not seriously considered as a text of Scripture). And the second part of this paper suggests that, in contrast to an earlier era when there was an assumption of "normative Judaism," the acceptance "as binding (authoritative) by Jewish tradition" appears to be a slightly later phenomenon. Is the proof there at a sufficiently early date to warrant such a claim for Judaism? And, even if warranted for Judaism, is the proof there that general Judaism had a clearly defined single text of each book at a sufficiently early date to warrant such a claim for Christianity?

Insofar as I understand the evidence, neither warrant is in place. I have been searching, without result, for over a decade for any evidence that any group prior to the Second Revolt consciously selected a certain text type on the basis of textual comparison. There seems to be no evidence that texts were compared for text-critical purposes to select a single text that would become standard. Then, like now, so it appears, the text was not subject to sectarian polemics, except for the SP. The text was pluriform, and creativity was allowed, but only for natural development, not for ideological polemics. If that be so, is the following a legitimate way to pose the question, both from a historical point of view and from a religious — Jewish and Christian — point of view: If the text was indeed pluriform and still developing near the end of the first century C.E. and perhaps into the second century, should not the object of the text-critical endeavor be the text as it truly was? That is, should not the object of the textual criticism of the Hebrew Bible be, not the single (and textually arbitrary?) collection of Masoretic texts of the individual books, but the organic, developing, pluriform Hebrew text — different for each book — such as the evidence indicates?

A historical example can illustrate the need for a revised view. Thirty years ago and perhaps still today, James Sanders stood in the minority in claiming that the Psalms Scroll from Qumran (11QPs^{a}) was truly a form of the Psalter, while a number of weighty voices declared that it was a secondary, post-biblical and non-biblical composition.[30] This demonstrates the need to refine the criteria for understanding the biblical text in the period of the formation of Rabbinic Judaism and Christianity. The case for the biblical character of that scroll has been strongly made now by Peter Flint, made freshly in light of the gains in understanding the nature of the biblical

30. See note 21 above.

text and in light of the full evidence of the Psalms material from the Judaean Desert.[31]

Thus, because the text of each book was produced organically, in multiple layers, determining "the original text" is a difficult, complex task; and arguably, it may not even be the correct goal. Historically, was there ever such a thing? Theologically, how do we decide which to select of the many layers that could claim to be the "original reading"? Often the more powerful religious meanings in a text are those that entered the text at a relatively late or developed stage; do we choose the "original" but less powerful reading or the later, more profound reading? In contrast, if a profound religious insight in an early stage of the text is neutralized later by a conventional formula, which do we select?

It is tempting to continue exploring the difficulties of seeking "the original text," by considering the relationship of text and canon.[32] One suggestive observation to consider here is that, beyond those books we now retrospectively consider Scripture, the בני ישראל were composing a wide library of religious literature, some of which was undoubtedly considered as serious, as holy, as some of those books that subsequently were included in the canons of the various heirs to the בני ישראל. One thinks of *Enoch* and *Jubilees, Sirach* and *Tobit,* and other books that were considered Scripture by some. All were composed in similar ways; the difference is due to later, reflexive judgments. But canon is a category of tradition, not of Scripture. Scripture, of course, began as tradition and only gradually *became* "Scripture"; and the collection of the Scriptures becomes canon retrospectively only through the historical developments of the community's ongoing trajectory of life, thought, and controversy that eventually gets labeled "tradition."

31. See the 4QPsalms editions by P. W. Skehan, E. Ulrich, and P. W. Flint in DJD 16 (forthcoming); Flint, *The Dead Sea Psalms Scrolls;* and E. Ulrich, "Multiple Literary Editions: Reflections Toward a Theory of the History of the Biblical Text," in *Current Research and Technological Developments on the Dead Sea Scrolls: Conference on the Texts from the Judean Desert, Jerusalem, 30 April 1995* (ed. D. W. Parry and S. D. Ricks; STDJ 20; Leiden: Brill, 1996) 78-105, esp. 99-101 (reprinted as Chapter 6 in this volume).

32. For discussion, see Sanders, *Canon and Community;* idem, *From Sacred Story to Sacred Text;* Ulrich, "The Canonical Process"; idem, "The Bible in the Making."

CHAPTER 2

The Bible in the Making: The Scriptures at Qumran

The first statement to make about the Bible at Qumran is that we should probably not think of a "Bible" in the first century B.C.E. or the first century C.E., at Qumran or elsewhere. There were collections of sacred scripture, of course, but no Bible in our developed sense of the term. Then, just as now, the precise list of books which were considered "Scripture" varied from group to group. When we say the word "Bible," there are at least three shapes to the idea — presuming that Christians would add a number of books (the New Testament) that Jews would not, and presuming that Catholics would add a number of books (the Apocrypha or Deuterocanonicals) that Protestants would not, and Greek Orthodox would add more.

In what follows I will attempt to offer a sharper and more accurate understanding of the Scriptures at Qumran, or our Bible in the shape it had during the Qumran period, from two perspectives. The first is the external shape of the collection, or collections, of Scripture in the late Second Temple period in Judaism, at the time of the birth of Christianity. What did the collection of the unrolled books of the Scriptures look like? The second is an internal perspective: once the scrolls are unrolled and read, what do we learn from their contents? What are the results — as we can see them now — of the analysis that my colleagues and I have done on the biblical scrolls so far? I will then conclude with some reflections upon the significance of these new data for a sharper view of our Bible today.

I must preface this discussion with a few preliminary remarks. First, here I am speaking primarily as a historian. I hasten to add that I think that all that follows is also easily compatible religiously. But the attempt here is to describe the nature of the Bible as it was in this crucial period of religious history — as seen through the ancient window, and bathed in the new light, provided from Qumran.

Secondly, some of what follows could be interpreted as less than respectful to the traditional *textus receptus* of the Hebrew Bible, called the Masoretic Text (MT). Let me assure you, that is not my intent. I have high respect for this most important of witnesses to the ancient Hebrew Bible. But the evidence from the ancient world — and not just that of the scrolls, but also that of the Samaritan Pentateuch (SP) and the Septuagint (LXX, i.e., the Greek translation of the Hebrew) — makes us see things a bit more clearly than we used to, and I have found that sometimes this new knowledge comes at the cost of some uneasiness or defensiveness concerning our time-honored views, whether those views are entirely accurate or not.

Thirdly, it is important to stick to our coign of vantage: to look at the evidence concerning the Scriptures that we actually find at Qumran, at times aided by evidence from the New Testament and the Mishnah and Talmud. But we should try to look with first-century eyes, not retrojecting later perspectives without warrant back onto first-century reality.

The Scrolls and the External Shape of the Collection(s) of Scripture

The Corpus of Scrolls of Scripture Found at Qumran

From the eleven caves at Qumran fragments from roughly 800 manuscripts were recovered.[1] Of these about 200, or 25 percent, were scriptural manu-

1. For principal publications and lists of the manuscripts, see: M. Burrows, ed., *The Dead Sea Scrolls of St. Mark's Monastery,* vol. 1 (New Haven: American Schools of Oriental Research, 1950); F. M. Cross et al., *Scrolls from Qumrân Cave I: The Great Isaiah Scroll, the Order of the Community, the* Pesher *to Habakkuk;* from photographs by John C. Trever (Jerusalem: Albright Institute of Archaeological Research and the Shrine of the Book, 1972); E. L. Sukenik, *The Dead Sea Scrolls of the Hebrew University* (Jerusalem: Hebrew University and Magnes Press, 1955); D. Barthélemy and J. T. Milik, *Qumrân Cave 1* (DJD 1; Oxford: Clarendon, 1955); P. Benoit, J. T. Milik, and R. de Vaux, *Les Grottes de Murabbaʿat.* 1: *Texte.* 2: *Planches* (DJD 2; Oxford: Clarendon, 1961); M. Baillet, J. T. Milik, and R. de Vaux, *Les 'Petites Grottes' de Qumrân.* 1: *Texte.* 2: *Planches* (DJD 3; Oxford: Clarendon, 1962); J. A. Sanders, *The Psalms Scroll of Qumrân Cave 11 (11QPs^{a})* (DJD 4; Oxford: Clarendon, 1965); M. Baillet, *Qumrân Grotte 4, III* (DJD 7; Oxford: Clarendon, 1982); E. Tov with R. A. Kraft, *The Greek Minor Prophets Scroll from Naḥal Ḥever (8ḤevXII gr)* (The Seiyâl

scripts. Cave 4 was by far the richest cave, with some 575 of those 800 manuscripts. Of the 575 manuscripts from Cave 4, roughly 127 were classified as "biblical," though as usual that designation needs some fine-print distinctions.[2] About 65 biblical manuscripts were recovered from the other ten caves combined. At least one copy of each of the books of the traditional Hebrew canon, except for Esther and Nehemiah, was found at Qumran, as were some of the books of the wider canon.[3] The three books represented by the most manuscripts were the Psalms (39 total from all the caves, including 22 manuscripts from Cave 4), Deuteronomy (32 total, including 21 manuscripts from Cave 4), and Isaiah (22 total, including 18 manuscripts from Cave 4). It is interesting, but not surprising, that these three books are also the most frequently quoted in the New Testament.

The Collection of Books of Scripture

The Qumran scrolls tell us many new and exciting things about the Scriptures. Why do I say Scriptures and not Bible? What is the difference? The Scriptures are a collection of sacred works that are considered authoritative for belief and practice within a religious community. The term "Bible," in the singular, adds the extra factor — linked with the idea of a "canon" — of inclusivity and exclusivity: these books are *in*, those books are *out*. From a visual perspective, the Bible is a single book with a front cover and a back cover, and a definite table of contents.

During the Qumran period, however, and more broadly during the closing centuries of the Second Temple period in Judaism, there were "volumes," not "books." Literary works were written on scrolls, not in codices. Our word "volume" comes from the Latin word *volumen*, "a rolled thing," from *volvo*, "to

Collection 1; DJD 8; Oxford: Clarendon, 1989); P. W. Skehan, E. Ulrich, and J. E. Sanderson, *Qumran Cave 4, IV: Palaeo-Hebrew and Greek Biblical Manuscripts* (DJD 9; Oxford, Clarendon, 1992); E. Tov, ed., *The Dead Sea Scrolls on Microfiche: A Comprehensive Facsimile Edition of the Texts from the Judean Desert, Companion Volume* (Leiden: Brill, 1993); F. García Martínez, "Lista de MSS procedentes de Qumran," *Henoch* 11 (1989) 149-232; J. A. Fitzmyer, *The Dead Sea Scrolls: Major Publications and Tools for Study* (rev. ed.; SBLRBS 20; Atlanta: Scholars Press, 1990); E. Tov, "The Unpublished Qumran Texts from Caves 4 and 11," *BA* 55 (1992) 94-104.

2. For a list and description of the biblical manuscripts from Cave 4, see E. Ulrich, "The Biblical Scrolls from Qumran Cave 4: An Overview and a Progress Report on their Publication," *RevQ* 14 (1989) 207-28. See also idem, "An Index of Passages in the Biblical Manuscripts from the Judean Desert (Genesis-Kings)," *DSD* 1 (1994) 113-29.

3. E.g., Sirach, Tobit, *Jubilees, Enoch,* the Epistle of Jeremiah, etc.

turn or roll." The codex, a stack of leaves or pages bound together, did not become the normal format for literary works until the third or fourth century C.E.[4] Our early large manuscripts of the Greek Bible, for example, dating from the fourth and fifth centuries of the common era, are codices.[5]

Thus, during the period of the Dead Sea Scrolls, the late Second Temple period, the time of Hillel and Christ, and several centuries beyond, our visual imaginations must conjure up books of the Scriptures inscribed on individual scrolls. When the pious community of the Covenant at Qumran studied the Scriptures, they unrolled individual scrolls. When Jesus stood up in the synagogue at Nazareth, the Gospel According to Luke narrates (4:16-20) that he unrolled a scroll of Isaiah — a scroll perhaps not too different from the Great Isaiah Scroll, found entirely intact in Cave 1 at Qumran and on display at the Shrine of the Book in Jerusalem. Although the entire Bible can be printed within a single book, it was impossible to copy all the Scriptures on a single scroll. Thus, we must imagine a collection of scrolls.

Exactly how many scrolls would have been included in this collection? It may help to envision a large jar of scrolls or a shelf of scrolls. Then, just as now, the precise list of books which were considered "Scripture" varied from group to group. Which scrolls belonged in the jar? Which were relegated to outside the jar? Which scrolls were to be shelved on the main shelf of "Scripture," as opposed to the lower shelf marked (proleptically) "Apocrypha and Pseudepigrapha"? We have no clear evidence that anyone was explicitly asking these questions yet. To be sure, the Samaritans seem to have settled conservatively on the five books of Moses alone as their authoritative Scriptures.[6] But what appears to have been the dominant view — shared by the Pharisees, the Qumran community, and the early Christians — included the Prophets as well.

1. So we come to our first conclusion: there was *no canon* as yet, no clearly agreed-upon list of which books were "Scripture" and which were not. This was the situation at least up to the fall of the Second Temple in 70 C.E., probably as late as the end of the first century, and arguably even up to the

4. Edward M. Thompson, *An Introduction to Greek and Latin Palaeography* (Oxford: Clarendon, 1912) 51-53.

5. The Septuagint manuscripts from Qumran, however, are scrolls, not codices; see DJD 3 and 9.

6. Some would conclude, on the basis of Josephus, the same position for the Sadducees. But James VanderKam ("Revealed Literature in the Second-Temple Period," forthcoming) argues that Josephus's statement must be interpreted "in a context in which he is distinguishing sources of authority for practice. . . ."

second Jewish revolt against Rome in 132-135 C.E., since we find Rabbi Aqiba having to argue strenuously that, yes, The Song of Songs is in fact Scripture.

2. But the *order* of the books was also unclear. This was usually no problem as long as the Scriptures were written on discrete scrolls. To be sure, the five books of Moses had achieved a recognized order; of the few manuscripts in which we find more than one book written on a single scroll, only one may possibly preserve the physical connection between two books of the Torah, and it appears to be in the traditional order.[7] Their fixed order, however, is partly set by the chronological structure of the story from creation down to Moses.

But it was a different matter for the Prophets. I am unaware of any scroll that contains more than one prophetic book,[8] and so our evidence at Qumran is limited. Nonetheless, the Former Prophets (the books of Joshua, Judges, Samuel, and Kings) most likely maintained that fixed order, since, as for the Torah, the order was primarily determined by the chronological structure of the story that the books narrate. For the Latter Prophets, however, Jewish and Christian lists[9] from antiquity display varying orders, and as late as the Talmud (fourth to fifth century), the Rabbis tell us "the order of the Prophets is . . . Jeremiah, Ezekiel, Isaiah. . . ."[10]

3. More importantly, it was unclear *which books* were included among the Prophets. One of the primary names for the Scriptures both at Qumran and in the New Testament is "The Law and the Prophets."[11] The *Rule of the Community* from Cave 1 at Qumran begins with the goal "that they may seek God with a whole heart and soul, and do what is good and right before Him as He commanded by the hand of Moses and all His servants the Prophets. . . ."[12] But which books were considered among the Prophets? Was Daniel? Were the Psalms? The *Florilegium* specifically mentions the "book of the prophet Daniel,"[13] and the Gospel According to Matthew calls Daniel a prophet.[14] Moreover, Josephus and Melito also think of him as a prophet, and

7. 4QpaleoGen-Exod[l] probably contains the end of Genesis, plus one partly blank and three fully blank lines, then the beginning of Exodus. The physical join between the end of one book and the beginning of the next is not preserved on 4QGen-Exod[a], 4QExod-Lev[f], or 4QLev-Num[a].

8. The twelve Minor Prophets evidently were considered to comprise one book.

9. A number of lists are reproduced in H. B. Swete, *An Introduction to the Old Testament in Greek* (rev. ed. by R. R. Ottley; New York: Ktav, 1968) 198-214.

10. *B. B. Bat.* 14b.

11. See, e.g., Luke 16:16, 29, 31; 24:27; Acts 26:22; 28:23.

12. 1QS 1:1-3; trans. G. Vermes, *The Dead Sea Scrolls in English* (3d ed.; London: Penguin, 1987) 62.

13. 4Q174 2:3 (DJD 5:54).

14. Matt 24:15; see also Mark 13:14.

in fact the first written evidence that places Daniel not among the prophets but among the Ketubim or Writings is the much later Talmud. So Daniel was among the prophets in Judaism generally in the first century.

Similarly, with respect to the Psalms, the Qumran community produced *pesharim,* or commentaries, evidently only on prophetic books; but there turn up a few *pesharim* on the Psalms,[15] and 11QPs[a] speaks of David as having composed the Psalms through prophecy.[16] If we find ourselves hesitating here, we can again look at the New Testament, which also interprets the Psalms prophetically.

4. What is more, apparently the category of "Prophets" was gradually perceived as being *stretched too far.* Though "the Law and the Prophets" (or "Moses and the Prophets") was a frequent designation for the Scriptures at Qumran and in the New Testament, 4QMMT at one point speaks of Moses, the Prophets, and David, parallel to Luke's speaking of "the Law and the Prophets and Psalms" (24:44). So the book of Psalms, which had been counted among the Prophets, began to establish a new category which eventually would be called the Ketubim or the Hagiographa. Other books as well, such as *Jubilees, Enoch,* Sirach, and a number of the other apocrypha or deuterocanonical works, were also being quoted or alluded to both at Qumran and in the New Testament in the same manner and the same contexts as other scriptural works.[17] And these, or some of these, became the Ketubim or the Hagiographa.

In short, though the books constituting the inner core of the collection, viz., the Torah and the main Prophets, were clearly considered authoritative works of Scripture, and their order was largely but not fully set, works nearer the periphery were still finding their place.

The Individual Books of Scripture as Seen from Qumran

The Text Encountered in the Individual Scrolls

What do the books of Scripture look like from within? When the individual books were unrolled in antiquity, did they look exactly like the text of the He-

15. 1Q16, 4Q171, 4Q173; 4Q172?

16. כול אלה דבר בנבואה אשר נתן לו מלפני העליון, 11QPs[a] 27:11 (DJD 4:48 and plate 16).

17. *Jub.* 23:11 is quoted as authoritative in CD 10:8-10 and its exact title, "The Book of the Divisions of the Times in their Jubilees and Weeks," occurs in CD 16:3-4. In addition, allusions to *Enoch* occur fourteen times in the NT.

brew Bible that we read or translate today? A healthy presumption is that no two manuscripts of any book in antiquity were ever exactly alike. Before the invention of the printing press in the fifteenth century and more recent photographic and electronic means of mass production of books, every copy of every book was indeed a copy, made individually by a more or less careful, but fallible, human being. But let's dismiss the individual minor variants and errors that populate every text. Let's also note but not get distracted by the differing systems or practices of orthography or spelling; much as in Elizabethan England, where spelling was more a creative art than a linguistic science, so too in the scrolls we find a variety of orthographic styles. These two categories of variation between manuscripts — individual minor variants and orthographic differences — usually do not make much of a difference in meaning. But there has emerged a third category that teaches us much about the composition and transmission of the ancient biblical text, namely, multiple literary editions of biblical books and passages.

Multiple Literary Editions of Biblical Books and Passages

Although in the traditional, pious, and popular imagination, the books of Scripture were composed by individual holy men from earliest times (Moses and Isaiah, for example), critical study of the text of Scripture demonstrates that the books are the result of a long literary development, whereby traditional material was faithfully retold and handed on from generation to generation, but also creatively expanded and reshaped to fit the new circumstances and new needs that the successive communities experienced through the vicissitudes of history. So the process of the composition of the Scriptures was organic, developmental, with successive layers of tradition. Ezekiel was commanded to eat a scroll and found that it was sweet as honey (Ezek 3:1-3), so perhaps I can be allowed to use the image of baklava for the composition of scriptural texts: many layers laid on top of one another by successive generations over the centuries, as the traditions were handed on faithfully but creatively adapted, and formed into a unity by the honey — sometimes heated — of the lived experience of the community over time.

At Qumran as in wider Judaism, we can see the scribes and their predecessors at work along two lines. Often the books of the Scriptures were simply copied as exactly as possible. But sometimes the scribes intentionally incorporated new material that helped interpret or bring home to their contemporary congregation in a new situation the relevance of the traditional text. These creative biblical scribes were actively handing on the tradition, but they were adding to it, enriching it, making it adaptable, up-to-date, relevant, multivalent. We must assume that by and large they knew explicitly what they were doing. Insofar as the scribes were handing on the tradition, they became part of the canonical process: handing on the tradition is a constitutive factor of the canonical process. James Sanders refers to this aspect as "repetition."[18] The repetition, in a sense, works like a hammer, pounding home again and again that this material is important. The texts were authoritative texts, and through the traditioning process they were being made more authoritative.

But the scribes were also updating the tradition, contemporizing it, making it relevant. That is, sometimes when the tradition was not adaptable, these scribes *made* it adaptable, thus giving it another of its canonical characteristics, a complementary factor that Sanders terms "resignification." That is, the tradition, important in its original setting, and important in itself beyond its importance for that original concrete situation, is found also to be important to me here and now in my present situation. The tradition proves adaptable, capable of having new significance in this new particular situation. The resignification — insofar as the tradition has proved useful or true — shows that indeed the tradition is *important in itself* (thus genuinely in the category of "tradition") and that it is *important to me* (thus genuinely in the category of "adaptable tradition"). The "authority" of such tradition is not an extraneous characteristic (authority imposed) but is intrinsic (the community recognizes the life-giving power of the tradition).[19]

Thus, we have gained a new window on the ancient world and the biblical text in the making. The Qumran manuscripts and the versions document the creativity of religious leaders and scribes who produced revised literary editions of many of the books of Scripture. But, as is often the case with new knowledge, this new illumination brings complications. If this was the way the Scriptures were composed, how do we isolate "the original text"? What level do we translate in our modern Bible translations? We will touch on those problems later. Here, let us simply note that such *composition-by-stages* is the method by which the Scriptures were produced from the beginning, and that for some of the latter stages we now have manuscript evidence docu-

18. James A. Sanders, *Canon and Community: A Guide to Canonical Criticism* (Philadelphia: Fortress, 1984) 22.

19. E. Ulrich, "The Canonical Process, Textual Criticism, and Latter Stages in the Composition of the Bible," in *Sha'arei Talmon: Studies in the Bible, Qumran, and the Ancient Near East Presented to Shemaryahu Talmon* (ed. M. Fishbane and E. Tov with W. W. Fields; Winona Lake, Ind.: Eisenbrauns, 1992) 267-91, esp. pp. 288-89 (reprinted as Chapter 4 in this volume).

menting two or more literary editions of some of the biblical books. We will describe these as we review the books at Qumran one by one.

A Review of Individual Books

The text of *Genesis* starts us off slowly and gently, like the beginning of a roller-coaster or Ferris-wheel ride, though the ride will become more textually interesting soon. It appears that the text of Genesis had become basically stable by the late Second Temple period. All our manuscripts exhibit basically the same text type; most of the variants are only minor or unintentional.[20]

The book of *Exodus*, however, provides a clear example of two editions of a biblical book. The different edition preserved in the Samaritan Pentateuch (SP) has been known since the seventeenth century, but its significance was capable of being dismissed, because the major differences were considered the work of the marginalized Samaritans. With the discovery of 4QpaleoExod^{m},[21] however, we see that the book of Exodus circulated in Judaism in two editions. One was the form traditionally found in the MT and translated in the LXX, and the other an intentionally expanded version with most of the features characteristic of the Samaritan version except the two *specifically* Samaritan features (namely, the addition of the commandment to build an altar on Mt. Gerizim, and the systematic use of the past, and not the future, of the verb in the formula "the place that the Lord has chosen" [not "will choose"]).[22]

The book of *Leviticus*, perhaps because it was a work containing specific cultic regulations, also seems to have stabilized early, and to my knowledge, we have only one major textual tradition.[23]

20. A possible exception is the chronological system. For editions of the Cave 4 manuscripts, see James R. Davila, "Unpublished Pentateuchal Manuscripts from Cave IV, Qumran: 4QGenEx^{a}, 4QGen$^{b\text{-}h,j\text{-}k}$" (Dissertation, Harvard University, 1988).

21. For the publication of 4QpaleoExod^{m} see P. W. Skehan, E. Ulrich, and J. E. Sanderson, DJD 9:53-130. For preliminary publication and analyses see P. W. Skehan, "Exodus in the Samaritan Recension from Qumran," *JBL* 74 (1955) 182-87; idem, "Qumran and the Present State of Old Testament Text Studies: The Masoretic Text," *JBL* 78 (1959) 21-25, esp. 25; J. E. Sanderson, *An Exodus Scroll from Qumran: 4QpaleoExod^{m} and the Samaritan Tradition* (HSS 30; Atlanta: Scholars Press, 1986); eadem, "The Contributions of 4QpaleoExod^{m} to Textual Criticism," in *Mémorial Jean Carmignac* = *RevQ* 13 (1988) 547-60; eadem, "The Old Greek of Exodus in the Light of 4QpaleoExod^{m}," *Textus* 14 (1988) 87-104.

22. Cf. Exod 20:17, and Deut 12:5, 11, 14, 18, etc.

23. For the publication of 4QLev^{c}, see the contribution of E. Tov in *Pomegranates*

The book of *Numbers* again exhibits variant editions. 4QNum[b], edited by Nathan Jastram, shows a number of expansions shared by the Samaritan text of Numbers, but it is not specifically Samaritan.[24] Again, it seems that there were at least two editions of Exodus and Numbers that circulated within Judaism in the Second Temple period, and the Samaritans simply took one of those (the expanded version) and used that as their Torah, making only a few changes in accord with their beliefs.

The book of *Deuteronomy* is one of the three most popular books at Qumran, just as it is in the New Testament.[25] It is too early to be able to give a definitive account of the textual nature of Deuteronomy, but there is a wide variety of textual variants preserved in the manuscripts from Qumran, and some manuscripts which preserve text that is totally from scripture were apparently not *biblical* manuscripts but manuscripts of biblical excerpts used for liturgical purposes.[26]

Once past the book of Deuteronomy, the number of scrolls preserved for each book diminishes. For some books, either such a small percentage survives at Qumran, or the analyses are so recent, that it is hazardous to proffer judgments about them, since such judgments would undoubtedly be quoted and passed on as "the assured results of scholarship" in settings that would only cause disinformation. For the book of Esther, for example, nothing survives (if the book had been there at all). Nothing survives of the book

---

and Golden Bells: Studies in Biblical, Jewish, and Near Eastern Ritual, Law, and Literature in Honor of Jacob Milgrom (ed. D. P. Wright, D. N. Freedman, and A. Hurvitz; Winona Lake, Ind.: Eisenbrauns, 1995). For 4QLev[d], see E. Tov, "4QLev[d] (4Q26)," in *The Scriptures and the Scrolls: Studies in Honour of A. S. van der Woude on the Occasion of His 65th Birthday* (ed. F. García Martínez et al.; VTSup 49; Leiden: Brill, 1992) 1-5 and plates 1-2.

24. N. Jastram, "The Book of Numbers from Qumrân, Cave IV (4QNum[b])" (Dissertation, Harvard University, 1990).

25. For editions of the Deuteronomy manuscripts see Sidnie Ann White, "A Critical Edition of Seven Manuscripts of Deuteronomy: 4QDt[a], 4QDt[c], 4QDt[d], 4QDt[f], 4QDt[g], 4QDt[i], and 4QDt[n]" (Dissertation, Harvard University, 1988); eadem, "The All Souls Deuteronomy and the Decalogue," *JBL* 109 (1990) 193-206; eadem, "Three Deuteronomy Manuscripts from Cave 4, Qumran," *JBL* 112 (1993) 23-42; Julie Ann Duncan, "A Critical Edition of Deuteronomy Manuscripts from Qumran, Cave IV: 4QDt[b], 4QDt[e], 4QDt[h], 4QDt[j], 4QDt[k], 4QDt[l]" (Dissertation, Harvard University, 1989); Esther Eshel, "4QDeut[n] — A Text That Has Undergone Harmonistic Editing," *HUCA* 62 (1991) 117-54; P. W. Skehan, "The Structure of the Song of Moses in Deuteronomy (Dt 32:1-43)," *CBQ* 13 (1951) 153-63, reprinted in P. W. Skehan, *Studies in Israelite Poetry and Wisdom* (CBQMS 1; Washington, D.C.: Catholic Biblical Association of America, 1971) 67-77; idem, "A Fragment of the 'Song of Moses' (Deut. 32) from Qumran," *BASOR* 136 (1954) 12-15; Skehan, Ulrich, and Sanderson, DJD 9.131-54.

26. E.g., 4QDeut[j] and 4QDeut[n].

of Nehemiah, unless Nehemiah was — this early — always considered as part of a single book of Ezra-Nehemiah. From the following books only small amounts survive, and judgment — beyond that given in the preliminary editions — should be held in abeyance until sufficient analysis has been completed: the books of *Judges,*[27] *Kings,*[28] *Ruth, Canticles, Qoheleth,*[29] *Lamentations,*[30] *Ezra,*[31] *Chronicles.*[32] The book of Ezekiel survives in only three small manuscripts,[33] the book of *Job* in only three,[34] and *Proverbs* in only two;[35] the text in these manuscripts appears to be generally similar to that of the traditional *textus receptus.*

The text of *Joshua* survives in only two manuscripts that are clearly the book of Joshua.[36] In addition, 4QpaleoParaJoshua (4Q123) is a manuscript

27. J. Trebolle Barrera, "Textual Variants in *4QJudg*[a] and the Textual and Editorial History of the Book of Judges," *RevQ* 14 (1989) 229-45.

28. J. Trebolle Barrera, "A Preliminary Edition of 4QKings (4Q54)," in *The Madrid Qumran Congress: Proceedings of the International Congress on the Dead Sea Scrolls, Madrid 18-21 March, 1991* (2 vols.; ed. J. Trebolle Barrera and L. Vegas Montaner; STDJ 11; Leiden: Brill; Madrid: Editorial Complutense, 1992) 1:229-46. Trebolle has developed a methodology for recovering an alternate edition of the books of Kings; see his "Redaction, Recension, and Midrash in the Books of Kings," *BIOSCS* 15 (1982) 12-35.

29. E. Ulrich, "Ezra and Qoheleth Manuscripts from Qumran (4QEzra, 4QQoh[a,b])," in *Priests, Prophets, and Scribes: Essays on the Formation and Heritage of Second Temple Judaism in Honour of Joseph Blenkinsopp* (ed. E. Ulrich et al.; JSOTSup 149; Sheffield: JSOT Press, 1992) 139-57.

30. F. M. Cross, "Studies in the Structure of Hebrew Verse: The Prosody of Lamentations 1:1-22," in *The Word of the Lord Shall Go Forth: Essays in Honor of David Noel Freedman in Celebration of His Sixtieth Birthday* (ed. Carol L. Meyers and M. O'Connor: Winona Lake, Ind.: ASOR/Eisenbrauns, 1983) 129-55.

31. Ulrich, "Ezra and Qoheleth Manuscripts."

32. J. Trebolle Barrera, "Édition préliminaire de 4QChroniques," *RevQ* 15 (1992) 423-29.

33. See the provisional transcription of 4QEzek[a] and 4QEzek[b] by Johan Lust, "Ezekiel Manuscripts in Qumran: Preliminary Edition of 4Q Ez a and b," *Ezekiel and His Book: Textual and Literary Criticism and Their Interrelation* (ed. J. Lust; Leuven: Leuven University Press, 1986) 90-100.

34. For 4QpaleoJob[c], see DJD 9:155-57.

35. See P. W. Skehan, "Qumran and Old Testament Criticism," in *Qumran: Sa piété, sa théologie et son mileu* (ed. M. Delcor; BETL 46; Paris: Duculot; Leuven: Leuven University Press, 1978) 163.

36. E. Ulrich, "4QJoshua[a] and Joshua's First Altar in the Promised Land," in *New Qumran Texts and Studies: Proceedings of the First Meeting of the International Organization for Qumran Studies, Paris 1992* (ed. G. J. Brooke with F. García Martinez; STDJ 15; Leiden: Brill, 1994) 89-104 and plates 4-6; E. Tov, "4QJosh[b]," in *Intertestamental Essays in Honour of Józef Tadeusz Milik* (ed. Z. J. Kapera; Kraków: Enigma, 1992) 205-12 and plate 1. For full critical editions of the Qumran texts of Deuteronomy, Joshua, Judges, and Kings,

with only four fragments surviving. They are so small that the work is difficult to identify, but the text is more reminiscent of the book of Joshua than of any other known work, and it is conceivable that it is simply a variant textual form of the biblical book.[37] Furthermore, 4QJosh[a] appears to present a variant edition of the text of that book. Though not fully certain, it is probable that the scroll contained an intentionally different order of the narrative in a highly significant matter — the building of the first altar in the newly entered promised land. The passage that occurs at the end of chapter 8 in the traditional MT (though suspiciously after 9:2 in the LXX) is placed before chapter 5 in 4QJosh[a]. What is more, one of our earliest witnesses to the biblical text, Josephus, similarly attests that Joshua built an altar at Gilgal immediately after crossing the Jordan and entering the Land.[38] The placement of the passage in the MT is admittedly odd, entailing the curious detour up to the otherwise insignificant Mt. Ebal. It is quite possible that 4QJosh[a] and Josephus retain the original story and that it has been changed in the MT tradition due to anti-Samaritan polemic.

The book of *Samuel* is somewhat more complex.[39] There do not appear to have been two separate editions of the entire book (or pair of books), but there are variant editions of certain passages. Insofar as Stanley Walters's analysis of 1 Samuel 1 is accepted, the argument can be made for a second, intentionally developed and changed edition of that narrative, perhaps due to

---

see now E. Ulrich, et al., *Qumran Cave 4, IX: Deuteronomy, Joshua, Judges, Kings* (DJD 14; Oxford Clarendon Press, 1996).

37. Ulrich, DJD 9:201-3.

38. Josephus, *Antiquities* 5.1.4 §20

39. For 4QSam[a], see F. M. Cross, "A New Qumran Biblical Fragment Related to the Original Hebrew Underlying the Septuagint," *BASOR* 132 (1953) 15-26; idem, "The Ammonite Oppression of the Tribes of Gad and Reuben: Missing Verses from 1 Samuel 11 Found in 4QSam[a]," in *The Hebrew and Greek Texts of Samuel: 1980 Proceedings IOSCS — Vienna* (ed. E. Tov; Jerusalem: Academon, 1980) 105-19. E. Ulrich, *The Qumran Text of Samuel and Josephus* (HSM 19; Missoula, Mont.: Scholars Press, 1978); a list of contents of the manuscript is given on p. 271. See also E. Tov, "The Textual Affiliations of 4QSam[a]," *JSOT* 14 (1979) 37-53, reprinted in *The Hebrew and Greek Texts of Samuel* (ed. E. Tov; Jerusalem: Academon, 1980) 189-205; J. Trebolle Barrera, "El estudio de 4Q Sam[a]: Implicaciones exegéticas e históricas," *Estudios bíblicos* 39 (1981) 5-18; and A. van der Kooij, "De tekst van Samuel en het tekstkritisch onderzoek," *Nederlands Theologisch Tijdschrift* 36 (1982) 177-204. For 4QSam[b], see F. M. Cross, "The Oldest Manuscripts from Qumran," *JBL* 74 (1955) 147-72; and for 4QSam[c], see E. Ulrich, "4QSam[c]: A Fragmentary Manuscript of 2 Samuel 14–15 from the Scribe of the *Serek Hay-yaḥad* (1QS)," *BASOR* 235 (1979) 1-25, reprinted in *The Hebrew and Greek Texts of Samuel* (ed. E. Tov; Jerusalem: Academon, 1980) 166-88.

theological and misogynist factors.[40] For the David-Goliath narrative in 1 Samuel 17–18 there are also two quite contrasting variant editions.[41]

The book of *Isaiah* is one of the three most richly attested books at Qumran.[42] The textual character of the book and its many manuscript witnesses from Qumran is too complex for adequate summary here. The scrolls do not seem to preserve evidence of different editions, but the multivalent poetic text shows at a number of points that the LXX faithfully translated an existing Hebrew text and was not "free," if free means tendentious or inventive.[43]

The book of *Jeremiah,* however, does provide evidence of two literary editions,[44] and this appears to be widely recognized. The LXX preserves the earlier, shorter edition, documented in Hebrew in 4QJer^{b}, and the MT a subsequent, longer edition, with rearranged text.

The Hebrew manuscripts of the *Twelve Minor Prophets* do not offer

40. Stanley D. Walters, "Hannah and Anna: The Greek and Hebrew Texts of 1 Samuel 1," *JBL* 107 (1988) 385-412.

41. For the detailed characteristics of the two editions, see D. Barthélemy, D. W. Gooding, J. Lust, and E. Tov, *The Story of David and Goliath: Textual and Literary Criticism: Papers of a Joint Research Venture* (OBO 73; Fribourg: Éditions Universitaires; Göttingen: Vandenhoeck & Ruprecht, 1986). I agree with the position of Tov and Lust and disagree with that of Barthélemy and Gooding. The correctness of either position, however, should not distract one from the main point that there are two editions of the biblical text.

42. M. Burrows, ed., *The Dead Sea Scrolls of St. Mark's Monastery,* vol. 1 (New Haven: American Schools of Oriental Research, 1950); F. M. Cross et al., *Scrolls from Qumrân Cave I: The Great Isaiah Scroll, the Order of the Community, the* Pesher *to Habakkuk;* from photographs by John C. Trever (Jerusalem: Albright Institute of Archaeological Research and the Shrine of the Book, 1972); E. L. Sukenik, *The Dead Sea Scrolls of the Hebrew University* (Jerusalem: Hebrew University and Magnes Press, 1955), supplemented by D. Barthélemy and J. T. Milik, DJD 1:66-68; J. Muilenburg, "Fragments of Another Qumran Isaiah Scroll," *BASOR* 135 (1954) 28-32; P. W. Skehan, "Qumrân et découvertes au désert de Juda: IV. Littérature de Qumrân. — A. Textes bibliques. B. Apocryphes de l'Ancien Testament," *DBSup* 9 (1979) cols. 805-28; esp. cols. 811-12. See also P. W. Skehan, "The Text of Isaias at Qumrân," *CBQ* 17 (1955) 158-63; Francis J. Morrow, Jr., "The Text of Isaiah at Qumran" (Dissertation, The Catholic University of America, 1973).

43. See, e.g., P. W. Flint, "The Septuagint Version of Isaiah 23:1-14 and the Massoretic Text," *BIOSCS* 21 (1988) 35-54.

44. E. Tov, "The Jeremiah Scrolls from Qumran," *RevQ* 14 (1989) 189-206; idem, "Three Fragments of Jeremiah from Qumran Cave 4," *RevQ* 15 (1992) 531-41; idem, "The Literary History of the Book of Jeremiah in the Light of Its Textual History," in *Empirical Models for Biblical Criticism* (ed. J. H. Tigay; Philadelphia: University of Pennsylvania, 1985) 213-37; J. Gerald Janzen, *Studies in the Text of Jeremiah* (HSM 6; Cambridge, Mass.: Harvard University Press, 1973) 173-84; F. M. Cross, *The Ancient Library of Qumran and Modern Biblical Studies* (rev. ed.; Grand Rapids: Baker, 1980) 186-87 and notes 37-38.

strong signs of significantly diverse textual traditions,[45] but the Greek scroll from Naḥal Ḥever displays a systematic revision of the Old Greek translation toward the Hebrew text of the proto-Rabbinic tradition (MT).[46]

The book of *Psalms* is again rich but difficult to summarize. More manuscripts of this book are preserved both at Qumran and in the Judaean Desert generally than of any other work.[47] 11QPs[a] is an extensively preserved manuscript. It both includes nine compositions not found in the MT edition and exhibits an order partly identical with the traditional order of the MT but also significantly at variance with it. One of the additional compositions is drawn from another Davidic section of the Hebrew Bible, four were psalms preserved in the Greek and Syriac traditions, and the remaining four were hitherto unknown. But significantly, all (except "David's Compositions") are composed like other biblical psalms; they stand in marked contrast to the *Hôdāyôt,* which sound post-biblical and reflect the theology of the Qumran commune. In "David's Compositions" a clear claim for the revelatory, and thus scriptural, character of the work is made by proclaiming that David composed all these psalms through God-given prophecy, as mentioned above.

I am very close to being convinced that there were (at least) two major editions of the Psalter. One is that found in the MT and more or less reflected in the LXX, though there are numerous minor variants as well as the single major variant that the LXX includes Psalm 151, whereas the MT ends with Psalm 150. A second Psalter — a second edition of the scriptural book of Psalms — is partly preserved in 11QPs[a]; this assertion is supported by the fact that a second manuscript (11QPs[b]) and perhaps a third (4QPs[e]) also seem to exhibit this edition, whereas there is "only one scroll from Masada (MasPs[b]), and none from Qumran, whose order *unambiguously* supports the Received Psalter against the 11QPs[a] arrangement."[48] It should also be noted that 11QPs[a] ends with Psalm 151, as does the LXX.

45. R. E. Fuller, "The Minor Prophets Manuscripts from Qumrân, Cave IV" (Dissertation, Harvard University, 1988), esp. pp. 152-54.

46. Tov with Kraft, *The Greek Minor Prophets Scroll* (DJD 8).

47. P. W. Skehan, "A Psalm Manuscript from Qumran (4QPs[b])," *CBQ* 26 (1964) 313-22; idem, "Qumrân et découvertes," cols. 805-28, esp. cols. 815-16; J. T. Milik, "Deux documents inédits du désert de Juda," *Biblica* 38 (1957) 245-68, esp. 245-55. For analyses, see Gerald H. Wilson, *The Editing of the Hebrew Psalter* (SBLDS 76; Chico, Calif.: Scholars Press, 1985); and Peter W. Flint, "The Psalters at Qumran and the Book of Psalms" (Dissertation, University of Notre Dame, 1993); see now the published form of Flint's dissertation: *The Dead Sea Psalms Scrolls and the Book of Psalms* (STDJ 17; Leiden: Brill, 1997).

48. Flint, "The Psalters," 147.

Finally, the eight manuscripts of the book of *Daniel* from Qumran teach us a great deal about the text, language, and orthography of the book.[49] Though the scrolls themselves do not, the Old Greek in comparison with the MT does exemplify variant literary editions of Daniel.[50]

Conclusions

1. Fifty years ago we had the Masoretic Text, the Samaritan Pentateuch, and the Septuagint, and our predecessors wrote "the history of the biblical text" on the basis of that evidence. Today we have a great deal of new information about the shape of the Bible before 135 C.E. From a general perspective, one could say that not much on the grand scale has changed, but when the focus is sharpened, some serious advances can be seen. Lines that were once obscure or perceived incorrectly are now noticeably clearer, though we could wish for yet greater clarity. Our knowledge has advanced, and so concomitant changes in our explanations will soon have to filter down.

2. The Scriptures were pluriform (as were Judaism and Christianity) until at least 70 C.E., probably until 100, and quite possibly as late as 135 or beyond. Thus, we must revise our imaginations and our explanations. Neither the external shape nor the internal shape of the Scriptures has changed, but our knowledge of them has. We can now know significantly more, and know it more precisely. Externally, we know more about which books were "in" and which "out," and which books were in which category. Internally, we can now see more clearly that there were multiple literary editions of many of the biblical books. And we can understand that, for example, the book of Jeremiah or Daniel was considered among the books of Scripture, but the spe-

49. See the editions of 1QDan[a] and 1QDan[b] by D. Barthélemy in DJD 1:50-52, and that of pap6QDan by M. Baillet in DJD 3:114-15 and plate 23. For 4QDan[a,b,c], see E. Ulrich, "Daniel Manuscripts from Qumran. Part 1: A Preliminary Edition of 4QDan[a]," *BASOR* 267 (1987) 17-37; idem, "Daniel Manuscripts from Qumran. Part 2: Preliminary Editions of 4QDan[b] and 4QDan[c]," *BASOR* 274 (1989) 3-26. See also Ulrich, "Orthography and Text in 4QDan[a] and 4QDan[b] and in the Received Masoretic Text," in *Of Scribes and Scrolls: Studies on the Hebrew Bible, Intertestamental Judaism, and Christian Origins Presented to John Strugnell on the Occasion of His Sixtieth Birthday* (ed. H. W. Attridge, J. J. Collins, and T. H. Tobin; College Theology Society Resources in Religion 5; Lanham, Md.: University Press of America, 1990) 29-42, now reprinted as Chapter 8 in this volume.

50. D. O. Wenthe, "The Old Greek Translation of Daniel 1–6" (Dissertation, University of Notre Dame, 1991), demonstrates that the edition of the book in the MT is the earliest complete edition available, but not the first edition of the biblical book of Daniel, and that the MT and LXX exhibit variant editions.

cific textual form was not a consideration. The process of the composition of the Scriptures was layered; some of the latter stages of that process — multiple literary editions of the books of Scripture — are demonstrated by our new extant evidence.[51]

3. Because the text of each book was produced organically, in multiple layers, determining "the original text" is a difficult, complex task; and theologically it may not even be the correct goal. How do we decide which of the many layers that could claim to be the "original reading" to select? Often the richer religious meanings in a text are those which entered the text at a relatively late or developed stage; do we choose the earlier, less rich reading or the later, more profound reading? In contrast, if a profound religious insight in an early stage of the text is toned down later by a standard formula or even a vapid platitude, which do we select? And must we not be consistent in choosing the early or the later edition or reading?

4. The Samaritans, the Jews, and the Christians ended up with three texts (not text types) and three collections of books because each group survived with a certain set of texts. Though their list of books was due to their religious principles and beliefs, the specific textual form of the individual books was accidental.

5. The Masoretic Text, like the Samaritan Pentateuch and the Septuagint, is not a univocal term or entity, but a collection of disparate texts, from different periods, of differing nature, of differing textual value. There is no reason to think of the Masoretic collection as a *unit* (a codex, a "Bible"), or as a *unity.* The collection is like the Septuagint, a collection of varied forms of the various books.

6. Thus, finally, the situation has changed concerning translations of "The Holy Bible." The *New Revised Standard Version* now contains a number of improved readings based on the biblical manuscripts from Qumran. It can even claim to be the first Bible to contain a paragraph missing from all Bibles for 2,000 years! It contains between chapters 10 and 11 in 1 Samuel a paragraph found at Qumran and attested by Josephus, but absent from all other Bibles over the past two millennia.

But we still need to revise our approach toward translating the Bible. On the one hand, I have argued elsewhere that it is legitimate for a specific religious community or a specific scholarly project to produce a translation of a

51. I have not yet studied 4Q364-367 in detail, but in light of this documented pluriformity of the developing text of the Scriptures, it may turn out that such works are more properly classified as "biblical" (i.e., scriptural) works rather than "paraphrases" or "reworked" biblical texts.

specific collection of texts as received within a faith tradition (e.g., the MT, the LXX, or the SP).[52] On the other hand, a Bible translation that claims to be a scholarly or academically sound translation of the Hebrew Bible must be based on a critically established text, not just a diplomatic text (such as the MT or the LXX). While saying this, I must note that this is a statement of principle; it is very difficult in practice, and we are just getting to the point of being able to articulate the need; we may not yet be at the point of implementing it.

Qumran has begun to teach us a great deal about the Bible and the history of its text. There is a great deal still ahead to be learned.

52. E. Ulrich, "Double Literary Editions of Biblical Narratives and Reflections on Determining the Form to Be Translated," in *Perspectives on the Hebrew Bible: Essays in Honor of Walter J. Harrelson* (ed. J. L. Crenshaw; Macon, Ga.: Mercer University Press, 1988) 101-16, esp. 111-13 (reprinted as Chapter 3 of this volume).

CHAPTER 3

Double Literary Editions of Biblical Narratives and Reflections on Determining the Form to Be Translated

The issues — theological, religious, political, historical, textual, philological, hermeneutical, and so on — that require consideration and decision before attempting a translation of the Bible are numerous and of so many different types that even to attempt to list them and their subdivisions, much less discuss them, would consume too much space.

In this study I wish to explore simply one aspect of Bible translation, an issue which plays an important role in Bible translation but is seldom discussed, at least as an issue and not just an ad hoc instance. I wish to explore the issue of double literary editions of biblical texts, in the hope of shedding some light on the criteria for determining which textual form of the biblical text should be selected for a translation of the Bible when there are two or more alternative forms.[1]

1. Terminology is unfortunately inadequate. When I use "Bible" in this paper I am generally meaning, and focusing on, the Hebrew Bible, or Tanak, or the Old Testament, but on none of these terms precisely with their particular connotations. That is, by "Hebrew Bible" I do not mean to exclude witnesses to the Hebrew text preserved only in Greek, Aramaic, Syriac, Latin, etc. Nor do I necessarily mean to exclude or include ancient Jewish writings in Greek that were considered sacred and authoritative but not accepted into the Rabbinic canon. And though my attention is on Tanak or the Old Testament, I do not think that all my remarks will be unrelated to the principles underlying a translation of the New Testament.

The "problem," as I see it, can be introduced by quoting the following criterion for selecting the specific form of the text to be translated:

> For the Old Testament the Masoretic Text is used, that is the text established in the eighth/ninth centuries AD by Jewish scholars who fixed its letters and vowel signs, the text reproduced by most manuscripts. Only when this text presents insuperable difficulties have emendations or the versions of other Hebrew manuscripts or the ancient versions (notably the LXX and Syriac) been used. . . .[2]

The general "problem" I am addressing, then, is whether the Masoretic Text (MT) is too often and too monolithically chosen or assumed as "the biblical text" to be translated. In cases of individual words or phrases in the MT, the usual provocation that draws attention to the problem is the existence of plausible variants in other textual witnesses. But the specific issue that I wish to explore is that of double literary editions of biblical texts, insofar as this phenomenon poses a difficulty for the a priori selection of any single text as the basis for a translation.

By double literary edition I mean a literary unit — a story, pericope, narrative, poem, book, and so forth — appearing in two (or more) parallel forms in our principal textual witnesses, which one author, major redactor, or major editor completed and which a subsequent redactor or editor intentionally changed to a sufficient extent that the resultant form should be called a revised edition of that text. The subsequent redactor or editor could, of course, be the same person who produced the original edition, as sometimes happens in literature, painting, music, or other art forms, but presumably the subsequent editor would be a different person.

Sometimes the scope of the pair of editions encompasses only a single story, narrative, chapter, or set of chapters. Sometimes the scope of the double edition extends to the entire biblical book, as in the case of Jeremiah. At the shorter end of the spectrum, if the scope of the variant tradition is smaller than a single pericope, then "literary edition" is too elevated a term and "textual variant," or "set of textual variants," is more appropriate. At the longer end of the spectrum, one could consider the double edition of the Deuteronomistic History.[3]

2. *The New Jerusalem Bible* (Garden City, N.Y.: Doubleday, 1985) xii. I am not singling out *The New Jerusalem Bible* for criticism; I randomly selected one of the many Bibles that sit on my shelf, and the introduction to the first Bible I picked up simply stated clearly and precisely the method that I think is at work, by reflective choice or by unreflective custom, as the principle underlying the work of many Bible translators.

3. See, e.g., Richard D. Nelson, *The Double Redaction of the Deuteronomistic History* (JSOTSup 18; Sheffield: JSOT Press, 1981).

For individual variants, the selection of a given reading in the MT, a Qumran manuscript, the Septuagint (LXX), or some other version usually does not have ramifications for the selection of variants in subsequent passages. For double literary editions of extended passages, however, unless a certain textual witness (for example, the MT) has been selected in principle as the single textual tradition to be translated throughout the whole Bible, then it may emerge that the study of double literary editions will logically require, if the MT has been selected for one passage, the selection of an alternate textual tradition for a subsequent passage. My hope is that analysis of this phenomenon will help illuminate the criteria by which Bible translators decide which form of the text is to be selected as "the text" to be translated as "The Holy Bible."

Double Literary Editions of Biblical Narratives

One of the best among recent books to put into graduate students' hands in order to let them watch the process of integrating textual and literary studies is *The Story of David and Goliath: Textual and Literary Criticism: Papers of a Joint Research Venture* by Dominique Barthélemy, David W. Gooding, Johan Lust, and Emanuel Tov.[4]

The book lets us watch four different scholars with different backgrounds, training, and specializations present their initial solution to a problem, respectfully learn from and critique each others' solution, and then present another attempt at solution.

One of the results that emerges from the book, or, rather, one of the facts that forms the problematic for the book, is the double edition of the story of David and Goliath. Someone in antiquity took a traditional form of the story of David and Goliath and intentionally interspersed another account of Davidic traditions into it, thereby creating a significantly different edition of the text in quantity and in content. The book thus confronts those who attempt translations of the Bible with a problem — a problem of riches — the fact of double literary editions of biblical texts.

The editorial procedure of weaving into one narrative a quite different version of the same or a similar narrative is well known. That is exactly what happened, for example, in the Flood narrative with the versions commonly

4. D. Barthélemy, D. W. Gooding, J. Lust, and E. Tov, *The Story of David and Goliath: Textual and Literary Criticism: Papers of a Joint Research Venture* (OBO 73; Fribourg: Editions Universitaires; Göttingen: Vandenhoeck & Ruprecht, 1986).

attributed to the Yahwist and the Priestly editions. But from the translator's point of view, that case is different because all major surviving witnesses to the text attest to the same composite secondary edition.

The David-Goliath story is a clear example of two different editions of a biblical narrative,[5] both attested in textual witnesses which in different eras have had long-standing and widespread claim as "the Bible." An earlier edition of the text with its own integrity and its own specific viewpoint is still found in the witnesses to the Old Greek (OG), and a second, later, developed edition is now found in the MT. The edition embedded in the MT has intentionally expanded the narrative with identifiably different types of material and different David traditions.[6]

One can list further examples within Samuel where there appear evidences, not just of variant words or phrases within the text, but of variant editions of portions of the book. For example, Professor Stanley Walters[7] has proposed that the story of Hannah, which has long been recognized as rich in textual variants, is not a single edition of the story with haphazard textual variants. He maintains that the variants form a pattern: that a portrait of Hannah is presented in the Masoretic Text in one light and that a different portrait of her is presented in an intentionally different and consistent light in the Septuagint. I will not give details here, but preliminarily I would agree with him. I think that in 1 Samuel 1–2, the Masoretic Text and the Septuagint may well present two different forms of the text, one intentionally different from the other, but each internally consistent.

In one sense, it does not matter whether the example of 1 Samuel 1–2 is verified as an instance of two intentionally different literary editions of that narrative, since literary and textual critics will probably continue to identify

5. For the detailed characteristics of the two editions, see Berthélemy, Gooding, Lust, and Tov, *The Story of David.* The detailed characteristics should not distract us here, nor should our judgment concerning the priority between the two editions (see the following note). It should also be pointed out for clarification that the issue here is not "earlier" or "later" in the origin of the traditions, but "earlier" or "later" in the redaction of the stories as they appear in the LXX and the MT.

6. Here I clearly side with Tov and Lust and disagree with Barthélemy and Gooding. The correctness of either position, however, should not deflect us from the main point that there do exist double literary editions of the biblical text, because (a) all four agree that this is an example of double literary editions, and (b) even if this particular example should fail, other examples would swiftly take its place.

7. Professor Walters gave an oral presentation entitled "Translating Samuel: Problems of the Text" to the Textual Basis for Bible Translation Group at the Society of Biblical Literature annual meeting in Boston on 7 December 1987. See now Stanley D. Walters, "Hannah and Anna: The Greek and Hebrew Texts of 1 Samuel 1," *JBL* 107 (1988) 385-412.

more examples of double literary editions. Thus, let us work on the hypothesis that 1 Samuel 1–2 is preserved in one edition in the MT and in another edition in the LXX, and that one of these two editions was intentionally re-edited from the other.

Insofar as that hypothesis can be verified, the critical reader of Samuel is confronted with a problem. The features of the two intentionally different literary editions of 1 Samuel 1–2 are not at all the same as the features of the two intentionally different literary editions of 1 Samuel 17–18. That is, the ways in which the MT and the LXX differ from each other in the Hannah story are quite different from the ways the MT and the LXX differ in the David and Goliath story.[8]

For 1 Samuel 1–2 we find in the earlier edition (the MT, I would preliminarily suggest) a straightforward account with one portrait of Hannah. In the secondary edition (the LXX) we find the intentional and consistent reshaping of that account, arguably for theological motives and possibly for misogynous motives, to give a changed portrait of Hannah. When we turn to 1 Samuel 17–18, in the earlier edition (the LXX) we find a single version of the story, whereas in the secondary edition (the MT) we find a composite version: the same version as in the LXX, basically unchanged, but now augmented with inserted components of a second version quite different in content, details, and style.[9]

The book of Samuel, of course, is not unique. If we look backward to the Torah, we quickly find other double editions, for example, in the book of Exodus; and if we look forward to the Latter Prophets and the Writings, we find double editions also, for example, in Jeremiah and Daniel. These are not new findings, just samples that quickly come to mind. In each of these books we find intentionally variant editions of the text.

Let us focus first on the book of Exodus. Here we meet a different type of intentionally different edition. Patrick Skehan published in 1955 a column from 4QpaleoExod^{m} containing fragments from Exodus 32.[10] Initially he referred to the character of its text as being "in the Samaritan Recension," but

8. For the present we will not digress to the larger issue of the editing of Chronicles from the sources of Samuel-Kings.

9. Even if Barthélemy and Gooding were correct, the point made here still holds: the rationale for the difference between the two literary editions of the Hannah story is different from the rationale for the difference between the two literary editions of the David-Goliath story.

10. P. W. Skehan, "Exodus in the Samaritan Recension from Qumran," *JBL* 74 (1955) 435-40. In the early days of Qumran research, the manuscript was designated 4QExod$^{\alpha}$ and was sometimes confusingly cited as 4QExod^{a}.

subsequently he refined his assessment: the scroll "has proved on further study to contain all the expansions of the Samaritan form of Exodus, with one notable exception: it did not contain the addition to the Ten Commandments after Exod 20:17, referring to the unhewn altar on Mt. Gerizim."[11]

Thus, in 4QpaleoExod^m we have a Jewish edition of Exodus. It displays a text type of Exodus intentionally reedited in conscious distinction from the Masoretic text type. That reedited text type was subsequently taken over by the Samaritans, perhaps uncritically, that is, without reflection on the different available text types of Exodus and without a conscious decision to use this text type as opposed to the different text type also transmitted in Jewish circles and eventually used by the Masoretes. The Samaritans then inserted a single additional expansion, referring to the altar on Mt. Gerizim, according to the same method by which the expansions characteristic of the edition in 4QpaleoExod^m were made.

But our focus here remains on the two Jewish text types of Exodus, the MT and 4QpaleoExod^m. What we see in the revised edition of Exodus found at Qumran is different from what we discovered in either of the revised editions in the Samuel narratives. In the secondary edition of the text of Exodus, we find neither an intentional reshaping of stories to give a changed emphasis or changed portrait (as in the Hannah story), nor an intentionally composite edition made by supplementing a single tradition with additional contents of sizable proportions from a quite different type of narrative (as in the David-Goliath story).[12] We find a text intentionally expanded by systematic harmonization[13] — by taking other parts of scripture and placing them virtually word-for-word in a new, related context, sometimes from nearby places in Exodus, sometimes from parallel passages in Deuteronomy. For the book of Exodus, the MT and the LXX preserve an earlier form of the text, whereas 4QpaleoExod^m preserves a secondary edition of the text produced — still presumably by Jews — on the principle of harmonization. To complicate matters, the MT and the LXX may well exhibit different editions of Exodus 35–40, but that we shall not explore here.

11. P. W. Skehan, "Qumran and the Present State of Old Testament Text Studies: The Masoretic Text," *JBL* 78 (1959) 21-25, esp. 22. Judith E. Sanderson, who collaborated with me on the completion of Skehan's edition of that scroll for publication in volume 9 of Discoveries in the Judaean Desert, has published an excellent analysis of the textual character of the scroll in *An Exodus Scroll from Qumran: 4QpaleoExod^m and the Samaritan Tradition* (HSS 30; Atlanta: Scholars Press, 1986).

12. Lust (*The Story of David,* 13-14) characterizes the material of the earlier, shorter edition as "heroic epic" material, and the supplemental material as "romantic epic" material.

13. Sanderson, *An Exodus Scroll,* 196-220.

The two editions of the book of Jeremiah have become widely known. 4QJer[b] and the LXX display a form of the story which Emanuel Tov[14] has labeled "edition I," and the MT, 2QJer, 4QJer[a], and 4QJer[c] display a subsequent, intentionally expanded edition, "edition II." Tov has outlined very convincingly the characteristics by which edition II goes beyond edition I. There are both editorial aspects and exegetical aspects. Under editorial aspects Tov lists the rearrangement of text, the addition of headings to prophecies, the repetition of sections, and so forth. Under exegetical aspects, he lists the clarification of details in the context, the making explicit of material that was implicit, minor harmonistic additions, and the emphasizing of ideas found in other parts of the book.[15] Thus the two editions of Jeremiah exhibit yet another type of contrast. Here the scope of the secondary edition is the entire book, and the method is basically rearrangement plus expansion — expansion not by relatively infrequent, large-scale harmonization (as in 4QpaleoExod[m]) but by routine minor explicitation, clarification, lengthened forms of titles, and so on.

When we turn to the book of Daniel, we find yet a fourth type of intentionally different editions in the biblical text. Though for most of the book the MT and the OG witness to the same edition, they exhibit two different editions of chapters 4–6. In chapters 4 and 6 the MT is considerably shorter than the OG, whereas in chapter 5 the OG is noticeably shorter than the MT. The least that can be said is that the same process is not consistently at work in these three chapters. But we can get much more specific. When we analyze the MT and the OG in parallel for each of the three chapters, the principal factors become clear. The differences in the quantity of text are not, as often in the MT of Samuel, caused by loss of sizable amounts of material through parablepsis. In Daniel 4–6 both the MT and the OG are apparently secondary, that is, they each expand in different directions beyond an earlier common edition that no longer survives. For example, for each of the three speeches in

14. Tov ("Some Aspects of the Textual and Literary History of the Book of Jeremiah," in *Le livre de Jérémie: Le prophète et son milieu, les oracles et leur transmission* [BETL 54; ed. P. M. Bogaert; Leuven: University Press, 1981] 145-67, esp. 146) correctly maintains that "the scroll resembles the LXX in the two major features in which the reconstructed *Vorlage* of that translation differs from the MT, namely, the arrangement of the text and its shortness as opposed to the longer text of MT. It should be remembered that the fragment is rather small, but the recognition of these two main characteristics in the fragment is beyond doubt." See also Tov's later formulation in "The Literary History of the Book of Jeremiah in the Light of Its Textual History," in *Empirical Models for Biblical Criticism* (ed. Jeffrey H. Tigay; Philadelphia: University of Pennsylvania, 1985) 213-37.

15. Tov, "Some Aspects," 150-67.

5:10-12, 13-16, 17-23, the edition preserved in the MT greatly expands for rhetorical and dramatic effect beyond the edition preserved in the OG. The variant editions for chapter 4, in contrast, are signaled by the differing arrangements of various components and are confirmed by expansions in the OG, such as the expansion (perhaps a Babylonian astrological motif) of the sun and moon dwelling in the great tree (4:8), and so forth.[16] Thus, the double editions found in Daniel 4–6 are two different later editions of the story, both secondary, both expanding in different ways beyond a no-longer-extant form which lies behind both.

In summary, then, we have shown examples of four different books of the Bible with text forms preserving intentionally variant editions of the biblical text. For the book of Exodus, the MT and the LXX preserve an earlier form of the text, whereas 4QpaleoExod^{m} (and subsequently the Samaritan text) preserves a secondary edition of the text produced on the principle of harmonization, spanning the majority of the book.

For the books of Samuel, we have one clear example and another plausible example, offering two different types of intentionally new edition of individual narratives. On the one hand, in 1 Samuel 1–2 the MT may be the earlier form, and the text translated in the LXX may witness to a secondary edition with an intentionally altered portrait for theological motives. On the other, in 1 Samuel 17–18 there are clearly two intentionally different editions, the Greek now displaying the earlier edition and the MT offering a second edition supplemented by diverse David traditions.

For the book of Jeremiah, the LXX displays an earlier edition of the entire book with one arrangement ("edition I") and the MT an expanded second edition ("edition II"), in substance basically unchanged, but with a variant arrangement and with systematic expansion by numerous, routine, minor additions.

For the book of Daniel, the MT and the OG exhibit two different editions of chapters 4–6, this time both apparently being secondary, that is, expanding in different directions beyond an earlier common edition that no longer survives.

16. For a detailed analysis of this material, see D. O. Wenthe, "The Old Greek Translation of Daniel 1–6" (Dissertation, University of Notre Dame, 1991).

Was the Second Edition Produced at the Hebrew Stage or by a Greek Translator?

Before proceeding, it may be helpful to determine whether the second of the two different literary editions in each of the four biblical books discussed above was produced at the Hebrew stage or by a Greek translator. And I would like to preface our analysis with two observations.

First, with regard to the question of "theological *Tendenz*" or "actualizing exegesis" on the part of LXX translators, I have yet to examine an allegation of a major interpretative translation by an OG translator and be convinced that the OG translator was responsible for a substantively innovative translation. Most who make such allegations have failed to distinguish the three stages of (i) the Hebrew *Vorlage* that was being translated into Greek, (ii) the results of the transformational process by the original Greek translator, and (iii) the subsequent transmission history within the Greek manuscript tradition.[17] In most cases the OG translators were attempting to produce a faithful, not innovative in content, translation of the sacred text.

Secondly, in contrast, it is methodologically important to examine the question for each instance, because it remains a possibility that, since the OG translators operated on partially differing applications of principles, a certain individual translator may turn out to have exercised substantively creative interpretation in the translation.

Examining now the four books we have just discussed, happily we find that the case is quite clear for the book of Exodus: the second edition was produced at the Hebrew stage, for the two texts that contain the later edition, 4QpaleoExod^{m} and the Samaritan, are both in Hebrew. And if confirmation be sought, the LXX of Exodus (at least up to chapter 35) is a faithful translation of a short, earlier Hebrew text very close to that in the MT.

In Samuel, for the David-Goliath story, Lust and Tov both considered the edition witnessed by the LXX as prior to that witnessed by the MT. And though both Barthélemy[18] and Gooding[19] began by leaving open the possibility that the secondary literary activity could have been at either the Hebrew

17. One clear example of such allegation and its subsequent correction is F. F. Bruce, "The Oldest Greek Version of Daniel," *OTS* 20 (1975) 22-40, corrected by Sharon Pace, "The Stratigraphy of the Text of Daniel and the Question of Theological *Tendenz* in the Old Greek," *BIOSCS* 17 (1984) 15-35; see, now more fully, Sharon Pace Jeansonne, *The Old Greek Translation of Daniel 7–12* (CBQMS 19; Washington, D.C.: Catholic Biblical Association, 1988).

18. *The Story of David,* 54, but inaccurately summarized by Gooding, 56.

19. Ibid., 83.

or the Greek stage, at the end both were largely, if not fully, convinced that Tov was correct that the second literary edition had been made at the Hebrew stage.[20] For the Hannah story, Professor Walters was not yet prepared to say whether he thought one version was earlier than the other, perhaps wisely so, since I am not sure that I have yet posed precisely the correct question. But for my part, I think I have shown in general that many variants found in the OG of Samuel (including some in the Hannah story) are identical with variant Hebrew readings in 4QSam^{a},[21] the bulk of those OG agreements with the Qumran Hebrew surely being faithful translations of a Hebrew *Vorlage* in that text tradition.[22]

For the book of Jeremiah, 4QJer^{b} provides in Hebrew an exemplar of the shorter text tradition of which the LXX is a faithful translation, while 4QJer^{a} and 4QJer^{c} present Hebrew texts that agree with the secondary edition found in the MT.

For the book of Daniel, the evidence is not yet conclusive, but it appears that the secondary editions were both made at the Aramaic level.[23] The MT and the OG seem to reflect the same edition through most of the book. Sharon Pace Jeansonne has demonstrated that the OG of 7–12 is a faithful translation of its Semitic *Vorlage*,[24] and the same seems true for chapters 1–2.[25] In chapters 4–6, however, we recall that the MT and the OG exhibit two different editions, this time both apparently being secondary, that is, expanding in different creative directions beyond an earlier common edition which no longer survives. But from the perspective of the OG as a single document, the OG of 4–6 appears to be woven from the same fabric as the OG translation of 1–2 and 7–12. Thus, the OG seems to be a consistent, unified document with a consistent translation technique. Therefore, the significant variation between the OG and the MT in 4–6 seems to indicate that the OG is a faithful translation of a different literary edition of these chapters. That would mean that again for Daniel the editorial activity resulting in secondary

20. Ibid., 138, 145.

21. E. Ulrich, *The Qumran Text of Samuel and Josephus* (HSM 19; Missoula, Mont.: Scholars Press, 1978) esp. 40-41, 48-49, 71-72.

22. We should also observe that the editing of Chronicles from the sources of Samuel-Kings took place at the Hebrew level.

23. We will not even attempt here to bring up the question of the larger book of Daniel with the "additions," further complicated by the appearance of that longer edition in the presumably Jewish recension, presumably based on a Hebrew-Aramaic *Vorlage*, attributed to Theodotion.

24. Jeansonne, *The Old Greek Translation of Daniel 7–12.*

25. For the moment I suspend judgment on the unclear case of chapter 3.

editions found in the MT and OG witnesses was done at the level of the original language. At the very least we can maintain that for the examples from Daniel 5 mentioned above the secondary literary activity was done at the Aramaic stage.

The point to bring out in our present discussion is that in a number of instances of double literary editions preserved in our textual witnesses, the secondary editorial work was already done at the Hebrew (or, for Daniel, Aramaic) level within the Jewish community and cannot be discounted as the unimportant or regrettable work of a Greek translator. The parallel editions were current, available forms of the biblical text in the original language, apparently with equally valid claims to being "the biblical text."

Reflections on Determining Which Form of the Biblical Text to Translate

If it is true that there exist double literary editions of biblical books and passages in our preserved textual witnesses to the Bible, that these alternate editions were produced in Hebrew in the Jewish community prior to the emergence of Christianity, and that our evidence shows that until and somewhat beyond the fall of the Second Temple they shared equally valid claims to being "the biblical text," then Bible translators are faced with a question: how do we go about selecting the form of the text that should be translated?

When we ask that question, several other questions immediately descend upon us, many fighting for first place. The preceding arguments have been largely in the scholarly, empirical arena; is that the starting point for deciding questions of Bible translation? How are the different arenas to be weighted? Upon what basis is the question to be decided: theological argument or empirical argument, denominational custom or ecumenical unity, and so on?

It is impossible to attempt to answer these questions properly in this short study. The questions and considerations bearing on a Bible translation for religious or denominational purposes[26] eventually diverge widely from those bearing on a translation for scholarly or study purposes. In this paper, therefore, we can focus only on the latter, hoping that what is said is not en-

26. Though for reasons of space the focus in this paper is restricted to the scholarly aspects, and cannot cover the theological or religious aspects of our topic, I want to say that I think there can be legitimate reasons within a religious community for choosing to translate a specific textual tradition.

tirely unrelated to the former. So I would like to focus on some of the criteria by which we determine which form of the text is to serve as the text to be translated for a "scholarly Bible." It is presumptuous to think that I can fully answer even this single question here. Rather, I offer some reflections — not considered as definitive but as one moment in an unfinished dialogue — that should be included among considerations of the issues of Bible translation. In fact, I am quite conscious that my reflections may end with more questions raised and left unanswered than questions answered. Perhaps, then, this can be read as a call for continuing and updated dialogue in light of our advancing knowledge and resources relative to the question of the textual basis for Bible translation.

We can begin by noting that it seems to be a defensible position (1) that different translations of the Bible can be produced as the result of legitimately differing scholarly judgments on historical or philological or other principles, (2) that different translations of the Bible can be produced as the result of legitimately differing theological positions or denominational needs, and (3) that both "scholarly Bibles" and "worship Bibles" have their place. The large number of recent translations would seem to corroborate this.

Since both in theory and in practice the MT is predominantly chosen, by conviction or otherwise, I think it important that we reflect on the basis for this choice. The specific issue I am trying to explore here is whether the optimum procedure for those who intend to produce a translation of the Bible based on scholarly principles is to use the MT as the textual basis except where that text is disturbed.[27]

For a scholarly Bible, either a specific text form must be selected a priori as the text to be translated, or parallel text forms must be examined throughout to determine which form is preferable as the basis of the translation. So that readers may know what kind of text they are dealing with, a decision should be made and announced in the introduction whether the translation is made from a particular manuscript or from a critically established text.

Should a specific text tradition be chosen a priori? Unless the goal is to produce a translation of the MT as a literary or religiously influential document, or to produce a translation of the LXX or another version as a literary or religiously influential document, then it would seem that the only reason for selecting a specific text form for a scholarly translation would be despair that a sufficiently solid basis can be found for a critically established text. An argument that usually accompanies this last position is that a diplomatic text, that is, the printing of the text found in a particular manuscript as opposed to

27. See, as an illustration, the quotation on p. 35 above.

a critically established or eclectic text, at least offers a text that actually existed and was used.[28]

A decision to translate the text form preserved in the MT can be made legitimately in principle (a priori), and can possibly — but subject to debate — be made as a result of examination of various text forms concluding that the MT is simply the best text (a posteriori).[29] A decision in principle to translate the MT specifically[30] is completely legitimate and desirable, on both scholarly and religious grounds. The MT is a literary document with a magnificent history, and it has been highly influential and carefully protected; we should all have available a modern translation worthy of this religious and cultural treasure. And there can be no question that the modern Jewish community, even if it were to have alternate translations, should possess a translation of the specific text form of the MT, which the Rabbis and the community have by conscious decision held sacred from antiquity. An analogous argument for a translation of the LXX can also be made.[31]

Most, however, appear to agree with the prevailing consensus that generally it is the "original" text that is to serve as the basis of translations; thus, if an a priori option for a specific text form were to be made, the MT would be the only viable candidate for that choice.

The MT does have the practical advantage of being a complete collection (unlike the Qumran scrolls) in Hebrew (unlike the versions) of texts of "the Hebrew Bible." Also, statistically it is probably true that a good, critical translation will in the main agree with the MT more than with any other single source. But it should also be kept in mind that "the Masoretic Text" is not a univocal term; it is a quite equivocal term. "The Masoretic Text" is not one text; it is a collection of texts — just as, for example, the LXX is — a collection of texts of divergent textual provenance, divergent stages of literary edition,

28. Though some find this a persuasive argument, I question its depth for several reasons. Here I will mention only one, noted by Tov ("The Text of the Old Testament," in *The World of the Bible* [ed. A. S. van der Woude; Grand Rapids: Eerdmans, 1986] 156-90, esp. 157): "Except in the case of photographic reproductions of the same text, no two editions of the Hebrew Bible are identical." We can now include also electronic reproductions, but neither detracts from the point that Professor Tov makes.

29. Even this idea of translating "the MT" is a highly complex issue; cf. M. Goshen-Gottstein, "The Textual Criticism of the Old Testament: Rise, Decline, Rebirth," *JBL* 102 (1983) 365-99.

30. E.g., the recent translation by the Jewish Publication Society.

31. E.g., Marguerite Harl's translation of the LXX as the Bible for Jewish and Christian readers in antiquity; cf. M. Harl, "Projet d'une traduction de la Septante en français," *BIOSCS* 13 (1980) 7-8; eadem, *La Bible d'Alexandrie: La Genèse: Traduction et Annotation des Livres de La Septante* (Paris: Cerf, 1986).

divergent literary merit, divergent textual quality, divergent text type, and so forth. For certain books, for example, Exodus, the MT proves to be the best single witness in general to the early text of the book.[32] For other books the case is different; for example, in Samuel, 4QSam$^{a, b, c}$ all prove to be superior in general to the MT,[33] though available only in very fragmentary condition, while the LXX proves to be superior in a large number of readings, though often resting on the basis of retroversion.[34]

But while agreeing that it is the "original" text that is generally to serve as the basis of translations, not all agree on the meaning of "original." My understanding of Jerome's position and the position of the translators in the early Reformation period is that their eye was on the "original" in the sense of the Hebrew as the original language in which the texts were written. Is there any cause to doubt that the "*Hebraica veritas*" they sought was the Hebrew scriptures in their original language, which they, without distinct awareness of alternate Hebrew forms, happened to equate with the MT? Are there any indications that they chose the MT in contradistinction to alternate Hebrew text forms of whose existence they were aware but which they passed over?

We know Augustine's choice (!), but if Jerome or the translators in the early Reformation period had had Hebrew texts available like 4QpaleoExod^{m}, 4QSam^{a}, 1QIsa^{a}, and 4QJer^{b} alongside "the Hebrew" they knew (namely, the MT), would they have chosen the MT? Here, of course, we can only speculate. But does it not surpass speculation to suggest that, like Origen, they would have compared the different texts and made some kind of choice on systematic principles? Thus, for example, if they thought that the shorter text (if sound) was usually preferable, would they not have chosen the shorter text in each case; if the longer, would they not have consistently chosen the longer, or if they thought that, as Jerome did for the book of Daniel, the more "messianic" text was preferable, then would they not have consistently chosen the more "messianic" text where available; and so forth? Insofar as this assumption is correct, does it suggest that we should consider readjusting our perspective on the MT?

32. Cf. Sanderson's careful, detailed analysis and assessment in *An Exodus Scroll*, 53-108, 307-11, esp. 309.

33. For 4QSam^{a}, cf. F. M. Cross, "A New Qumrân Biblical Fragment Related to the Original Hebrew Underlying the Septuagint," *BASOR* 132 (1953) 15-26; and Ulrich, *The Qumran Text*. For 4QSam^{b}, cf. Cross, "The Oldest Manuscripts from Qumran," *JBL* 74 (1955) 147-72. For 4QSam^{c}, cf. Ulrich, "4QSam^{c}: A Fragmentary Manuscript of 2 Samuel 14–15 from the Scribe of the *Serek Hay-yaḥad* (1QS)," *BASOR* 235 (1979) 1-25.

34. Cf. E. Tov's judicious treatment of the problem of retroversion in *The Text-Critical Use of the Septuagint in Biblical Research* (Jerusalem Biblical Studies 3; Jerusalem: Simor, 1981).

Let us for a moment allow our imaginations to indulge in a bit of fantasy. Let us imagine that we discovered scores or hundreds of ancient biblical manuscripts in Hebrew, similar to the Qumran scrolls, but all complete and intact. Or let us imagine that the roughly 170 biblical manuscripts from the Qumran caves were all complete and intact. If either were the case, should we still translate simply the MT except where its text seems disturbed? Or should we carefully collate and examine all the parallel texts to determine which form of the text, verse by verse and book by book, is preferable as the basis for our translation?

Reluctantly taking leave of the world of fantasy and returning to our real situation, we find that our current situation, though highly impoverished, is more similar than dissimilar to our fantasy situation. Though we do not have an abundance of complete manuscripts in the original language, we do have some poor but proud replacements in the fragmentary manuscripts from the Judaean wilderness and in the complete but once-removed or twice-removed versions — once-removed for the original translation, and twice-removed for versional manuscripts that have suffered in their transmission history and for the sub-versions.

An encouraging number of individuals and committees who set out to produce biblical translations do use the witness of available Hebrew manuscripts and the versions when pondering individual textual variants. But what happens when the variant is not an individual word or phrase protruding rebelliously in a verse or passage that is otherwise in textual harmony? What happens when the variant is a variant edition of a full literary unit?

The collection of literary texts that constitute the Hebrew Bible exists in a variety of conditions. One of those conditions which occurs intermittently is that of parallel editions in the different textual witnesses of a given passage. Again, the Masoretic collection of texts contains different types of literary editions of the biblical books; that is, the distinguishing features of the editions that happen to be embedded in the textual traditions preserved in the various books in the MT are inconsistent in the manner of their variation from the distinguishing features of the editions embedded in other textual witnesses. Consequently, the particular editions in the MT — depending upon the criteria adopted by a single translator, a translation committee, or the community — will sometimes be seen as superior to the editions preserved in other witnesses, sometimes as different but equally good, sometimes as inferior.

If, for purposes of specific illustration, we were to decide that the textual basis of our translation should be the earliest careful edition of a text produced by an author or major editor and preserved in our textual witnesses, then for Exodus we would in general select the MT-LXX tradition, bypassing the 4QpaleoExod^{m}-Samaritan tradition (though choosing for individual variant readings whichever of the various witnesses offers the best reading). For Jeremiah, in contrast, we would set aside the MT edition and translate the OG edition in general (though correcting the OG at specific points by means of the MT and other versions insofar as they exhibit superior readings within that edition). And though selecting the MT for the Hannah story in Samuel, we would still select the OG for the David-Goliath story later in the same book.

If, on the other hand, we were to decide that the textual basis of our translation should be the latest careful edition of a text accepted as authoritative by a community, then we would select the MT for the book of Jeremiah and for the David and Goliath story. But we would pass over the MT to select the proto-Samaritan text form (that is, the Jewish text form, as in 4QpaleoExod^{m}, subsequently adopted and preserved by the Samaritans, but without the specifically Samaritan changes) for Exodus and Numbers. And though selecting the MT for the David-Goliath story, we would select the OG for the Hannah story earlier in the same book.

For Daniel 4–6 we would, on either the "earliest" or the "latest" principle, still lack a criterion for deciding which form of the text to use for translation. Both the OG and the MT display secondary, developed editions of the narratives; and as yet I do not see a way to decide in favor of either edition as "the final adopted edition" of Daniel.

Conclusion

It is legitimate and desirable to produce translations of specific textual traditions of the Bible, such as the MT and the LXX. But insofar as the purpose of a scholarly Bible translation is to produce a translation based on a critically established text, the method of procedure must be the full and systematic comparison of the major textual traditions — in both microcontexts (verse-by-verse) and macrocontexts (each book or section as a whole). It is quite probable that the spectrum of classifications of textual variation will be so widely differentiated as to make a fully consistent policy impossible. And it is quite probable that it will prove very difficult to decide in many cases into which category an individual variant fits. Nonetheless, there should still be a discussion of the principles by which the selection is to be made. And the principles should be spelled out, as is usually done, in the introduction, so that users can know in advance the principles of selection.

It seems clear now from the evidence of double literary editions of biblical passages, just as it has long been clear from the evidence of individual variants, that a translation of the Bible which claims to be made on scholarly principles must rest on a critically established text. Serious thought should be given to the types of data briefly presented in the first and second parts of this paper and to consideration of the options sketchily presented in the third part. Presumably, consideration of the options will result in a reasoned and consistent approach to establishing that text. Just as there has probably never existed a perfect single written exemplar of "the biblical text," so too we will probably never produce a perfect single translation of "the biblical text," If we think otherwise, we need only wait until the next generation, or look more widely to broader sections of the believing community, to realize that we have not in fact produced a perfect translation. What we must strive for is the best that the human mind and human methods can produce within our particular culture and our own generation.

CHAPTER 4

The Canonical Process, Textual Criticism, and Latter Stages in the Composition of the Bible

In antiquity there were certain scribes engaged in the process of handing on the texts of the Hebrew Scriptures who intentionally went beyond the simple copying of the text. They worked creatively on the traditional sacred text, dared to augment it and enrich it for the community, and thus became contributors to the composition of the scriptures. Shemaryahu Talmon has described this type of scribe as "a minor partner in the creative literary process."[1]

The present generation of textual critics has made a major contribution to our understanding of the history of the biblical text, and I hope to show how recent textual study of the Hebrew Bible has opened a window on a previously dark stage in the composition of the Bible. James Sanders is correct that study of the areas of text and canon can be mutually illuminating.[2] Tex-

1. S. Talmon, "The Textual Study of the Bible — A New Outlook," in *Qumran and the History of the Biblical Text* (ed. F. M. Cross and S. Talmon; Cambridge, Mass.: Harvard University Press, 1975) 321-400, esp. 381.

2. James A. Sanders, *From Sacred Story to Sacred Text* (Philadelphia: Fortress, 1987).

I wish to thank Professor Shemaryahu Talmon for inviting me to give an earlier version of this paper at a symposium he organized on "The Hebrew Bible — From Literature to Canon," held at the National Humanities Center, Research Triangle Park, N.C., April 27-29, 1989.

tual study has illumined some of the latter stages in the composition of the Bible, stages that (depending upon terminology) we cannot yet call "canon," but stages that have been termed "the canonical process."

In my view, "the canon" as such is a post-biblical topic. The work that I have been doing over the past years has focused on the way that the canon was formed, or more precisely, on aspects of the canonical process — tracking the tradents and scribes as they developed and handed on their sacred, traditional literature. There are various aspects in the canonical process: the process by which the individual traditions were collected and composed as present books of the Bible, the process by which books of a similar nature were collected into groupings as sections of our present canon, and the process by which differing parties within Judaism struggled for the supremacy of the section of the canon they believed to be more important (e.g., the Law or the Prophets).

Here I wish to explore the stage in the canonical process between the completion (more or less) of one early edition of what we could recognize as a given biblical book and the completion of a later (sometimes the final) version or edition of that book. Thus, just as it is important to consider the earlier stages of growth and collection in *books* such as Genesis or Isaiah or Proverbs, and the stages of growth and collection in *sections* such as the narrative or legal or prophetic or wisdom collections, so too I would like to consider the latter stages of the composition of the biblical text in general, stages common to the majority of the books and extending widely through the materials in the various collections or sections of the Bible.

Specifically, I wish to explore how textual study of the Bible helps one see what the creative scribes (those "minor partners" in the biblical process) were doing, what their contribution was to the Bible as we know it today. As I see it, our exploration will erase even more the line between "higher criticism" and "lower criticism," which has been disappearing for some time.[3] That is, the outmoded distinction between higher criticism and lower criticism has as its premise that the major authors of a book wrote and did their creative work and completed a book, and then accurate or sloppy scribes copied that completed work accurately or sloppily. Higher criticism works on the side of the line marked "composition," and lower criticism operates on the side of the line marked "copying." The data presented below will make the attempt to draw such a line yet more difficult.

Because of the widespread absence of agreement concerning terminol-

3. Cf. E. Ulrich, "Horizons of Old Testament Textual Research at the Thirtieth Anniversary of Qumran Cave 4," *CBQ* 46 (1984) 613-36, esp. 616-18.

ogy related to canon, I must preface my remarks with some reflections and clarifications. Hopefully these will help advance our thinking about canon, but in any case they will at least make clear the sense in which I am using the terms. I then want to focus on one form of the creative activity of the scribes of the Second Temple period, what I will term "multiple literary editions" of biblical texts. Perhaps it would be more factual to say "double literary editions," since we seldom have more than two editions that are extant for any particular example; but I wish to focus our attention, not simply on the data that happen to be still extant, but on the general phenomenon that I believe was multiple. An examination of this phenomenon will probably suffice both to show heuristically what other similar creative activities of the scribes were like, and to show that the procedures of these scribes were equivalent to the procedures of those tradents we normally think of as the successive composers of the Scriptures.

Terminology Concerning "Canon"

Recent literature and debates demonstrate a need for a thorough and nuanced definition and description of "canon" and related terms: canonical process, Scripture, canonical text, authoritative text, etc.[4] Brevard Childs states that the "initial difficulty in discussing the issue of the canon arises from the ambiguity of the terminology,"[5] but though he discusses a number of the aspects of the complexity, he does not arrive at a satisfactory definition.[6] Sid Leiman has offered a definition of "a canonical book": "A canonical

4. A somewhat sustained attempt at some definitions and distinctions, with bibliography, can be found in T. A. Hoffman, "Inspiration, Normativeness, Canonicity, and the Unique Sacred Character of the Bible," *CBQ* 44 (1982) 447-69, esp. 454, 463-65. In addition to the general complexity of the issue, the welcome setting of ecumenical searching and dialogue compounds the difficulty of the task but at the same time offers the possibility of more penetrating and accurate results. We are all forced to ask ourselves to what extent, and to what advantage or disadvantage, our presuppositions and views are influenced by denominational histories and approaches, and even within these to distinguish between traditional understandings and attempts at modernization in light of new discoveries and vantage points.

5. B. S. Childs, *Introduction to the Old Testament as Scripture* (Philadelphia: Fortress, 1979) 49.

6. I tend to agree with Professor Bruce Metzger, *The Canon of the New Testament: Its Origin, Development, and Significance* (Oxford: Oxford University Press, 1987) 36, "Since [Childs's] use of the word 'canon' has three distinct meanings (as a fixed collection of books, as the final form of a book or group of books, and as a principle of finality and au-

book is a book accepted by Jews as authoritative for religious practice and/or doctrine, and whose authority is binding upon the Jewish people for all generations. Furthermore, such books are to be studied and expounded in private and in public."[7] But there are many complex factors involved. Does Leiman's definition include all the factors that ought to be included? Can we properly speak of canon at periods before the sacred writings were commonly considered and widely agreed by reflexive judgment to be canonical? That is, do not all the characteristics that constitute canon have to be present before we can legitimately speak of canon? Historical evidence is usually lacking for decisive answers. Is it at all meaningful to speak of an "open canon"? That is a contradiction in terms according to some views. The issue of canon is both a historical and a theological issue, and these two perspectives cannot be either totally fused or totally kept separate.[8]

Johann Gottfried Eichhorn said that "it would have been desirable if one had never even used the term canon" — but nonetheless he did.[9] Furthermore, his division is unfortunate: he divides between "general" and "special" matters — treating text and canon under general and individual books under special. This division is unfortunate, because issues of text and canon must be probed also for individual books and sections, and the individual books have certain constitutive characteristics that are best studied as a general phenomenon (e.g., the editorial history of prophetic books).

As far as terminology is concerned, I have not yet been persuaded to agree with anyone more than with James Barr, who holds that the canon is a later concept and term, and that it is a technical term requiring precise definition and precise usage.[10] It seems that we must adopt a definition of canon

---

thority), the reader is struck by the seemingly indiscriminate way in which the word 'canonical' is attached to a vast range of words, creating a kind of mystique." Also, Gerald H. Wilson's book, *The Editing of the Hebrew Psalter* (SBLDS 76; Chico, Calif.: Scholars Press, 1985), would have been stronger if he had more thoroughly examined "canonicity," (pp. 88-89) and pushed the questions more penetratingly (p. 64).

7. Sid Z. Leiman, *The Canonization of Hebrew Scripture: The Talmudic and Midrashic Evidence* (Transactions of the American Academy of Arts and Sciences 47; Hamden, Conn.: Archon Books, 1976) 14; cited by Wilson, *The Editing of the Hebrew Psalter,* 88.

8. In the original context in which this paper was read (a symposium on the making of the Hebrew Bible), the parallel issue of the canon of the New Testament (and in certain views even the Mishnah and the Talmud) need not raise greater confusion, but perhaps we should not forget that views on canon with respect to the Hebrew Bible ought to remain plausible in the latter contexts as well.

9. Cited in Childs, *Introduction to the Old Testament as Scripture,* 36.

10. J. Barr, *Holy Scripture: Canon, Authority, Criticism* (Philadelphia: Westminster, 1983) 50.

that is either on the broad side or on the strict side. A broad definition will include the notions of traditional, sacred texts considered authoritative, but not necessarily the notions of a reflexive, articulated decision that specific texts and not others belong to a special category and are binding for all believers for all time. A strict definition of canon will also include these latter concepts: conscious decision, unique status, necessarily binding.

I had sanguinely hoped, in the process of constructing this study, to sort out all these issues and come to a clear decision. But I rather quickly learned that that task was impossible in the time available and that it would require book-length treatment.[11] Among other things in dealing with canon, we have a problem similar to that of "midrash," where the term traditionally referred to "biblical interpretation in the rabbinic milieu," but, because it "has clear analogues with respect to presuppositions, procedures, and functions in literature outside and prior to the rabbinic movement," the term has broadened considerably in the last forty years to include "the study of the origin, evolution, and varieties of biblical interpretation in early Judaism, including the NT."[12] This is not the place to discuss whether the broadening of the definition of midrash is legitimate. But, because I think that the use of strict definitions in general requires us to bring greater sharpness to our thinking and thus greater advances in common knowledge, I continue to hold, tentatively, for the stricter definition of canon.

"Canon" is a technical term with an established usage in theological discourse. Nonetheless, it is important to begin discussion of its meaning, not within the context of Jewish or Christian religious literature, but within the broader context of Hellenistic culture. Although in Greek it had a concrete original meaning and then metaphorical uses, in Latin and derivative languages and literatures the word has a range of metaphorical uses. H. W. Beyer's article in *TDNT* correctly summarizes that in secular use the Greek word had the figurative sense of "norm" or "ideal": in sculpture, the "perfect form of the human frame"; in philosophy, the "basis . . . by which to know what is true and false"; in law, "that which binds us, . . . specific ideals"; and also a "list" or "table."[13]

It is significant that the term does not occur in the LXX in any sense rel-

11. It is unfortunate that, for all the commendable industry that went into Roger Beckwith's *The Old Testament Canon of the New Testament Church* (Grand Rapids: Eerdmans, 1985), the project fails on the level of judgment; see also the review by Albert C. Sundberg Jr., "Reexamining the Formation of the Old Testament Canon," *Int* 42 (1988) 78-82.

12. Merrill P. Miller, "Midrash," *IDBSup*, 593-97, esp. 596-97.

13. H. W. Beyer, "κανών," *TDNT*, 3:596-602.

evant to this discussion,[14] just as it is significant that there is no Hebrew word for canon even long after the biblical period. Galatians 6:16 seems to be the only New Testament use that is relevant for our purposes, and there it is used in the rather general sense of "measure of assessment, norm of one's own action, norm of true Christianity."[15] Until the fourth century, the term was used in Christian circles

> generally to emphasise what is for Christianity an inner law and binding norm. . . . After the 4th century the general use was supplemented by the description of certain things in the Church as κανών or κανονικός. . . . Most significant is the fact that from the middle of the 4th century the term canon came to be used for the collection of the sacred writings of the OT, which had been taken over from the Synagogue, and of the NT, which had already taken essential shape from *c.* 200. . . .[16]

Even were we to agree on the meaning of canon in Christian usage, it is not a necessary next step to argue that the same precise usage should hold concerning the canon of the Hebrew Bible. Nonetheless, I think it functionally expedient to appeal to consistency here and to use the term according to its traditional, strict definition as the collection or list of books of the Scriptures.[17]

There are three aspects of the technical use of canon that I think it will be important to note: (1) it represents a reflexive judgment, (2) it denotes a closed list, and (3) it concerns biblical books. Thus, I would argue that there is no canon as such in Judaism prior to the end of the first century C.E. or in Christianity prior to the fourth century, that it is confusing to speak of an "open canon," and that "the canonical text" is an imprecise term, at best an abstraction (not a text one could ever pick up and read). In what follows I do

14. Beyer (ibid., 596) notes that it does occur in Judith for "bed-post"; in Micah 7:4 with no clear meaning; and in 4 Macc 7:21 in a philosophical context.

15. Ibid., 598, 600.

16. Ibid., 600-601. Beyer continues: "The use of κανών in this sense was not influenced by the fact that Alexandrian grammarians had spoken of a canon of writers of model Greek. Nor is the decisive point the equation of κανών and κατάλογος, formal though the use of the term may be. What really counted was the concept of norm inherent in the term, i.e., its material content as the κανὼν τῆς ἀληθείας in the Christian sense. The Latins thus came to equate *canon* and *biblia.*" These conclusions, however, need further scrutiny in the light of the texts and descriptions given by Metzger, *Canon of the New Testament,* 312-13 and 210-12.

17. Note also the dictionary definitions: "The collection or list of books of the Bible accepted by [Jews or] the Christian Church as genuine and inspired" *(Oxford English Dictionary),* and "a collection or authoritative list of books accepted as holy scripture" *(Webster's Third New International Dictionary).*

not claim to solve the issues but rather note aspects of the problem in the hope of eliciting finer resolution in the future.

(1) In philosophical terms a reflexive judgment is a judgment that is made in retrospect, self-consciously looking backward and recognizing and explicitly affirming that which has already come to be. It represents the difference between sense experience and judgment, the difference between living and "the examined life." It represents the difference between pre-conceptual knowledge, which animals share, and post-insight ("aha!," "click!") human knowledge, the difference between the habitual conviction that the sunrise will be there in the morning and the scientific knowledge about the physical rotation of the earth on its axis. Thus, for a long while the community handed down sacred writings that increasingly functioned as authoritative books, but it was not until questions were raised and communal or official agreements made that there existed what we properly call a canon. The simple practice of living with the conviction that certain books are binding for our community is a matter of authoritativeness. The reflexive judgment when a group formally decides that it is a constituent requirement that these books which have been exercising authority are henceforth binding is a judgment concerning canon.

(2) Canon denotes a closed list. Exclusion as well as inclusion is important; as Bruce Metzger says, the process by which the canon was formed "was a task, not only of collecting, but also of sifting and rejecting."[18] He is speaking of the New Testament, of course, but the same process was at work with respect to the Hebrew Bible. The simple judgment that certain books are binding for one's community is again a matter of authoritativeness; the reflexive judgment that these books *but not those books* are binding is a judgment concerning canon. Thus, I would argue that it is confusing to speak of an open canon. That there were disagreements on the extent of the canon reflects not so much a toleration of an open canon but a lack of agreement concerning which particular closed list was to be endorsed.

(3) Canon concerns biblical books, not the specific textual form of the books. One must distinguish two senses of the word "text": a literary opus and the particular wording of that opus. It is the literary opus, and not the particular wording of that opus, with which canon is concerned. Both in Judaism and in Christianity it is books, not the textual form of the books, that are canonical. For the Rabbis it was scrolls, that is, books, that made the hands unclean (*m. Yadayim* 3:5; 4:6). The Mishnah discusses the permissibility of

18. Metzger, *Canon of the New Testament*, 7. Note Athanasius's directive (cited by Metzger, 212): "Let no one add to these; let nothing be taken away from them."

diverse languages for the biblical scrolls (*m. Megilla* 1:8, 2:1; *m. Yadayim* 4:5), the script ("Assyrian" [= square], not "Hebrew" [= Palaeo-Hebrew]), the materials (ink, and leather [presumably not papyrus]; *m. Yadayim* 4:5), and even the blank spaces that border a scroll (*m. Yadayim* 3:4); but to my knowledge there is no discussion of a distinction between textual forms. Similarly for Christian writers:

> Eusebius and Jerome, well aware of such variation in the witnesses, discussed which form of text was to be preferred. It is noteworthy, however, that neither Father suggested that one form was canonical and the other was not. Furthermore, the perception that the canon was basically closed did not lead to a slavish fixing of the text of the canonical books.
>
> Thus, the category of "canonical" appears to have been broad enough to include all variant readings (as well as variant renderings in early versions). . . .
>
> In short, it appears that the question of canonicity pertains to the document *qua* document, and not to one particular form or version of that document.[19]

Thus, "the canonical text" is an imprecise term, an abbreviated expression for "the text of a canonical book" or "the text of the canonical books." It is an ideal, referring to the text of a book or books without focus on any particular form of the text. It is an abstraction, not a text that one can pick up and read.[20] It appears that Childs would agree at least partially:

> However, the point needs to be emphasized that the Masoretic text is not identical with the canonical text, but is only a vehicle for its recovery. There is no extant canonical text. Rather, what we have is a Hebrew text which has been carefully transmitted and meticulously guarded by a school of scribes through an elaborate Masoretic system. . . . The canonical text of first-century Judaism is now contained within a post-canonical tradition. Therefore, even though the expressed purpose of the Masoretes was to preserve the canonical text unchanged, in fact, a variety of factors make clear that changes have occurred and that a distinction between the MT and the canonical text must be maintained.[21]

19. Ibid., 269-70.

20. The later decisions by diverse believing communities to endorse a specific text form, or (perhaps more precisely) a form of the Bible in a specific *language*, were juridical, probably sociopolitical, and possibly polemical, but not critical, decisions; and they are conceptually distinct from the decisions concerning the books as canonical.

21. Childs, *Introduction to the Old Testament as Scripture*, 100.

I would agree with Childs that there is no extant canonical text but disagree with him insofar as he holds that the ideal canonical text is necessarily within the Masoretic textual tradition, especially insofar as he is speaking as a Christian theologian. And I would further suggest that the canonical text is a term usually used improperly and, in light of terminological confusion, should be avoided.[22]

I will conclude this section on the canon with some comments to support my earlier view that the canon as such is a post-biblical topic. According to the criteria outlined above, I think that the canon represents a reflexive judgment, denotes a closed list, and concerns biblical books. Thus I think that Childs is theologically seeking something that historically is not yet there.[23] He appears to focus rather rigidly on

> that official Hebrew text of the Jewish community which had reached a point of stabilization in the first century A.D., thus all but ending its long history of fluidity. From that period on, the one form of the Hebrew text of the Bible became the normative and authoritative expression of Israel's sacred scripture. Stabilization marked the point which separated the text's history into two sharply distinguished periods: a pre-stabilization period marked by a wider toleration of divergent text types, and a post-stabilization period characterized by only minor variations of the one official text.[24]

There is, to my knowledge, no evidence prior to the late first century C.E., either in Judaism or in Christianity, to suggest that there was either a *fixed list* of books, or a *fixed text* either of individual books or *a fortiori* of the unified collection of books.[25] Thus, prior to the end of the first century, we do not have a canon in either Judaism or Christianity. We have a canon-in-the-making, but we do not have a canon. We have, well documented by practice, the concept of authoritative sacred books that are to be preserved very faithfully. And we have a "canonical process," that is, the activity by which the books later to become accepted as the canon were produced and treated as sacred and authoritative. But we do not have a canon or a canonical text before the end of the first century. Nor do we have such until noticeably later, except

22. That is, except in those rare instances in which someone is discussing precisely that which the term denotes.

23. This and what follows would hold *a fortiori* with regard to Beckwith's position.

24. Childs, *Introduction to the Old Testament as Scripture*, 100.

25. Even Childs (ibid., 102) agrees concerning the absence of a fixed text: "The period of textual fluidity extended from at least 300 B.C. to A.D. 100."

possibly within rabbinic Judaism insofar as the Masoretic stream of textual tradition was seen as the only legitimate textual form of the canonical books; but is there evidence to show that diaspora Judaism or even widespread Palestinian Judaism generally accepted, prior to the middle third of the second century, the proto-Masoretic stream that emerged as exclusive?[26]

Do we have a canonical list prior to the end of the first century? Yes and no: Torah — yes; Prophets — mostly; Writings — partly. Can the entries on the list change? If, using the technical definition, one answers "no," then there cannot be a canon until the middle of the second century at the earliest. Those who would choose to use the broader definition could answer "yes," but they would always have to add quickly that that list was not stable and that contemporary believers were not fully conscious of, and were not in agreement on, this aspect of the sacred texts. It is better to describe the situation this way: there was a category of sacred, authoritative books to which further entries could be added, and this category contained a number of books that were always included and always required to be included (the five books of Moses, Isaiah, Psalms, etc.), even though others could also be included (Ezekiel, Song of Songs, Esther, *Jubilees,* etc.). If so, then one would say that there was a canon-in-the-making, but there was not yet a canon.

Some of the contents (e.g., the Torah and, for most, the Prophets) would, of course, have met widespread agreement as a central core. But for other books, there would not have been agreement on whether they were meant to be included (such agreement had not been reached well into the second century in Judaism, nor even until later in Christianity). More importantly, the multiplicity of "titles" and the general lack of concern about expressly naming and delimiting the contents forcefully indicate that the many authors who referred to this anthology of literature with such diverse and generic designations were obviously unconcerned about the issue concerning which later Jews and Christians made decisions and still later called canon.[27]

The contents of "the Law" seem clear: the five books of Moses. But what about the contents of "the Prophets"? Was the book of Daniel included? Was the book of Psalms included?[28] Since at that time books were generally separate entities, written on individual scrolls, not sequentially ordered in codices,

26. The Masada and Murabbaʿat manuscripts positively document a proto-Masoretic text tradition, but the assumption of an official, definitive rejection of other textual forms is an *argumentum e silentio.*

27. *Contra* Beckwith, *Old Testament Canon,* 1, 105-10.

28. See Barr, *Holy Scripture,* 54-55. In this regard, Talmon's oral observation at the symposium is very pointed: at Qumran the only books for which *pešarim* are extant are books of the prophets and the Psalms (considered to be included among the prophets?).

it is one step more difficult to answer that question. But Barr's view has much to recommend it, namely, that "instead of the three-stage organization familiar to us, there probably was for a considerable time a two-stage conception, using only the two terms, the Torah and the 'Prophets'. Some books, which to us are in the Writings, may well have been in the Prophets. . . ."[29] Indeed, Daniel is considered among the prophets at Qumran, by Josephus (*Antiquities* 10.249, 266-67), and in the New Testament, whereas the rabbinic tradition that resulted in the present arrangement of the MT presumably did not consider the book among the Prophets (cf. *b. Baba Batra* 14b) but rather among the wise (cf. *b. Baba Batra* 14b; *b. Yoma* 77a).[30] If the content of the Prophets was unclear, how can one even entertain the notion that the content of "the Writings" would have been clear?

Again, I do not claim to have solved the issues but rather to have pointed out what I see as issues to be clarified, how I think they might be further pursued, and pragmatically where I position myself in the terminological haze. I can now turn to an examination of the scribes' contribution to the growth of the text that would become the canon.

Examples of the Editorial Work of the Scribes

Shemaryahu Talmon has noted "that a great number, probably an overwhelming majority, of Qumran [and other] variants in biblical scrolls and in Bible quotations resulted from insufficiently controlled copying and/or sometimes represent diverging *Vorlagen*."[31] Indeed, the scribes of scriptural manuscripts often intended simply to produce a new copy of an older *Vorlage*, and from time to time they made mistakes. But let us grant general amnesty to all scribes for their errors and corruptions. Let us concentrate on what they were trying to accomplish beyond simple copying. Let us examine the creative role of these

29. Barr, *Holy Scripture*, 54.

30. For the Qumran reference, see J. M. Allegro, *Qumrân Cave 4, I (4Q158-4Q186)* (DJD 5; Oxford: Clarendon, 1968) 54, 4Q174 2:3: [<כ>אש]ר כתוב בספר דניאל הנביא. Matt 24:15, the only place where Daniel is mentioned in the NT (and secondarily in some manuscripts in the parallel in Mark 13:14), refers to "[the book of] Daniel the prophet." Note also the speculation in *b. B. Bat.* 14b that the book of Hosea was perhaps not written on a separate scroll and placed before Jeremiah, Ezekiel, and Isaiah [*sic*] because it is small and could possibly have gotten lost. It is interesting now to speculate further that, since the book of Daniel is not so much larger than the book of Hosea, the book of the Twelve could have been arranged in such a way as to include it.

31. Talmon, "Textual Study of the Bible," 380.

scribes in helping to compose what we now call the Bible. Textual criticism has revealed some of the details of what they were doing, and their role in the composition of the Bible at least partially constitutes the canonical process.

I am not the first, of course, to take up this project. Shemaryahu Talmon devoted most of his long and rich article on "The Textual Study of the Bible" to what he terms "biblical stylistics" contrasted with what are normally seen as textual variants. In it he was engaged in demonstrating "that an undetermined percentage of these *variae lectiones* derive from the impact of ongoing literary processes of an intra-biblical nature."[32] One can learn much also from Emanuel Tov's article on biblical harmonization.[33] And many further aspects of this creative activity are illumined by the approach designated "comparative midrash."[34]

Let me briefly recall some of the types of scribal creativity that Talmon analyzed, and then focus on another major type of creative scribal activity. He presented examples of stylistic and textual interchangeability of words, stylistic and textual conflation, and stylistic metathesis and textual inversion. Each of these he considered as "fundamental formative elements which assumedly were operative on the author level as stylistic patterns and in the transmission-stage as their editorial and textual modification."[35]

Here I would like to focus on yet another major type of creative scribal activity, namely, multiple literary editions of biblical texts. Now the usual scenario for textual variants is the recognition of plausible variants in other textual witnesses for individual words or phrases in the MT, thus *individual variant readings*, and it is generally this type that Talmon studied, presenting us

32. Ibid. See also Talmon, "DSIa as a Witness to Ancient Exegesis of the Book of Isaiah," *Annual of the Swedish Theological Institute* 1 (1962) 62-72; and idem, "Aspects of the Textual Transmission of the Bible in the Light of Qumran Manuscripts," *Textus* 4 (1964) 95-132. Both of these essays are reprinted in *Qumran and the History of the Biblical Text* (ed. F. M. Cross and S. Talmon; Cambridge, Mass.: Harvard University Press, 1975) 111-26, 226-63.

33. E. Tov, "The Nature and Background of Harmonizations in Biblical Manuscripts," *JSOT* 31 (1985) 3-29.

34. R. Bloch, "Écriture et tradition dans le judaisme: Aperçus sur l'origine du midrash," *Cahiers sioniens* 8 (1954) 1-34; idem, "Midrash," in *Approaches to Ancient Judaism: Theory and Practice* (ed. W. S. Green; Missoula, Mont.: Scholars Press, 1978); "R. Le Déaut, "A propos d'une définition du midrash," *Bib* 50 (1969) 395-413; M. D. Herr, "Midrash," *EncJud,* 11:1507-14; Miller, "Midrash"; Sanders, "Torah and Christ," in *From Sacred Story to Sacred Text,* 41-60; idem, "Work to Do," in *Canon and Community: A Guide to Canonical Criticism* (Philadelphia: Fortress, 1984) 61-68. See also James L. Kugel and Rowan A. Greer, *Early Biblical Interpretation* (Philadelphia: Westminster, 1986).

35. Talmon, "Textual Study of the Bible," 334.

with a veritable textbook or chrestomathy of text-critical cases and analyses. But the specific type of textual variant that I wish to explore is that of *variant editions,* multiple literary editions of biblical texts.[36]

By multiple literary editions I mean a literary unit — a story, pericope, narrative, poem, book, etc. — appearing in two or more parallel forms (whether by chance extant or no longer extant in the textual witnesses), which one author, major redactor, or major editor completed and which a subsequent redactor or editor intentionally changed to a sufficient extent that the resultant form should be called a revised edition of that text. The subsequent redactor or editor could, of course, be the same person who produced the original edition, as sometimes happens in literature, painting, music, or other art forms, but presumably the subsequent editor would be a different person. In fact there are seldom more than two parallel forms of subsequent editions of biblical passages; but that is chiefly an accident of history, and the process I am intending to describe was a much richer and more frequent process, especially when viewed from a canonical-process perspective, and so I will speak of multiple editions.

Sometimes the scope of the variant editions encompasses only a single story, narrative, chapter, or set of chapters. Sometimes the scope extends to the entire biblical book, as in the case of Jeremiah. At the shorter end of the spectrum, if the scope of the variant tradition is smaller than a single pericope, then "literary edition" is too elevated a term; "textual variant," or "set of textual variants," is more appropriate.[37] At the longer end of the spectrum, one could consider the double edition of the entire Deuteronomistic History.[38]

I would like to reflect on samples of multiple editions found in the vari-

36. Much of the content in this section appeared as part of an earlier article in which I explored the same data in a different direction: the ramifications of preserved double literary editions for selecting the form of the biblical text which the Bible translator should translate; see E. Ulrich, "Double Literary Editions of Biblical Narratives and Reflections on Determining the Form to Be Translated," in *Perspectives on the Hebrew Bible: Essays in Honor of Walter J. Harrelson* (ed. James L. Crenshaw; Macon, Ga.: Mercer University Press, 1988) 101-16 (now reprinted in Chapter 3 of the present volume.)

37. For individual variants, the selection of a given reading in the MT, a Qumran manuscript, the LXX, or some other version usually does not have ramifications for the selection of variants in subsequent passages. For variant literary editions of extended passages, however, the process of selection must begin with the selection of the *edition* to be used (i.e., the edition as encountered in a certain textual witness, e.g., the MT, the LXX, etc.), and only then should individual variants be considered, and only insofar as they are textual variants within the textual form of that edition.

38. See, e.g., Richard D. Nelson, *The Double Redaction of the Deuteronomistic History* (JSOTSup 18; Sheffield: JSOT Press, 1981).

ous parts of the Hebrew Bible: from the Torah, the book of Exodus; from the *Nebi'im Ri'šonim* (or historical books), the books of Samuel; from the *Nebi'im 'Aḥronim* (or prophetic corpus), the book of Jeremiah; and from the *Ketubim* (or wisdom corpus), the book of Daniel. I propose to explore the phenomenon of multiple literary editions of these books and then reflect on what it tells us about the process by which the canonical books were produced.

The Book of Exodus

For the book of Exodus, the MT presents a form of the book that I call "edition I," because we have no texts which preserve an earlier edition of the book as a whole.[39] A subsequent edition has generally been recognized in the Samaritan Pentateuch, an intentionally reedited form based on the form transmitted in the MT. In 1955 Patrick Skehan published some fragments from 4QpaleoExod^{m} containing Exodus 32.[40] Initially he described the character of its text as "in the Samaritan Recension," but subsequently he refined his assessment: the scroll had "proved on further study to contain all the expansions of the Samaritan form of Exodus, with one notable exception: it did not contain the addition to the Ten Commandments after Exod 20:17, referring to the unhewn altar on Mt. Gerizim."[41] Thus, this text of Exodus appears to be positioned between the form found in the MT and that found in the Samaritan Pentateuch. Is it a different edition?

If Skehan is correct (and after spending several years on that scroll I will affirm that he is), then it seems that there are two Jewish editions of Exodus, one in the MT and a second in 4QpaleoExod^{m}. Judith Sanderson, who collaborated with me on the completion of Skehan's edition of this scroll, has published an excellent analysis of its textual character in *An Exodus Scroll from Qumran: 4QpaleoExod^{m} and the Samaritan Tradition*.[42] Her analysis demon-

39. The Old Greek of Exodus witnesses to an earlier form of the text for at least eight individual readings, but those readings are sporadic and do not constitute an earlier "edition"; cf. Judith E. Sanderson, "The Old Greek of Exodus in the Light of 4QpaleoExod^{m}," *Textus* 14 (1988) 87-104.

40. P. W. Skehan, "Exodus in the Samaritan Recension from Qumran," *JBL* 74 (1955) 182-87. In the early days of Qumran research, the manuscript was designated 4QExod$^{\alpha}$ and was on occasional confusingly cited as 4QExod^{a}.

41. P. W. Skehan, "Qumran and the Present State of Old Testament Text Studies: The Masoretic Text," *JBL* 78 (1959) 21-25, esp. 22. See also the following note.

42. Judith E. Sanderson, *An Exodus Scroll from Qumran: 4QpaleoExod^{m} and the Samaritan Tradition* (HSS 30; Atlanta: Scholars Press, 1986).

strates that the scroll is a descendant of a text of Exodus similar to that of the MT. But one or possibly more scribes took the edition of Exodus as found now in the MT and intentionally developed it. The scroll displays a text type of Exodus intentionally reedited in conscious distinction from the Masoretic text type. The Samaritans subsequently used that reedited text type, perhaps uncritically. That is, I think it probable that the Samaritans used the text type as in 4QpaleoExod^{m} without conscious reflection on the different available text types of Exodus and without a conscious decision to use this text type as opposed to the different text type that was also transmitted in Jewish circles and eventually used by the Masoretes. The Samaritans then inserted a single additional expansion, referring to the altar on Mt. Gerizim, and they did this according to the same method by which the expansions characteristic of the edition in 4QpaleoExod^{m} were made. I would hesitate to say that the Samaritan text constitutes yet a third edition of Exodus on the basis of this single, though monumental, expansion. But we need not decide the Samaritan issue here.

My point is that we possess two Jewish editions of Exodus, that found in the MT and that found in 4QpaleoExod^{m}. The revised edition of Exodus from Qumran is a text intentionally expanded by *systematic harmonization.*[43] A scribe enriched the traditional edition of Exodus by excerpting and minimally rewording parts of the scriptural text and inserting them virtually word-for-word in a new, related context. Sometimes the text was from nearby places in Exodus, sometimes it was from parallel passages in Deuteronomy. Thus one has in the MT and the LXX an earlier form of the text, but in 4QpaleoExod^{m} a secondary edition of the text produced in Hebrew by Jewish tradents on the principle of harmonization.[44]

The Books of Samuel

In the books of Samuel one meets a different type of editorial activity contributing to the composition of the biblical text. Some ancient scribe took a traditional form of the story of David and Goliath and intentionally interwove into it another account of Davidic traditions, thereby creating a significantly different edition of the text in quantity and in content. The David-Goliath story is a clear example of two different editions of a biblical nar-

43. Ibid., 196-220; Tov, "Harmonizations in Biblical Manuscripts," 7, 13-14.

44. To complicate matters, the MT and the Old Greek may well exhibit a different type of variant editions for Exodus 35–40, but I shall not explore this here.

rative, both attested in textual witnesses that have had long-standing and widespread claim as "the Bible" in different communities.[45] An earlier edition of the text with its own integrity and its own specific viewpoint is still found in the witnesses to the Old Greek, and a second, later, developed edition is now found in the MT.[46] The edition embedded in the MT has intentionally expanded the narrative with identifiably different types of material and different David traditions.[47]

One can list further examples within Samuel where there is evidence, not just of variant words or phrases within the text, but of variant editions of portions of the book. For example, the story of Hannah in 1 Samuel 1–2, which has long been recognized as rich in textual variants,[48] is probably not a single edition of the story with haphazard textual variants. A striking number of the Greek variants against the MT are quite probably faithful reflections of a different Hebrew text as exemplified now by the somewhat later and very fragmentary 4QSam[a].[49] My strong suspicion is that a number of the variants coalesce to constitute a pattern indicating that the Hebrew text which lay behind the Old Greek may well have been a variant edition from that which has been transmitted through the Masoretic *textus receptus.*

Professor Stanley Walters has recently proposed "the thesis that M and B [the MT and the LXX Codex Vaticanus] are alternate versions of the story

45. For the detailed characteristics of the two editions, see D. Barthélemy, D. W. Gooding, J. Lust, and E. Tov, *The Story of David and Goliath: Textual and Literary Criticism: Papers of a Joint Research Venture* (OBO 73; Fribourg: Editions universitaires; Göttingen: Vandenhoeck & Ruprecht, 1986). The detailed characteristics should not distract one here, nor should one's judgment concerning the priority of either of the two editions (see the following note). It should also be pointed out for clarification that the issue here is not "earlier" or "later" in the origin of the traditions, but "earlier" or "later" in the redaction of the stories as they appear in the LXX and the MT.

46. Here I clearly agree with Tov and Lust and disagree with Barthélemy and Gooding. The correctness of either position, however, should not deflect one from the main point that there do exist double literary editions of the biblical text, because (a) all four scholars agree that this is an example of double literary editions, and (b) even if this particular example should fail, other examples will swiftly take its place.

47. Lust (*Story of David and Goliath,* 13-14) characterizes the material of the earlier, shorter edition as "heroic epic" material, and the supplemental material as "romantic epic" material.

48. See the commentaries of Thenius, Wellhausen, Driver, McCarter, Gordon, and Klein.

49. See F. M. Cross, "A New Qumran Biblical Fragment Related to the Original Hebrew Underlying the Septuagint," *BASOR* 132 (1953) 15-26; and E. Ulrich, *The Qumran Text of Samuel and Josephus* (HSM 19; Missoula, Mont.: Scholars Press, 1978) 39-41, 48-49, 62, 71-72.

of Samuel's birth. The texts of each, while not in perfect condition, can be given a reasonable and internally consistent reading which shows them to be discrete narratives, each with its own interests and design."[50] One need not agree with all the individual arguments adduced by Walters or with his interpretation of the significance of the individual variants in order to espouse his general conclusion that, as I would rephrase it, in 1 Samuel 1 the MT and the LXX (in basic fidelity to its Hebrew *Vorlage*) may well present two different editions of the text, one intentionally different from the other, each internally consistent.[51]

In one sense, it does not matter whether the example of 1 Samuel 1–2 is verified as an instance of two intentionally different literary editions of that narrative, since literary and textual critics will probably continue to identify

50. Stanley D. Walters, "Hannah and Anna: The Greek and Hebrew Texts of 1 Samuel 1," *JBL* 107 (1988) 385-412, esp. 408. Walters goes on to say (p. 409), and with this view I heartily concur, that since "M and B are discrete narratives, each with its own *Tendenz*, . . . any use of either to correct the other must be guided by a very precise and exacting method." See my n. 37 above.

51. I will mention only two examples where I disagree. The reading "Her distress was equal to the depression caused by {her} a co-wife [*sic*]. So she would become depressed on account of . . ." (LXX B) is listed by Walters ("Hannah and Anna," 389) as if it were a divergent element of the narrative from the reading "Her co-wife used to vex her bitterly in order to . . ." (MT). I think that methodologically it is more sound to view these readings as parallel: to see the Greek as attempting to offer a translation of a consonantal text close (at the time of translation, but later augmented by a conflation in the transmission process) to the text now reflected in the received Hebrew: וכעסתה צרתה גם כעס בעבור. It is possibly, but not necessarily, correct to assume that the reading of the early Hebrew text has been accurately transmitted in the medieval Codex Leningradensis. Walters also sees the need to posit a variant Hebrew *Vorlage* for the Greek (pp. 394-96). The question is, were the particular variations in the text here made *intentionally* in order to produce variant editions so that it is meaningful to maintain that "in M it is the harassment that goes on and on; in B it is Anna's passive resistance that goes on and on. And neither feature is found in the other story. In M there is provocation but no response; in B there is depression but no provocation" (p. 392). I would not agree that the Greek translation here is due to an intent to paint the portrait of Hannah in a different character. Second, I do not think that the B addition (from its *Vorlage?*) ἰδοὺ ἐγώ, κύριε can bear the weight of the interpretation as "extreme deference" (p. 392). One needs only to hear the potent quadruple echo of ἰδοὺ ἐγώ in Samuel's call narrative (1 Sam 3:4, 5, 6, 8) and to hear the proud and confident Bathsheba as favored wife address the failing David as κύριε (1 Kgs 1:17) in order to demur with respect to the interpretation that "M portrays Hannah more positively than B, giving to her person — both words and actions — a more substantive importance" (p. 392). It is true that communities hearing the two stories separately would get slightly different impressions of Hannah; the question is whether the difference is due to an editor's intention to paint a different portrait.

more examples of variant literary editions. Thus, I work on the hypothesis that 1 Samuel 1–2 is preserved in one edition in the MT and in another edition in the LXX, and that one of these two editions was intentionally reedited from the other.[52]

The critical reader of Samuel, comparing the scribes' work in producing multiple editions, will note that the features distinguishing the two intentionally different literary editions of 1 Samuel 1–2 are not at all the same as the features distinguishing the two intentionally different literary editions of 1 Samuel 17–18. That is, the ways in which the MT and the LXX differ from each other in the Hannah story are quite different from the ways the MT and the LXX differ in the David and Goliath story.[53]

For 1 Samuel 1–2 one finds in the earlier edition (perhaps the MT) a straightforward account with one portrait of Hannah. In the secondary edition (perhaps the LXX) one finds the intentional and consistent *reshaping* of that account, arguably for theological motives, to give a *changed portrait* of Hannah. But for 1 Samuel 17–18, in the earlier edition (this time the LXX) one finds a single version of the story, whereas in the secondary edition (the MT) one finds a *composite* version: the same version as in the LXX, basically unchanged, but now augmented with inserted components of a second version quite different in content, details, and style.[54]

What we had found in the revised edition of Exodus from Qumran is different from what we discover in either of the revised editions in the Samuel narratives. The secondary edition of the text of Exodus was characterized primarily by *harmonization;* in Samuel we find intentional *reshaping* of stories to give a changed emphasis or *changed portrait* (in the Hannah story), and an intentionally *composite* edition made by supplementing a single tradition with additional contents of sizable proportions from a quite different type of narrative (in the David-Goliath story).

52. It is not necessary to assume that the edition in the MT and the one in the Old Greek or its *Vorlage* are directly related. But except for some extraneous variants and for those variants which coalesce to form the variant edition, the texts are close enough to hold a direct relationship as a point of departure for a working hypothesis.

53. For the present we will not digress to the larger issue of the editing of Chronicles from the sources of Samuel-Kings.

54. Even if Barthélemy and Gooding were correct, the point made here still holds: the rationale for the difference between the two literary editions of the Hannah story is different from the rationale for the difference between the two literary editions of the David-Goliath story.

The Book of Jeremiah

The two editions of the book of Jeremiah have become widely known. 4QJer[b] (now probably to be divided as 4QJer[b] and 4QJer[d]) and the LXX display a form of the story that Emanuel Tov has labeled "edition I," and the MT, 2QJer, 4QJer[a], and 4QJer[c] display a subsequent, intentionally expanded edition, "edition II."[55] Tov has outlined very convincingly the characteristics by which edition II goes beyond edition I, including both editorial aspects and exegetical aspects. Under editorial aspects, Tov lists the rearrangement of text, the addition of headings to prophecies, the repetition of sections, etc. Under exegetical aspects, he lists the clarification of details in the context, the making explicit of material that was implicit, minor harmonistic additions, and the emphasizing of ideas found in other parts of the book.[56] Thus the two editions of Jeremiah exhibit yet another type of contrast. Here the scope of the secondary edition is the entire book, and the method is basically rearrangement plus expansion — expansion not by relatively infrequent, large-scale harmonization (as in 4QpaleoExod[m]) but by routine minor explicitation, clarification, lengthened forms of titles, etc.

The Book of Daniel

Turning to the book of Daniel, one finds yet a fourth type of intentionally different editions in the biblical text. The text type of Daniel reflected in the MT is well documented from the early period of its textual transmission. Qumran provides eight exemplars of the book (as compared with only six of Jeremiah), one of which dates from the end of the second century B.C.E., only about a half century after the book's composition.[57] And all eight, insofar as

55. E. Tov, "Some Aspects of the Textual and Literary History of the Book of Jeremiah," in *Le livre de Jérémie: Le prophète et son milieu, les oracles et leur transmission* (BETL 54; ed. P.-M. Bogaert; Louvain: University of Louvain Press, 1981) 145-67, esp. 146, correctly maintains that "the scroll resembles the LXX in the two major features in which the reconstructed *Vorlage* of that translation differs from the MT, viz., the arrangement of the text and its shortness as opposed to the longer text of MT. It should be remembered that the fragment is rather small, but the recognition of these two main characteristics in the fragment is beyond doubt." See also Tov's newer formulation in "The Literary History of the Book of Jeremiah in the Light of Its Textual History," in *Empirical Models for Biblical Criticism* (ed. Jeffrey H. Tigay; Philadelphia: University of Pennsylvania Press, 1985) 213-37; and "The Jeremiah Scrolls from Qumran," *RevQ* 14 (1989) 189-206.

56. Tov, "Textual and Literary History of the Book of Jeremiah," 150-67.

57. The editions of 1QDan[a] and 1QDan[b] are in D. Barthélemy and J. T. Milik,

the fragmentary evidence allows one to judge, are generally in the same textual tradition in which the MT stands. I hasten to qualify that in some of the individual variants the MT is clearly secondary, just as each of the Qumran manuscripts also displays secondary readings vis-à-vis the MT. But my point is that, even though there are many minor discrepancies among the various scrolls and between each and the MT, the Qumran manuscripts display the same general *edition* as that in the MT. There are no witnesses to the additions of Susanna, Bel and the Dragon, the Prayer of the Three Youths, etc., or to the alternate order as found in Papyrus 967.[58]

I will also mention, though it is not my main point here, that for certain individual readings the scrolls provide in Aramaic or Hebrew the *Vorlage* of certain individual Old Greek readings; but again, the general *edition* of each of the scrolls appears to be that of the MT, not that of the Old Greek.

For most of the book, when the MT and the Old Greek are compared, they both witness to the same edition. They do exhibit, however, significant discrepancy in chapters 4–6, and the Old Greek translator of Daniel has been severely criticized.[59] The dissertation of Dean Wenthe, however, on the Old Greek intends to demonstrate that August Bludau, J. A. Montgomery, and Sharon Pace Jeansonne were correct in exonerating the Old Greek translator with regard to the book in general, and in considering chapters 4–6 of a different order.[60] I agree with Montgomery that "careful study re-

---

Qumrân Cave 1 (DJD 1; Oxford: Clarendon, 1955) 150-52; that of pap6QDan in M. Baillet, J. T. Milik, and R. de Vaux, *Les "Petites Grottes" de Qumrân* (DJD 3; Oxford: Clarendon, 1962) 114-15, plate 23. See also the recent editions by Ulrich, "Daniel Manuscripts from Qumran, Part 1: A Preliminary Edition of 4QDan[a]," *BASOR* 268 (1987) 17-37; and idem, "Daniel Manuscripts from Qumran, Part 2: Preliminary Editions of 4QDan[b] and 4QDan[c]," *BASOR* 274 (1989) 3-26. 4QDan[d] and 4QDan[e], both very small, will be published in a later volume of DJD.

58. I will not even attempt here to bring up the question of the variant editions in the larger book of Daniel with the "additions," further complicated by the appearance of that longer edition in the presumably Jewish recension, possibly based on a Hebrew-Aramaic *Vorlage,* attributed to Theodotion.

59. See the discussion by J. A. Montgomery, *A Critical and Exegetical Commentary on the Book of Daniel* (ICC; Edinburgh: Clark, 1927) 35.

60. D. O. Wenthe, "The Old Greek Translation of Daniel 1–6" (Dissertation, University of Notre Dame, 1991); August Bludau, *Die alexandrinische Übersetzung des Buches Daniel und ihr Verhältniss zum massorethischen Text* (BibS[F] 2/2-3; Freiburg im Breisgau: Herder, 1897) 31; Montgomery, *Daniel,* 35-37; Sharon Pace, "The Stratigraphy of the Text of Daniel and the Question of Theological *Tendenz* in the Old Greek," *BIOSCS* 17 (1984) 15-35; and, now more fully, Sharon Pace Jeansonne, *The Old Greek Translation of Daniel 7–12* (CBQMS 19; Washington, D.C.: Catholic Biblical Association of America, 1988).

lieves much of the odium that has been cast upon the translation."[61] When the entire book is carefully studied, one finds that for chapters 1–2, perhaps 3, and 7–12 the Old Greek translation is a faithful translation of a Semitic text close to that in the MT and the scrolls. In chapters 4 and 6, however, the MT is considerably shorter than the Old Greek, whereas in chapter 5 the Old Greek is noticeably shorter than the MT. The least that can be said is that the same process is not consistently at work in these three chapters. But one can get much more specific. When one analyzes the MT and the Old Greek in parallel for each of the three chapters, the principal factors become clear. (1) I have already mentioned that occasionally the scrolls demonstrate that the MT incorporates secondary readings. (2) Though for chapters 4–6 the Old Greek is noticeably different from the MT, the nature of the Greek in those chapters is the same as that in the remainder of the book; that is, the Greek of chapters 1–12 is of one piece. (3) The differences in the quantity of text are not, as often in the MT of Samuel, caused by loss of sizable amounts of material through parablepsis. Rather, in Daniel 4–6 *both* the MT and the Old Greek are apparently secondary, that is, they each expand in different directions beyond an earlier common edition that no longer survives. For example, for each of the three speeches in 5:10-12, 13-16, 17-23, the edition preserved in the MT greatly expands for rhetorical and dramatic effect beyond the edition preserved in the Old Greek. In contrast, the variant editions for chapter 4 are signaled by the differing arrangements of various components and are confirmed by expansions in the Old Greek, such as the expansion (perhaps a Babylonian astrological motif) of the sun and moon dwelling in the great tree (4:8), etc. The conclusion to be drawn, but still to be demonstrated in detail, is that the Old Greek translator translated the entire book faithfully from his Semitic *Vorlage;* he simply had a version of the book that contained a variant edition of the text for those three chapters. Furthermore, the variant editions found in the MT and in the Old Greek for Daniel 4–6 appear to be two different later editions of the story, both secondary, both expanding in different ways beyond a single form which lies behind both but which is no longer extant.

In summary, then, we have shown examples of four different books of the Bible with text forms preserving intentionally variant editions of the biblical text. For the book of Exodus, the MT and the LXX preserve an earlier form of the text, whereas 4QpaleoExod^{m} (and subsequently the Samaritan text) pre-

61. Montgomery, *Book of Daniel,* 36.

serves a secondary edition of the text produced on the principle of *harmonization,* spanning the majority of the book.

For the books of Samuel, we have one clear example and another plausible example, offering two different types of an intentionally new edition of individual narratives. On the one hand, in 1 Samuel 1–2 the MT may be the earlier form, and the text translated in the LXX may witness to a secondary edition with an *intentionally altered portrait* for theological motives. On the other, in 1 Samuel 17–18 there are clearly two intentionally different editions, the Greek now displaying the earlier edition and the MT a secondary edition *supplemented by diverse traditions* about David.

For the book of Jeremiah, the LXX displays an earlier edition of the entire book with one arrangement ("edition I") and the MT an expanded second edition ("edition II"), in substance basically unchanged, but with a *variant arrangement and systematic expansion* by numerous, routine, minor additions.

For the book of Daniel, the MT and the Old Greek exhibit two different editions of chapters 4–6, this time *both* apparently being *secondary,* that is, *expanding in different directions* beyond an earlier common edition which no longer survives.

All the editorial work I have been discussing was done at the Hebrew stage.[62] That is, the second of the two different literary editions in each of the four biblical books discussed above was produced at the Hebrew (or, for Daniel, Aramaic) stage, not by a Greek translator. That is important for our consideration of the creative activity of the scribes. But let me add a tangential *obiter dictum.*

With regard to the question of "theological *Tendenz*" or "actualizing exegesis" on the part of LXX translators, I have yet to examine an allegation of a major interpretative translation by an Old Greek translator and be convinced that the Old Greek translator was responsible for a substantively innovative translation. Most who make such allegations have failed to distinguish the three stages of (a) the Hebrew *Vorlage* that is being translated into Greek, (b) the results of the transformational process by the original Greek translator, and (c) the subsequent transmission history within the Greek manuscript tradition.[63] In most cases the Old Greek translators were at-

62. See Ulrich, "Double Literary Editions," 108-10.

63. One clear example of such allegation and its subsequent correction is F. F. Bruce, "The Oldest Greek Version of Daniel," in H. A. Brongers et al., *Instruction and Interpretation: Studies in Hebrew Language, Palestinian Archeology, and Biblical Exegesis* (Oudtestamentische Studiën 20; Leiden: Brill, 1977) 22-40, corrected by Pace, "Stratigraphy of the Text of Daniel," 28-32.

tempting to produce a faithful translation of the sacred text, not to produce an interpretation remarkably innovative in content. Nonetheless, it is methodologically important to examine the question for each instance, because it remains a possibility that, since the various Old Greek translators operated on partially differing applications of principles, a certain individual translator may turn out to have exercised substantively creative interpretation in the translation.

The point to bring out in this present discussion is that in a number of instances of multiple literary editions, some of which are still preserved in our textual witnesses, the creative, secondary editorial work was already done at the Hebrew (or, for Daniel, Aramaic) level within the Jewish community and cannot be discounted as the unimportant or regrettable work of a Greek translator. The parallel editions were current, available forms of the sacred text in the original language, and apparently up to the end of the first century of the common era they were seen as having equally valid claims to being "the biblical text."

Aspects of the Canonical Process

The canonical process is that series of actions, or complex of activity, viewed both individually and as an organic whole, by which the collection of sacred books now recognized as the canonical books was produced, especially with regard to the characteristics by which it became the canon as such. That activity includes, as James Sanders says, selectivity and repetition with interpretation — tradition being retold and reshaped faithfully but creatively.[64]

Sanders compares the canonical process to comparative midrash, and I would like to go further and add the very composition of Scripture as another equivalent, and to suggest moreover that the homiletical, liturgical, and spiritual use of Scripture involves a similar process.

In an article published in 1980, I suggested that there was a dynamic operative in modern theological reflection that had its roots in the very process by which the Scriptures were composed. Using an analysis of the biblical account of the exodus, I made the claim that the method of composition of the Scriptures is "a *process* and that the process of the development of Scripture is dialectical — Scripture, which began as experience, was produced through a process of tradition(s) being formulated about that experience and being reformulated by interpreters in dialogue with the experience of their communi-

64. Sanders, *Canon and Community,* 33.

ties and with the larger culture."[65] Using the exodus as an example, it seems clear that what (according to the documentary view) the Yahwist, the Elohist, and the Priestly editions were doing was each taking the tradition and *repeating it faithfully* but *reshaping it creatively* in the light of the exigencies of their current cultural situation.

Since the biblical narratives are usually not eyewitness accounts of events but "classic retelling(s)" of the traditions, one must carefully analyze and differentiate the epistemological levels from experience or "raw event" to the final written text: experience, understanding, and judgment, followed by explicit articulation of the judgment. We usually do not have direct witnesses to "what really happened," but later communities' proclamations of the significance of what had been experienced. Even the very early layers of the biblical text are already selected and interpreted repetitions of Israel's traditions.

Thus, though the events behind the biblical account of the exodus began in human experience, they were not limited to raw, unreflective experience. It was human experience recognized in faith as shaped by God's presence and purpose. That is, it was interpreted and formulated in traditional religious categories, and it was told and retold, shaped and reshaped, in light of the developing needs and worldviews of the believing communities.[66]

I continue with the modern analogy because it is similar to the attitudes and methods of the creative scribes in antiquity who were at once handing on and composing the scriptural text. "Reading the Bible in the process of theological reflection today is also an event of dynamic interaction between the minister and the text. . . . The dynamic interaction includes several elements: the text and the reader or hearer, each with a definite worldview and each in a particular concrete situation. . . ."[67] The use of Scripture — whether homiletical or liturgical, whether ancient or contemporary — involves a tripolar dynamic of interaction between the traditional text, the contemporary cultural situation, and the experience of the minister within the community. This tripolar dynamic is a reflection of, and is in faithful continuity with, the process by which the Scriptures were composed.[68]

65. Eugene Ulrich and William G. Thompson, "The Tradition as a Resource in Theological Reflection — Scripture and the Minister," in J. D. Whitehead and E. E. Whitehead, *Method in Ministry: Theological Reflection and Christian Ministry* (San Francisco: Harper & Row, 1980) 31-52, esp. 36.

66. Ibid., 38-39.

67. Ibid., 40-41.

68. This, by the way, I would see as the theological basis or warrant, if needed, for "conjectural emendation." When Bible translators see ambiguous Hebrew expressions, they must make a decision, an interpretation; they must use their God-given minds to de-

Returning to the creative biblical scribes, these tradents were actively handing on the tradition, but they were adding to it, enriching it, making it adaptable, up-to-date, relevant, multivalent. We must assume that by and large they knew explicitly what they were doing. Insofar as the scribes were handing on the tradition, they became part of the canonical process: handing on the tradition is a constitutive factor of the canonical process. Sanders refers to this aspect as "repetition."[69] The repetition, in a sense, works like a hammer, pounding home again and again that this material is important. The texts were authoritative texts, and through the traditioning process they were being made more authoritative.[70]

But the scribes were also updating the tradition, contemporizing it, making it relevant. That is, sometimes when the tradition was not adaptable, these scribes *made* it adaptable, thus giving it another of its canonical characteristics, a complementary factor that Sanders terms "resignification."[71] That is, the tradition, important in its original setting, and important in itself beyond its importance for that original concrete situation, is found also to be important to me here and now in my present situation. The tradition proves adaptable, capable of having new significance in this new particular situation. The resignification — insofar as the tradition has proved useful or true — shows that indeed the tradition is *important in itself* (thus genuinely in the category of "tradition") and that it is *important to me* (thus genuinely in the category of "adaptable tradition"). The "authority" of such tradition is not an extraneous characteristic (authority imposed)[72] but is intrinsic (the community recognizes the life-giving power of the tradition).

termine as best they can what the meaning is. Translation is an attempt to understand the intention of the "author." The translator must be attentive to the tradition, must understand the culture in which the text originated and has been transmitted, and must rely on his or her experience. There are clearly instances where none of our few surviving witnesses preserves the original reading or intended meaning of the author. In such instances the translator must first listen to the three resources just mentioned and then have them vigorously interact and debate with each other. It then becomes the translator's duty to provide the best possible reading, whether by chance attested or not.

69. Sanders, *Canon and Community,* 22.

70. This provides another argument, though not a conclusive argument, against calling the material "canonical" at this stage: insofar as the composition is canonical, it should not be changed; it should already be "tradition" and should already be "adaptable" as it is. Also, paradoxically, insofar as the scribes thought they were copying "Scripture," they did not create Scripture; insofar as they thought they were handing on and developing sacred textual traditions, they were creatively producing Scripture.

71. Sanders, *Canon and Community,* 22.

72. One entire avenue that I have not had time to explore here but that deserves ex-

Conclusion

It remains, then, to sum up how I see textual criticism illuminating the very composition of the canonical Scriptures, that is, illuminating the scribal procedures which in turn constitute an important aspect of the compositional process for the texts of the books that eventually became our canon of Scripture.

The canon as such, as I now see it, is a topic that belongs to the period after the close of the composition of the Scriptures. But aspects of the canonical process can be charted by text-critical research. Textual critics, sparked by the discoveries in the Judaean Desert, have been quite active in recent decades. One area of results that I think particularly suggestive is the demonstration that creative scribes produced multiple literary editions of various biblical passages. Though we are grateful for the manuscript remains that we have from the period 250 B.C.E. to 70 C.E., one must remember that we have but a tiny percentage of the textual activity on biblical literature. Research on the small sampling of surviving evidence shows that this creative scribal activity took different forms — easily recognized in that each of these forms corresponds to well-known procedures by which in even earlier times many parts of the biblical text were produced.

Studying the book of Exodus displays harmonization of texts, that is, what we could call "biblical" text added to "biblical" text. The books of Samuel exhibit both the interweaving of "nonbiblical" supplementary traditions into a "biblical" account and possibly the changing or reshaping of a story to present a theologically different portrait. The book of Jeremiah contains systematic amplification of the entire book of routine minor expansion, although this did not greatly alter the book's overall meaning. In one section of the book of Daniel, all the extant editions of the book display one or other of two alternative revised editions, both of which are based on an earlier edition no longer preserved.

Many of the procedures that characterize "the canonical process" can be found very early in the composition of the biblical literature and continued to be exercised until well past the latest books accepted into the canon. This is true for the Torah; true for the Former Prophets (it is easier to see if we think rather of "the Deuteronomistic History"); true for the Latter Prophets (con-

ploration is the approach to canonical criticism which sees that part of the present arrangement and certain parts of the content of the text are a direct result of the tradents or scribes vying to establish or enhance the authority of the books or sections they considered more important. Joseph Blenkinsopp has developed this idea in his *Prophecy and Canon* (Notre Dame, Ind.: University of Notre Dame Press, 1977).

sider redactional layers of the book of Amos, the book of Isaiah, etc.);[73] true for Psalms, Job, Proverbs, Daniel, etc.[74]

The creative scribal work of harmonization and transplanting of text that we observed in Exodus can be seen also in other passages, namely, Isa 2:2-4//Mic 4:1-4; Obadiah 1-10//Jer 49:7-22, etc.[75]

The editorial procedure of weaving into one narrative a quite different version of the same or a similar narrative, observed in 1 Samuel 17–18, is also well known. That is exactly what happened, for example, in the Flood narrative with the versions commonly attributed to the Yahwist and the Priestly editions, and indeed in much of the composition of the Torah and in the far-reaching compositional work of the Deuteronomistic editors. And insofar as I am correct concerning 1 Samuel 1–2, one must assume that a number of biblical passages in their present form similarly resulted from a later editor's reshaping of earlier, now lost, narratives for theological motives.

Finally, the general type of creative scribal work that characterizes the revised editions now found in the MT and in the Old Greek of Daniel 4–6 is pervasive and can be seen throughout the Bible. It is, in fact, similar to the secondary edition of Jeremiah on a larger scale. This "later edition" activity represents one of the major ways in which the latter stages of the many texts that came to form our Bible were composed.

Thus, the methods of the late scribes are basically similar to the methods we recognize in the earlier "authors" and tradents who produced the Scriptures. They were interweaving into traditional materials other material, either their own insightful creations or other available traditions, which they considered important to add for what would now become "the text." These are early and late forms of the same phenomenon, at the early and late stages of the canonical process.[76] What they can teach us with a high degree of reli-

73. See Robert B. Coote, *Amos among the Prophets: Composition and Theology* (Philadelphia: Fortress, 1981). Note the subtitle of William L. Holladay's book, *Isaiah: Scroll of a Prophetic Heritage* (Grand Rapids: Eerdmans, 1978). Note also the description by O. Kaiser, *Isaiah 1–12* (OTL; 2d ed.; trans. J. Bowden; Philadelphia, 1983) 7-8, of the composition by successive layers in the first portion of the book of Isaiah.

74. This is also true, of course, for the Gospels.

75. Harmonization presupposes that both texts are important in the same or compatible ways, and it presupposes the unity or homogeneity of the two. To put it baldly: sometimes the presupposition behind harmonization is that this text can be juxtaposed to that text because God is the author of both. That presupposition is clearly behind some of the Qumran, New Testament, and rabbinic texts.

76. Insofar as this is true, it is another argument for hesitating to speak of "the canonical text" in Childs's sense. The stabilization of the text, which in a developed form we inherit as the Masoretic *textus receptus*, was — not religiously speaking, but textually and

ability is that this process was intermittently at work in the development of many parts of the texts of the canonical books where there is no direct evidence to prove it.

---

historically speaking — an accident of history. I am not aware of any evidence demonstrating that, for each of the books, the choice of specifically those textual forms included in the Masoretic collection was made on any kind of literary, or theological, or other objective criteria. As Childs (*Introduction to the Old Testament,* 103) remarks, the MT was not selected because it was "the best, or the most original, Hebrew text."

CHAPTER 5

Pluriformity in the Biblical Text, Text Groups, and Questions of Canon

Introduction

Complutum, the impressive and respected seat of scholarship which nearly five centuries ago gave such innovative impetus to the textual study of the Bible by producing the Complutensian Polyglot, the first biblical polyglot in 1514-1517, has once again, through the international congress Manuscritos Mar Muerto Madrid, made a significant contribution to the textual study of the Bible, this time to the publication and interpretation of the biblical and other religious manuscripts from the Dead Sea Scroll community.[1]

1. Scholars from the Universidad Complutense de Madrid and neighboring institutions have been very active in areas important for the text and versions of the Hebrew Bible. Here it is possible to give only a few recent examples:

Julio Trebolle Barrera, *Salomón y Jeroboán: Historia de la recensión y redacción de*

Both personally and on behalf of the editors of the Qumran manuscripts, I would like to express sincere gratitude to Her Majesty the Queen Doña Sofía, and their Excellencies the Minister of Education and Science, the Minister of Culture, the President of the Autonomous State of Madrid, and the Rector of the Complutensian University, for making this congress possible, and for their lavish hospitality. Also to Professors Julio Trebolle Barrera, Luis Vegas Montaner, and Javier Fernández Vallina for the immense amount of work and planning required to make this congress possible and make it function so smoothly. I am truly grateful because the congress succeeded in providing a significant impetus to the publication of the scrolls as well as valuable interaction and communication of knowledge among the individuals publishing and interpreting the scrolls.

In this paper I will attempt to contribute toward the illumination of the nature and history of the text of the Hebrew Bible. A number of scholars have dealt with this subject in the past, and several contributors to this congress have utilized the new evidence discovered in the Judaean Desert to advance the topic in a major, constructive, and very valuable way. The remarks that follow will not have surveyed all the new data (though that possibility is not too distant), nor present a comprehensive theory, nor, to be sure, constitute the final word on the topic. That, as we all know, is not the way knowledge develops. Despite our ambitious desires to penetrate and solve a problem once and for all, we all know that scholarship seldom, if ever, works that way. It works progressively, with new hypotheses proposed, shedding fresh light upon our common endeavor, but then eventually critiqued. The correct aspects remain, the limitations are pruned, and a better picture has been provided.

The question dominating the discussion of the history of the biblical text is how to explain the pluriformity observable in the biblical manuscripts from Qumran, the MT, and the versions. Are the manifold variations between texts simply due to sporadic errors and changes by isolated scribes, or are there rational patterns that can be detected and described? If the lat-

---

1 Reyes 2–12; 14 (Bibliotheca Salmanticensis Dissertationes 3; Salamanca: Universidad Pontificia, 1980); idem, "Redaction, Recension, and Midrash in the Books of Kings," *BIOSCS* 15 (1982) 12-35; idem, "From the 'Old Latin' through the 'Old Greek' to the 'Old Hebrew' (2 Kings 10:23-35)," *Textus* 11 (1984) 17-36; idem, "Textual Variants in 4QJudg[a] and the Textual and Editorial History of the Book of Judges," in *The Texts of Qumran and the History of the Community: Proceedings of the Groningen Congress on the Dead Sea Scrolls (20-23 August 1989)*, vol. 1: Biblical Texts (ed. F. García Martínez; Paris: Gabalda [= *RevQ* 14/2, no. 54-55] 1989) 229-45; idem, *Centena in libros Samuelis et Regum: Variantes textuales y composición literaria en los libros de Samuel y Reyes* (Textos y Estudios "Cardenal Cisneros" 47; Madrid: Instituto "Arias Montano" C.S.I.C., 1989).

Luis Vegas Montaner, *Biblia del Mar Muerto: Profetas Menores* (Textos y Estudios 29; Madrid, 1980); idem, "Computer-Assisted Study on the Relation between 1QpHab and the Ancient (Mainly Greek) Biblical Versions," in *The Texts of Qumran* [= *RevQ* 14/2, no. 54-55 (1989)] 307-18.

N. Fernández Marcos and A. Sáenz-Badillos, eds., *Theodoreti Cyrensis Quaestiones in Octateuchum: Editio Critica* (Textos y Estudios 17; Madrid, 1979); N. Fernández Marcos and J. R. Busto Saiz, eds., *Theodoreti Cyrensis Quaestiones in Reges et Paralipomena: Editio Critica* (Textos y Estudios 32; Madrid, 1984); N. Fernández Marcos, ed., *La Septuaginta en la investigación contemporánea (V Congreso de la IOSCS)*, (Textos y Estudios 34; Madrid, 1985); N. Fernández Marcos and J. R. Busto Saiz, eds., *El Texto Antioqueno de la Biblia Griega I. 1-2 Samuel* (Textos y Estudios 50; Madrid, 1989).

Ciriaca Morano Rodríguez, *Glosas marginales de* Vetus Latina *en las Biblias Vulgatas españolas: 1-2 Samuel* (Textos y Estudios 48; Madrid, 1989).

ter, can we discover the intentional attitudes and activities of the tradents and scribes who developed and handed on the text to succeeding generations and localities?

To make advances in the study of the history of the biblical text and the "mapping" of text groups, we need (1) to amass and analyze the manuscript data, studying the character of each of the individual manuscripts; (2) to construct a number of overarching theories that could possibly explain the data, because each of us usually sees important factors involved, but, at least at first, only a limited number of the factors; and then (3) to judge which theory, or which combination of them, best fits and explains the textual evidence.

The first part of this study will discuss the *status quaestionis,* the dominant theories concerning the history of the text, and will offer some attempts to clarify and advance the discussion. The second part will examine the different categories of textual variation, some of which are caused by factors in the canonical process. The third part will discuss the problem of terminology. This study is not a finished "position paper" seen from the end of the road but only an interim perspective in a dialogue that needs to be continued.

The State of the Question: Theories on the History of the Text

I will not rehearse the history of scholarship dealing with the text of the Hebrew Bible. Emanuel Tov has already surveyed that territory in his article "A Modern Textual Outlook Based on the Qumran Scrolls," which appeared in 1982.[2] I will rather join in the discussion as it had progressed about a decade ago. The three prominent voices are those of Frank Moore Cross,[3] Shemaryahu Talmon,[4] and Emanuel Tov.[5] In a paper I wrote in 1982 that appeared in 1984, I briefly outlined their three positions, which are sufficiently well-known that they need not be repeated here, and I suggested that a "critique of these three positions of local texts, *Gruppentexte,* and the denial of text-types

2. E. Tov, "A Modern Textual Outlook Based on the Qumran Scrolls," *HUCA* 53 (1982) 11-27.

3. F. M. Cross, "The Evolution of a Theory of Local Texts," in *Qumran and the History of the Biblical Text* (ed. F. M. Cross and S. Talmon; Cambridge, Mass.: Harvard University Press, 1975) 306-15.

4. S. Talmon, "The Textual Study of the Bible — A New Outlook," in *Qumran and the History of the Biblical Text* (ed. F. M. Cross and S. Talmon; Cambridge, Mass.: Harvard University Press, 1975) 321-400.

5. E. Tov, "A Modern Textual Outlook."

now becomes a clear desideratum for the near future."[6] That future is now in progress: David Hart, a doctoral student at Vanderbilt University, is devoting his dissertation to this topic.[7] Also Tov and I have, each from our own perspectives, been working on the topic, though advances come slowly and only after a great amount of work on particular texts and specific aspects of the problem. In the discussion that follows, Tov's more recently developed articles should be borne in mind.[8]

All three of those views are partly correct and constitute important elements in the more complex map, which I believe will eventually be more filled out to explain the history of the biblical text and the interrelationships of our extant manuscript witnesses. Each has provided a very important advance, and without their insight we would still be in a chaos of widely divergent manuscripts. In light of my immersion in analyzing text after text, I will attempt to sift out some of the insights that make a permanent contribution, that contribute a lasting piece in the eventual mosaic that now we can only impressionistically see and proleptically call "the history of the biblical text."

At this point, I think that only one of these, viz., Cross's position, really constitutes a "theory" of the history of the biblical text. The other two do not appear to be "theories" in the sense that they do not elaborate a large-scale schema that explains sample after sample of amassed data; rather, they identify new and important factors that help explain significant facets of the total picture. Thus, they seem more properly classified as astute, important ideas or observations that correct and advance our understanding. Both Talmon and Tov, of course, have analyzed great quantities of Qumran and related textual data, and they are two of the most prominent scholars who have enriched our understanding in the textual area. Their contributions illumine a number of areas, but they have not elaborated a comprehensive theory of the *history* of the text as such.

Though the three views are often seen as contradicting each other, to me they rather seem simply to focus on different aspects. Briefly stated: Cross has

6. E. Ulrich, "Horizons of Old Testament Textual Research at the Thirtieth Anniversary of Qumran Cave 4," *CBQ* 46 (1984) 613-36, esp. 624.

7. Hart presented a paper on this topic entitled "Some Recent Approaches to the History of the Biblical Text" at the Society of Biblical Literature meeting in New Orleans on November 18, 1990.

8. E. Tov, "Hebrew Biblical Manuscripts from the Judaean Desert: Their Contribution to Textual Criticism," *JJS* 39 (1988) 5-37; idem, "Groups of Texts Found at Qumran," in *Time to Prepare the Way in the Wilderness: Papers on the Qumran Scrolls by Fellows of the Institute for Advanced Studies of the Hebrew University, Jerusalem, 1989-1990* (STDJ 16; ed. D. Dimant and L. H. Schiffman; Leiden: Brill, 1995) 85-102.

focused on the *origins* or originating causes of the different text types — how the different types came to be or were produced. Talmon has focused on the *final stages* — how we end up with only three main texts or text types. Tov has focused on the *complexity* of the textual witnesses in the manuscript remains.

The evidence from Qumran highlights some limits in each of the three views. Our common problem is that only a very small percentage of the textual data from antiquity is available, and thus we are in the mode of reconstruction. If we envision a stemma, extant manuscript witnesses function as a number of dots to be connected, and the question is how to draw the lines to connect the dots.

First, Cross is partly correct, but there is more. There clearly existed three major centers of Judaism in the Second Temple period, and the text certainly developed to some degree in each of them. But the Qumran evidence partly argues against the purity or sufficiency of a local-text theory. At Qumran, a single locality, we have a wide variety of quite diverse texts and text types in what was a rather strong-minded and single-minded group, and this situation apparently spanned two centuries. Furthermore, I think we must presume that there were several parties (as there were from Hasmonaean times on, and still are today) in each locality, differing ideological groups or parties, and different texts.

Specifically, why designate as "Egyptian" the Hebrew text type used for the OG of Jeremiah, if, for example, $4QJer^{b}$ is found at Qumran? In favor of the designation is the likelihood that the Greek translators probably faithfully translated the Hebrew text they had available, and for many or most books the translation probably took place in Egypt. But would not other text types alongside the one used as the basis for the translation also be found in Egypt? Again, $4QJer^{b}$ and $4QSam^{a}$ were copied presumably in Palestine after those books had been translated into Greek in Egypt. Thus, copies of the text similar to the *Vorlage* of the OG translation produced in Egypt apparently continued to circulate in Palestine a century or so later. Lawrence Schiffman has also suggested that the Hillel traditions used for Babylonian aspects of the hypothesis must pass critical study.[9]

So Cross is correct that the different major localities of Judaism clearly gave direction to the varying text types. More research is now needed to determine whether each of the isolated localities was unidimensional or multidimensional, whether we can find specific tendencies due to specific localities, and how specifically the isolated localities shaped their texts.

9. His suggestion during the congress discussions referred to the critical work of J. Neusner in sorting out the relative reliability of various types of rabbinic traditions.

Second, Talmon's point is that the MT, the SP, and the LXX were preserved out of a much larger assortment of texts because the Rabbis, the Samaritans, and the Christians each preserved their own text, while the other rival texts perished with their adherents. This observation contributes an additional important piece of the puzzle. But can we push farther and ask whether there is evidence that any of those groups intentionally edited or reformulated their specific text in major ways? An earlier view attributed the expansionism attested in the SP to specifically Samaritan editorial activity. But 4QpaleoExod^{m} indicates that most of the characteristics associated with the SP were already in one commonly available edition of the text, and that the Samaritans merely added two textually limited changes: the addition of the final commandment about the altar on Gerizim and the use of the past instead of the future tense for the Lord's choice of the central shrine.[10]

In fact, the choice of text type appears to have been accidental in nature. Each community chose *something* — some aspect or characteristic — but they did not intentionally make a choice for a certain text type on a specifically textual basis. The choices appear to have nothing to do with the nature or quality of the text as such or the theology or ideology of that specific group. The Samaritans chose a *script* (the ancient Israelite or Palaeo-Hebrew script), probably for conservative reasons, just as they (and apparently the Sadducees)[11] were conservative in adhering to the Torah alone, without the Prophets. But the text type appears to have been simply one of the several text types available in the Hasmonaean era, perhaps accidentally chosen because it, like the text type displayed in 4QpaleoExod^{m}, was in the script they preferred.[12]

The Rabbis chose a *language* in opposition to the Christians, who chose the other language. The Christians chose the Scriptures in Greek possibly because of the spreading "mission to the Gentiles" in predominantly Greek-

10. See P. W. Skehan, "Qumran and the Present State of Old Testament Text Studies: The Masoretic Text," *JBL* 78 (1959) 21-25; and Judith E. Sanderson, *An Exodus Scroll from Qumran: 4QpaleoExod^{m} and the Samaritan Tradition* (HSS 30; Atlanta: Scholars Press, 1986), 235.

11. See the discussion of the positive and negative evidence with respect to the Sadducees in Roger Beckwith, *The Old Testament Canon of the New Testament Church* (Grand Rapids: Eerdmans, 1985) 86-91. This book amasses an immense amount of valuable material, even if one is not able to accept its general conclusions; see the review by Albert C. Sundberg, Jr., "Reexamining the Formation of the Old Testament Canon," *Int* 42 (1988) 78-82.

12. For a full treatment of all the variants of 4QpaleoExod^{m} and the scroll's relationship to the SP and MT, see Sanderson, *An Exodus Scroll.*

speaking regions. It would be naive to suppose that polemics played no role in this division of languages, but neither group significantly altered the older text as it appeared in that language.[13]

The Rabbis also chose a *text type*, the short one, as opposed to the longer text type already chosen (unintentionally) by the Samaritans, and they chose a *script* (the Aramaic or Jewish script) as opposed to the archaic script already chosen by the Samaritans. The Rabbis' choice of the short text type was presumably intentional, but that intentional choice apparently centered on religious self-definition and not on textual considerations of the text type itself.

Thus what Talmon observes is true and important, but until now that phenomenon appears to be by accident rather than by intention. What is also true, and derivative from his insight, is that religious groups probably did develop the text intentionally. But most of the observable variation does not seem to be confessional or based on distinctive ideas associated with particular groups.[14] Research is now needed to find evidence documenting which groups did what, where, and when. Did the various socioreligious groups intentionally or ideologically shape their specific forms of the text, and how did they do so?

Third, Emanuel Tov has sounded the clear trumpet call that the Qumran texts have "taught us no longer to posit MT at the center of our textual thinking."[15] Furthermore, he has pointed out a wealth of other significant facts, for example, that the Qumran biblical manuscripts reflect the situation in wider Jerusalem and Palestine, and that the prevalence of the MT at Masada and Naḥal Ḥever is not due to the "victory" of the MT but to an "accident" of survival.

My views are generally quite close to Tov's. Three points where they differ from his involve (1) his understanding of what he terms "Qumran orthography," (2) his reductionist or minimal view of text types, and (3) his conclusions about a majority of Qumran biblical manuscripts belonging to a "proto-Masoretic group." I hasten to say that he himself has expressed cautious qualifications of these views, but it is hard to escape the impression that he agrees more with his primary statements and formulations than with his caveats, and those formulations get absorbed into other scholars' quicker and

13. Charges of alteration, of course, were eventually made, and such alteration may have occurred, leading Aquila, for example, to attempt revisions of the LXX; but that was much later in the stage of textual transmission.

14. For a minor example of an ideological variant, see the Gerizim/Ebal variant in the SP and MT at Deut 27:4.

15. Tov, "Hebrew Biblical Manuscripts," 7.

less cautious conclusions.[16] I will develop the first two of these ideas further below; the third is sufficiently complex to require more space than is available here.

Categories of Textual Variation and the Canonical Process

What are the *main types of differences* that we observe when we examine the wide array of biblical manuscripts? What are the principal categories for classifying the differences observable among manuscripts? There are several ways of classifying the many types of variants, but I suggest that it is useful for our purpose of discussing text groups to divide them into the following three principal categories: (1) orthographic differences, (2) individual variant readings, and (3) variant editions of works. For the first two classifications, the differences can be major or minor and can be accidental or intentional; for the third classification, a variant edition of a book or passage is necessarily major and intentional.

Orthography

Orthographic differences can be simply defined, for our purposes, as alternate ways of spelling the same word. Usually they are the least important of the three main types of variation between manuscripts because they usually do not constitute differences in the meaning of the text. It is useful to distinguish three subclassifications of phenomena that are usually included under the term "orthography." The first is exemplified by the absence or presence of a *mater lectionis* (e.g., כל vs. כול, or לא vs. לוא). Insofar as these are alternate ways of spelling the same word, they do not affect the meaning of the text. From the point of view of historical grammar, they can be viewed either as errors or as a new practice of signaling historically short vowels or doubly signaling long vowels. The second subclassification is exemplified by the shorter or longer suffixes (e.g., ך– vs. כה–, or ת– vs. תה–). This is more properly a morphological, rather than an orthographic, phenomenon, since it involves two alternate morphological forms, each of which is spelled correctly. But with regard to the Qumran scrolls, it is more practical to include it with discussion of orthography, since, like the first subclassification, it does not affect

16. E.g., L. Schiffman's popular summary, "The Significance of the Scrolls," *Bible Review* 6/5 (1990) 18-27, esp. 27.

the meaning of the text. The third subclassification is exemplified by the insertion of a *mater lectionis,* which provides an indication of interpretation (e.g., expanding כתב to כותב). It can, of course, affect the meaning, and at times its purpose is to ensure one possible interpretation rather than another for exegetical or theological purposes.[17]

Although orthographic differences usually do not constitute differences in the meaning of the text, they can be important indicators for a number of aspects of textual history. For example, orthography can be an indicator of an earlier or later stage in the transmission history, insofar as the use of *matres lectionis* in general tended to expand during the Second Temple period. Orthography can also serve as the genesis of textual groupings. That is, text groups are determined by common variant readings, and orthography can originate variant readings insofar as particular spellings sometimes force a choice of one specific interpretation, over against another, of forms that had been ambiguous. Thus, as an example of the third subclassification above, the ambiguous form תורתי could mean "my Torah" (תּוֹרָתִי: singular noun) or "my instructions" (תּוֹרֹתַי: plural noun). If a scribe subsequently spells it תורותי, then all manuscripts copied or translated accurately from that more specific orthographic form will (at least for this reading) be in the same subgroup.

Tov has suggested that orthography can be a clue indicating whether a manuscript was copied outside Qumran or at Qumran.[18] And he goes further to describe the orthographic system that reflects a "scribal school" at Qumran.[19] I hope that we can gain some clear and helpful conclusions from studying the orthography of the Qumran manuscripts, and I think that the notion of a scribal school at Qumran is worth pursuing,[20] but I cannot persuade myself that Tov is correct on his proposal of "Qumran orthography." Though I could be wrong, it seems to me that at our present stage little can be determined conclusively on the basis of orthography alone, for two reasons. First, the more expansive orthography is found in Palestine outside Qumran and in Egypt.[21] Second, at Qumran scribes who were simply "copyists" would

17. If the *mater lectionis* is used merely for purposes of phonetic spelling rather than intentional interpretation, it is more properly placed in the first subclassification.

18. E. Tov, "The Orthography and Language of the Hebrew Scrolls Found at Qumran and the Origin of These Scrolls," *Textus* 13 (1986) 31-57; idem, "Hebrew Biblical Manuscripts," 23-25; idem, "Groups of Texts Found at Qumran."

19. Tov, "Hebrew Biblical Manuscripts," 25.

20. A limitation, however, is that fluidity in orthography is a characteristic of the Second Temple period. As in the Elizabethan era, there were several acceptable ways to spell words. Ability to write exceeded knowledge of historical spelling and grammar.

21. As examples of the widespread patterns, both יהד and יהוד are found on coins

reproduce a text — whether in traditional or contemporizing[22] orthography — exactly as they encountered it. Insofar as they were "updaters,"[23] they might produce a text with expanded orthography whether the source text was in traditional or contemporizing orthography. Both of the mentalities attributed to "copyists" and "updaters" were clear, distinct, and acceptable in antiquity, as they are now. It is an attractive idea that there was a scribal school at Qumran, whether it was by design a school or by custom the equivalent of a school. But I question whether the principles or practices of the scribes at Qumran differed significantly from those of other contemporary Jewish scribes.[24] In the third part of this paper, I will discuss the orthographic data provided by 4QDan[a] and 4QDan[b].

---

of similar date, and the Nash Papyrus from Egypt spells לוא with *waw;* see, e.g., J. Naveh, *Early History of the Alphabet: An Introduction to West Semitic Epigraphy and Palaeography* (2d rev. ed.; Jerusalem: Magnes, 1987) 116, 163. The difference in expansive orthography exemplified by forms such as כיא is of degree, not of kind.

22. I am not suggesting that "traditional" (or "conservative") and "contemporary" (or "contemporizing" or "modernizing" or "baroque") orthography are fully satisfactory terms. They are employed here to describe the shorter, *"defective"* (also an unsatisfactory term) spelling system more characteristic of the late monarchic and early postexilic periods, in contrast to the longer, *plene* system progressively more characteristic of the late Second Temple period. Though perhaps not fully satisfactory, I think that they may more accurately describe the situation than "non-Qumran" and "Qumran" orthography. See the remarks on this point in Cross, "The Evolution of a Theory of Local Texts." Insofar as I was able quickly to absorb Cross's discussion of orthographic terminology, it appears that he was concerned primarily with the pronominal suffixes, thus the morphological (my second) subclassification, and I accept his explanation as another solid advance. At this point I still think that two distinguishing factors in the properly orthographic aspects (esp. my first subclassification) are the faithful copying of a basically traditional spelling with more sparing use of *matres lectionis* and the expansion (sometimes inadvertent, sometimes intentional) of spelling in a style that was increasingly widely used in the Second Temple period.

23. See the distinction made between "copyists" and "updaters" by F. I. Andersen and A. D. Forbes, *Spelling in the Hebrew Bible* (BibOr 41; Rome: Biblical Institute Press, 1986) 115. An example of an "updating" scribe is the scribe of 4QSam[c]; see E. Ulrich, "4QSam[c]: A Fragmentary Manuscript of 2 Samuel 14–15 from the Scribe of the *Serek Hay-yaḥad* (1QS)," *BASOR* 235 (1979) 1-25.

24. See E. Ulrich, "The Palaeo-Hebrew Biblical Manuscripts from Qumran Cave 4," in *Time to Prepare the Way in the Wilderness: Papers on the Qumran Scrolls by Fellows of the Institute for Advanced Studies of the Hebrew University, Jerusalem, 1989-1990* (STDJ 16; ed. D. Dimant and L. H. Schiffman; Leiden: Brill, 1995) 103-29, now reprinted below as Chapter 7 in this volume. The evidence is neither abundant nor strongly conclusive, but with regard to the four categories of the physical characteristics, the palaeography and date, the orthography, and the textual character of those manuscripts, "there seems to be no great distinction in any of those four categories between manuscripts copied outside Qumran (or predating Qumran) and manuscripts copied at Qumran."

Individual Variant Readings

Individual or isolated variant readings constitute the primary category in most discussions of textual criticism. This is the first category that commonly comes to mind and is the category into which most differences in the text are lumped unless there is a reason to classify them otherwise. The vast majority of treatments of textual criticism revolves predominantly on individual variant readings, and thus further discussion is not necessary here.

Variant Literary Editions of Scriptural Books or Passages

Just as orthographic differences and individual textual variants contribute in two basically different ways to the textual diversity manifest in our extant textual witnesses, so do variant literary editions of scriptural books or passages cause a fundamentally different category of textual diversity. A revised literary edition of a sacred composition that eventually becomes accepted into the canon is an intentional reworking of an older form of the book for a specific purpose or according to identifiable editorial principles. The process by which the canonical books were formed has direct effects on the text and textual variation of the books; the discernment of variant editions thus becomes an essential step in understanding and classifying certain kinds of textual variants.

I must introduce this section with several preliminary observations, a number of which border on the canonical process.[25] A consideration of how the Scriptures were composed, how they were viewed and used, and how they were copied and transmitted will prove to be an important dimension in understanding the history of the biblical text and therefore in understanding text groups.

First, if we try to achieve a historical perspective on the text of the Bible, the first step is not to talk about a Bible. The word Bible evokes the image of a unified book, a codex, a unit, a collected anthology; but this was not the case in the late Second Temple period. There were sacred compositions or books that were viewed more or less widely as classical and authoritative. Physically,

25. See E. Ulrich, "The Canonical Process, Textual Criticism, and Latter Stages in the Composition of the Bible," in *Sha'arei Talmon: Studies in the Bible, Qumran, and the Ancient Near East Presented to Shemaryahu Talmon* (ed. M. Fishbane and E. Tov with W. W. Fields; Winona Lake, Ind.: Eisenbrauns, 1992), now reprinted as Chapter 4 in this volume. See also Julio Trebolle Barrera's remarks on canon in *Centena in libros Samuelis et Regum*, 34-36.

these were on separate scrolls, not yet combined into a single codex, so that linkage between, and order of, the units of the whole were not strong factors. Conceptually, certain subgroups were considered to be linked together in varying degrees. The five books of Moses, for example, were clearly viewed as a connected group, and sometimes one of these books was copied on the same scroll as another (e.g., 4QGen-Exod[a] and probably 4QpaleoGen-Exod[l]); I do not know of an ancient example of all five books being copied together on a single scroll, though the Pentateuchal Paraphrases (4Q364-367) may indicate such. At any rate, it is clear that the Torah was considered a unit of combined sacred books. The "Prophets" were also viewed as a collection by the latter part of the Second Temple period. We can assume that the Former Prophets and the Latter Prophets were perceived as subgroups as well. The Minor Prophets scroll from Murabbaʿat and the Greek Minor Prophets scroll from Naḥal Ḥever both display "The Twelve" Minor Prophets as a single scroll, but these were probably viewed as a single collection or "book"; I know of no example where two prophetic books were copied on the same scroll.

Moreover, conceptually, there was probably felt to be a traditional order for some of the books or small groups of books. That is, the books of the Torah would naturally have occurred in the order familiar to us, and this is what we find on the scrolls that contain more than one book. Similarly, the Torah would surely have been mentally arranged in a position preceding the Prophets. But as late as the Talmud, we find statements such as "the order of the Prophets is . . . Jeremiah, Ezekiel, Isaiah. . . ."[26] Thus, instead of envisioning a "Bible," a single-volume anthology bound with the books in a permanent order, we might more accurately envision a jar of scrolls. A majority of influential leaders would implicitly or explicitly have believed that most of those scrolls belonged in the jar. The ideological center of the collection, the type of scrolls that could by no means be withdrawn, would have been the Torah, and the scrolls of prophetic books would have had strong support. But the status of the scrolls near the periphery was not so clear; long beyond the fall of the Temple there was, both in explicit debate and in practice, uncertainty as to the status of books such as Qoheleth, the Song of Songs, Sirach, *Enoch*, and *Jubilees*. In short, the question of "canon" had not yet fully been raised and settled. By the end of the Second Temple period there were works that were considered "Scrip-

26. See *b. B. Bat.* 14b; also note the varying orders still found in Jewish and Christian lists, conveniently reproduced in H. B. Swete, *An Introduction to the Old Testament in Greek* (rev. ed. by R. R. Ottley; New York: Ktav, 1968) 198-214.

ture," a canonical process, and a canon-in-the-making, but there was not yet a canon.

Second, it is important to note that, though "the Prophets" were viewed as a collection, the contents and limits of that collection were quite elastic. The Scriptures, or the collection of the sacred books, were referred to as "the Law and the Prophets." Clearly, there were many books beyond the Torah that were explicitly or implicitly considered as Scripture but that are now not classified among the Prophets. The book of Daniel, for example, was considered prophetic at Qumran, in the New Testament, by Josephus, by Melito, and indeed, to judge by the evidence, by all.[27] The first written evidence of Daniel as among the Ketubim apparently comes relatively late, from the Talmud.[28] Moreover, the book of Psalms was viewed as prophetic at Qumran.[29] But, though Psalms texts continued to be interpreted as prophetic (e.g., in the Epistle to the Hebrews and the Gospels), eventually the book of Psalms was understood to be in a classification beyond the Law and the Prophets. The Halakhic Letter from Qumran (4QMMT) speaks in a way that groups together in a single breath the book of Moses, the Prophets, and David;[30] this parallels the Gospel According to Luke, which customarily refers to the Law (or Moses) and the Prophets (Luke 16:16, 29, 31; 24:27; cf. Acts 26:22; 28:23), but which once speaks of the Law and the Prophets and Psalms (Luke 24:44). Evidence for a third classification in addition to the Law and the Prophets is commonly seen in the Prologue to Ben Sira, but it is important to note that the identification of the third classification there is not certain, while other clear references to a third classification do not appear, or do not appear again, until the first century C.E.[31]

Third, it is also important to remember how the biblical books were composed. It is commonly known that the Torah was produced by a series of what we might call revised editions of earlier traditions. That is, the premonarchic ancestral traditions were reformulated in a theological frame-

27. See 4Q174 2:3 (DJD 5:54); Matt 24:15 (cf. Mark 13:14); Josephus, *Antiquities* 10.11.1 §§249, 266-67; and Melito *apud* Eusebius, *Ecclesiastical History* 4.26.14.

28. *B. Baba Batra* 14b.

29. 11QPs^a (col. 27, line 11) records that all the 3,600 psalms (including those preserved in the MT) and 364 songs written by David "he spoke through prophecy given him by the Most High." Furthermore, the Qumran community produced pesharim, a genre apparently confined to prophetic material, on Psalms texts (4Q171, 4Q173; 4Q172?).

30. I thank Profs. John Strugnell and Elisha Qimron for discussion of this text at the Institute for Advanced Studies at the Hebrew University in Jerusalem, and Prof. Jacob Milgrom for bringing the phrase to my attention in this context.

31. I thank Charles Miller for this observation and that about the Lukan usage.

work by early monarchic editors, classically termed the Yahwist and the Elohist;[32] these in turn were combined by a subsequent editor later in the monarchic period; and a yet later editor combined the Priestly material with it probably in the early postexilic period. The prophetic books were compiled in the same way, both the Former Prophets (or the Deuteronomistic History) and the Latter Prophets (cf. the successive revised editions of the books of Amos, Isaiah, etc.). The same process holds true for the Writings. My point is not the validity of the detailed theories or terminology here, but that the process of the composition of the Scriptures can be seen as part of the canonical process. It was a dialectic process of editors taking up older sources and reworking them in dialogue with the needs or views of their contemporary situation.

Fourth, as Talmon has observed, even in the late Second Temple period, there were many individual scribes who worked as "a minor partner in the creative literary process"[33] who, like "the Chronicler, or for that matter the author of Daniel, . . . related to the biblical literature from within."[34] Talmon also maintains "that an undetermined percentage of . . . *variae lectiones* derive from the impact of ongoing literary processes of an intra-biblical nature. . . ."[35]

Developing Talmon's ideas, I have made the point that the compositional creativity of these late creative scribes is of the same nature as the compositional creativity of the early tradents.[36] That is, the composition of the individual biblical books involved a sequence of revisions of traditional materials — a succession of new editions. This ongoing process, different for each book, started early and continued for some books up through the late Second Temple period. "The text" was evolutionary. Its development is organic and logical, but unpredictable. We basically expect it to stay the same. Sometimes it does, and this accounts for its continuity and stability. Sometimes it does not, and then we must investigate the changes — basically the types of variation described in the second part of this chapter. If the individual variant readings are not isolated but form a coherent pattern, this can signal a variant literary edition. Each edition is a moment in the development of each book. The cut-off point where the text was frozen for each book and in

32. For the sake of clarity, for the point I am making, the classical documentary hypothesis is used. I think that any revision required for that hypothesis will probably incorporate some form of the idea being here presented.

33. Talmon, "Textual Study," 381.

34. Ibid., 379.

35. Ibid., 380.

36. Ulrich, "The Canonical Process." See also the insightful contributions of Julio Trebolle Barrera linking compositional, redactional, and textual layers.

each religious tradition is arbitrary or accidental. Thus, there were multiple editions of some, perhaps many, of these sacred works, and unless we have indication to the contrary, we must assume that — just as today — it was the sacred work or book that was important, not the specific edition or specific wording of the work.[37] In discussion of the canon, it thus becomes important to remember that, for both Judaism and Christianity, it was books, not specific textual forms of the books, that were canonical.[38]

The point of these observations is to set a context for our understanding of variant literary editions of scriptural books and passages. What we later envision as the canon of "the Bible" was, during the late Second Temple period, a collection — not clearly defined — of individual sacred compositions. We should not begin our thinking with a vision of a unified *Biblia Hebraica* or modern Bible, but rather with an image of a flexible number of sacred scrolls with varying degrees of closeness or distance from a center called "Torah," whose periphery was vague. The history of composition of these books developed through a series of revised editions of the traditional material. The types of new composition and new editions produced in the late Second Temple period are of the same nature as the types of composition produced in the monarchic, exilic, and early postexilic periods. The timetable for each book grew independently, and the text type found in one book often had no relation to that in another. Moreover, the use by both Jews and Christians of diverse forms of texts in the first century shows that neither community thought that a fixed text was necessary for an authoritative book; evidently, differing forms of the text were acceptable.

Elsewhere I have developed detailed examples of multiple literary editions in representative books in the Torah (Exodus), the Former Prophets (Samuel) and Latter Prophets (Jeremiah), and the Writings (Daniel).[39] Those specific examples even show different types of intentionally variant editions of the scriptural text formed on different editorial principles.[40] I will not repeat here the details but only the conclusion that the pattern of composition is one of multiple literary editions of many (if not all) of the books of the Bi-

37. See Talmon ("Textual Study," 326): "The limited flux of the textual transmission of the Bible appears to be a legitimate and accepted phenomenon of ancient scribal tradition."

38. Ulrich, "The Canonical Process"; Trebolle, *Centena in libros Samuelis et Regum*, 34-36.

39. Ulrich, "The Canonical Process."

40. The different types include harmonization, intentional alteration of a portrait, supplementation of one narrative with diverse traditions from another, variant arrangement, and systematic minor expansion.

ble, thus forming plural text types (see below). This process of successive variant editions continues up to the period in which manuscripts witnessing to the variant editions survive. Unfortunately, few survive. But the surviving manuscripts do confirm the abundant lessons in this regard that the Samaritan Pentateuch, the Septuagint, and the other versions have long since offered.

What I have attempted to do in this second part of the paper is to distinguish three main categories of textual variation in biblical manuscripts and to suggest a relationship between the canonical process and certain text groups. This was done in the hope that those distinct categories can aid in the discernment of different levels of text groups, and that the process of composition for the books that eventually formed the canon of Scripture can illumine editorial activity that resulted in distinct text groups. To the correlation of these factors and the terminology for describing them we now turn.

Text Groups and Terminology

To show how the three types of manuscript variation fit together to help advance understanding of the history of the text, let us now move to a discussion of terminology. David Gooding in 1976 registered "An Appeal for a Stricter Terminology in the Textual Criticism of the Old Testament."[41] But we must, I think, ask him to continue to be patient. We cannot make our terminology precise until our understanding of the material we are describing is precise. We have been making advances toward that goal, but we have not yet achieved it.

At this point I do not think that it is advisable to borrow the terminology of New Testament textual criticism[42] because of the vast differences in the evidence: there are thousands of well-preserved manuscripts of the New Testament, while there are very few complete witnesses to the Hebrew Bible. Thus, there is a great deal of evidence by which to group manuscripts of the New Testament, but very little by which to group manuscripts of the Hebrew Bible. Rather, I offer one suggestion for terminology and one for further research and refinement. I will attempt to demonstrate my suggestion for fur-

41. D. W. Gooding, "An Appeal for a Stricter Terminology in the Textual Criticism of the Old Testament," *JSS* 21 (1976) 15-25.

42. James R. Davila, however, made a good advance on this problem in a paper entitled "Text-Type and Terminology: The Book of Genesis as a Test Case" at the Society of Biblical Literature meeting in New Orleans on November 18, 1990. I have not yet succeeded in integrating his suggestions into the proposal developed here.

ther research by analyzing the text of Daniel and correlating the data provided by the textual analysis of Daniel with the proposed terminology.

Terminology

With regard to terminology, we are in a position only to propose tentative terms. Enough of the biblical material from Qumran has been published for all to have a good understanding of the general picture, though we must leave room for the possibility that more long-term study of the fully published texts will require revision and refinement of the way we see and describe things now. From our present vantage point, I suggest the following terms and categories:

Text family — a relatively small set of manuscripts that display close agreement in idiosyncratic or unique readings that are secondary (e.g., errors, distinctive additions, etc.)

Text type — a relatively large set of manuscripts that display general agreement despite differences in details, but where the emphasis is on affiliation (thus the horizontal dimension on a stemma)

Text tradition — a relatively large set of manuscripts that display general agreement despite differences in details, but where the emphasis is on the development or history of the text (thus the vertical dimension on a stemma)

Text group — a general term that covers any or all of the above when speaking generally or when the evidence is insufficient to use the other terms.

Further Research

With regard to further research, it will be important to correlate three factors, and to do so, analyses or probes should be made to see how the proposed (or any revised) terminology fits the data. The three factors are the types of variation presented by the manuscript witnesses (orthographic differences, individual textual variants, and variant editions), the types of lines on a stemma, and terminology. As an example, let me use the two larger manuscripts of Daniel from Qumran, 4QDan^{a} and 4QDan^{b}.[43]

43. For editions of these manuscripts, see E. Ulrich, "Daniel Manuscripts from

Analysis. With respect to orthography, it must be said that there is no consistent orthographic system in either of these two manuscripts or, for that matter, in the MT of Daniel.[44] There are orthographic tendencies or general patterns in each, but nothing close to a consistent system; in each, the same words or morphemes are spelled in differing ways.[45] Granted that, certain patterns nonetheless emerge. 4QDan^a and the MT are found to share similar orthographic practices in common against the generally more liberal use by 4QDan^b of *matres lectionis.* There are six orthographic differences where both 4QDan^a and 4QDan^b are extant, and in all six the pattern is 4QDan^a = MT ≠ 4QDan^b. For these orthographic matters, the Greek evidence is of no consequence.

With respect to individual textual variants, however, the pattern is reversed. There are four textual variants in the material where the two Qumran manuscripts have extant fragments that overlap, and in all four the pattern is 4QDan^a = 4QDan^b ≠ MT. In other words, 4QDan^a and 4QDan^b consistently present the same text in contrast to the MT.[46] All four variants "are pluses relative to the MT, all (with [one] quite possible exception . . .) are secondary additions, and all (with [one] possible exception . . .) are predictable."[47] For these individual textual variants the Greek evidence is as follows: twice OG = 4QDan^a 4QDan^b ≠ MT; once OG = MT ≠ 4QDan^a 4QDan^b; and once OG ≠ 4QDan^a 4QDan^b ≠ MT.

With respect to variant literary editions, there are two editions of the book of Daniel as a whole still preserved: the shorter, earlier edition found in the MT and evidently in all eight manuscripts of Daniel from Qumran Caves

Qumran. Part 1: A Preliminary Edition of 4QDan^a," *BASOR* 268 (1987) 17-37; idem, "Daniel Manuscripts from Qumran. Part 2: Preliminary Editions of 4QDan^b and 4QDan^c," *BASOR* 274 (1989) 3-27.

44. See E. Ulrich, "Orthography and Text in 4QDan^a and 4QDan^b and in the Received Masoretic Text," in *Of Scribes and Scrolls: Studies on the Hebrew Bible, Intertestamental Judaism, and Christian Origins Presented to John Strugnell on the Occasion of His Sixtieth Birthday* (ed. Harold W. Attridge, John J. Collins, and Thomas H. Tobin; College Theology Society Resources in Religion 5; Lanham, Md.: University Press of America, 1990) 29-42, now reprinted below as Chapter 8 in this volume.

45. Ibid., 41: "Though for an individual reading, comparison with a Qumran manuscript may show the MT as displaying a certain orthographic feature, the MT not infrequently displays in another verse the contrasting feature that marked the Qumran reading."

46. Ibid.: "Due to the fragmentary nature of the evidence, only one agreement is fully certain, but strong evidence is extant for the other three and the most cogent interpretation is surely to conclude that 4QDan^a and 4QDan^b agree in four longer readings against the MT."

47. Ibid.

1, 4, and 6;[48] and the longer, expanded edition including "the additions" found in the OG and in the text attributed to Theodotion. This last note is interesting, of course, insofar as the Theodotionic text presumably resulted from revision to conform to a current, or the current, Hebrew-Aramaic text.

Correlation. At first, one might be tempted to consider the Qumran, Masoretic, and Greek texts of Daniel simply "independent texts" because the patterns go in all directions. But let us consider the following partial reconstruction of the history of the text of Daniel. Edition *N* of the book of Daniel,[49] found in the MT and the eight Qumran manuscripts, was revised to include "the additions" (probably in Hebrew-Aramaic), thus becoming Edition *N+1* found in the OG and Theodotion. The manuscripts copied or translated from Edition *N* form one "text type," and those copied or translated from Edition *N+1* form a second "text type." Due to the minor clarifications, errors, and other changes of the subsequent Hebrew-Aramaic copyists, of the Greek translator, and of the Greek copyists, there developed individual variant readings within each text type. Thus, the texts found at Qumran and the text eventually preserved in the MT, though of the same text type, display minor variants against each other; in this case 4QDan[a] and 4QDan[b] happen to display four secondary pluses relative to the MT (though the medieval MT also has secondary pluses at other points). Due either to the cross-influence of texts or to the simple, predictable nature of those pluses, two of those same four secondary pluses become inserted into exemplars of Edition *N+1*, whether in a Hebrew-Aramaic text, or in a developed form within the transmission history of the Greek text.

Thus far, the MT and the Qumran manuscripts are part of one "text type" in contrast to another text type that includes the OG. 4QDan[a] and 4QDan[b] are part of a "text family" or subgroup within that first "text type," closely sharing secondary additions and even unique readings, and due to accident or dependence the OG exhibits minor agreements with them.

The scribe who inscribed 4QDan[a] faithfully copied the text (with its secondary pluses) in the same traditional orthographic style that generally

48. For the manuscripts from Caves 1 and 6, see the editions of 1QDan[a] and 1QDan[b] by D. Barthélemy in DJD 1:150-52, and that of pap6QDan by Baillet in DJD 3:114-15 and plate 23. The possibility should be kept in mind that Cave 4 fragments still labeled "unidentified" may be Hebrew or Aramaic portions of the Danielic material otherwise transmitted only through the Greek.

49. I shall use *N* to designate the unknown number (second, third, etc.) in the series of editions of the book of Daniel. See D. O. Wenthe, "The Old Greek Translation of Daniel 1–6" (Dissertation, University of Notre Dame, 1991), which demonstrates why the edition of the book contained in the MT, though the earliest preserved complete edition, is not the first edition of the biblical book of Daniel.

characterizes the text preserved in the Masoretic *textus receptus*. But the scribe who copied the later scroll, 4QDan[b],[50] decided to operate not simply as a "copyist" but as an "updater" at the level of orthography, and faithfully copied the text (and therefore the distinctive details of the text family) of 4QDan[a] or another scroll in the same text family, but did so using the more contemporary expanded orthography.

Thus, we have identified contrasting "text types" based on the *variant literary editions* of the book of Daniel, contrasting "text families" based on a series of *individual variant readings* shared by closely related manuscripts within one text type, and contrasting *orthographic differences* based on the preference for the expanded orthography that increasingly characterized writing practices in the late Second Temple period. We have also identified contrasting "text traditions" insofar as the various witnesses can be correlated in a chronological dimension. Finally, a general term that may serve to describe the subject of the above discussion or aspects where data for more precise terminology are lacking is "text groups."

Conclusion

This essay has attempted to illumine the history of the biblical text, especially in the realm of text groups. The three dominant positions on the topic were reviewed in the light of subsequent work on the Qumran manuscripts, suggesting which features continue to prove helpful, which features need refinement, and which areas of future research offer promise. An analysis of the types of textual variation observable in the Qumran manuscripts, the Masoretic *textus receptus,* and the Septuagint and other versions served to distinguish factors that led to a clearer vision for the mapping of text groups. The canonical process — the process of composition, including a succession of revised literary editions, of the canonical books — proved to be a helpful key in discerning text types. Tentative terminology with respect to text families, text types, and text traditions was suggested in light of the categories of textual variation, in the hope that — if future probes find it to be appropriate for the material and useful for clarity — we may reach greater precision in the use of terminology for the textual criticism of the Hebrew Bible.

50. 4QDan[a] is dated palaeographically in the mid–first century B.C.E., and 4QDan[b] about 20-50 C.E., thus later by about a century or somewhat less. Moreover, "4QDan[b] in both palaeographic script and orthographic profile — including the active insertion of supralinear *matres lectionis* by the scribe — is a later and more developed manuscript than 4QDan[a]" (Ulrich, "Orthography," 42).

CHAPTER 6

Multiple Literary Editions: Reflections Toward a Theory of the History of the Biblical Text

Perennially fascinating to the human mind are questions regarding the genesis and development of important elements that constitute our world, our existence, our physical, psychological, or spiritual life. The historical-critical study of theBible is one such assay in exploring the origins and development of a predominant influence on Western culture and Jewish-Christian values and traditions.

Various new forces provide stimuli for reconsidering and rethinking current perspectives on origins, such as a new invention with wide-ranging possibilities, a new Zeitgeist with fertile potencies for seeing familiar subjects from a fresh viewpoint, or the discovery of a new body of evidence that offers a fresh coign of vantage for reevaluation of traditional theories.

The two hundred biblical manuscripts[1] discovered at Qumran offer,

1. For a list and discussion of the biblical scrolls from Cave 4, see E. Ulrich, "The Biblical Scrolls from Qumran Cave 4: An Overview and a Progress Report on Their Publication," *RevQ* 14/2, no. 54-55 (December 1989) 207-28. For updates of that list plus a list of manuscripts from the other caves and their publication data, see E. Tov et al., eds., *The Dead Sea Scrolls on Microfiche: A Comprehensive Facsimile Edition of the Texts from the Judaean Desert, Companion Volume* (2d ed.; Leiden: Brill, 1995). For publication of the Cave 4 biblical scrolls, see DJD 9 (manuscripts in palaeo-Hebrew or Greek), DJD 12 (Gen-

I am especially grateful to Professors Noel B. Reynolds and Donald W. Parry, the Foundation for Ancient Research and Mormon Studies, and the Jerusalem Center for Near Eastern Studies of Brigham Young University for the invitation to contribute to their Judaean Desert Scrolls Conference 1995 and for their gracious hospitality.

among many other benefits, the possibility of a great advance in the area usually labeled "the history of the biblical text." Discussions of this topic are usually confined to the closing centuries of the Second Temple period, and understandably so, since we have no textual evidence prior to about the middle of the third century B.C.E. But such constriction tends to distort the picture and even to distort approaches to the picture. Moreover, lack of extant evidence, though regrettable and daunting, should not excessively intimidate us, for history is essentially a process and an art of reconstruction. Lack of extant evidence should certainly cause us to proceed cautiously, but that lack should not prevent us from proceeding. On the one hand, frequent and widespread archaeological discoveries of large depositories have documented highly developed literary activity throughout the ancient Near East in the second and first millennia B.C.E. On the other hand, intense and voluminous literary and historical-critical study of the biblical literature over several centuries has solidly grounded the assumption of a rich and continuous literary history of Israel spanning more than a millennium. And, although it was in existence, it was not until our generation that the documentation of that amazingly large cache of literary remains found near the tiny commune of Qumran happened to become available.

Thus the topic of the discussion about the history of the biblical text should not be limited to the evidence that we happen to have available, or we will not succeed in the task of reconstructing that history, since all the evidence and all logic point to a much larger scope of biblical literary activity throughout the monarchic and postexilic periods. The following proposal will attempt to situate the discussion in the larger context of the history of the composition of the biblical books. After a review of some of the evidence from Qumran, I will attempt an exposition of variant literary editions as a key to the history of the biblical text.

The Evidence from Qumran

Before examining the Qumran evidence, it is helpful to recall that before the Qumran discoveries we had the primary clues necessary for outlining the fol-

esis-Numbers), DJD 14 (Deuteronomy-Kings), DJD 15 (Isaiah-Minor Prophets), plus the forthcoming DJD 16 (Psalms-Chronicles), and DJD 17 (Samuel). For an index of the biblical passages preserved in these manuscripts, see E. Ulrich, "An Index of Passages in the Biblical Manuscripts from the Judean Desert (Genesis-Kings)," *DSD* 1 (1994) 113-29; idem, "An Index of Passages in the Biblical Manuscripts from the Judean Desert (Part 2: Isaiah-Chronicles)," *DSD* 2 (1995) 86-107.

lowing proposal, namely, the Samaritan Pentateuch (𝔪) and the Septuagint (𝔊) alongside the Masoretic Text (𝔐). By reconsidering scholarly use of the Samaritan and Septuagintal evidence, we may also gain valuable insight for today.

Ever since its rediscovery in 1616, the Samaritan Pentateuch has provided us with examples of an alternate edition of the traditional biblical text. In the books of Exodus and Numbers[2] it displays an only slightly altered version of an edition that is similar to, derived from, and more developed than our traditional text. It tells us a great deal about the Jewish texts of the Scriptures at the time of Jesus and Paul, Hillel and Shammai, and Qumran's Teacher of Righteousness. This valuable information we had available, but we simply paid little or no attention to it because of religious prejudice against the marginalized Samaritans. Those variant editions were viewed simply as the product of the perverse Samaritans, and, as in racist or other prejudiced groups, scholars colluded, collectively agreeing, without real thought, that the evidence was of little worth.

Similarly, 𝔊 preserves editions of some biblical books or passages that are different from those found in 𝔐. 𝔊 is the earliest translation of the Hebrew Bible, a translation that started with the Torah probably around 280 B.C.E. and was gradually completed over the next two centuries or so. But the function of 𝔊 in biblical scholarship until the middle of this century was often polemical. Catholics tended to use it because it had been the Bible of the Church from the beginnings, until the Vulgate replaced it. Jews tended to ignore it in favor of the traditional Hebrew, and Protestants tended to dismiss it in view of the renewed interest in the "original Hebrew," partly as a result of the Renaissance return to the original languages for all classics. Thus, major differences between the text of 𝔊 and that of the "original" Hebrew were mainly seen as corruptions or deliberate changes from the inspired text. 𝔊 was charged with being a poor translation or a loose paraphrase, and its witness, along with that of 𝔪, lay dormant because it was marginalized. However, the Qumran scrolls are a thousand years older than what was known in the fifteenth century as the "original Hebrew" text, and the scrolls demonstrate that in fact multiple forms of the "original Hebrew" text existed, and that the various books of 𝔊 — far from being corrupt translations or poor paraphrases — should be viewed as gen-

2. For the books of Genesis, Leviticus, and perhaps Deuteronomy, 𝔪 and 𝔐 share the same literary edition, although in Genesis 5:18-32 and 11:10-32 𝔐, 𝔊, and 𝔪 appear to have intentionally variant forms of the numerical schemata; for further references see E. Tov, *Textual Criticism of the Hebrew Bible* (Minneapolis: Fortress, 1992) 337-38.

erally faithful translations of ancient, alternate Hebrew forms of texts unknown throughout the Middle Ages but now rediscovered and fragmentarily attested at Qumran.

Perhaps the modern recognition both of the value of 𝔪 and 𝔊, and of the scholarly misjudgment due to preconceived denominational loyalties, can provide us with an instructive lesson. We should first pay serious attention to our new data, try creatively to allow various possible interpretations to emerge and be sufficiently explored, and only then come to a judgment between competing interpretations. In other words, we should let our judgments flow logically from the data and not superimpose an interpretation prompted by "what we already know" from traditional theological systems.

Turning now to the Qumran evidence, I would like to begin by presenting an illustration that may serve as a point of reference in the ensuing discussion: four lines from 4QpaleoExod^{m} (see p. 103). Although the full column that begins with this text was published by Patrick Skehan in 1955,[3] to my knowledge no one has made the detailed points and distinctions that follow.

The primary feature to notice is that the scroll exhibits the same basic textual form as 𝔪 (see lines 1-2). After an examination of the larger patterns of 4QpaleoExod^{m}, 𝔪, 𝔐, and 𝔊, it becomes clear that this textual form is a revised and expanded *variant edition* of the base text generally shared by all four. Thus, 4QpaleoExod^{m} and 𝔪 share the same literary edition of Exodus, a secondary edition expanded (in this case from Deuteronomy 9:20) beyond the earlier edition exhibited by 𝔐 and 𝔊. Although the picture gets more complicated, it should be mentioned that for Exodus 35–39 𝔐 probably contains an edition that, in comparison with the earlier edition of 𝔊, was secondarily revised and rearranged. If we also decide that the final text of the Samaritans qualifies as yet another variant edition of Exodus — not because of quantitative mass but because of the significance of the two kinds of change introduced[4] — then we have isolated four variant editions of the book of Exodus that are extant, beyond the many creative new editions that preceded our surviving textual witnesses.

3. P. W. Skehan, "Exodus in the Samaritan Recension from Qumran," *JBL* 74 (1955) 182-87; for full publication, see P. W. Skehan, E. Ulrich, and J. E. Sanderson, *Qumran Cave 4, IV: Palaeo-Hebrew and Greek Biblical Manuscripts* (DJD 9; Oxford: Clarendon, 1992) 53-130.

4. The two major changes marking the specifically Samaritan Torah are the commandment to build an altar at Shechem and the use of the perfect בחר "has chosen" [Shechem] in contrast to the future יבחר "will choose" [Jerusalem] to designate the central shrine.

4QpaleoExod^{m} (Exodus 32:10-11)

1 או[תך] לגוי גדול [ובאהרון התאנף יה]וה מאד להשמידו[ ]
2 ו[י]תפלל משה בעד א]הרון [ ] [11ו] [ ]
3 י[חל] משה את [פנ]י [יהוה אלהיו ויאו]מר למ[ה]יהוה יחר א[פך]
4 בעמ[ך]אשר [הו]צ[את מארץ מצרים בכח גדול ו]בזרוע חזק[ה]

Samaritan Pentateuch

1 אתך לגוי גדול ובאהרן התאנף יהוה מאד להשמידו
2 ויתפלל משה בעד אהרן
3 [11]ויחל משה את פני יהוה אלהיו ויאמר למה יהוה יחר אפך
4 בעמך אשר הוצאת ממצרים בכח גדול ובזרוע נטויה

Masoretic Text

1 אותך לגוי גדל
2
3 [11]ויחל משה את פני יהוה אלהיו ויאמר למה יהוה יחרה אפך
4 בעמך אשר הוצאת מארץ מצרים בכח גדול וביד חזקה

Translation (Exodus 32:10-11; cf. Deuteronomy 9:20)

1 (. . . but I will make) you a great nation. But against Aaron
the LORD was very angry, (enough) to destroy him;
2 so Moses prayed on behalf of Aaron.
3 [11]Moses entreated the Lord his God and said,
"Why, O LORD, does your anger burn
4 against your people whom you have brought out of
the land of Egypt with great power and a mighty arm?"

A second feature to notice in the example is the variety in patterns of agreement and disagreement between the three texts in *individual textual variants:* 4QpaleoExod^{m} and 𝔪 agree against 𝔐 in one individual variant, the verb יחר in line 3; in contrast, 4QpaleoExod^{m} and 𝔐 agree against 𝔪 in a second individual variant, מארץ מצרים in line 4; whereas in the final variant all three texts disagree among themselves.

A third feature to notice is that 4QpaleoExod^{m} and 𝔐 agree in *orthography* against 𝔪 with respect to the first word א(ו)תך, whereas they presumably differ regarding אהר(ו)ן, since the scroll habitually has אהרון elsewhere, while 𝔐 and 𝔪 habitually have אהרן.[5]

It is easy to understand why one could view this and numerous analogous examples as simply "independent" or "nonaligned" texts.[6] But we should never assume that any particular text encountered is a "pure form" of the literary edition or text type. Individual variants arise spontaneously or influence other texts ad hoc, without regard to literary editions. Moreover, orthography was expanding generally in Palestine in the latter Second Temple period; expanded use of *matres lectionis* was the tendency, and it would be a healthy assumption that the practice of introducing *matres lectionis* into a text for greater clarity happened independently of text type.[7]

As additional data for the theoretical considerations that follow, I would like to offer a few more examples from Qumran biblical manuscripts — focusing on the Former Prophets or Deuteronomistic history, mainly because, as I write, those are the books that happen to be in the final process of publication in Discoveries in the Judaean Desert.

4QJosh^{a} possibly provides an example of a variant literary edition of the book of Joshua.[8] The quantity and scope of the evidence are small, and so

5. See another example of the variety of patterns for literary edition vs. individual textual variants vs. orthography in the book of Daniel illustrated in E. Ulrich, "Orthography and Text in 4QDan^{a} and 4QDan^{b} and in the Received Masoretic Text," in *Of Scribes and Scrolls: Studies on the Hebrew Bible, Intertestamental Judaism, and Christian Origins Presented to John Strugnell on the Occasion of His Sixtieth Birthday,* (ed. H. W. Attridge, J. J. Collins, and T. H. Tobin; Lanham, Md.: University Press of America, 1990) 29-42, now reprinted below as Chapter 8 in the present volume.

6. E. Tov, "Hebrew Biblical Manuscripts from the Judaean Desert: Their Contribution to Textual Criticism," *JJS* 39 (1988) 5-37, has correctly stated that the Qumran texts have "taught us no longer to posit MT at the center of our textual thinking" (p. 7). He does, nonetheless, continue to use the term *nonaligned* in *Textual Criticism,* 116-17. Perhaps we should rethink the use of such terms, since 𝔐, 𝔪, and 𝔊 are not "texts" or "text types," and thus are not consistent standards by which other manuscripts of individual books are to be measured for proper "alignment."

7. See, e.g., the supralinear insertion of *matres lectionis* in 4QSam^{c} in E. Ulrich, "4QSam^{c}: A Fragmentary Manuscript of 2 Samuel 14–15 from the Scribe of the *Serek Hay-yaḥad* (1QS)," *BASOR* 235 (1979) 1-25. Note also the expanded orthography of 4QDan^{b} in contrast to that of 4QDan^{a}, though the two apparently share the same text type and the same individual variants; see Ulrich, "Orthography and Text in 4QDan^{a}," 41-42.

8. See E. Ulrich, "4QJoshua^{a} and Joshua's First Altar in the Promised Land," in *New Qumran Texts and Studies: Proceedings of the First Meeting of the International Organization for Qumran Studies, Paris 1992* (ed. G. J. Brooke with F. García Martínez; Leiden: Brill, 1994) 89-104, plates 4-6; and E. Ulrich, "47. 4QJosh^{a}," in DJD 14:143-52.

it is uncertain whether this scroll represents a variant edition of the full book of Joshua or only of the extant passages. However, the sizable extent of the differences between 𝔐 and 𝔊 makes it plausible that multiple editions of the full book did exist.[9] At any rate, the scroll presents the narrative of Joshua's building of the first altar in the newly entered promised land in a sequence quite different from that found in 𝔐 and 𝔊. In the traditional text the first altar is built curiously on Mt. Ebal (Joshua 8:30-35 [𝔊 9:3-8]) after the fall of Jericho and the destruction of Ai. In 4QJosh^a, however, Joshua apparently builds the first altar at Gilgal immediately after crossing the Jordan. The scroll's narrative, seemingly supported by Josephus,[10] may well be an earlier form of the story, in contrast to a revision in 𝔐 based on cultic polemics.[11]

4QJudg^a, to my knowledge the oldest manuscript of the book of Judges, dating from about 50-25 B.C.E., survives in only a single fragment, measuring 7.6 cm high and 4.8 cm wide (or roughly half the size of the palm of one's hand).[12] It contains bits of text from Judges 6:2-6, followed directly by verses 11-13. In other words, what our traditional Bible lists as Judges 6:7-10 is not present. Two explanations are possible: first, either the scribe made a mistake and accidentally omitted four verses that were in the text from which he was copying; or, second, this ancient manuscript contains an early form of the text, which was secondarily expanded by a late addition attested in our surviving manuscript tradition.

With reference to the second possibility (i.e., that the scroll witnesses to an earlier form of the text, while 𝔐 and 𝔊 transmit a subsequent enrichment of the tradition), all the evidence points to this explanation. First, Judges 6:7-10 forms a cohesive unit in a style different from what precedes and what follows; second, it is introduced by a resumptive clause (repeating Judges 6:6), just as many secondary additions are introduced — and some 𝔐 manuscripts, 𝔊, the Peshitta, and the Vulgate all lack this resumptive clause; third, it has for more than a century been regarded as a secondary addition in the text by scholars such as Wellhausen, Gray, Bodine, and Soggin; and fourth, it is set off within 𝔐 by major paragraph markers *(petuḥot)* as a separate unit.

9. See L. Mazor, "The Septuagint Translation of the Book of Joshua," *BIOSCS* 27 (1994) 29-38.

10. Josephus, *Antiquities* 5.1.4 §20; cf. 5.1.14 §45-57.

11. Ulrich, "47. 4QJosh^a," in DJD 14:145-46.

12. See J. Trebolle Barrera, "49. 4QJudg^a," in DJD 14:161-64; idem, "Textual Variants in 4QJudg^a and the Textual and Editorial History of the Book of Judges," in *The Texts of Qumran and the History of the Community: Proceedings of the Groningen Congress on the Dead Sea Scrolls (20-23 August 1989)*, vol. 1: Biblical Texts (ed. F. García Martínez; Paris: Gabalda [= *RevQ* 14/2, no. 54-55] 1989) 229-45.

Thus, 4QJudg[a] is probably a witness to an earlier, shorter form of the text, and the other witnesses attest to a secondarily expanded and enriched form of the text. Since this is all that survives of this oldest manuscript of Judges, we cannot be sure whether this is a singular phenomenon or whether it represents an earlier complete edition of the book, but Julio Trebolle Barrera presents additional evidence from the Old Greek and the Vetus Latina supporting a variant edition of the book.

4QSam[a], in contrast, provides a dramatic paragraph that is not found in any other biblical text, though it was present in the text used by Josephus.[13] This paragraph does not appear to be related to any other variants in the manuscript, but was probably lost through a single error, and thus it does not constitute a variant *edition*. The omission of it, however, does create an alternate text type, insofar as subsequent manuscripts will either have the reading or lack it.

Variant Literary Editions as a Key to the History of the Biblical Text

The view that I proposed at Madrid in 1991, and have been gradually developing since, is a theory of "new editions" of biblical books or passages.[14] Two preliminary steps are necessary to understand the main lines of the history of the text. These two steps are designed to dispel the sense of "chaos" engendered when confronted with a variety of manuscripts. First, it is helpful to sift

13. This paragraph was first described in the private notes of F. M. Cross and was heralded in the footnotes to the New American Bible by P. W. Skehan. See the textual and literary discussion in E. Ulrich, *The Qumran Text of Samuel and Josephus* (Missoula, Mont.: Scholars Press, 1978) 69 and 166-70. The fragment was published by Cross, "The Ammonite Oppression of the Tribes of Gad and Reuben: Missing Verses from 1 Samuel 11 Found in 4QSamuel[a]," in *History, Historiography, and Interpretation* (ed. H. Tadmor and M. Weinfeld; Jerusalem: Magnes, 1983) 148-58. It has subsequently been adopted into the New Revised Standard Version.

For my present purposes, it would not matter whether the longer passage is original or, as A. Rofé, "The Acts of Nahash according to 4QSam[a]," *IEJ* 32 (1982) 129-33, has suggested, a secondary midrashic addition, since in either case we would have two significantly different forms of the text. Although I disagree with my friend in this instance, he is surely correct that numerous sections of the biblical text arose in precisely the manner he describes.

14. See E. Ulrich, "Pluriformity in the Biblical Text, Text Groups, and Questions of Canon," in *Proceedings of the International Congress on the Dead Sea Scrolls, Madrid, 18-21 March 1991* (ed. J. Trebolle Barrera and L. Vegas Montaner; Leiden: Brill, 1992) 37-40. This paper is now reprinted as Chapter 5 in the present volume.

out the orthographic differences between texts (these are usually relatively insignificant); and then second, to study, but then also sift out for a moment, the individual textual variants that populate every manuscript (they should be studied first and brought back into consideration after the next step). Then, with the distracting orthographical and minor variants out of the way, the larger picture becomes more clear. The three different categories of variation arise at different moments or different stages in the history of the text, because of different causes.

Thus I propose that the main lines in the picture of the history of the biblical text were formed by the deliberate activity of a series of creative scribes who produced the new or multiple literary editions of the books of the Bible. These multiple literary editions have been demonstrated for us over the past forty-five years in the biblical manuscripts from Qumran; they have been under our noses for centuries in the new literary editions preserved in 𝔐 and 𝔊 or attested in Josephus; and they have been described for us by literary and historical critics since the Enlightenment as the successive literary editions constituting the history of the very composition of the Scriptures from the beginning.

After the main lines become clear through sorting out variant literary editions, study then moves back to the individual variants in order further to delineate text types, text traditions, and text families, and even to orthography, which can possibly give detailed clues concerning text families. The proposal presented here follows those three main levels.

Variant Literary Editions

As usual, it will be helpful to begin by defining terms:

> By multiple literary editions I mean a literary unit — a story, pericope, narrative, poem, book, etc. — appearing in two or more parallel forms (whether by chance extant or no longer extant in our textual witnesses), which one author, major redactor, or major editor completed and which a subsequent redactor or editor intentionally changed to a sufficient extent that the resultant form should be called a revised edition of that text. . . . In fact we seldom have more than two parallel forms of subsequent editions of biblical passages; but that is chiefly an accident of history, and the process I am intending to describe was a much richer and more frequent process.[15]

15. E. Ulrich, "The Canonical Process, Textual Criticism, and Latter Stages in the Composition of the Bible," in *Sha'arei Talmon: Studies in the Bible, Qumran, and the An-*

The fundamental principle guiding this proposal is that the Scriptures, from their shadowy beginnings until their final, perhaps abrupt, freezing point of the Masoretic tradition, arose and evolved through a process of organic development. The major lines of that development are characterized by the intentional, creative work of authors or tradents who produced new, revised editions of the traditional form of a book or passage.

It is well known that many parts of Scripture began as small, oral units and were told and retold, grouped into small collections of related material, and gradually written down. The oral and written forms were occasionally reformulated to meet the varied needs of the times and were handed down and repeated faithfully for generations.

But every once in a while, an occasion arose that sparked reflection on the traditional literature and readaptation of its traditional thrust in order to illuminate the current situation with its dangers or possibilities, to help the people see the situation more clearly and to motivate them to act in the way the authors or tradents considered necessary or proper.

Equally well known is the evolutionary development of the principal literary works that comprise the Scriptures: the Pentateuch, with its several sources interwoven, each of which was itself a quilt of earlier materials; the Deuteronomistic history, a large redactional unit compiled from variegated national sources and itself reedited during the Exile; the prophetic collections, many of which have a multilayered compositional and redactional history; the Psalter and Proverbs, both magnets that attracted numerous individual units and small collections over the centuries. This process had already started in Israel's early existence and continued over the centuries until the Roman threat and the growing division between the Rabbinic Jews and the Christian Jews finally brought a halt to the process. By then new anthologies of religious literature in new forms had begun to emerge: the New Testament and the Mishnah.

The emergence of each fresh literary edition occasioned variant versions of the literature that would coexist for some time. Variant text types were thus caused by revised literary editions.

When we turn to the textual transmission level, we must always remember that we have lost most of the ancient evidence. The witnesses that have survived attest to the continuation of this process of faithful transmission occasionally punctuated by evolutionary leaps to a new, revised, and expanded edition of biblical books. Our extant witnesses are the scrolls from the

---

cient Near East Presented to Shemaryahu Talmon (ed. M. Fishbane and E. Tov with W. W. Fields; Winona Lake, Ind.: Eisenbrauns, 1992) 278. This paper is now reprinted as Chapter 4 in the present volume.

Judaean Desert, 𝔐, 𝔖, 𝔊, and the versions (not necessarily the specific manuscripts but the text forms they transmit), and all apparently derive from the last four hundred years — roughly the last one-third — of Israel's major period of literary formation from national literature to sacred Scriptures.

We do, and we do not, see serious movement in the growth of the text. The base text of most books remained relatively stable, although new, variant editions were being produced or handed on side by side with the older editions. Some variant editions may well go back several centuries — we have little or no criteria or data for determining this — but it also appears that others were created within the late Second Temple, or Qumran, period. The farther back, the more important this phenomenon is, because it represents a more deeply established and accepted aspect of the Jewish consciousness of "authoritative books" that would eventually result in canonical decisions.

For example, the edition of Exodus transmitted in 𝔐 and 𝔊 and the revised and expanded edition exhibited in 4QpaleoExod^m could both conceivably go back to the fifth century; it is unlikely that the edition in 𝔊, perhaps revised in 𝔐 for Exodus 35–39, is much later than the fifth century. But the edition in 4QpaleoExod^m could be as late as the early second century B.C.E., though not later, because it was apparently sufficiently known and accepted in Judaism to be the form of that scriptural book taken and utilized by the conservative Samaritans, with only a handful of changes, for their Scriptures.

Individual Textual Variants

Although the primary lines in the history of the text are determined by variant literary editions, another significant determining factor can be major individual variants. The smaller lines are caused by the introduction, frequently intentional, of individual expansions, clarifications, interpretations, and even errors.[16] Major variants, such as those discussed earlier — the passage involving the first altar in 4QJosh^a suggesting a transposition in 𝔐, the lack of the Deuteronomistic passage in 4QJudg^a, the Nahash passage in 4QSam^a —

16. The errors, of course, are usually unintentional, but sometimes they are intentional — not as errors but as changes that happen to involve error. An example of an intentional change that is in fact erroneous is the introduction of the king's name in 𝔐^L Jer 27[34𝔊]:1. The earlier Greek edition has no elaborate introduction, but the expanded edition 𝔐^L has added an introduction similar to that in Jer 26:1, complete with the name Jehoiachim. The correct name, however, is Zedekiah, as 27:3, 12 and 28:1 [𝔊 34:2, 10; 35:1] indicate, and as three 𝔐 manuscripts attest, according to *BH*^{3}; for illustration and discussion see Tov, *Textual Criticism,* 11, 322.

could theoretically be either part of a pattern constituting a revised literary edition or simply isolated variants. If simply individual variants, they would certainly give rise to variant text families in the subsequent transmission. The individual textual variants of an entire book or section must be studied both singly and synoptically in order to determine whether they are truly "individual" textual variants or part of the pattern constituting a variant edition. For example, Goliath's height (1 Samuel 17:4) is given at four cubits in one text group (4QSam^{a}, $\mathfrak{G}$, Josephus),[17] five cubits in another ($\mathfrak{G}^{N}$), and six cubits in yet another ($\mathfrak{M}$, $\mathfrak{G}^{O}$, σ'). Most textual critics, viewing that evidence alone, would probably judge that "four cubits" was the earlier reading and that the height was exaggerated in subsequent recitations. But is that an isolated variant or part of the larger pattern in which $\mathfrak{G}$ of 1 Samuel 17–18 displays an earlier, shorter form of the narrative and $\mathfrak{M}$ $\mathfrak{G}^{O}$ display a secondary, expanded variant edition?[18] But again, texts and their variants have a rich life, and individual variants can and do cross the boundaries between variant editions. Thus those who say simply that texts exhibiting different editions should not be used to correct individual variants in the other begin with a good premise but are also likely to be mistaken as often as they are correct.

Orthographic Differences

Similarly, the orthographic profile of a manuscript generally appears to be unrelated or incidental to its textual character.[19] Although orthographic dif-

17. Josephus, *Antiquities* 6.9.1 §171.

18. In their collaborative volume, *The Story of David and Goliath: Textual and Literary Criticism: Papers of a Joint Research Venture* (OBO 73; Fribourg: Éditions Universitaires; Göttingen: Vandenhoeck & Ruprecht, 1986), Dominique Barthélemy, David W. Gooding, Johan Lust, and Emanuel Tov split over the question of the variant editions of $\mathfrak{G}$ and $\mathfrak{M}$. Barthélemy and Gooding attempt to demonstrate that the shorter $\mathfrak{G}$ edition of the David-Goliath narrative in 1 Samuel 17–18 is a pruned version of a more original $\mathfrak{M}$ version, but the explanations of Tov and Lust are decidedly more persuasive. Texts are usually foreshortened through error, often by parablepsis, the loss of material through inadvertent skipping from one occurrence of a word or phrase to another; in contrast, it is usually intentional change that lies behind either expansions or quantitatively equal substitutions of a preferable word for a less preferable.

19. See Ulrich, "Orthography and Text in 4QDan^{a}"; idem, "The Palaeo-Hebrew Biblical Manuscripts from Qumran Cave 4," in *Time to Prepare the Way in the Wilderness: Papers on the Qumran Scrolls by Fellows of the Institute for Advanced Studies of the Hebrew University, Jerusalem, 1989-1990* (STDJ 16; ed. D. Dimant and L. H. Schiffman; Leiden: Brill, 1995) 103-29, now reprinted as Chapter 7 in the present volume.

ferences are sometimes significant for identifying stemmatic relationships, this does not usually seem to be the case. Studying orthography helps sort out the "chaos of texts," but often more through sifting out the orthographic factor temporarily to keep it from cluttering the textual variants.

The Qumran scrolls have taught us much about orthography in the late Second Temple period. One area especially attracts discussion, if only to urge greater clarity and less uncritical adoption by others. Emanuel Tov speaks of a "Qumran practice"[20] of orthography and morphology that is "unique" and claims that "it appears that the texts belonging to this group were copied by the Qumran covenanters themselves."[21] He concedes that the term "is somewhat misleading" and that it "merely indicates that as a scribal system it is known mainly from a number of Qumran scrolls, without implying that this orthography was not used elsewhere in Palestine."[22]

I think the term "Qumran practice" is sufficiently misleading that it should be abandoned, for at least two reasons. First, the features noted are encountered only erratically in the scrolls, and most of them are not unique to Qumran but are also found either in 𝔐 itself or in other texts, often biblical. For example, for the pleonastic **א** in **כיא** note the same double marking in **נקיא** in 𝔐 at Joel 4:19 and Jonah 1:14; the Targums also attest analogous forms such as **–אית** (e.g., **ואיתגלי**) for **–את**. For *waw* to mark short *o* or *u*, note **לכול** in 𝔐 at Jeremiah 33:8 (though a *qĕrê* also attests a variant **לכל**) as well as forms such as **גוברא** and **מגובר** in the Targums; **כול** also occurs in both absolute and suffixal forms in an Aramaic inscription from Hatra.[23] **לוא** appears in the Nash Papyrus from Egypt. Further, how is **מושה** in some scrolls vs. **משה** in 𝔐 (and some other scrolls) different from **דויד** in 𝔐 of Chronicles vs. **דוד** in 𝔐 of Samuel; or for that matter from **יהד** on some coins vs. **יהוד** on others? Rather, it appears preferable to agree with E. Y. Kutscher that "we may assume that many of those points in which the Scroll [1QIsa^a] differs linguistically from the Masoretic Isaiah represent characteristics of the literary Hebrew of the last centuries of the first millennium B.C.E."[24]

Second, the term "Qumran practice" in fact misleads. It is increasingly

20. E. Tov, "The Orthography and Language of the Hebrew Scrolls Found at Qumran and the Origin of These Scrolls," *Textus* 13 (1986) 31-57; idem, *Textual Criticism,* 107-9.

21. Tov, *Textual Criticism,* 107.

22. Ibid., 108.

23. H. Donner and W. Röllig, *Kanaanäische und Aramäische Inschriften,* vol. 1 (Wiesbaden: Harrassowitz, 1966) 49, no. 256.

24. E. Y. Kutscher, *A History of the Hebrew Language* (Jerusalem: Magnes, 1982) 95.

quoted without Tov's nuance, and is thus proclaimed as established fact rather than as tentative hypothesis. For example, the most recent use of it I have seen simply states:

> In addition to the three already known text families [𝔐, 𝔪, and 𝔊], there exist at Qumran biblical manuscripts of a type unique to this collection. Many Qumran manuscripts are written in an orthography (spelling system) and morphology (grammatical form) characteristic of the Qumran sect. This writing method is used in virtually all the documents that can be directly attributed to the sect and that contain its teachings. Texts composed elsewhere but preserved at Qumran do not exhibit the special characteristics of the language of Qumran.
>
> It stands to reason that the biblical texts written in the unique Qumran style were copied by the sectarians, perhaps at Qumran, although the geographic location cannot really be proven and is not of great importance.[25]

We may presume that some biblical and some nonbiblical manuscripts were copied at Qumran, but we may also presume that many or most were penned outside Qumran. Very little evidence exists to demonstrate that any specific biblical manuscript was copied there. The text represented in 4QpaleoExod^{m}, for example, was a Jewish text, known outside Qumran, for we may be confident that the Samaritans did not come to Qumran to acquire it for their base text.

Nonetheless, some biblical texts probably were copied at Qumran. On the one hand, it is virtually certain that the manuscript 4QSam^{c} was indeed copied there, because it is very likely that the distinctively inexpert scribe who copied it also copied the *Community Rule* (1QS), one of the community's "foundation documents." But on the other hand, there is no reason to suspect that the text presented in 4QSam^{c} does not reflect its *Vorlage* from Jerusalem or elsewhere in Palestine. In fact, 4QSam^{c} is textually closer than 𝔐 is to 𝔊 and Josephus, which have nothing to do with Qumran.

The orthography and morphology of the scrolls (and of 𝔐) do indeed exhibit intriguing aspects, but it is far more likely that the range of tendencies (neither "method" nor "characteristic") observed in the scrolls is generally typical of contemporary Palestinian copyists rather than specific to the copyists at Qumran. Even if this were not so, I would still argue that orthographic style is usually unrelated to the textual character of a biblical book, and there-

25. L. H. Schiffman, *Reclaiming the Dead Sea Scrolls: The History of Judaism, the Background of Christianity, the Lost Library of Qumran* (Philadelphia: Jewish Publication Society, 1994) 171.

fore that the orthography displayed in the Qumran biblical scrolls tells us little about the nature of the text in those scrolls.[26]

Returning to consideration of the main lines of the history of the text, we may again temporarily bracket orthography and individual variants to focus on what may be called the base text.[27] The base text may be thought of as the form of the text, or the literary edition, of any particular book that was current (during any given period) prior to a new, creatively developed literary edition.

The base text functions with respect to subsequent variant editions in a manner analogous to an original or correct reading in relation to variant readings, whether expansions, revisions, or errors. That is, it is what one expects to find — the "default reading" — and so its occurrence is unremarkable. In a sense, all witnesses of a given book exhibit the base text; the material that indicates a variant literary edition is the coordinated pattern of intentional variants intended by a creative author. Thus, again, one can see why the key to seeing the stemma properly is not to use 𝔐, 𝔪, and 𝔊 as the three principal lines. Those three are not properly "texts" or "text types" or "recensions." The only one that possibly comes close is 𝔪, and that is because 𝔪 is restricted to only the five books of the Torah, and because it used texts containing the expanded editions for the two books, Exodus and Numbers, for which seriously expanded editions were circulating. Neither 𝔐, nor 𝔪, nor 𝔊 is properly "a text" in the sense that the nature of their text has any consistency or related character from book to book. Nor are they "text types" or "recensions" in the sense that they were planned and designed or carefully edited according to textual principals or textual criteria. They are rather *collections* of individual scrolls the nature of whose text varies from scroll to scroll, apparently quite without regard to any criterion. This is not a problem as long as one recognizes the phenomenon and does not treat the collections as though they were unities.

It may prove helpful to pause and remember two things. First, the shape of all collections of Scripture until around the third century C.E. was a collection of individual scrolls, not a codex or book. Second, 𝔐 is a nonunified collection of texts, the nature of which varies from book to book. Scholarship has gained considerable clarity in our century by recognizing the aggregate or collection aspect of the texts that constitute the anthology labeled 𝔊; many

26. See Ulrich, "The Palaeo-Hebrew Biblical Manuscripts"; idem, "Orthography and Text in 4QDan^{a}."

27. The term *base text* may advance the discussion beyond what is sometimes referred to as the *Urtext,* which gives the impression of a single, static entity.

problems have been clarified by understanding that the text of 𝔊 varies from book to book. We can expect similar gains in clarity if we realize that the text of 𝔐 also varies from book to book. Clearly the books were copied with a care and fidelity that fills us with awe and admiration, but no evidence before 135 C.E. has been forthcoming that intentional consideration was given to the precisely textual criteria governing the selection of individual texts.[28]

If we can work with the supposition that proto-𝔐 was a collection of texts whose textual character varied from book to book, then we may have advanced a step in focusing with increased acuity on the history of the biblical text. We should not look to 𝔐 as the standard by which to judge the text of the various books, but to the base text, or earliest available literary edition of each. The base text of each book, that is, the earliest edition of that book attested in our extant witnesses, must be individually assessed and determined. It already stands late in the succession of reworked editions of that book, but for the sake of general applicability we can call the first extant edition of each book the base text. For some books only one edition appears to be attested, and for those books one can skip to the level of individual textual variants to refine the interrelationship of preserved manuscripts. But for many books our witnesses document variant literary editions. Normally, the interrelationship of variant editions can be determined somewhat easily, since the barometer of quantity seldom fails. That is, the tendency was to expand the scriptural text, not to remove anything that had come to be considered God's word, though of course this barometer must be used cautiously.[29]

Thus, I would propose for consideration that the goal of textual criticism is not 𝔐, as Emanuel Tov proposes, the text of that edition of each book which Rabbinic Judaism eventually chose, but rather the ancient Hebrew text, which was in fact a developing text, not a static, fixed text. It is certainly legitimate, for religious or historical purposes, to decide to focus a specific text-critical project on 𝔐, but I propose that the goal of the general project labeled "textual criticism of the Hebrew Bible" is exactly that — textual criticism of the ancient Hebrew Bible, not of the Masoretic or, more accurately, the proto-Masoretic texts. And it must focus on the text of the ancient Hebrew Bible as it was, namely, diachronic and pluriform. Thus, the target of "textual criticism of the Hebrew Bible" is not a single text. The purpose or function of textual criticism is to reconstruct the history of the texts that eventually became

28. Evidence against such consideration is the problematic state of texts such as 𝔐 of Samuel and Hosea; if the texts had been compared and selected on the basis of superior text form, it is dubious that the texts of those two books would have been selected.

29. See note 16.

the biblical collection in both its literary growth and its scribal transmission; it is not just to judge individual variants in order to determine which were "superior" or "original." "The original text" is a distracting concept for the Hebrew Bible;[30] in a very real sense, there was no "original text," at least none accessible, except for those relatively late parts contributed by redactors. Late layers or additions often have as much claim to being important tesserae in the biblical mosaic as do "original" or "early" elements of the developed text, since this cumulative aspect characterizes the nature of the biblical text from its very beginnings.

It is important to see the distinctions in the gradual development of Israel's "literature" into its becoming "Scripture" and then its becoming "Bible" or canon of Scripture. And this development was different for the various books, or at least for various groups of books. In its early stages Israel's national religious literature was probably treated not very differently from the way other peoples treated their own national religious literature. Near the closing of the creative period, the Torah and the main Prophets had long since become "Scripture," that is, sacred and authoritative works, but their individual texts were still in a somewhat creative stage. The Writings were still mainly "literature," though some books would have been considered by some Jews as "Scripture." The debates over Qoheleth and the Song of Songs highlight the important transition being made.

Recently, Lawrence Schiffman has proposed an alternate view of the nature of the biblical manuscripts from Qumran. His interpretation of the data leads to serious differences in judgments about the Qumran evidence: are "the biblical scrolls" truly biblical in our sense of the term, or are they only biblically related, or were they considered biblical by only one insignificant "sect"?

Here we have space to focus only on one example, 11QPs^a.[31] This beautiful and extensive scroll from Cave 11 is regarded by Schiffman, following noted authorities in the earlier generation of Qumran scholars, as nonbiblical.[32] He considers 11QPs^a a "liturgical" scroll, denying its biblical status. Earlier scholars had rejected its biblical status for the following reasons:

a. It presents the biblical psalms in an order notably different from 𝔐, the *textus receptus*.

30. The term is, of course, a valuable concept for works entirely composed by a single author, as is often the case in classical studies.

31. See P. W. Flint, *The Dead Sea Psalms Scrolls and the Book of Psalms* (STDJ 17; Leiden: Brill, 1997), which discusses 11QPs^a more extensively.

32. Schiffman, *Reclaiming the Dead Sea Scrolls,* 165-69, 178-80.

b. It has additional psalms not contained in 𝔐.
c. Within one biblical psalm (Psalm 145) it repeatedly adds an antiphon not found in the 𝔐 version.
d. It has a prose composition near, but not at, the end of the scroll.
e. The divine name is inscribed, not in the normal Jewish ("square") script, but in the palaeo-Hebrew script.

In response I would say that the 𝔐 Psalter is by its very nature a liturgical scroll and that all of the above features are contained either in 𝔐 at other loci or in other manuscripts that are undeniably biblical.

a. The 𝔐 text of Jeremiah is generally recognized as a secondarily revised edition of the book as found in 𝔊, and it presents major blocks of the book in a variant order.[33]
b. The Greek and especially Syriac Psalters include psalms that were clearly originally Hebrew psalms but are not contained in 𝔐.
c. The antiphon "Blessed be the Lord and blessed be his name forever and ever" is totally derived from verse 1 of Psalm 145 and is systematically repeated in the identical manner in which the antiphon "For his faithfulness endures for ever" is repeated in Psalm 136 in 𝔐.
d. The prose composition, called "David's Compositions," is an explicit claim to scriptural status for the Psalter, and may have functioned as a colophon found at the end of this collection at an earlier stage. It records that David composed all his psalms "by prophecy that was given to him from before the Most High,"[34] and it is through "prophecy" that it makes the transition from being the hymnbook of the Temple to being Scripture, that is, an integral part of "the Law and the Prophets." This passage follows the song (also found in 2 Samuel 23:[1-]7), the "Last Words of David," which speaks of "the man raised on high, the anointed of the God of Jacob, and the sweet singer of Israel." In turn, the "Last Words of David" follows Psalms 149 and 150 and the closing "Hymn to the Creator." Later, a few more related passages were added (as happened at the end of the books of Samuel, Isaiah, Amos, etc.). And in fact, 11QPs[a] ends with the same extra Psalm 151 with which the 𝔊 Psalter ends. In sum, the problem with Schiffman's conclusions is that

33. See the commentaries and E. Tov, "Some Aspects of the Textual and Literary History of the Book of Jeremiah," in *Le livre de Jérémie: Le prophète et son milieu, les oracles et leur transmission* (ed. P.-M. Bogaert; Leuven: Leuven University Press, 1981) 145-67.

34. DJD 4:48 and plate 16.

current evidence challenges earlier judgments about the character of biblical texts.

e. The use of the palaeo-Hebrew script for the divine name in a text principally written in the Jewish script had earlier been viewed as a sign that the text was not biblical. As with the previous points, that view was understandable in light of the early evidence, but it should be laid to rest now that a number of scrolls, all judged to be biblical, and one (4QIsa[c]) indisputably biblical, have attested the practice. I will close by describing several of these scrolls (see Plates 1 and 2 on pp. 118-19).[35]

1. 11QPs[a]: The top two lines contain the end of Psalm 134. After a paragraph break Psalm 151 begins; the empty leather to the left shows that the manuscript ended with the same "extra" Psalm with which the Greek Psalter concludes. The first word at the top right corner is the Tetragrammaton written in the ancient palaeo-Hebrew script, found also three words to the left, as well as the third and fifth words in the next line, and the second word in the last line shown.

2. 2QExod[b]: In the third line of this small fragment (the line below the blank space), the last three letters of the Tetragrammaton are preserved, though the first is lost in the hole.

3. 4QExod[j]: In the third line, at the right edge of the fragment, only the left side of the final letter of the Tetragrammaton is preserved, but the three horizontal lines are distinctive enough to make the letter certain, and the word occurs exactly where the divine name is expected.

4. 4QLev[g]: This manuscript is difficult to read, but in the next-to-last line (above the number "4") the Tetragrammaton can be seen in the palaeo-Hebrew script.

5. 4QDeut[k2]: The Tetragrammaton in the palaeo-Hebrew script can be seen in the center of the next-to-last line. This manuscript contains text from Deuteronomy 19–26, which indicates that it is a manuscript of the book of Deuteronomy, not merely excerpts from that book.

6. 4QIsa[c]: At the end of the third line in the column to the right, and in lines seven and nine in the column to the left, the Tetragrammaton is written in the palaeo-Hebrew script. This is a generously preserved manuscript, with portions of chapters 9–55 extant, and parts of two contiguous columns are displayed to show clearly that this is indeed a full biblical manuscript.

35. Photographs courtesy of the Palestine Archaeological Museum, the Israel Antiquities Authority, Oxford University Press, Professor John C. Trever, and the American Schools of Oriental Research.

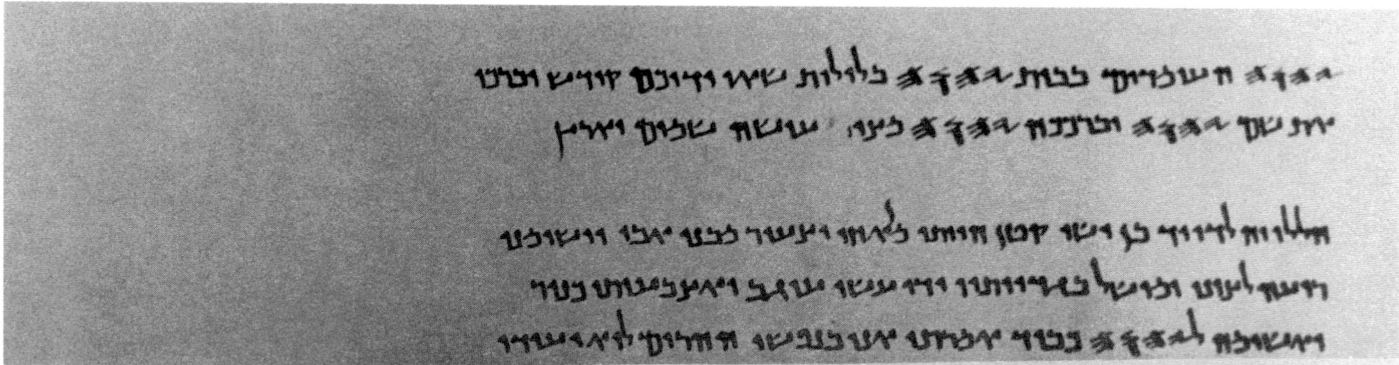

1

5

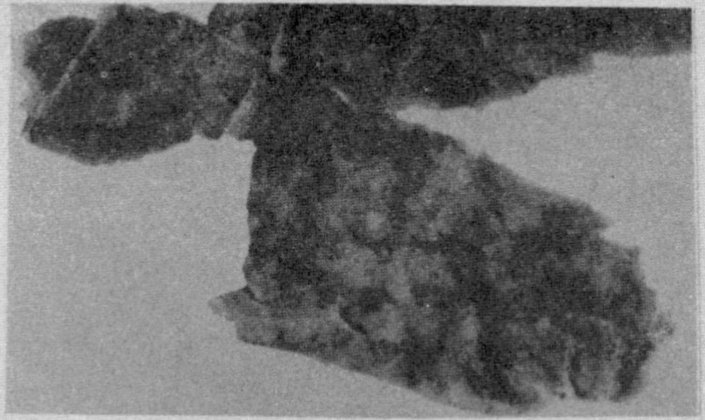

4

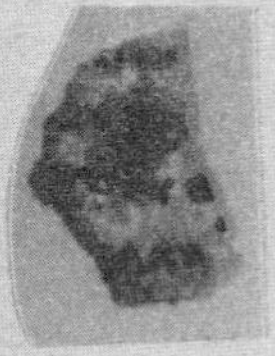

3

2

PLATE I: 1. *11QPs*^{a}. 2. *2QExod*^{b}. 3. *4QExod*^{j}. 4. *4QLev*^{g}. 5. *4QDeut*^{k2}.

6

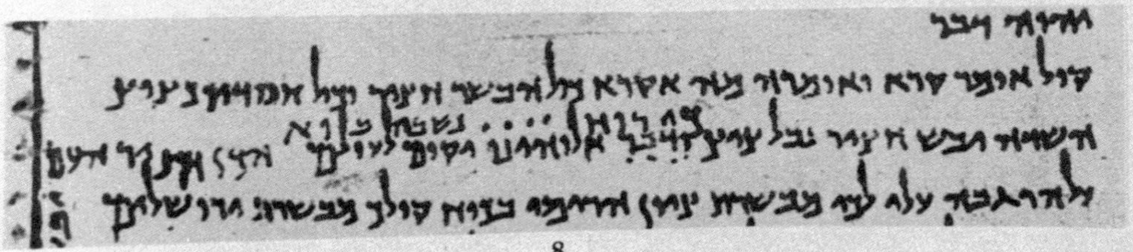

8

7

PLATE II: 6. 4QIsa[c]. 7. 4QSam[c]. 8. 1QIsa[a].

7. 4QSam^{c}: The scribe of this biblical manuscript employed an analogous device — four dots in lieu of the four letters — for preventing the pronunciation of the divine name. In the small fragment at the right, three of the dots can be seen before the fragment breaks off, losing the fourth, and further along the same line the phenomenon recurs, though here the first dot has been lost in the lacuna, and so again only three dots can be seen.

8. 1QIsa^{a}: Above the third line pictured here the same scribe who penned 4QSam^{c} inserted a supralinear correction, clearly using the four dots to replace the divine name.

Thus 4QIsa^{c} clearly demonstrates within a biblical manuscript in the regular Jewish script the practice of using the ancient palaeo-Hebrew script for the Tetragrammaton, just as 4QSam^{c} and the correction in 1QIsa^{a} demonstrate the use of four dots in a biblical manuscripts. This and the arguments above press for the revision of earlier views and the acceptance of 11QPs^{a} as a truly biblical manuscript, though a variant edition, of the Psalter. 11QPs^{a} and the other manuscripts described above should be viewed as variant editions of the biblical books that had full claim to being authoritative Scripture.

CHAPTER 7

The Palaeo-Hebrew Biblical Manuscripts from Qumran Cave 4

In 1955, Patrick W. Skehan published a preliminary report on a fragmentary Qumran manuscript that can claim a place as one of the most significant biblical manuscripts in this already spectacular collection of scrolls.[1] It was inscribed in the palaeo-Hebrew script, which made one automatically think that it might be connected with the Samaritan Pentateuch, and in fact Skehan

1. P. W. Skehan, "Exodus in the Samaritan Recension from Qumran," *JBL* 74 (1955) 182-87 [= col. XXXVIII, Exod 32:10-30]. For a detailed analysis of the significance of the scroll, see J. E. Sanderson, *An Exodus Scroll from Qumran: 4QpaleoExod^{m} and the Samaritan Tradition* (HSS 30; Atlanta: Scholars Press, 1986). I wish to acknowledge the part that both Skehan and Sanderson have played in the editions and, by extension, in this article. The work is truly one of homogenized collaboration by now, and a number of the ideas and formulations contained in this article are theirs. I also thank Emanuel Tov and Esti Eshel for a number of helpful corrections and clarifications in this article and in the editions of the palaeo-Hebrew manuscripts.

It is a pleasure to thank the Institute for Advanced Studies at the Hebrew University, Jerusalem, whose invitation, efficiency, and cordiality made possible a serious advance in the publication of the scrolls, and also the University of Notre Dame and the National Endowment for the Humanities for their support of the long-term work which this paper represents.

The editions of the manuscripts treated below have been published in P. W. Skehan, E. Ulrich, and J. E. Sanderson, *Qumran Cave IV, Palaeo-Hebrew and Greek Biblical Manuscripts* (DJD 9; Oxford: Clarendon, 1992). As a service to scholars interested in these texts, generous amounts of the descriptions of these scrolls have been excerpted or digested from those editions.

initially presented it as such. But already by 1959 he had refined his view as he studied it in relation to other manuscripts in the palaeo-Hebrew script.[2]

Fragments from thirteen (or fourteen?) biblical manuscripts in the palaeo-Hebrew script were found in the eleven caves at Qumran, plus three other manuscripts that are possibly biblical or biblically related. Three (or four?) were in Cave 1, one in Cave 2, two in Cave 6, and one in Cave 11,[3] while Cave 4 held fragments from an additional six biblical manuscripts and three others that resist identification:

1Q3	1QpaleoLev^{a}	4QpaleoGen-Exod^{l}
1Q3	1QpaleoLev^{b}	4QpaleoGen^{m}
1Q3	1QpaleoNum	4QpaleoExod^{m}
2Q5	2QpaleoLev	4QpaleoDeut^{r}
6Q1	6QpaleoGen	4QpaleoDeut^{s}
6Q2	6QpaleoLev	4QpaleoJob^{c}
11Q1	11QpaleoLev^{a}	4Q123 (paraphrase of Joshua?)
		4Q124 (unidentified)
		4Q125 (unidentified)

The manuscripts from all but Cave 4 had been published before 1992, and those from Cave 4 appeared in volume 9 of Discoveries in the Judaean Desert (DJD). Skehan had prepared an edition of each of the six biblical (but not the

2. P. W. Skehan, "Qumran and the Present State of Old Testament Text Studies: The Masoretic Text," *JBL* 78 (1959) 21-25.

3. The publications of the biblical scrolls in the palaeo-Hebrew script from the other caves are as follows:

1Q3 = 1QpaleoLev^{a}, 1QpaleoLev^{b}, 1QpaleoNum: Barthélemy in D. Barthélemy and J. T. Milik, *Qumrân Cave 1* (DJD 1; Oxford: Clarendon, 1955) 51-54 and plates VIII-IX [it is unclear whether 1Q3 is the remains of three or four manuscripts];

2Q5 = 2QpaleoLev: Baillet in M. Baillet, J. T. Milik, and R. de Vaux, *Les 'petites grottes' de Qumrân* (DJD 3; Oxford: Clarendon, 1962) 56-57 and plate XII;

6Q1 = 6QpaleoLev: Baillet, DJD 3.106 and plate XX;

11Q1 = 11QpaleoLev^{a}: D. N. Freedman and K. A. Mathews, *The Paleo-Hebrew Leviticus Scroll (11QpaleoLev)* (Winona Lake, Ind.: ASOR/Eisenbrauns, 1985); see also D. N. Freedman, "Variant Readings in the Leviticus Scroll from Qumran Cave 11," *CBQ* 36 (1974) 525-34; E. Tov, "The Textual Character of 11QpaleoLev," *Shnaton* 3 (1978-79) 238-44 (Hebrew); F. García Martínez, "Texts from Cave 11," in *The Dead Sea Scrolls: Forty Years of Research* (ed. D. Dimant and U. Rappaport; Leiden: Brill; Jerusalem: Magnes Press and Yad Ishak Ben-Zvi, 1992) 18-26; and esp. É. Puech, "Notes en marge de 11QPaléoLévitique: Le Fragment L, des fragments inédits et une jarre de la grotte 11," *RB* 92/2 (1989) 161-83 and plates I-III.

nonbiblical) manuscripts prior to his death on September 9, 1980. Some he had prepared noticeably earlier than that date, and for several reasons Judith Sanderson and I have revised and augmented them, approximately doubling their size. One reason, of course, is that Skehan himself would have done a final revision and proofreading of his editions before sending them to the press. A second reason is that with the deepening and broadening of Qumran scholarship over the past decade or two, a richer battery of questions is being asked of the material. The detailed consideration of these questions is important not only for the eventual reader but also for the editor, in order to understand the document more thoroughly and thus be able to present it to scholars more intelligibly, and to offer them greater potential for their own use of the scrolls. Moreover, the vast majority of those who will use the DJD volumes cannot come to Jerusalem to consult the original manuscripts for a resolution of the ambiguities in the photographs; it is the duty of the editor to inform those who will work from the photographs whether, for example, a dark line is the ink of a letter or a meaningless shadow or defect.

The original extent of these six manuscripts cannot be determined with certainty. The first probably contained both Genesis and Exodus and conceivably contained the entire Torah. The second survives in only one fragment from Genesis. The third — one of the two most extensively preserved biblical manuscripts from Qumran — contains fragments of Exodus from all but the first five and last three chapters. The fourth has a modest sampling of fragments from much of Deuteronomy. The fifth has only one fragment of Deuteronomy, and the sixth preserves but three small fragments from the book of Job. It will be observed that with the exception of the last, they are all from the books of Moses, as is the case for the other seven manuscripts in palaeo-Hebrew from the other Qumran caves. The appearance of Job in this script may well be due to an ancient tradition, later recorded in *b. Baba Batra* 14b, 15a, that attributed the book of Job to Moses.

There are three more palaeo-Hebrew manuscripts from Cave 4, but they will not be treated here. They are not clearly identifiable as "biblical" in the traditional sense. The third is merely a single small scrap with at most a single letter identifiable on each of two lines and a couple unidentifiable letters on two other lines. The second is more extensive but yields no intelligible connected text. The first, however, though surviving only in four small fragments, finds its closest identity to known texts in Joshua 21. This suggests, of course, that the palaeo-Hebrew script may well have been reserved for, or used especially for, what was considered the writings of Moses and his contemporaries. This, in turn, may help focus the work toward identification of the second, as yet unidentified, palaeo-Hebrew manuscript.

The purpose of this study is to examine the six biblical manuscripts from Cave 4 in the palaeo-Hebrew script together,[4] in order to learn what we can from the similarities and contrasts and to see whether these manuscripts form a distinctive group of texts or are simply varied samples of the biblical scrolls in general, not to be distinguished from the other biblical manuscripts except for their script. Full treatments of these scrolls are provided in the editions; here we must limit our focus to selected features of the manuscripts, the palaeography and date, the orthography, and the textual character of the manuscripts.

The Individual Manuscripts

4QpaleoGen-Exod^l

Features of the Manuscript

The extant fragments of 4QpaleoGen-Exod^l (previously designated as 4QpaleoExod^l or as 4QpaleoExod^n) preserve letters from what is probably the final verse of Genesis and portions of text from Exodus 1–4; 8–12; 14; 16–20; 22; 25–28; 36; and 40(?).[5] Thus, the original scroll probably contained the entire book of Exodus and quite possibly the entire book of Genesis as well.

The first fragment preserves a right margin with holes from stitching, two letters on the first line followed by almost four blank but ruled lines, and then the beginning of the book of Exodus (Exod 1:1-5). The holes show that this was not the first column of the original scroll, despite the fact that the text is from the beginning of Exodus. The four ruled lines show that this was not the top margin of the column — significantly, no fragments from the top margin have been preserved, and the two fragments that preserve a bottom margin show, as expected, an unruled margin. The second to fourth lines have presumably been left completely blank. At the right margin of the first line of the fragment are visible parts of two letters that perfectly match the final word of Genesis, and given Qumran practices such as lack of colophons, it is difficult to imagine what this would be if not from the end of Genesis. If the

4. See also the earlier article by K. A. Mathews, "The Background of the Paleo-Hebrew Texts at Qumran," in *The Word of the Lord Shall Go Forth,* (ed. C. Meyers and M. O'Connor; Winona Lake, Ind.: Eisenbrauns, 1983) 549-68.

5. See P. W. Skehan, "The Biblical Scrolls from Qumran and the Text of the Old Testament," *BA* 28 (1965) 88, 99 [reprinted in *Qumran and the History of the Biblical Text* (ed. F. M. Cross and S. Talmon; Cambridge, Mass.: Harvard University Press, 1975) 265, 276].

analysis is correct, the format comes within one word of matching the rule found in later rabbinic sources (*b. Baba Batra* 13b; *m. Soperim* 2:2; *y. Megilla* 1:9[8]), calling for four blank lines between books of the Torah. Confirming evidence, however, is available from even closer sources. Another scroll from Cave 4 in the Jewish script, 4QGen-Exod[a], also contains this pair of books, and both Leviticus and Numbers are included on 4QLev-Num[a]. Moreover, although the transition from the end of one book to the beginning of the next is not preserved for either 4QGen-Exod[a] or 4QLev-Num[a], the practice of leaving a number of blank lines between books on the same scroll is documented at Murabbaʿat (in the Minor Prophets Scroll) and Naḥal Ḥever (in the Greek Minor Prophets Scroll).[6]

The height of the scroll on which 4QpaleoGen-Exod[l] was copied can only be estimated. No column has been preserved from top to bottom, but two factors provide a reasonable estimate. The distance between the horizontal rulings for lines of script is fairly regular, at ca. 0.5 cm, and larger fragments preserving text from two contiguous columns allow an estimation of ca. 55-60 lines of text per column. Thus, the height of the inscribed part of a column was 28-30 cm, and, allowing about 4 cm each for top and bottom margins, the height of the scroll can be estimated at about 36-38 cm.

The full width of only one column is preserved, and it contains 50-56 letters per line, measuring ca. 10 cm. In columns where measurement is not possible but letters per line can be estimated, the number varies considerably, for example, from 46-53 in one column to 66-73 in others. Only two letters are missing from the width of another column, but there the end of the skin forced the scribe to make the column narrow. That column has only 38-44 letters per line, and its estimated width is only 8.1 cm; for purposes of calculation of the size of the scroll, this column should be considered an exception.

The height of this scroll and the width of its columns are not unusual in comparison with other biblical scrolls. But the very large number of lines per column is unusual, and that large number of lines plus the small, compact size of the letters makes it fully plausible that the scroll contained both Genesis and Exodus. It is not inconceivable that it contained the entire Torah, though there seems to be no way to ascertain that.

It was customary, in manuscripts inscribed in the palaeo-Hebrew script, as also often in inscriptions in the Phoenician script, to use dots or small vertical or diagonal strokes to serve as word dividers. Similarly, one

6. See Mur XII in DJD 2:182, 192, 197, 200, 202, 205; plates LXI, LXVI, LXIX, LXXI, LXXII; and 8ḤevXII gr in DJD 8:3; plates I, IV.

finds occasionally that a word at the end of a line is divided and the second part of the word starts the next line. Neither the word-division dots nor the divisions of words between lines is normally found in biblical scrolls in the Jewish script.[7]

The scribe signaled divisions between paragraphs in four ways. Ten times the remainder of a line is left blank at the close of one section, and the new section is begun at the right margin of the next line. Six times that same pattern is followed plus the addition of another completely blank line, whereas eight times simply one blank line is left. Finally, six times a short interval is left within the line.[8] It is probably legitimate to consider the first three types as various equivalents to the divisions in Masoretic manuscripts classified as "open" (פתוחה, sometimes marked פ), and the fourth type as equivalent to that classified as "closed" (סתומה, sometimes marked ס). 4QpaleoGen-Exod^l, however, shows no particularly strong relationship between its divisions and the open and closed divisions as handed down in Masoretic manuscripts. Of the twenty-four long intervals in the scroll, only seven correspond to the open divisions recorded in the Masoretic Text (= 𝔐).[9] Of the scroll's six short intervals, only one (or possibly two) corresponds to the closed division in 𝔐. Furthermore, the Samaritan (= 𝔪) manuscripts, which generally seem to have only one main type of division (קצה), frequently do, but often do not, correspond to those recorded in Masoretic manuscripts. The scroll's divisions are also at variance with those of 𝔪 nine times.

Thus, it would probably be illegitimate to envision an ancient ideal of a fixed pattern of divisions between sections. Rather, the ancient scribes simply appear to have made or handed on logical divisions between sections to help

7. The Aramaic script used for international correspondence during the Persian period developed into various national scripts after the fall of the Persian empire. These included the Nabataean, Palmyrene, and Jewish scripts, the last being the form of the Aramaic script adapted and developed within Jewish scribal traditions. See F. M. Cross, "The Development of the Jewish Scripts," in *The Bible and the Ancient Near East: Essays in Honor of William Foxwell Albright* (ed. G. E. Wright; Garden City, N.Y.: Doubleday, 1961) 133-202, esp. 189-90, n. 5; and J. Naveh, *Early History of the Alphabet: An Introduction to West Semitic Epigraphy and Palaeography* (2d rev. ed.; Jerusalem: Magnes, 1987) 9-11.

8. In these statistics and occasionally elsewhere in this article, the attempt is to provide a useful impression of the features of the scrolls. A few examples are sometimes omitted due to ambiguous evidence or to the disproportionate length required for descriptions of tortuous but pointless complications.

9. Both in the editions and in this article, the data concerning 𝔐 are calculated from the representation in *BHS*, and the data concerning 𝔪 are calculated from the von Gall edition.

the reader, not to have been tradents of a pattern of standardized divisions that were viewed as a part of the text as were the words themselves.

Palaeography and Date

The palaeography of the palaeo-Hebrew manuscripts from Qumran has been described by Mark D. McLean in a 1982 Harvard dissertation written under the direction of Frank Moore Cross. McLean provides a palaeographic chart of the script of 4QpaleoGen-Exod^{l} and a discussion of the features of the script, suggesting a date in "the first half or first three-quarters of the first century BCE."[10]

Orthography

The orthography of a number of the books as they appear in the Masoretic collection and in the manuscripts of the Samaritan Pentateuch is inconsistent.[11] It is helpful to begin by noting that 𝔐 in Exodus uses both short and *plene* forms of the same words: אלכם (5:4; 7:9) and אליכם (11:9); אלהן (1:19) and אליהן (1:17); לשתת (17:1) and לשתות (7:21); קלת (9:23, 28) and הקלות (9:29). Even within the same verse 𝔐 has both הכנים and הכנם (8:14).

The orthography of many of the biblical scrolls from Qumran is also inconsistent, though — as also in the case of 𝔐 and 𝔪 — there are certain tendencies observable in the orthographic practice. So it is for 4QpaleoGen-Exod^{l}, which strikes a moderate balance between conservative and full orthography, whereas 𝔐 in Exodus tends to be somewhat more conservative. In common with 𝔐 and 𝔪 it spells אלהים, אהרן, כל, and לא without *waw.* On the other hand, it is apparent, just as in the Masoretic texts, that the scribe was not attempting to put into practice a grammatically standardized orthography. A few examples of divergent spellings are presented here to illustrate the inconsistency in orthography in the various texts:

10. M. D. McLean, "The Use and Development of Palaeo-Hebrew in the Hellenistic and Roman Periods" (Dissertation, Harvard University, 1982) plate 3, lines 8-10, and pp. 66-71, 78, esp. 66 [designated 4QpaleoExod^{n}].

11. See my discussion of "Orthography and Text in 4QDan^{a} and 4QDan^{b} and in the Received Masoretic Text," in *Of Scribes and Scrolls: Studies on the Hebrew Bible, Intertestamental Judaism, and Christian Origins Presented to John Strugnell* (ed. H. W. Attridge, J. J. Collins, and T. H. Tobin; Lanham, Md.: University Press of America, 1990) 29-42. This article is now reprinted as Chapter 8 in this volume.

Exodus	Gen-Exod^{l}	𝔐	𝔐^{q}	⅏^{ed}	⅏^{mss}
16:2	ו]ילנו (var.?)	וילינו	וילונו	וילנו	
16:7	תלינו (var.?)	תלונו	תלינו	תלנו	תלינו
16:30	הש]ביעי	השבעי		השביעי	
23:11	והשביעית	והשביעת		והשבעית	והשיבעת, והשביעית
25:18	כרובים	כרבים		כרובים	
25:19	וכרב	וכרוב		וכרוב	

But more typical patterns are illustrated in these examples:

Exodus	Gen-Exod^{l}	𝔐	𝔐^{q}	⅏^{ed}	⅏^{mss}
9:28	קלות	קלת		קולות	
11:6	גדולה	גדלה		גדלה	
12:4	מהיות	מהית		מהיות	
12:4	נפשות	נפשת		נפשות	
12:7	המזוזות	המזוזת		המזוזת	המזזות, המזוזות
16:30	הש]ביעי	השבעי		השביעי	
18:21	עליהם	עלהם		עליהם	

Textual Character and Affiliation

4QpaleoGen-Exod^{l} appears, on the basis not of preserved evidence but of probable reconstruction, not to have the typological features of the Exod^{m}⅏ tradition. It would be incorrect, however, to characterize the scroll simply as agreeing with 𝔐. Skehan's early (1965) judgment that it is "quite near to the received text, with only slight concessions to the tendency towards expanded readings for the sake of clarity and smoothness" (p. 99) now needs to be refined on the basis of his own, and Sanderson's, and my research.

Gen-Exod^{l} belongs to the general textual tradition of the book of Exodus, which I term "edition I" (because we have no earlier editions extant) and which is represented also by both 𝔐 and the text base from which 4QpaleoExod^{m} and ⅏ developed. The "revised edition" (or "edition II") of Exodus, witnessed by 4QpaleoExod^{m} and the text that the Samaritans accepted for their Scriptures, was produced by the addition of sixteen major expansions and a different order of text in two places.[12]

While the reconstruction of this scroll strongly suggests that it did not

12. 4QpaleoExod^{m} agrees with ⅏ in thirteen extant typological readings and in five reconstructed typological readings. For a detailed discussion of both similarities and differences between 4QpaleoExod^{m} and ⅏, see Sanderson, *An Exodus Scroll,* 196-220.

contain any of the major expansions, the remains are too fragmentary to demonstrate that conclusively. But it is a conservative and careful text that, though probably agreeing with 𝔐𝔊 in its textual *edition*, agrees in *individual* variants sometimes with 𝔐, sometimes with ⅏, sometimes with Exod^{m}, and sometimes preserves a unique reading. It exhibits a slight tendency to expand by one word or element of a word (approximately eight times beyond 𝔐), as do most texts, including 𝔐 (approximately four times beyond Gen-Exod^{l}) and ⅏ (approximately nine times beyond Gen-Exod^{l}).

In the edition, those readings are catalogued among the "variants" that are extant on the leather and for which any one of the four Hebrew witnesses (Gen-Exod^{l}, Exod^{m}, 𝔐, or ⅏) shows disagreement beyond pure orthography. Gen-Exod^{l} preserves fifty such variants. Only one of them involves a major feature of the Exod^{m}⅏ tradition: after Exod 26:35 the scroll agrees with 𝔐 against Exod^{m} and ⅏ in lacking the passage containing the instructions for the incense altar. 𝔐 places that passage at Exod 30:1-10, but Gen-Exod^{l} is not extant at that point, and though it is possible, one cannot be certain whether the scroll originally had it at that point. Only six of the fifty variants involve a phrase (e.g., א[יש אל אחיו with 𝔐 rather than אחד א[ל אחד with Exod^{m}⅏, 25:20). The remaining forty-three variants involve only a single word (e.g., the Tetragrammaton with 𝔐 rather than אלהים with ⅏, 3:4; נח[שת with ⅏, which is lacking in 𝔐, 27:12). Thus Gen-Exod^{l} does not offer much of significance with regard to textual content.

In twenty-six variants Gen-Exod^{l} agrees with 𝔐 against ⅏, in nine it agrees with ⅏ against 𝔐, in fourteen it disagrees with both, and in one it agrees with both against Exod^{m}. But it is interesting to push a bit further and note that in eleven of those twenty-three disagreements with 𝔐, the scroll agrees with either 𝔐^{q} or 𝔐^{mss}, and in three agreements with 𝔐 it disagrees with either 𝔐^{q} or 𝔐^{mss}.

There are very few passages where both Gen-Exod^{l} and Exod^{m} are preserved, only nine variants of the total of fifty: in two Gen-Exod^{l} agrees with Exod^{m}𝔐; in one with 𝔐⅏; in one with Exod^{m}⅏; in three with 𝔐 alone; in one with ⅏ alone; and in one Gen-Exod^{l} preserves a unique reading.

Thus, the most that can be said here is that there are an early and a revised edition of the book of Exodus, that 𝔐𝔊 and probably 4QpaleoGen-Exod^{l} are witnesses to the early edition, and that 4QpaleoExod^{m} and ⅏ are witnesses to the revised, expanded edition, but that each of the texts shows some development beyond the main lines of its textual parentage.

4QpaleoGen^m

Features of the Manuscript

Of 4QpaleoGen^{m} only a single small fragment, containing ten (or nine) complete words and eight (or nine) parts of words from Gen 26:21-28, survives. The fragment is only 4.5 cm high and 2.9 cm wide. Horizontal ruling with dry lines is visible and perhaps vertical ruling; the distance between lines is 0.6 cm. As was customary in scrolls inscribed with the palaeo-Hebrew script, the scribe used a dot to divide between words and probably divided words between lines. There are about seventy-three letters per line (but see below concerning lines 4 and 5).

Palaeography and Date

The manuscript displays a regular, practiced palaeo-Hebrew hand. McLean offers a palaeographic chart and a description of the script. He considers this manuscript one of the three earliest biblical manuscripts in the palaeo-Hebrew script, together with 4QpaleoDeut^{s} and 4QpaleoJob^{c}, although he thinks that 4QpaleoGen^{m} has developed beyond the other two. His suggested date is "in the middle of the second century" B.C.E.[13]

Orthography

The orthography of 4QpaleoGen^{m} differs from that of 𝔐⅏ in three of its eighteen words:

26:22 אׄחרית ⅏$^{\text{ed. Ken, mss}}$ (cf. also 26:21) } אחרת
𝔐 ⅏$^{\text{ed. vGall, mss}}$ (var. or orth.?)
26:22 ולוא } ולא 𝔐 ⅏
26:25]ויטי } ויט 𝔐 ⅏

The phonological orthography seen in]ויטי is paralleled, for example, in:[14]

13. McLean, "The Use and Development," plate 3, line 3, and pp. 57-60, esp. 60 [designated 4QpaleoGen].

14. See A. Sperber, *A Historical Grammar of Biblical Hebrew* (Leiden: Brill, 1966) 486 (§65); and R. Macuch, *Grammatik der samaritanischen Hebraïsch* (Berlin: de Gruyter, 1969) 36 (§14d). I am grateful to Esti Eshel for searching out these parallels.

Num 24:4 𝔐 𝔪 יחזה] 𝔪^{mss} יחזי
Gen 6:14 𝔐 𝔪 עשה] 𝔪^{ms} עשי
Gen 29:35 𝔐 𝔪 אודה] 𝔪^{mss} אודי

Textual Character and Affiliation

The small amount of text preserved is frustrating. For one word in Gen 26:21, the manuscript has ו[ייחפר] and then breaks off at the left edge of the fragment, still within the *reš;* thus it cannot be determined whether the word here was plural with 𝔐 𝔪 ℭ 𝔖 𝔙 or singular with 𝔊; note that in the next verse 𝔐 has ויחפר and 𝔪 has ויחפרו. Though we cannot determine some details such as that, for some other questions speculation becomes a bit more possible. The ends of seven lines from the left side of a column do allow an attempt at least at quantitative reconstruction of the text that had been present. For most lines, the corresponding text in 𝔐 𝔪 has about seventy-three letter spaces per line (counting both letters and the spaces between words). But for line 4 the number of letters in 4QpaleoGen^{m} is ten less than that in the corresponding text in 𝔐 𝔪, whereas for the next line the count is about fourteen letters longer in 4QpaleoGen^{m} than in 𝔐 𝔪. It is probably safer to conclude that in line 4 the manuscript possibly had a interval, because, although 𝔐 has no interval, 𝔪 does have קצה. For line 5, however, one is forced to conclude that the manuscript simply had a shorter reading than 𝔐 𝔪, omitting a phrase (perhaps such as והרביתי את זרעך) entirely or possibly inserting an omitted phrase supralinearly.

With so little text preserved, it is nearly impossible to determine or describe the textual character in any meaningful way. Some might say that it is "like 𝔐 with a few minor exceptions." A less misleading description, however, using more accurate terminology, would be to say, first, that though there is too little text to support major conclusions, 4QpaleoGen^{m} appears to be in general a witness to the same general text tradition to which 𝔐 in Genesis is also a later witness. But it is important to note that, in the small amount of text preserved, it disagrees orthographically with 𝔐 rather frequently (in three out of eighteen words) and is thus comparatively more divergent from 𝔐 than 𝔪 is from 𝔐.

4QpaleoExod^{m}

Features of the Manuscript

4QpaleoExod^{m} has justifiably received a good deal of advance announcement concerning its great significance.[15] It was originally designated 4QEx$^{\alpha}$, Greek superscripts having been provisionally chosen to denote scrolls in the palaeo-Hebrew script. It is one of the most extensively preserved of the biblical scrolls from Cave 4. Fragments from forty-three out of forty-five consecutive columns are preserved, spanning from Exod 6:25 to Exod 37:16.[16]

The introduction to the edition of this scroll extends to about seventeen pages. Here we can note only a few items of interest. 4QpaleoExod^{m} was originally a beautiful scroll of fine, thin, creamy tan leather. Reconstruction of the layout of the full scroll suggests that seven columns would have preceded the first of the forty-five columns partly preserved, and that five columns would have followed, thus totaling fifty-seven columns for the complete book. The height of the scroll is estimated at 35 cm or slightly more, the inscribed portion measuring ca. 25-27.5 cm, with a top margin of at least 3.3 cm and a bottom margin of at least 4.5 cm. The number of lines per column was thirty-two, or in some columns thirty-three. The distance between ruled lines for script fluctuates from 0.7-1.0 cm, averaging 0.85 cm. The width of the columns varies within an estimated range of 12.2-14.7 cm. Note that the height of this scroll is about the same as that of 4QpaleoGen-Exod^{l} (36-38 cm), but that the latter has almost double the number of lines per column (55-60).

Preliminary study of the patterns of physical deterioration of the scroll suggests that the conclusion of Exodus was at the center of the scroll as it lay rolled in the cave. This would preclude the possibility that the text of Leviti-

15. See the bibliography in the edition, especially: P. W. Skehan, "Exodus in the Samaritan Recension"; idem, "Qumran and the Present State"; idem, "The Biblical Scrolls from Qumran and the Text of the Old Testament," *BA* 28 (1965) 87-100, esp. fig. 14 on p. 98 [= cols. I-II, Exod 6:25–7:19] [reprinted in *Qumran and the History of the Biblical Text* (ed. F. M. Cross and S. Talmon; Cambridge, Mass.: Harvard University Press, 1975) 264-77]; "Fragments of Another Exodus Scroll," in *Scrolls from the Wilderness of the Dead Sea* (A Guide to the Exhibition *The Dead Sea Scrolls of Jordan,* Arranged by the Smithsonian Institution in Cooperation with the Government of the Hashemite Kingdom of Jordan and the Palestine Archaeological Museum; London: Trustees of the British Museum, 1965) 16, 26 [= cols. I-II, Exod 6:25–7:19]; Sanderson, *An Exodus Scroll;* E. Tov, "Proto-Samaritan Texts and the Samaritan Pentateuch," in *The Samaritans* (ed. A. D. Crown; Tübingen: Mohr Siebeck, 1989) 397-407.

16. For the full list of contents of the manuscript, see Sanderson, *An Exodus Scroll,* 321-23.

cus followed but would leave open the possibility that the text of Genesis preceded (cf. 4QGen-Exod^{a} and 4QpaleoGen-Exod^{l}), though there is no evidence or any particular reason to think that the scroll contained Genesis.

There was a patch stitched on the bottom of column VIII to repair it during the Qumran period. It is grayish tan (whereas the leather used for the original scroll was creamy tan), roughly circular, ca. 6.5 cm in diameter, and was sewn behind the original leather. Both the script and the orthography on the patch differ from those of the main scribe.

The scribe used dots for word division, and occasionally split words at the end of a line.

There were several methods of signaling paragraph divisions. The largest divisions were signaled by a threefold pattern: (1) leaving the remainder of the line at the end of a section blank, (2) with an enlarged palaeo-Hebrew *waw,* the initial letter of the new section, usually placed at the approximate center of that interval, and (3) the rest of the first word following at the right margin of the next line.[17] Again, it is probably legitimate to consider this an equivalent of the "open" section (פ) in 𝔐. But of the approximately twenty-three times that this pattern occurs in 4QpaleoExod^{m}, only seventeen times does it correspond to an "open" section in 𝔐, whereas twice it occurs where 𝔐 has only the *'atnaḥ*. Twice 𝔐 has no interval, once it lacks the entire passage (a major expansion), and once it has a "closed" section (ס). All twenty-three times ɯ agrees with 𝔐 and thus also disagrees with 4QpaleoExod^{m} six times. There are three places where divisions in 4QpaleoExod^{m} overlap with those in 4QpaleoGen-Exod^{l}, and all four Hebrew texts agree in a large division at all three points.

Lesser divisions were signaled by a short interval with the first word of the new section on the same line. Of the nineteen occurrences of this type of division in the scroll, only twice does 𝔐 have a "closed" section (ס), and only once does ɯ have קצה. 𝔐 again lacks one of the passages. In the remaining sixteen occurrences 𝔐 has: an unmarked interval once (after 6:27), merely verse division twelve times, only the *'atnaḥ* twice, and a larger "open" section (פ) once.

There are several other patterns for larger divisions that occur less frequently, but the general conclusions drawn concerning 4QpaleoGen-Exod^{l} continue to apply to 4QpaleoExod^{m}, as indeed they apply to most of the biblical scrolls in general.

17. See column I line 6 for a clear example: in P. W. Skehan, "The Biblical Scrolls from Qumran," fig. 14 on p. 98.

Palaeography and Date

McLean suggests a date in "the first half or first three-quarters of the first century BCE" for 4QpaleoExod^{m} as well as for Gen-Exod^{l} and a third unidentified manuscript (4Q124), but of these three he considers Exod^{m} to "display the latest features and the greatest number of novel features which will see subsequent development."[18]

Orthography

The orthography of 4QpaleoExod^{m}, like that of 𝔪 and 𝔐, is at the same time mixed yet prone toward characteristic features. It tends toward a more full orthography, but remains in the moderate range. For example, the words **אלהים**, **כל**, and **לא** are consistently spelled without *waw*, whereas **אהרון**, **אותך**, and **לאמור** are consistently spelled with *waw* (𝔪 and 𝔐 both normally have **אלהים**, **אהרן**, **כל**, and **לא**).

On the other hand it is apparent, just as it is in 𝔐, that the scribe was not attempting to put into practice a grammatically systematic orthography. He wrote **ויאמר**, without *mater lectionis,* five times on the extant fragments where the lack of *waw* is clear, once where the *waw* is probably lacking, and once in the plural, **ויאמרו**, where the long *o* is no longer accented. In contrast, he also wrote **ויאומר**, with *mater lectionis,* five times where the *waw* is extant and clear, and once where it is probable.[19]

In the few places where 4QpaleoGen-Exod^{l} and 4QpaleoExod^{m} overlap, 4QpaleoExod^{m} always displays the fuller reading:

Exodus	Gen-Exod^{l}	Exod^{m}	𝔐	𝔪
16:33	**אתו**	**אותו**	**אתו**	**אתו**
18:21	**שנאי**	**ש]וׄנאי**	**שנאי**	**שנאי**
19:24	**ואה]רן**	**ואהרון**	**ואהרן**	**ואהרן**

Another interesting feature that at first appears to be an orthographic matter turns out to be illuminating. As in 𝔪 and 𝔐, so in this manuscript the expected form **מצרים** often occurs (6:26, 27bis, 28, 29; $7:4^{bis}$; etc.), meaning "[the land of] Egypt" (occasionally preceded by **ארץ** or **מלך**). In contrast to 𝔪 and 𝔐, in this manuscript another form, **מצריים**, also occurs five times

18. McLean, "The Use and Development," plate 3, line 12, and pp. 73-78, esp. 78 [designated 4QpaleoExod^{m}].

19. The subsequent scribe of the patch wrote 𐤅 **יאמר** in its sole occurrence there (VIII 28).

where the double *yod* is sufficiently clear (7:18^{b}; 9:5^{b}, 6; 12:35, 36), ɯ 𝔐 invariably reading מצריים (always vocalized in 𝔐 מִצְרַיִם, or pausally מִצְרָיִם). This is not simply a pair of orthographic alternatives, but two morphologically distinct forms. In all the latter five instances, "the Egyptians" (the people, as opposed to the land) is either the clear meaning or a reasonable interpretation, and in all five 𝔊 and 𝔖 have the plural Αἰγυπτιοι and *mṣry'*, as opposed to Αιγυπτος and *mṣryn* (7:18^{b} and 9:5^{b} are major expansions in 4QpaleoExod^{m} and ɯ, thus not in 𝔊 𝔖, but 𝔊 𝔖 have the plural in the source texts, 7:18 and 9:4, for those expansions). In further confirmation ℭ has מצראי at 7:18, 9:4, and 9:6.

Textual Character and Affiliation

4QpaleoExod^{m} is the only scroll found at Qumran that combines all three of these distinctive characteristics: palaeo-Hebrew script, relatively fuller orthography, and text in the proto-Samaritan tradition. It is a carefully copied scroll with only four scribal errors in the portions of the forty-three columns that have been preserved, as well as five other unique cases of shorter text that may either reflect parablepsis or retain the preferable, unexpanded text.

The text of Exod^{m} belongs to the text-type or tradition, which previously was known to us only in its later representative, the Samaritan Exodus. The scroll shares all major, typological features with ɯ with the single exception of the new tenth commandment regarding the altar on Mount Gerizim inserted in the Samaritan Exodus 20 from Deuteronomy 11 and 27. Thus, the expanded textual tradition now known to us as the Samaritan Pentateuch, rather than being a creation *de novo* of the community that worshiped at Gerizim, is instead a somewhat later representative of a tradition that was already known elsewhere in Palestine and was used in other communities without special allegiance to Gerizim. The presence of 4QpaleoExod^{m} in Cave 4 at Qumran is evidence that a somewhat earlier representative of the same expanded textual tradition was presumably accepted and used by at least some in the Qumran community. The Gerizim expansion, proper to Samaritan theology, was made only in the Samaritan community, and this was the only major expansion that it made in Exodus.

To determine the detailed relationship between 4QpaleoExod^{m} and ɯ and their contrast with 𝔐, it is necessary to look at the pattern of both agreements and disagreements, in secondary, preferable, and synonymous variants, among all four witnesses, Exod^{m}, ɯ, 𝔐, and 𝔊. To describe all this adequately requires great length and nuance, and fortunately Sanderson has already published such a description.[20]

4QpaleoDeut^{r}

Features of the Manuscript

4QpaleoDeut^{r} has forty-four extant fragments with identifiable text from chapters 7, 10–15, 19, 22–23, 28, and 31–34, and other fragments possibly from chapters 1, 17, 21, 29, and 30.

4QpaleoDeut^{r} in most ways is similar to the other scrolls. There are approximately thirty-two lines per column, and the distance between lines of script is fairly uniform, at 0.8-0.9 cm. Its height is thus approximately 27.2 cm for the inscribed portion, plus ca. 3 cm for the top and the bottom margins, totaling ca. 33 cm. The width of the columns is difficult to assess, but where the evidence is clearest, the estimate is 10.2 cm. Deuteronomy 32 was apparently written stichometrically, with two hemistichs to the line.

The scribe occasionally split words at the ends of lines. Unlike the scribe of 4QpaleoDeut^{s}, who observed the left marginal ruling so scrupulously that he divided individual words, leaving a single letter at the end or beginning of a line, this scribe followed the custom of other scribes and left at least two letters together, at least in the three instances that have been preserved.

However, it also has a number of unusual characteristics: its scribe did not use dots for word division as all the other scribes writing palaeo-Hebrew did, but separated words only by leaving a space of ca. 0.2 cm; its surface appears to crumble in a manner not common at Qumran; and one of its fragments has a right angled cut that may have been made deliberately (otherwise, it is an amazingly coincidental geometric happenstance!). With respect to the lack of dots for word division, one should bear in mind that some inscriptions in the Phoenician script also did not use word dividers.

The paragraph divisions of this scroll are difficult to assess because of its fragmentary nature. Only one type is extant, a short interval with a line. Of the five such occurrences, 𝔐 has a "closed" section all five times and ⅏ has קצה twice. One larger interval, of about a half line prior to chapter 34, is mostly reconstructed, but there 𝔐 also has a "closed" section, while ⅏ has קצה. On the other hand, there is one place where 𝔐 has an "open" section not

20. For a full analysis of the textual character and textual affiliation of this scroll, see Sanderson, *An Exodus Scroll.*

shared by Deut^{r}, and two places where 𝔐 has a "closed" section not shared by Deut^{r}.

Palaeography and Date

The palaeo-Hebrew script is written in a small, firm, and practiced hand, employing fairly thick, even strokes. For some reason McLean does not seem to have known or studied this manuscript. It is, however, closely akin to the hand of 4QpaleoExod^{m}, but the hand of 4QpaleoDeut^{r} is slightly more compact and rounded than that of 4QpaleoExod^{m}. The features of the script indicate a date roughly contemporary with 4QpaleoExod^{m}, thus approximately in the first half or first three-quarters of the first century B.C.E.

Orthography

The orthography of 4QpaleoDeut^{r} is similar to that of 4QpaleoGen-Exod^{l}, that is, a moderate balance between conservative and full in its use of *matres lectionis,* and not fully consistent. The forms **אלהיך**, **כל**, and **לא** are consistently spelled so (but **הלוא** is spelled with *waw,* as expected in 32:6, as it is in 𝔐 there), and the divergent forms found in the manuscript are such as one customarily encounters at other places in 𝔐 𝔪. Often the forms in this manuscript are longer than those of 𝔐, but sometimes they are shorter (note **בצים** [22:6] and **וחפרת** (vid) [23:14]). This manuscript tends to use *waw* noticeably more frequently than either 𝔐 or 𝔪 (though often 𝔪^{mss} attest the same fuller form) to mark long *o,* especially in the feminine plural and the *Qal* participle, and infrequently to mark long or short *u.* But again, the orthographic practice is not systematic, since, for example, unaccented long *o* sometimes is, and sometimes is not, represented by *waw.* The manuscript also uses *yod* somewhat more than do 𝔐 (but again note **בצים**) or 𝔪, especially for the *Hif'il.* Though either 𝔐 or 𝔪 occasionally has a *mater lectionis* when this manuscript does not, there seems to be no instance in which both 𝔐 and 𝔪 have one when 4QpaleoDeut^{r} does not.

Textual Character and Affiliation

4QpaleoDeut^{r} appears to have agreed with 𝔐𝔊 in lacking the typological features of the Samaritan Deuteronomy. In minor variants the manuscript most often presents a unique reading, less often agrees with 𝔪, and least often agrees with 𝔐.

Though the scroll has not been preserved in any of the passages where ɯ has a typologically significant reading, there are two fragments that at least allow reconstruction at such a variant and that suggest that the manuscript did not belong to the ɯ tradition. The reconstruction at Deut 11:30 suggests that מול שכם as in ɯ was probably lacking; and that at Deut 12:5 suggests that this manuscript read יב]חר with 𝔐 rather than ב]חר with ɯ (and therefore, presumably, at the other twenty similar passages in Deuteronomy).

There are twenty-three variants preserved in this scroll. Though twenty-two involve only one word or part of a word, one variant involves an entire verse. Deut^{r} uniquely lacks 28:19. This could be seen as an omission, because the verse occurs in a series of curses introduced by ארור. But since it is the last of the series and its content quite jejune, it is also possible that Deut^{r} is original and the curse of verse 19 merely a generic addition. Of the twenty-three variants, in three minor variants Deut^{r} agrees with 𝔐 against ɯ. In eight minor variants Deut^{r} agrees with ɯ against 𝔐. In ten variants Deut^{r} disagrees with both 𝔐 and ɯ (in the one significant absence of verse 28:19 plus nine minor variants). In the final two variants Deut^{r} disagrees with 𝔐 and ɯ, which also disagree with each other.

Thus reconstruction suggests that Deut^{r} agreed with 𝔐 𝔊 against ɯ in lacking both the "sectarian" features and one moderate expansion of the latter tradition. But in minor variants the scroll agrees with ɯ against 𝔐 eight times, agrees with 𝔐 against ɯ only three times, and most often (twelve times) presents a unique reading.

Out of the forty-four identified fragments of this manuscript, there is very little overlap with the Cave 4 scrolls of Deuteronomy in the Jewish script edited by Sidnie White and Julie Duncan. In those few places a preliminary reading sees the texts as almost identical, except for some minor orthographical differences. Two textual variants tentatively emerged: in one manuscript there is one metathesis of two letters in a word where this commonly happens, and in another there is the substitution of one common preposition for another synonymous one.

4QpaleoDeut^{s}

Features of the Manuscript

Of 4QpaleoDeut^{s} only a single small fragment survives, measuring only 4.2 by 4.4 cm and containing only six complete and five partly preserved words from Deut 26:14-15. Word dividers are used regularly, and the left marginal ruling is so strictly followed that the word at the end of each of the three extant lines is divided. There is one interval of approximately a half line following Deut 26:15, which would normally be considered an "open" section but at this point 𝔐 has a "closed" section (ס); ⅏ has קצה.

Palaeography and Date

This manuscript is inscribed in a slender, practiced bookhand, written higher along the ruling than normal. To McLean 4QpaleoDeut^{s} appears to be the earliest of the biblical scrolls in the palaeo-Hebrew script. According to his typological schema, it is "roughly contemporary with or slightly older than" 4QpaleoJob^{c}.[21] Though seven letters are not available for comparison because it is so small, he notes the relationship with the *yhd* coins, especially for *dalet* and *yod,* and judges that "Overall, the available forms seem earlier than" those of 4QpaleoJob^{c}, thus indicating a date "in the second half of the third century BCE."[22] This would mean, of course, that the manuscript was copied elsewhere and brought about a century later to Qumran.

Orthography and Textual Character

Again, there are only six complete and five partial words extant. Both the orthography and the text are very ordinary and straightforward, and both agree with the orthography and text of both 𝔐 and ⅏ for those few words.

4QpaleoJob^{c}

Features of the Manuscript

Of 4QpaleoJob^{c} only three small fragments survive, containing Job 13:18-20, 23-27; 14:13-18. The three fragments seem to have been from well-prepared leather and retain their flexibility, ruling, and clarity of script. The distance between lines of script was 0.8-0.9 cm, and one can estimate approximately twenty-five lines per column. The text was written stichometrically, with each stich beginning a new line, and the dots customary for word division in palaeo-Hebrew manuscripts were used. No instances are preserved where a word is split between lines, but that observation is meaningless, since the

21. McLean, "The Use and Development," plate 3, line 2, and pp. 53-57, esp. 53 [designated 4QpaleoDeut$^{\beta}$].

22. Ibid., 57.

fragments are from a poetic passage written stichometrically, and the scribe may well have split words in the narrative sections.

Palaeography and Date

McLean considers this manuscript one of the two earliest biblical scrolls in the palaeo-Hebrew script, roughly contemporary with, but with a few tendencies slightly later than, 4QpaleoDeut^{s}. He detects "little development in either form or stance . . . from the sixth century BCE formal scripts," though he pinpoints five characteristics which "indicate a passage of time." He suggests an "approximate date between 225 and 150 BCE with an emphasis on the earlier end of the scale."[23]

Orthography

4QpaleoJob^{c} displays a very conservative orthography, using no internal *matres lectionis* except possibly in ימ]וֹת (14:14, which may reflect the radical), and in ידיך (14:15, which may reflect the historical spelling of the diphthong, *yadayk*). In contrast, for the few words preserved, 𝔐 has *waw* six times to indicate long *o* or long *u:*

13:24 𝔐 לאויב] ל]איב
13:26 𝔐 עונות] עונת
13:26 𝔐 נעורי] נערי
13:27 𝔐 ארחותי] ארחתי
14:16 𝔐 תספור] תספר[
14:17 𝔐 בצרור] ב]צרר

Textual Character and Affiliation

There is only one variant of one letter preserved, in 14:14. Its reading is clearly different from 𝔐, but it involves a single letter at the edge of the fragment, and the determination and significance of the disagreement involved are admittedly speculative. One cannot base any detailed arguments on this variant.

23. Ibid., plate 3, line 1, and pp. 47-52, esp. 52 [designated 4QpaleoJob^{x}].

The Manuscripts Compared

Features of the Manuscripts

Most or all of the features observed on these manuscripts fit into the patterns already familiar from the broader spectrum of manuscripts found at Qumran.

The leather prepared and used for the palaeo-Hebrew manuscripts, except possibly for 4QpaleoDeut^{r}, appears to be similar to that used for the biblical manuscripts inscribed in the Jewish (square) script, and no differences are apparent between those manuscripts predating the Qumran settlement and those possibly copied at Qumran. For example, the ink used for 4QpaleoGen-Exod^{l} had acid in it, just as the ink for some other manuscripts did, such as 4QLev^{d} and 4QDan^{d}.

4QpaleoDeut^{r} has a number of unusual characteristics: its scribe did not use dots for word division as did all the other scribes writing palaeo-Hebrew; its surface appears to crumble in a manner not common at Qumran; and one of its fragments has a right-angled cut with straight edges along the top and left sides that seems too geometrically regular to be unintentional. Nonetheless, its size, format, and text can be considered normal for a Qumran manuscript. Moreover, ancient inscriptions in the Phoenician script sometimes did not use dots for word division, and the surface crumbling of 4QpaleoDeut^{r} could be due to unrelated factors such as type of damage or deterioration.

Concerning paragraph divisions, all the manuscripts except the tiny 4QpaleoGen^{m} and 4QpaleoJob^{c} are at variance with both 𝔐 and 𝔪 in their distribution. The conclusion that emerges from comparison of the extant divisions with the divisions preserved in 𝔐 and 𝔪 is that there was a common practice in the late Second Temple period of separating sections by longer and shorter divisions, but that the placement of these divisions was made more on a free and logical basis than according to a traditional schema that was standardized and widely accepted.

The palaeo-Hebrew *waw* used systematically by 4QpaleoExod^{m} for division of some larger sections is used in 1QS at the top right of column V, apparently to mark the new section (though the square script *waw* is "repeated" in the initial word). A similar palaeo-Hebrew *waw* is found in 1QIsa^{a}, though both its placement and its function are unclear. It appears at line 22 between columns V and VI, and though it has been interpreted as marking column V,[24]

24. See E. Tov, "Hebrew Biblical Manuscripts from the Judaean Desert: Their Contribution to Textual Criticism," *JJS* 39 (1988) 5-37, esp. 26.

it is possible that its placement may rather indicate (as in 1QS) reference to column VI at its left. Its function is not clear, but possibly it marks either the new section at 6:1 (if for column V) or the new oracle at Isa 7:7 (if for column VI).

Palaeography and Date

The palaeography of the six palaeo-Hebrew biblical manuscripts reveals six different hands, all well practiced. They display a familiarity with the script and an ability to write with "grace and speed,"[25] which mark it as a reasonably common practice, not an unusual exercise. Though the palaeo-Hebrew script was probably a minority script, the minimalist view concerning its use needs to be revised, as McLean has noted, since all the main groups (except eventually the Pharisees) seem to have used it: the so-called "normative community" under the Sadducees[26] and Hasmonaeans, the Qumran community, the Samaritans, and those of the First and Second Revolts.[27] Naveh makes the point, even if perhaps too strongly, that there was "a strong bond between a language and its script."[28] In the Persian period, Jews used both languages and both scripts — presumably the palaeo-Hebrew script for biblical texts and the Aramaic script for administration and trade. According to Naveh, the old script was in use well into the Hellenistic era.[29] On the other hand, insofar as McLean is also correct, there is scarcely a gap that separates the common use of that script in the early Hellenistic era from manuscripts such as 4Qpaleo-Deut^s, copied in the palaeo-Hebrew script ca. 250-200 B.C.E.

The dating of the manuscripts by McLean was done according to a typological schema, anchored at both ends by inscriptional evidence. Typological dating is open to some degree of questioning, but it must be remembered that with undated manuscripts there are only two avenues of estimating the date, palaeography and archaeology. Archaeology can provide a *terminus ante quem,* the reliability of which depends upon the reliability of the methods,

25. F. M. Cross, "The Development of the Jewish Scripts," 189, n. 4.

26. D. Diringer, "Early Hebrew Script versus Square Hebrew Script," in *Essays and Studies Presented to S. A. Cook* (London: Taylor's Foreign Press, 1950) 46-49.

27. McLean, "The Use and Development," 20.

28. Naveh, *Early History of the Alphabet,* 114.

29. "The various national versions of the Aramaic script began to appear only about a century after the fall of the Persian empire. . . . The Aramaic script was at that time so deeply implanted that the various nations continued to use it. . . . Different nations began to develop their own versions. . . . It seems likely that the Jews began to write Hebrew texts in the Aramaic script only when they felt that their form of the Aramaic script was distinctively Jewish" (Naveh, *Early History of the Alphabet,* 122).

and luck, of the archaeological dating. The results of McLean's typological analysis of the scrolls fit with the archaeological dates. The dates assigned to some of the manuscripts predate the Qumran settlement (ca. 150 B.C.E.), but so do some of those in the Jewish script, for example, 4QExod^{f}, 4QSam^{b}, 4QJer^{a}, 4QXII^{a}, and 4QQoh^{a}. This is not problematic, since most agree that some of the scrolls, especially biblical scrolls, were copied elsewhere, in Jerusalem or broader Palestine, and imported into Qumran as people came to join the community.[30] The fact that there are no clear distinguishing features between the general Palestinian Jewish scrolls and the particularly Qumran scrolls suggests that scrolls were produced at Qumran according to conventions similar to those common in Jerusalem and Palestine in general.

The chronological order of the manuscripts in McLean's (and Cross's) view is 4QpaleoDeut^{s}, 4QpaleoJob^{c}, 4QpaleoGen^{m} (all three predating the Qumran settlement), 4QpaleoGen-Exod^{l}, 4QpaleoExod^{m}. McLean did not analyze 4QpaleoDeut^{r}, but in my view it should be dated roughly contemporary with 4QpaleoExod^{m}. Thus, the simple conclusion would be that the first three were presumably copied somewhere in Palestine outside Qumran and that the latter three could have been copied either at Qumran or elsewhere in Palestine. Since there were a number of other palaeo-Hebrew manuscripts in four other caves at Qumran, and since no physical features distinguish these manuscripts from the other manuscripts in Jewish script (a number of which must have been copied at Qumran), there is no evidence to rule out a conclusion that some of the palaeo-Hebrew manuscripts were also copied at Qumran. If this is true, the further conclusion is also logical, that there appear to be no characteristic differences between those palaeo-Hebrew manuscripts copied at Qumran and those imported into Qumran. I must reiterate that we do not have strong evidence to support this as a firm conclusion, but the conclusion is logical and plausible.

Most or all of the palaeographic features observed on these manuscripts also fit into the patterns that indicate no observable differences between manuscripts copied outside Qumran (i.e., those assigned dates prior to the settlement at Qumran) and manuscripts presumed to have been copied at Qumran. But it is necessary to consider this conclusion from the perspective of orthography as well.

30. The last clause clearly distances my view from that proposed by N. Golb, "Khirbet Qumran and the Manuscripts of the Judaean Wilderness: Observations on the Logic of Their Investigation," *JNES* 49 (1990) 103-14.

Orthography

Study of the orthography of each of the larger three palaeo-Hebrew manuscripts tells us something also about 𝔐. The orthographic practice at work in the Qumran manuscripts, just as in 𝔐, shows somewhat distinctive tendencies but also a degree of inconsistency in each manuscript and in the various books in 𝔐.

The orthography of the six palaeo-Hebrew manuscripts can be charted on a spectrum arranged this time, not primarily by chronology, but by fullness in use of internal *matres lectionis.* The most conservative use of internal *matres lectionis* is in 4QpaleoJob^{c}, which arguably has none. Perhaps 4QpaleoDeut^{s} may be ranked next, insofar as it has no spellings fuller than 𝔐 or ⅏, but this is uncertain and almost meaningless. 4QpaleoGen-Exod^{l} and 4QpaleoDeut^{r} display a slightly fuller use, and 4QpaleoExod^{m} a yet fuller use, though still within a fairly moderate range. Perhaps 4QpaleoGen^{m} should be placed with or slightly beyond 4QpaleoExod^{m} on this spectrum, but we have too little evidence for a firm decision. 4QpaleoGen^{m} alone among these manuscripts writes לוא with *waw,* whereas 4QpaleoExod^{m} writes לא without *waw;* but 4QpaleoExod^{m} sometimes, for example, writes ויאומר with *waw,* while we do not know whether 4QpaleoGen^{m} may have written ויאמר without *waw.* At any rate, though there is a spectrum of orthographic practice in the Qumran manuscripts, virtually all forms found are of a type routinely found in other known biblical manuscripts, including 𝔐, ⅏, and other Qumran manuscripts in the Jewish script.

If we then compare the chronological spectrum charted by the palaeographically assigned dates with the spectrum drawn according to orthographical usage, we get — not a logically satisfying correlation that shows a regular chronological development of orthographic practice — but a picture that is actually more real and believable. In the short period with which we are concerned, a moderate range of orthographic practice seems to have been acceptable. 4QpaleoJob^{c} cooperates best by having a very conservative orthography that most would tend to date early, and by having one of the earliest palaeographical dates. Analogously, 4QpaleoExod^{m} has a more liberal orthographic profile together with a date near the later end of the spectrum. But 4QpaleoGen^{m} has what we often think of as a later orthographic style, while being dated palaeographically as early. We should recall, however, that the Nash Papyrus also writes the negative as לוא, and it is commonly dated to the second half of the second century,[31] roughly contemporary with the date sug-

31. See W. F. Albright, "A Biblical Fragment from the Maccabaean Age: The Nash Papyrus," *JBL* 56 (1937) 145-76; Naveh, *Early History of the Alphabet,* 162 and fig. 147.

gested by McLean for 4QpaleoGen^{m}. The conclusion to be drawn here, just as for the scrolls in the Jewish script, is that though earlier manuscripts may tend to have more conservative spelling, that is only a rule of thumb, a tendency. The common view — that Hebrew orthography was never rigidly standardized, and that it reached its fullest style of spelling in the Hasmonaean era — is exactly what one observes in the palaeo-Hebrew manuscripts from Cave 4.

Orthography at Qumran is probably not to be distinguished from general orthographic practice in contemporary Palestine (4QpaleoGen^{m}) and even perhaps in Egypt (Nash Papyrus). Emanuel Tov speaks of Qumran orthography and amasses impressive data to offer us a more multidimensional perspective.[32] But he is careful to say that we do not have sufficient evidence to know whether "'Qumran' orthography was practiced widely in Palestine."[33] Though there is little evidence available, nonetheless there is some, and it is quite diverse. There are, for example, fourth-century jar handles alternating between **יהד** and **יהוד**; the Nash Papyrus from Egypt uses **לוא**; and even the Masoretic texts of Chronicles and of Samuel in their parallel passages display more and less *plene* styles, respectively, though a form of Samuel was used as a source by the Chronicler. In light of these diverse sources, I think it may be preferable to expand the nomenclature of orthographic categories from "Qumran" and "non-Qumran" orthography to terms that would cover the entire late Second Temple period, or Hasmonaean-Roman period, since it appears that the fuller orthography reached its characteristic features then. I would then characterize the different orthographic approaches in biblical manuscripts as "traditional" vs. "contemporary," or "conservative" vs. "modernizing" — depending upon whether the scribes continued to copy the Persian-period texts in the old orthography or (like the scribes of 4QSam^{c}, 4QIsa^{c}, and 4QDan^{b})[34] modernized them in accord with contemporary practices. In short, just as I detect no difference in physical features or palaeography of the palaeo-Hebrew biblical scrolls between those produced throughout Palestine and those produced at Qumran, neither do I see any characteristic difference between them in orthography, except insofar as

32. E. Tov, "The Orthography and Language of the Hebrew Scrolls Found at Qumran and the Origin of These Scroll," *Textus* 13 (1986) 31-57; idem, "Hebrew Biblical Manuscripts," esp. 23-25.

33. Tov, "Hebrew Biblical Manuscripts," 24.

34. See E. Ulrich, "4QSam^{c}: A Fragmentary Manuscript of 2 Samuel 14–15 from the Scribe of the *Serek Hay-yaḥad* (1QS)," *BASOR* 235 (1979) 1-25; idem, "Daniel Manuscripts from Qumran. Part 2: Preliminary Editions of 4QDan^{b} and 4QDan^{c}," *BASOR* 274 (1989) 3-27.

scribes had to make a decision whether to modernize or not to modernize the orthography of their manuscripts as they made new copies.

Textual Character and Affiliation

The Masoretic Text, when one is speaking in scholarly rather than religious terms, should more properly be termed the Masoretic collection of texts. It has now become common knowledge that the Septuagint differs from section to section and from book to book, and sometimes even within a given book. The case is the same with the assortment of texts gathered into the Masoretic collection. The textual profile of the individual books varies significantly, both with regard to the soundness of the text (i.e., sound texts such as Genesis and Exodus vs. problematic texts such as Samuel and Hosea) and with regard to the successive editions transmitted (i.e., early editions for the book of Exodus and for the Hannah narrative in Samuel vs. revised editions for the David-Goliath narrative also in Samuel and for the book of Jeremiah).[35] Thus, one cannot simply compare texts from various books of the Bible to "the text" of 𝔐.

The palaeo-Hebrew manuscripts exhibit what one would expect: they are primarily in agreement with the editions we have known, with predictable types of minor expansions, transpositions, errors, and other features that distinguish them in minor ways from the specific texts that happen to have been preserved. One could point out that only 4QpaleoExod^{m} has a demonstrably proto-Samaritan text type, whereas the remainder are close to 𝔐. But it must be remembered that this distinction is irrelevant for one of the six manuscripts (4QpaleoJob^{c}), is unable to be determined for two others (4QpaleoGen^{m} and 4QpaleoDeut^{s}), and is reached primarily by reconstruction for the remaining two (4QpaleoGen-Exod^{l} and 4QpaleoDeut^{r}, though one can rely on the conclusion about the latter two with reasonable confidence). Thus, we are left with the ratio of two texts in the same early edition as that in 𝔐 to one text in the revised edition as in 𝔪. A base that narrow cannot support very weighty conclusions. As is all too often the case, the fragmentary evidence is not extant where it is needed or sought. There is almost no overlap of the

35. See E. Ulrich, "Double Literary Editions of Biblical Narratives and Reflections on Determining the Form to Be Translated," in *Perspectives on the Hebrew Bible: Essays in Honor of Walter J. Harrelson* (ed. J. L. Crenshaw; Macon, Ga.: Mercer University Press, 1988) 101-16, reprinted as Chapter 3 in this volume; idem, "The Canonical Process, Textual Criticism, and Latter Stages in the Composition of the Bible," in *Sha'arei Talmon: Studies in the Bible, Qumran, and the Ancient Near East Presented to Shemaryahu Talmon* (ed. M. Fishbane and E. Tov with W. W. Fields; Winona Lake, Ind.: Eisenbrauns, 1992) 267-91, reprinted as Chapter 4 in this volume.

palaeo-Hebrew scrolls with each other or with other Cave 4 scrolls, and when there is, there is very little of significance in the contrast.

In sum, except for their script, the palaeo-Hebrew biblical manuscripts from Qumran Cave 4 do not appear to form a group distinguishable from the other biblical scrolls in either physical features, date, orthography, or textual character. Moreover, though certainty is even more elusive for this contrast, there seems to be no great distinction in any of those four categories between manuscripts copied outside Qumran (or predating Qumran) and manuscripts copied at Qumran.

CHAPTER 8

Orthography and Text in 4QDan^a and 4QDan^b and in the Received Masoretic Text

For certain ancient manuscripts, the authors, editors, or scribal copyists had such an acute knowledge of grammar and orthography that it is possible and profitable to describe their orthographic system in detail. If such manuscripts are fragmentary or damaged, letters that are difficult to read can sometimes be more accurately and confidently restored. The Ben Sira scroll from Masada is an example of such a manuscript. Professor John Strugnell was able to describe the system of orthography employed by the scribe and thus gain greater control for determining a number of damaged letters in that scroll.[1]

With regard to the text of the Bible, though the Masoretic Text is used as the common standard text, it has been amply demonstrated for a number of books that the ancient manuscripts discovered at Qumran sometimes provide us with more sound, preferable readings than does the MT, the *textus receptus* from medieval times.

The purpose of this study is, first, to explore the orthography of the

1. John Strugnell, "Notes and Queries on 'The Ben Sira Scroll from Masada,'" in *Eretz-Israel* 9: *W. F. Albright Volume* (ed. A. Malamat; Jerusalem: Israel Exploration Society, 1969) 109-19. For the publication of the Ben Sira scroll, see Y. Yadin, *The Ben Sira Scroll from Masada* (Jerusalem: Israel Exploration Society and the Shrine of the Book, 1965), Hebrew, pp. 1-45, English, pp. 1-49, and plates I-IX (anticipatory reprint from *Eretz-Israel* 8 [1967]).

two larger manuscripts of Daniel from Qumran and that of the MT, and secondly, to examine some of the variants in those texts, in order to understand the text of Daniel better than either the Qumran or the Masoretic texts alone would allow. The chapter will offer, not an exhaustive study, but a number of highlights from our recently gained vantage point on the book of Daniel.

Three of the Qumran caves have yielded a total of eight manuscripts of the book of Daniel from the late Second Temple period, providing us with a good glimpse of the shape of the book at the beginning of the common era. Two manuscripts on leather were found in Cave 1, five in Cave 4, and one on papyrus in Cave 6.[2]

The Qumran manuscripts, of course, are by no means flawless, but they do demonstrate that the MT of Daniel is also not flawless, and comparison of the Qumran texts with the MT gives us a better perspective on the sound parts of each and the less sound parts of each. Similarly, the Qumran biblical texts in general have exonerated the Old Greek translation of many books, showing that the OG is usually not an erroneous or willfully tendentious translation, but often a faithful translation of what is simply an alternate — sometimes more, sometimes less, preferable — Hebrew text of which in the past we had been simply unaware.

In order to put the present study in a larger context, we can recall some conclusions already generally available from study of the Qumran manuscripts and the MT concerning the early form of the text of Daniel. First, with regard to textual variants, there are no major departures from the early Hebrew-Aramaic text that is handed down to us in the Masoretic *textus receptus*. All twelve chapters of the traditional short edition of the book are attested in Cave 4, whereas — at least to date — there appears to be no manuscript evi-

2. The critical editions of the individual manuscripts are available in the following sources:

1QDan[a] and 1QDan[b]: D. Barthélemy, *Qumrân Cave I* (DJD 1; Oxford: Clarendon, 1955) 150-52. Because of time factors, these fragments had to be published without photographs; the photographs were subsequently published by J. C. Trever, "Completion of the Publication of Some Fragments from Qumran Cave 1," *RevQ* 5 (1964-66) 323-44.

4QDan: E. Ulrich, "Daniel Manuscripts from Qumran. Part 1: A Preliminary Edition of 4QDan[a]," *BASOR* 268 (1987) 17-37; idem, "Daniel Manuscripts from Qumran. Part 2: Preliminary Editions of 4QDan[b] and 4QDan[c]," *BASOR* 274 (1989) 3-26. 4QDan[d] and 4QDan[e] survive in only a few small scraps and will be published in the last of the biblical volumes in the DJD series.

Pap6QDan: M. Baillet, *Les 'Petites Grottes' de Qumrân. 1: Texte. 2: Planches* (DJD 3; Oxford: Clarendon, 1962) 114-16 and plate XXIII.

dence[3] of the longer edition attested in the Greek versions.[4] In the five manuscripts of the book of Daniel found in Cave 4, the first eleven of the twelve chapters of the book as transmitted in the MT are attested, and the twelfth chapter is quoted in the *Florilegium* (4Q174).

Secondly, the curious shift from Hebrew to Aramaic at 2:4a in the MT also is confirmed by the ancient manuscripts 1QDan[a] and 4QDan[a], and the shift from Aramaic back to Hebrew at 8:1 is confirmed by 4QDan[a] and 4QDan[b]; furthermore, all the extant fragments of all the Daniel manuscripts display the expected distribution of languages. Thirdly, though early conjectures suggested otherwise, it is now recognized that the book of Daniel was considered as a sacred and authoritative book at Qumran, on a level with other books later considered canonical scripture.[5]

In this study we will be able to deal only with the two most extensively preserved manuscripts, 4QDan[a] and 4QDan[b]. 4QDan[a] is inscribed in a formal script of the Hasmonaean period or the transition to the Herodian period, and thus may be assigned a date approximately in the middle of the first century B.C.E., about a century or so after the composition of the book.[6] It has sixteen identifiable fragments preserved, seven of which are from columns 2-6 of the original scroll. Column 4 is almost entirely preserved, containing the text of Dan 2:19-33, and it is followed by fragments in the next column from almost every verse of 2:33-46.

4QDan[b] is inscribed in a "developed Herodian formal script" and may be assigned to approximately 20-50 C.E.,[7] almost a century later than 4QDan[a]. It contains nineteen identifiable fragments, spanning Daniel 5–8,

3. There are, of course, fragments of what can be called a Daniel cycle, plus countless unidentified and "parabiblical" fragments. In this connection we should also note that 4QDan[e] has fragments of the Hebrew prayer in Daniel 9, and that 4QTestLevi has, in Hebrew, the prayer that is in Greek in the *Testament of Levi* (M. de Jonge, ed., *The Testaments of the Twelve Patriarchs: A Critical Edition of the Greek Text* [Leiden: Brill, 1978] 17, 19). This raises the possibility that some unidentified fragments may have in Aramaic (or Hebrew) the prayers now found only in the Greek versions of Daniel.

4. It remains an intriguing question why the Theodotionic text, which was supposedly revised according to the current rabbinic text, contains the longer edition of the book.

5. See the discussion in the 4QDan[a] edition, p. 19. Throughout this paper, see the respective editions for fuller discussion and fuller presentation of the myriad details of each manuscript.

6. See the 4QDan[a] edition, p. 20.

7. Cf. F. M. Cross, "The Development of the Jewish Scripts," in *The Bible and the Ancient Near East: Essays in Honor of William Foxwell Albright* (ed. G. E. Wright; Garden City, N.Y.: Doubleday, 1961) 173-81, and the chart on p. 139, figure 2, line 6; cf. also the 4QDan[b] edition, p. 5.

with a large fragment containing generous portions of two columns from Daniel 6.

The following passages from Daniel are extant on the two manuscripts:[8]

4QDan^{a}	*4QDan^{b}*	*4QDan^{a}*	*4QDan^{b}*
1:16-20			6:8-22, 27-29
2:9-11, 19-49		7:5-7	7:1-6, 11?
3:1-2		7:25-28	7:26-28
4:29-30		8:1-5	8:1-8, 13-16
5:5-7	5:10-12	10:16-20	
5:12-14	5:14-16	11:13-16	
5:16-19	5:19-22		

The lack of text shared in common by the two manuscripts is frustrating; see especially the distribution in chapter 5. Fortunately, however, the two manuscripts have modestly large fragments from Dan 8:1-5 which overlap, and we will examine these below. With this general perspective on the Daniel manuscripts, we may now center our focus on the orthography of the MT and the two larger manuscripts found at Qumran.

Orthography

Although for certain ancient manuscripts the authors, editors, or copyists employed a consistent system of orthography, nonetheless for many manuscripts there is no consistent system. The copyists simply copied the text as they found it, as faithfully as they could (though occasionally adding errors and intentional minor changes). If there was no consistent system on the part of the authors or major editors or scribal editors, then, unless the scribal copyists were both very learned and sufficiently confident to "correct" the spelling,[9] the text reproduced by the copyists will have been as inconsistent as the original. When the orthography of a biblical manuscript is inconsistent, a practical procedure is simply to list the differences between that manuscript and the MT, which usually serves as the standard text for comparison.

As we shall see below, it is necessary to distinguish between using the

8. For a complete list of all the contents of the published Daniel manuscripts, see Figure 1 in the 4QDan^{a} edition, p. 18.

9. Consistency in orthography is not, of course, universally regarded as important, as is evident from inspection of sources as diverse as the manuscripts of Shakespeare and the maps and road signs of Jerusalem.

MT as a standard in the sense of a common, convenient source of reference, and using it with the assumption that it is the standard in the sense of the original or perfect or normative text.[10]

The Orthography of the MT

When we survey the Hebrew-Aramaic manuscripts of the book of Daniel from Qumran, we notice that there is no consistent system of orthography operative in the form of the book as we meet it. Comparison with the Masoretic *textus receptus* reveals the fact that the MT also lacks a consistent orthographic system.

A thorough analysis of the orthographic practice in the MT of Daniel is surely a desideratum, but that is beyond what we can attempt in the confines of this study. If it were indeed consistent, then it could be described in short compass, but the greater its inconsistency, the more lengthy and complicated its description necessarily becomes. Thus the lists that follow are meant to be illustrative of the inconsistency in the orthographic practice of those responsible for the MT of Daniel as we receive it. It can be said, of course, that the MT has certain orthographic tendencies: it strikes a moderate balance between a sparse use and a full use of *matres lectionis*. For example, in both the Aramaic section and the Hebrew section, one always finds כל, never כול, and when long *o*- occurs in two successive syllables, usually only one, not both, are marked with *waw*.[11] There are, however, numerous inconsistencies — possibly due to the different hands involved in the composition and editorial history of the book and to the many hands who over the centuries copied the finished book. Again, the lists are not intended to be exhaustive, not all occurrences are listed, and prefixed articles and prepositions are ignored.

10. For a discussion of some of the issues involved, see E. Ulrich, "Jewish, Christian, and Empirical Perspectives on the Text of Our Scriptures," in *Hebrew Bible or Old Testament? Studying the Bible in Judaism and Christianity* (ed. R. Brooks and J. J. Collins; Christianity and Judaism in Antiquity 5; Notre Dame: University of Notre Dame, 1990) 69-85.

11. Note, however, occasional forms such as כרצוֹנוֹ in 11:16, 36 (but כרצֹנוֹ in 8:4).

MT: The Aramaic Section	
גלֵא 2:22, 28	גלֵה 2:47
גֹב 6:8, 25	גוֹב 6:13
רעיֹנהי 5:6	רעיוֹני 2:30; רעיוֹנך 2:29
רעינֹהי 5:6	חדוֹהי ודרעוֹהי 2:32
כתבא 5:8, 16, 17	כתבה 5:7
פשרא 2:4; 5:8, 17	פשרה 2:5; 5:7, 12, 16[12]
מקרֵא 5:8, 16; אקרֵא 5:17	יקרֵה 5:7; יתקרֵי 5:12
קיתרס 3:7	קיתרוס 3:5
סבכא 3:5	שׂבכא 3:7
בלאשצר 7:1	בלשאצר 5:1, 22, 29, 30
נבכדנצר 5:11	נבוכדנצר 2:28, 46 (cf. Heb.)
MT: The Hebrew Section	
עֹמד 8:3, 6, 15; 12:1	עוֹמד 11:16
נֹגע 9:21; 10:16	נוֹגע 8:5
גדֹלה 9:12; 10:7, 8;	גדוֹלה 8:8, 21
כֹח 1:4; 10:8, 16, 17; 11:15	כוֹח 11:6
רצֹנו 8:4	רצוֹנו 11:16, 36
מלאת 10:3	מלאות 9:2
שלש 8:14; 12:12	שלוש 1:1, 5; 8:1; 10:1
לקרֹא 2:2; לעמֹד 1:4; 11:15	לבוֹא 11:17
בנָו 11:10	לפנָיו 8:4
משמם 9:27	משומם 11:31
חמֻדות 10:3, 11, 19; 11:38	חמוּדות 9:23
האֻבל 8:3, 6	אוּבל 8:2
נבכדנצר 2:1	נבוכדנאצר 1:1 (cf. Aram.)

With even such a partial list, one need not continue the quest to describe "the orthographic system of the MT of Daniel."[13] Rather, having seen this illustration of non-systematic usage in the MT, we will now survey the orthographic practice in the scrolls from Qumran.

12. The (probably medieval) Masoretic vocalization is a secondary effort to make sense of the consonantal orthography, morphology, and syntax; it is not necessarily an accurate indication of the original form; see פשרה especially at 5:12, and כתבה at 5:7.

13. That quest would be a lengthy and complex undertaking. Perhaps it would lead nowhere. But one imaginable, although unlikely, possibility is that the early author or editor of the book of Daniel may have employed a consistent orthographic system and that a different consistent system may have been used by later editors or scribes; such a discovery would be of significant value in understanding the composition and editorial history of the book.

4QDan^a

The orthographic system[14] of 4QDan^a is also not consistent, but the orthographic practices of 4QDan^a are usually close to those of the MT (in contrast to those of 4QDan^b, as we shall see below); for example, the words לא, כל, and אלהים are never spelled with *waw.* There are, however, eleven orthographic differences between 4QDan^a and the MT. 4QDan^a has *waw* twice where the MT lacks it:

	4QDan^a	*MT*
5:6	ו֯ר֯עינוהי֯	ורעינהי
8:4	כרצו[נו]	כרצנו

has *yod* for *'alep* in the MT once:

	4QDan^a	*MT*
2:32	רישה	ראשה

and *he* twice where the MT has *'alep:*

	4QDan^a	*MT*
2:24	[ופשר]ה	ופשרא
5:17	ופשרה	ופשרא

On the other hand, the MT has *waw* four times where 4QDan^a lacks it:

	4QDan^a	*MT*
2:20	ו֯גברתא	וגבורתא
2:30	ורעיני	ורעיוני
2:32	ודרעה֯י	ודרעוהי
8:5	נגע	נוגע

and *yod* twice where 4QDan^a lacks it:

14. These descriptions of the orthography are distilled from those in the editions of 4QDan^a, p. 21, and 4QDan^b, pp. 5-6. See the editions for a number of minor qualifications on the orthography that would be more distracting than necessary in the present paper.

	4QDan^a	*MT*
2:44	[א]לן̊	אלין
5:17	ונבזבתך	ונבזביתך

Though these are the patterns where 4QDan^a happens to be extant, notice that some of the examples contrast with each other, and for yet others one can find the reverse patterns elsewhere in 4QDan^a and the MT.

4QDan^b

The orthography of 4QDan^b is fuller than that of the MT and of 4QDan^a for both the Hebrew and the Aramaic sections. In 4QDan^b the word כול, for example, is always spelled with *waw*, and לוא is always spelled with *waw* in the Hebrew section. There are twenty-three orthographic[15] differences extant between 4QDan^b and the MT. Six of these are preserved on both 4QDan^b and 4QDan^a, and 4QDan^b is almost always fuller. 4QDan^b has the longer reading five times against the combined 4QDan^a and MT: once using the "cohortative" equivalent of the indicative,[16] and four times adding *waw*. It is only in one instance of *yod* as a *mater lectionis* that 4QDan^b has the shorter reading against the combined 4QDan^a and MT:

	4QDan^b	*4QDan^a = MT*
8:3	ואׄשאה	ואשא
8:3	עומד	עמד
8:3	באחׄרונׄהׄ	באחרנה
8:4	וכול	וכל
8:4	לוא	לא
8:4	[ו]הׄגדל	והגדיל

In other instances where 4QDan^a is not extant, 4QDan^b never adds *yod* where the MT lacks it but does add *waw* nine times where the MT lacks it, two of which are inserted by the original scribe supralinearly:

15. For the use of longer pronominal suffixes and other minor morphological variants that can be considered together with orthographic differences, see the 4QDan^b edition.

16. See note 18 below. This is properly a morphological, rather than orthographic, variant.

	*4QDan^b^*	*MT*
6:9	ותרש'ם	ותרשם
6:13	כול	כל
6:14	קודם	קדם
6:18	ושוֹמת	ושמת
8:7	[ויר]מ֯'ס֯ה֯ו֯	וירמסהו
8:7	ולוא	ולא
8:13	וקודש	וקדש
8:14	קודש	קדש
8:15	[בר]א֯ותי	בראתי

4QDan^{b} has *'alep* twice where the MT has *he:*

	*4QDan^b^*	*MT*
6:11	[ב]ע֯ליתא	בעליתה
6:19	להיכלא	להיכלה

but it has *he* for the emphatic state once where the MT has *'alep:*

	*4QDan^b^*	*MT*
6:21	[חי]ה	חיא

4QDan^{b} has *'alep* for a III-*'alep* verb once where the MT has *yod:*

	*4QDan^b^*	*MT*
5:12	[?יתקר]א	יתקרי

has *he* for III-weak verbs three times where the MT has *'alep:*

	*4QDan^b^*	*MT*
6:9	[תעד]ה	תעדא
6:15	הוה	הוא
6:18	תשנה	תשנא

and finally, it has *'alep* for the *'Itpe'el* once where the MT has a *Hitpa'el* in the Aramaic section:

	*4QDan^b^*	*MT*
6:20	ובאתבה[לה]	ובהתבהלה

Thus, 4QDan^{b} has twenty-three orthographic (plus minor morphological) differences from the MT. In all six of the instances for which 4QDan^{a} is extant, the latter agrees with the MT against 4QDan^{b}. For clear perspective, however, we should note that the MT exhibits at other points most of the features of orthographic variation that have been observed in 4QDan^{b}. We should also recall that the MT does not have a consistent system of orthography, that neither 4QDan^{a} nor 4QDan^{b} has a consistent system, and indeed that the inconsistencies in each can often be found exemplified in the other.

Textual Variants

When attempting to assess the textual agreement or variation between 4QDan^{a} and 4QDan^{b} in order to see the textual relationship between the two Qumran scrolls and then the textual relationship between them and the MT, we find that we do not have much data to work with. We find two interesting passages.

Daniel 8:1-5

The largest overlap of text between 4QDan^{a} and 4QDan^{b} is at Dan 8:1-5 (see the synopsis on the next page). But there the two manuscripts overlap for only fourteen words that are preserved completely on both manuscripts and seventeen that are preserved only partly on one or both manuscripts. In order to concentrate on the question of textual variants for 4QDan^{a}, 4QDan^{b}, and the MT, let us first note and then eliminate the orthographic differences in this passage. 4QDan^{a} has only a single *mater lectionis* that is not found in 4QDan^{b}: the *yod* in **והגדיל** at the end of 8:4 (= MT, see above). The orthographic practice of 4QDan^{b}, in contrast, is fuller, and in this passage it uses *waw* four times where 4QDan^{a} does not: **עומד** and **באחרונה** (8:3), **וכול** and **לוא** (8:4) — all characteristic of this manuscript.[17] 4QDan^{b} also once has the longer "cohortative" form, **ואשאה** at 8:3, which at Qumran functions as an alternate form of the indicative.[18] We may recall that 4QDan^{a} agrees with the MT against 4QDan^{b} in all these minor differences.

17. In addition, it should be noted, even though the word is not extant in 4QDan^{b} at 8:4, that **וכול ח[י]ות** (= MT, without the article) is to be reconstructed, whereas 4QDan^{a} has **וכל החיות**.

18. E. Qimron (*The Hebrew of the Dead Sea Scrolls* [HSM 29; Atlanta: Scholars Press, 1986] #310.122, p. 44) describes the form: "It is a well-known feature of DSS Hebrew that

When we return to the larger question of the textual content of this passage, we note that there are three significant variants, which are underlined in the following synopsis.[19]

Synopsis
The Text of Daniel 8:1-4 in 4QDan[a], 4QDan[b], and the MT

4QDan[a]

61 [בשנת שלוש למלכות בלאשצר]המ[לך ~~ד]בר נגלא~~ חזון נראה אלי אני דניא[ל]

60 [אחרי הנראה אלי בתחלה 2]ואראה בחזון ויהי בראתי ואני בשושן הבירה

61 [אשר בעילם המדינה ואראה]בחזון ואני הייתי על אובל אולי 3ואשא עיני

53 [ואראה והנה איל אחד גד]וׄל עמד לפני האבל ולו קרנים קרנים

51 [והקרנים גבהות והאח]ת גבהה מן השנית והגבהה עלה באחרנה

54 [4ראיתי את האיל מנגח י]מה ומזרחה צפונה ונגבה וכל החיות לא

4QDan[b]

57 [בשנת שלוש למלכות בלאשצר המלך חזון נראה אלי אני ד]ניאל אחׄ[רי]

60 [הנראה אלי בתחלה 2ואראה בחזון ויהי]בׄרׄאׄ[ותי ואני בשו]שן הבירה אׄשר

59 [בעילם המדינה ואראה בח]זׄון וׄאני היׄ[יתי על אובל]אׄולי 3וׄאשאה עיני

55 [ואראה והנה איל א]חׄד גׄדול עומד לׄ[פני האובל ו]לׄוׄ קרנים קׄ[ר]נׄים

52 [והקרנים גבהות והאחת גב]הה מן השׄ[נית והגב]הׄה עלה באחׄרונׄהׄ

55 [4ראיתי את האיל מנגח ימה ומזרחה צפונה ונגב]ה וכול [חי]ות לוא

MT

57 בשנת שלוש למלכות בלאשצר המלך חזון נראה אלי אני דניאל אחרי

59 הנראה אלי בתחלה 2ואראה בחזון ויהי בראתי ואני בשושן הבירה אשר

58 בעילם המדינה ואראה בחזון ואני הייתי על אובל אולי 3ואשא עיני

42 ואראה והנה איל אחד עמד לפני האבל ולו קרנים

51 והקרנים גבהות והאחת גבהה מן השנית והגבהה עלה באחרנה

47 4ראיתי את האיל מנגח ימה וצפונה ונגבה וכל חיות לא

---

cohortative forms נ/אקטלה denote the indicative alongside the forms נ/אקטל, as in the late books of the Bible and the Samaritan Pentateuch." In confirmation, note the "cohortative"-as-indicative וָאֹמְרָה in the MT at 10:19, where 4QDan[a] has the expected "Biblical Hebrew" form וׄאמר.

19. The synopsis lists (1) the extant text of 4QDan[a] for the part of its column where it overlaps with 4QDan[b], plus a reconstruction of the destroyed portion of those lines. Then it similarly presents (2) the extant and reconstructed text of 4QDan[b]. The arrangement of the six lines for each manuscript is dictated by the format of the extant fragments; it is unusually fortunate that the left ends of the lines are extant here for both manuscripts. The synopsis then presents (3) the MT in an arrangement parallel to the format of the scrolls, for facility of comparison.

From analysis of the foregoing synopsis we can make the following observations:

Line 1. 4QDan^b and the MT are identical in text and letter count.[20] The scribe of 4QDan^a added two words probably suggested by the parallel introductory formula of chapter 10, recognized that they were incorrect here, crossed out the two erroneous words,[21] continued with the correct introduction for chapter 8, and wrote אחרי on the next line.

Line 2. 4QDan^b and the MT are identical (except for the assumed fuller spelling of בראותי in 4QDan^b). 4QDan^a, because of the error in line 1 and the subsequent shift of אחרי to line 2, shifts אשר to line 3.

Line 3. 4QDan^b and the MT are identical (except for the longer form ואשאה in 4QDan^b). 4QDan^a begins with אשר but ends with the same word as in 4QDan^b and the MT.

Line 4. The longer reading קרנים קרנים is extant in both 4QDan^a and 4QDan^b, and the longer reading גׄדול is extant clearly in 4QDan^b and probably in 4QDan^a. Thus, our analysis must begin with this evidence. The smaller letter count for 4QDan^a and 4QDan^b is partly due to a slightly shorter line in both manuscripts and partly due to the slightly more spacious script in 4QDan^a in this line.[22] But the smaller letter count means that 4QDan^a very probably had all the text that the MT has plus the additions as in 4QDan^b.

Line 5. The three texts are identical (except that 4QDan^b has the fuller באחרונה). The short letter count means that והקרנים must be reconstructed at the beginning of line 5 in both 4QDan^a and 4QDan^b in agreement with the MT. This in turn proves that the second קרנים in line 4 is truly a plus in 4QDan^a and 4QDan^b, not a shorter variant replacing והקרנים in line 5.

Line 6. 4QDan^a and 4QDan^b are identical (except for the fuller spellings וכול and לוא in 4QDan^b, partly counterbalanced by the article in החיות in 4QDan^a). Again, 4QDan^a clearly has the addition ומזרחה, and 4QDan^b probably had it also. If 4QDan^b did not have ומזרחה, then its line would have contained only forty-eight letters, and that implausibly short count would necessitate some alternate irregularity in this line of the manuscript.

Thus, 4QDan^a presents two certain pluses relative to the MT and one probable plus: קרנים 2°, ומזרחה, and [גד]ול. 4QDan^b clearly preserves the

20. At the left side of each line, the number of letters per line is given, serving as one control for the quantitative reconstruction of missing text. Since it is primarily width, not number of letters, that is being measured, spaces between words are counted in the "letter" count, unless two words are written together without space for word division (as, e.g., ואשאעיני in 4QDan^a at 8:3, line 3).

21. See the photograph of the fragment of 4QDan^a and the edition.

22. See the photograph.

קרנים 2° plus and preserves clearly the plus that is only "probable" in 4QDan[a] (גֹּדול); it must have preserved also the remaining clear plus in 4QDan[a] (ומזרחה) — unless we posit some even less predictable variant. In support, πρὸς ἀνατολάς (= ומזרחה) in the Old Greek translation of the verse, in combination with the occurrence of the plus μέγαν (= גדול) in agreement with 4QDan[b] in the preceding verse, also argues in favor of the likelihood of ומזרחה in 4QDan[b]. Prescinding from the minor and customary orthographic differences in 4QDan[b] and the article in 4QDan[a], the text of the two Qumran manuscripts stands in complete mutual agreement against the MT in the three variants that occur, whereas neither Qumran manuscript preserves an agreement with the MT against the other Qumran manuscript in this or any of the other Daniel fragments. In fact, let us examine one further example.

Daniel 5:12

At Dan 5:12 4QDan[a] has another variant from the MT. Of the small, four-line fragment, the few words in the first two lines share the same basic text with the MT, though with three minor, single-letter variants. The third line differs completely from the MT, while the fourth line is of little help, having only the top of a *lamed*. The variant in the third line reads וֹכֹּתבא יקרא, and it occurs in the place where one would expect the last two words of the MT reading כען דניאל יתקרי ופשרה יהחוה. If, however, the "writing-interpretation" formula is studied for all of chapter 5, the 4QDan[a]-MT variant becomes clear. There are five occurrences in the chapter, at 5:7, 8, 12, 16, and 17. In the MT, the double clause "read the writing and make known the/its[23] interpretation" occurs in four of the five instances, and the exception is here at 5:12, where only the second clause, but not the first, occurs. The scroll should be reconstructed to read:

[כען דניאל יתקרא[24]]וֹכֹּתבא יקרא[ופשרה יהחוה].

Critics, I am sure, will delight in debating whether this was a set formula, part of which was omitted by parablepsis from the MT tradition, or whether the text tradition from which the Qumran manuscript was copied inadvertently

23. For the ambiguous orthography and Masoretic pointing, see the Aramaic orthography chart above and the orthography and variants in the 4QDan[a] and 4QDan[b] editions.

24. Or, less likely, יתקרי with the MT; see the text of 4QDan[b] below.

or intentionally filled in a routine expansion in an originally shorter text.[25] Whatever the judgment on the superiority of the reading, 4QDan^a in fact has]וׄכׄתבא יקרא[at the point where it should follow יתקרי in 5:12.

4QDan^b has an even smaller fragment, but with equally clear and important results. The two-line fragment has only one complete letter and eight partial letters. Fortunately, all but one of the partial letters can be identified with near certainty, and, though not one letter of line 2 agrees with the MT, the fragment must be placed at 5:12.[26] Line 1 agrees with both 4QDan^a and the MT. Line 2 reads]א וכתׄ[, and, based on the spatial controls provided by three other nearby fragments in the same column, its text may be restored as:

[כען דניאל יתקר]א וכתׄ[בא יקרא ופשרה יהחוה].

The results of this second pair of overlapping fragments provide strong confirmation of our earlier finding — that 4QDan^a and 4QDan^b share variant readings in common against the MT. Indeed, it may be asserted now that 4QDan^a and 4QDan^b stand in agreement against the MT in four readings, all of which are pluses relative to the MT, all (with the quite possible exception of וכתבא יקרא) are secondary additions, and all (with the possible exception of קרנים 2°) are predictable. In contrast, neither of the two Qumran manuscripts ever agrees with the MT in a textual variant against the other Qumran manuscript, whereas the Old Greek agrees with 4QDan^a and 4QDan^b against the MT in two of the four readings.

Conclusion

We have examined the orthography of the Masoretic Text and of the two larger manuscripts of Daniel from Qumran, 4QDan^a and 4QDan^b, and then inquired into the nature of the interrelationship of these texts at points where all three are extant and able to be compared.

We found that 4QDan^a and 4QDan^b each have orthographic tendencies but that they do not have a consistent orthographic system. The examination also revealed that the MT has orthographic tendencies but that it too does not have a consistent orthographic system. Though for an individual reading, comparison with a Qumran manuscript may show the MT as displaying a

25. An interesting, but not decisive (because of general orthographic inconsistency), factor is that ופשרה appears incorrect in the MT without כתבא preceding. It could, of course, be argued casuistically that the queen may be speaking elliptically.

26. For the detailed argument see the 4QDan^b edition, p. 7.

certain orthographic feature, the MT not infrequently displays in another verse the contrasting feature that marked the Qumran reading. Thus, orthography in both the Qumran manuscripts and the MT of Daniel is partly stable but somewhat fluid. A specific conclusion that emerged is that 4QDan^a and the MT have similar orthographic practices in common against the generally more liberal use by 4QDan^b of *matres lectionis.* In all six orthographic differences where both 4QDan^a and 4QDan^b are extant, 4QDan^a agrees with the MT against 4QDan^b.

That pattern of agreement changed dramatically when we moved from orthography to textual interrelationships. Although in orthography 4QDan^a always agrees with the MT against 4QDan^b, in all four textual variants that occur where the two Qumran manuscripts have extant fragments which overlap, 4QDan^a and 4QDan^b always share the same text against the MT. Due to the fragmentary nature of the evidence, only one agreement is fully certain, but strong evidence is extant for the other three, and the most cogent interpretation is surely to conclude that 4QDan^a and 4QDan^b agree in four longer readings against the MT.

Moreover, since neither Qumran manuscript agrees with the MT in a single reading against the other Qumran manuscript, we can conclude that 4QDan^a and 4QDan^b stand in one text tradition over against that exemplified in the Masoretic *textus receptus.*

We can venture further, now beyond the area of what can be documented, and suggest the following possibility. We have seen that in textual affiliation 4QDan^a and 4QDan^b stand in one text tradition in contrast to the MT, and that 4QDan^b in both palaeographic script and orthographic profile — including the active insertion of supralinear *matres lectionis* by the scribe — is a later and more developed manuscript than 4QDan^a. Given this pair of facts, the fertile suggestion arises that 4QDan^b may have been copied[27] from 4QDan^a (or at least from a very closely related manuscript)[28] by a scribe who was intent upon reproducing the text in the more contemporary, more full and clear and interpretative orthography of the late Second Temple period.

27. Though by no means conclusive, it is an additional supporting argument that for the eight lines where the two Qumran manuscripts overlap in the Dan 8:1-5 passage, five lines actually end with exactly the same word. And if the scribe of 4QDan^a had not erred by confusing the introduction to chap. 8 with the introduction to chap. 10 — an error that the scribe of 4QDan^b would have immediately recognized and not copied — seven of those eight lines would exactly coincide.

28. If from "a closely related manuscript," of course that would add a third, probably Qumran, manuscript to the 4QDan^a-4QDan^b text family.

PART 2

THE SCROLLS, THE SEPTUAGINT, AND THE OLD LATIN

CHAPTER 9

The Septuagint Manuscripts from Qumran: A Reappraisal of Their Value

There were eight Septuagint or Septuagint-related manuscripts found at Qumran and, though none was found at Masada or Murabbaʿat, a ninth was found at Naḥal Ḥever (Wadi Ḥabra):

4Q119	4QLXXLev[a]	[Rahlfs 801]
4Q120	pap4QLXXLev[b]	[Rahlfs 802]
4Q121	4QLXXNum	[Rahlfs 803]
4Q122	4QLXXDeut	[Rahlfs 819]
4Q126	4QUnid gr	
4Q127	pap4QparaExod gr	
7Q1	pap7QExod	[Rahlfs 805]
7Q2	pap7QEpJer	[Rahlfs 804]
	8ḤevXIIgr	[Rahlfs 943]

It is a pleasure to thank the Rev. Prof. Barnabas Lindars, SSF, and Dr. George Brooke for their invitation to present this paper at the University of Manchester, and to thank the University of Notre Dame and the National Endowment for the Humanities for their support of the long-term work that this paper represents.

The editions of the LXX manuscripts have been accepted by Oxford University Press. As a service to scholars, variants and other information from the editions are presented here. Although the present article may appear before the more complex DJD volume does, the rights remain with Oxford University Press.

All these Greek manuscripts have been published or submitted for publication in Discoveries in the Judaean Desert.[1] Patrick Skehan had prepared editions of 4QLXXLev[a], pap4QLXXLev[b], and 4QLXXNum and published editions of the first and the last prior to his death on September 9, 1980. I published 4QLXXDeut along with a list of all the variants of the LXX manuscripts from Qumran in 1984. The larger fragments of the unidentified papyrus with the Exodus motif (4Q127) have recently been published in the Festschrift honoring our colleague and symbolic ἄρχων in the world of the Septuagint, Robert Hanhart. Maurice Baillet published the tiny fragments from Cave 7 in 1982. And Emanuel Tov's publication of the Greek Minor Prophets scroll appeared in 1990.

John Wevers, with whom both Skehan and I communicated and shared our work on the Cave 4 LXX manuscripts as it developed, included that evidence in his Göttingen editions of *Leviticus* and *Numeri*,[2] and in 1982 he published an article that examined the variants in 4QLXXNum.[3] I am un-

1. The publications of the Greek scrolls are as follows:

4QLXXLev[a]: P. W. Skehan, "The Qumran Manuscripts and Textual Criticism," in *Volume du congrès, Strasbourg 1956* (VTSup 4; Leiden: Brill, 1957) 148-60, esp. 157-60;

4QLXXNum: P. W. Skehan, "4QLXXNum: A Pre-Christian Reworking of the Septuagint," *HTR* 70 (1977) 39-50; partial publication: Skehan, "The Qumran Manuscripts and Textual Criticism," esp. 155-57;

4QLXXDeut plus the variants from all the LXX Exodus-Deuteronomy scrolls: E. Ulrich, "The Greek Manuscripts of the Pentateuch from Qumrân, Including Newly-Identified Fragments of Deuteronomy (4QLXXDeut)," in *De Septuaginta: Studies in Honour of John William Wevers on His Sixty-Fifth Birthday* (ed. A. Pietersma and C. Cox; Mississauga, Ont.: Benben, 1984) 71-82;

pap4QparaExod gr: E. Ulrich, "A Greek Paraphrase of Exodus on Papyrus from Qumran Cave 4," in *Studien zur Septuaginta — Robert Hanhart zu Ehren* (ed. D. Fraenkel, U. Quast, and J. W. Wevers; Göttingen: Vandenhoeck & Ruprecht, 1990) 287-94;

pap7QExod and pap7QEpJer: Baillet in M. Baillet, J. T. Milik, and R. de Vaux, *Les 'petites grottes' de Qumrân* (DJD 3; Oxford: Clarendon, 1962) 142-33 and plate 30;

8ḤevXIIgr: Emanuel Tov with R. A. Kraft, *The Greek Minor Prophets Scroll from Naḥal Ḥever (8ḤevXIIgr)* (DJD 8; Oxford: Clarendon, 1990); preliminary publication: D. Barthélemy, *Les devanciers d'Aquila* (VTSup 10; Leiden: Brill, 1963) 163-78.

2. J. W. Wevers, ed., *Leviticus* (Septuaginta: Vetus Testamentum Graecum II.2; Göttingen: Vandenhoeck & Ruprecht, 1986); *Numeri* (Septuaginta: Vetus Testamentum Graecum III.1; Göttingen: Vandenhoeck & Ruprecht, 1982).

3. J. W. Wevers, "An Early Revision of the Septuagint of Numbers," *Eretz-Israel* 16: *H. M. Orlinsky Volume* (Jerusalem: Israel Exploration Society, 1982) 235*-39*.

aware that anyone, with the single exception of Wevers, has analyzed the list of variants from the Qumran Greek manuscripts published in 1984 and used its evidence for refining our knowledge of the history of the LXX. I described the purpose of that article as "simply the attempt at objective presentation of the data, not the analysis of their significance . . ." and confessed that I would "undoubtedly fail to resist proposing such an analysis in a future study."[4]

In this article I now propose to analyze some of those variants. First, the variants of 4QLXXLev^a will be studied methodically. Secondly, as a result of that study some reflections will be required concerning the Hebrew text(s) that lay behind the Old Greek translation (OG) and other Greek witnesses. Thirdly, some of the variants of 4QLXXNum will be studied. And finally, conclusions will be offered reevaluating the significance of the variants of these two manuscripts.

At least one caveat should preface this analysis. Throughout the article texts will be compared and terms used such as "the scroll," "the Masoretic Text," and "the LXX." In order not to become engulfed in a constant quagmire of qualifications, it will be necessary to focus on a particular Qumran text, on the MT, and on the edition of the LXX edited by John Wevers ($\mathfrak{G}^{ed}$). But it must constantly be borne in mind that all texts are quite stratified — they contain many original readings, a certain number of unique errors, a certain number of errors inherited from parent texts, usually some intentional expansions or clarifications, and often some revisions (whether fresh or inherited) for a variety of purposes. It is perfectly logical, therefore, to maintain that the same text is original in one reading and secondary in the very next reading. We need not, however, accept the hypothesis that correction of the original Greek toward the Hebrew text that became dominant in the Masoretic *textus receptus* is randomly scattered. For example, it is a plausible hypothesis that 4QLXXLev^a might represent a revision toward proto-MT of a text like that transmitted in the fourth-century Codex Vaticanus ($\mathfrak{G}^B$); conversely, it is also a plausible hypothesis that the text in $\mathfrak{G}^B$ might represent a revision toward proto-MT of a text like that in 4QLXXLev^a. But it is implausible that both 4QLXXLev^a and $\mathfrak{G}^B$ could each be revised toward proto-MT in 40 to 50 percent of their readings. That is, although all texts are to a certain degree mixed texts and systematic revision toward the eventually dominant MT is to be expected in certain early texts, such revision is not to be expected to have permeated one text in half measure and a different text in different half measure.

4. Ulrich, "The Greek Manuscripts," 82.

The Variant Readings of 4QLXXLev^{a}

For the purposes of this article a "variant reading" will be any reading, beyond the purely orthographical, preserved on the extant Qumran fragments which differs from 𝔊^{ed}, 𝔊^{B}, or the MT. There are sixteen such variants in 4QLXXLev^{a}.[5] For each variant the lemma will present the reading of 4QLXXLev^{a}; the readings of 𝔊^{ed}, the MT, the Samaritan Pentateuch (𝔪), and other relevant versions will be distributed as their affiliation dictates. Comments will follow on aspects of the translation and variants, especially the question whether an alternate Hebrew text might lie behind the OG or might have influenced the Greek variants. Then the following pair of contrasting possibilities will be explored and articulated: (a) If the reading in 𝔊^{ed} represents the original Old Greek translation (OG), then how is the reading in 4QLXXLev^{a} to be explained? (b) If the reading in 4QLXXLev^{a} is the OG, then how is the reading in 𝔊^{ed} to be explained? A decision between the possibilities will be postponed until all the variants have been reviewed and the reflections in the second part of the essay have been considered.

Lev 26:4 [τον υετον τ]ηι γηι υμων 𝔗^{J} (מיטריא דארעכון)] τον υετον υμιν 𝔊^{ed} = **גשמיכם** MT𝔪 (cf. Ezek 34:26)

𝔊^{ed} is a correct, but not completely literal, translation of the Hebrew as represented in MT𝔪, whereas 4QLXXLev^{a} can be seen as a free translation of the sense of the same Hebrew. Occurrences, however, such as **מטר־ארצך** = τον υετον τη γη σου in the similar list of covenant blessings in Deut 28:12, demonstrate that 4QLXXLev^{a} could also be reflecting more literally a different Hebrew *Vorlage. Targum Pseudo-Jonathan* could also be a reflection of the same Hebrew that lay behind 4QLXXLev^{a}, or it could be a similar but independent expansion.

(a) If 𝔊^{ed} is original, then it should be seen as a translation of a text like MT𝔪, and 4QLXXLev^{a} is either a legitimate, free translation of the same Hebrew or a literal reflection of a slightly different Hebrew *Vorlage.* (b) If 4QLXXLev^{a} is original, then 𝔊^{ed} is probably the result of a revision toward MT.

5. Only fifteen variants are listed in Ulrich, "The Greek Manuscripts," 78-79. The additional variant (see και εσομ[αι] in Lev 26:12 below) occurs on a tiny fragment identified subsequently to that 1984 article.

Lev 26:4 τον ξυλινον καρ∘[ ] (καρπον?) } τα ξυλα (ξυλινα G-426) των πεδιων αποδωσει τον καρπον αυτων $\mathfrak{G}^{ed}$ = (ו)עץ השדה יתן פריו MT𝔪

$\mathfrak{G}^{ed}$ is again a correct, almost literal, translation of MT𝔪, whereas 4QLXXLev^{a} is a free translation of the sense, though it would apparently have read "the land will give its produce and its arboreal fruit" in contrast to "the land will give its produce, and the trees of the fields will give their fruit." With regard to the Hebrew *Vorlage*, the similar phrase του καρπου του ξυλινου = מפרי העץ in the next chapter (Lev 27:30) shows that 4QLXXLev^{a} may depend upon a slightly different Hebrew text.

(a) If $\mathfrak{G}^{ed}$ is original, then it would be a literal translation of a text like MT𝔪, and the scroll would be either a free translation of the same Hebrew or possibly a literal reflection of a different Hebrew *Vorlage*. (b) If the scroll is original, then it is either a legitimate, free translation of the same Hebrew as MT𝔪 or possibly a literal reflection of a different Hebrew *Vorlage*, and $\mathfrak{G}^{ed}$ is probably the result of a revision toward the MT.

Lev 26:5 αμητος A B* 121 MSS Philo Aeth } αλοητος $\mathfrak{G}^{ed}$ = דיש MT𝔪

דיש as a noun (= αλοητος, "threshing") is a *hapax legomenon* in the MT, occurring only here. The verbal root (דוש = αλοαν) occurs five times, including twice in Judges (8:7 and 8:16). In the latter two instances the meaning is metaphorical, and $\mathfrak{G}^{A}$ translates metaphorically with καταξαινειν "crush to pieces," a correct but more free rendering instead of the more literal αλοαν. Illustrating the problems we are dealing with throughout, the MT in Judg 8:16 presumably errs with a divergent Hebrew reading, וידע for וידש (*ʿayin* for *šin*).[6] Note also מתאב, an error in the MT for מתעב at Amos 6:8, discussed under Lev 26:11 below.

αμητος is most often used for קציר ("harvest"). It is possible that קציר occurred in the Hebrew *Vorlage* (or was mistaken for בציר two words later), though there is no proof. But in principle, there is no more reason to suspect that the substitution of "harvest" for "threshing" or vice versa should occur at the Greek stage than at the Hebrew stage. If the word (whether דיש or קציר) was clear in the Hebrew text being translated, the translator certainly knew both the meaning of the Hebrew word and the proper Greek word for it, and could have produced a precise translation. If there was no paleographic error

6. For an alternate, well-argued explanation based on the root ידע II "be submissive," see Barnabas Lindars, "Some Septuagint Readings in Judges," *JTS* [n.s.] 22 (1971) 1-14; and earlier, D. Winton Thomas, "The Root ידע in Hebrew," *JTS* 35 (1934) 298-306.

(ΑΛΟΗΤΟΣ > ΑΛΛΗΤΟΣ), then the substitution was made on the basis of sense or common usage. Note similar variation in Amos 9:13, some of which might be due to cross-influence.

Either (1) αλοητος is the OG, correctly translating the Hebrew preserved in MT$\mathfrak{m}$, but then the variant αμητος is difficult to explain except as a revision toward an undocumented Hebrew variant; or (2) αμητος is the OG, attested by the earliest witnesses, and αλοητος is a revision toward MT$\mathfrak{m}$.

(a) If $\mathfrak{G}^{ed}$ is original, then it is simply the accurate translation of a Hebrew text like MT$\mathfrak{m}$, and the scroll is either a paleographic error, or a smoothing of the text (from the less frequent to the more frequent expression), or even a correction toward a Hebrew text with קציר in place of דיש. (b) If the scroll is original, then $\mathfrak{G}^{ed}$ would be a revision toward the MT.

Lev 26:5, 6 [κ]αι πολεμος — [υμων 3°] ad fin 6 *O* mss La^{100} (πολεμος] *gladius* La^{100}) Arab Co Syh = MT$\mathfrak{m}$ (και πολεμος] וחרב MT$\mathfrak{m}$) } ad fin 5 $\mathfrak{G}^{ed}$; ad fin 5 et 6 A B^{mg} F M′ mss

This clause fits better at the end of verse 6, but it fits adequately at the end of either verse, while arguments can also be adduced against its position at the end of either verse. The best way to explain the variant positions in $\mathfrak{G}$ is to see the problem at the Hebrew stage. On the one hand, the clause may have been a secondary insertion into the early Hebrew; the "few chasing many" motif is found without the "war" motif in Deut 32:20, Josh 23:10, and Isa 30:17. On the other hand, the clause may have been original but omitted through parablepsis (בארצכם⁀בארצכם if at the end of verse 5; ורדפ־⁀וחרב if at the end of verse 6) and reinserted in the margin of a Hebrew text; then Hebrew manuscripts could have inserted it in either of the two places. The point of interest here is that the OG would have translated it at whichever point it occurred in the OG *Vorlage*, and subsequent Greek manuscripts would have placed it wherever their respective Hebrew texts (if any) had it.[7]

(a) If $\mathfrak{G}^{ed}$ is original, I would suggest that its order is due to its being translated from a Hebrew *Vorlage* that had that order; then the scroll would be seen as a correction toward a Hebrew text whose order was that attested by the MT. (b) If the scroll is original, then it should be seen as an accurate translation of a Hebrew text like the MT, and $\mathfrak{G}^{ed}$ would be either an unintentional

7. For the issue of the placement of this clause at the end of v. 6 or v. 5, the detailed question whether πολεμος is a free rendering of חרב or possibly a more literal rendering of קרב (see Job 38:23; Ps 68[67]:31[30]; 78[77]:9; Dan o′ θ′ 7:21; Qoh 9:18) need not be settled here.

displacement or a correction toward an early variant Hebrew that similarly could be an unintentional displacement.

Lev 26:6 [ο]εκφοβων / υμας F MSS Arm Syh (υμας sub ÷) = 𝔗^{P} } tr 𝔊^{ed} (sub ÷ G); > υμας Bo = **מחריד** MT𝔪𝔗^{O}

On one level this is an insignificant reading, for it seems unrelated to the Hebrew. In none of the twelve occurrences of **ואין מחריד** throughout the MT is there a direct object expressed in Hebrew, and usually the Greek does not include one. But the OG here appears to have added the direct object for sense (cf. also 𝔊Jer 26[MT46]:27), and the alternate tradition appears to have transposed for reasons of style. On another level, however, this reading serves to illustrate another type of variant that must be kept in mind — purely inner-Greek variants. This means that extra caution must be used, for at times variants may be purely inner-Greek yet independently happen to agree with the MT or some ancient manuscript and thus be assigned to false causes.

Lev 26:8 πεντε υμων Syh (π. εξ υ.) } εξ υμων πεντε 𝔊^{ed}; **מכם חמשה** MT𝔪

Both are correct translations of MT𝔪, but the reading of the scroll appears more natural, whereas that of 𝔊^{ed} is a more closely literal reflection of the MT. Is a variant Hebrew *Vorlage* for the scroll's reading likely? It is possible, but there is no reason to suppose so.

(a) If 𝔊^{ed} is original, then the scroll is to be seen as a stylistic revision. (b) If the scroll is original, then 𝔊^{ed} is probably a revision toward the MT.

Lev 26:9 [και εσται μο]υ η διαθηκη εν υμιν[ ] } και στησω την διαθηκην μου μεθ υμων (διαθ. υμιν *b; . . . pactum meum in uobis* Arm^{te}) 𝔊^{ed} Aeth Arm Bo = **והקימתי את בריתי אתכם** MT𝔪

The nominative in the scroll requires that η διαθηκη be the subject of its verb. The scroll's reading probably reflects a Hebrew not far from **והי(ת)ה בריתי בתוככם** (cf. Ezek 37:26) or **ובריתי אתכם** — note **והרביתי אתכם** (!) just before **והקימתי** in the MT.

(a) If 𝔊^{ed} is original, then it is to be seen as a literal translation of a text like the MT, and the scroll is either a revision toward an alternate, undocumented Hebrew, a revision for style or theological nuance, or an error. (b) If the scroll is original, then 𝔊^{ed} quite probably must be seen as a revision toward the MT.

Lev 26:10 [εξοισετ]ε μετα των νεων] εκ προσωπου νεων εξοισετε $\mathfrak{G}^{ed}$ = מפני חדש תוציאו MT𝔪

4QLXXLev^{a} could be freely translating a Hebrew text identical with the MT, a slightly different text, or even a text such as תוציאו עם חדש, whereas $\mathfrak{G}^{ed}$ is a virtually literal reflection of the MT.

(a) If $\mathfrak{G}^{ed}$ is original, then the scroll could be seen as an early revision toward a Hebrew text such as that just suggested (less likely) or as a revision for style. (b) If the scroll is original, then $\mathfrak{G}^{ed}$ quite probably must be seen as a revision toward the MT.

Lev 26:11 βδελυξομαι 126 (βδελλυξωμαι) Arab] βδελυξεται η ψυχη μου $\mathfrak{G}^{ed}$ = תגעל נפשי MT𝔪

Both readings occur in both Hebrew and Greek — βδελυσσομαι = מתאב (read מתעב, Amos 6:8) and εβδελυξατο η ψυχη αυτων = תתעב נפשם (Ps 107[$\mathfrak{G}$106]:18) — so it is difficult to decide whether the difference here is due to *Vorlage,* style, or theological influence.

(a) If $\mathfrak{G}^{ed}$ is original, then it is a literal reflection of a text like the MT or possibly a free translation of a text with אגעל, and the scroll could be seen as an early revision toward a Hebrew text with אגעל or as a revision for style. (b) If the scroll is original, then it is probably a translation from a Hebrew text such as אגעל or possibly a free translation of a text like the MT, and $\mathfrak{G}^{ed}$ probably must be seen as a revision toward the MT or as a euphemistic revision.

Lev 26:12 και εσομ[αι]] και εμπεριπατησω εν υμιν και εσομαι υμων θεος $\mathfrak{G}^{ed}$ = והתהלכתי בתוככם והייתי לכם לאלהים MT𝔪; και εμπ. εν υμιν ad fin tr 131

The scroll did not have και εμπεριπατησω εν υμιν at the beginning of this verse. It has space for about four short words to follow, but there is no way to determine whether the two clauses were transposed (with 131) or some other covenantal formula followed. In either case it is possible that it followed a different Hebrew *Vorlage.*

(a) If $\mathfrak{G}^{ed}$ is original, then it is to be seen as a close translation of a text like the MT, and the scroll presents an error (parablepsis or transposition), a revision toward an undocumented variant Hebrew text, or a theologically or stylistically altered text. (b) If the scroll is original, then it is a translation of an undocumented variant Hebrew text or an error (parablepsis or transposition), and $\mathfrak{G}^{ed}$ quite probably must be seen as a revision toward the MT.

Lev 26:12 μοι εθν[ος] } μου (μοι MSS) λαος (εις λαον *b* Arm^{te}) 𝔊^{ed} La Arm Bo 2 Cor 6:16; לי לעם MT𝔐

The preponderant usage of both the LXX and the later recensions is λαος for עם (when referring to Israel), and εθνος for גוי and for עם (when referring to peoples other than Israel). The LXX does use εθνος, however, to refer to Israel, at least once in Leviticus (19:16) where the Hebrew probably had עם, as well as in the promises to the ancestral bearers of the covenant (cf. Gen 18:18; 46:3). These latter translate גוי, it is true, but the point is that the LXX has established the occasional use of εθνος to refer to Israel, even to reflect עם. In contrast, it is very difficult to imagine εθνος being substituted — intentionally or in error — for an original λαος. Moreover, Wevers does endorse εθνος as the OG at Lev 19:16 for עם referring to Israel. Thus it would appear that εθνος was the OG translation here at 26:12, with λαος as the routine revisional substitution.

(a) If 𝔊^{ed} is original, then the scroll can only be seen as an uncanny error or unusual substitution. (b) If the scroll is original, then 𝔊^{ed} is a secondary, routine lexical revision toward the MT.

Lev 26:13 τον ζυγον το[υ δεσμου] MSS La^{100} } τον δεσμον του ζυγου 𝔊^{ed} Aeth Arm Bo; מטת על(כם) MT𝔐 (מטות עול-)

There are too many possibilities for these readings to allow a firm conclusion regarding the original translation and its subsequent fate. There are both literal and figurative meanings of both nouns in addition to both literal and figurative meanings as understood by later editors and later copyists at the transmission stage, plus the possibility of interference from Ezek 34:27. Thus, the reading is best left as questionable and able to be decided in either direction.

Lev 26:14 μου 2° MSS La^{100} Aeth Bo } + ταυτα 𝔊^{ed} Arm = האלה MT𝔐

The scroll reads well without ταυτα, and there is no reason to suspect it was intentionally or accidentally omitted, whereas the word seems superfluous in 𝔊^{ed} and is best interpreted as a revision toward the MT.

Lev 26:15 αλ[λα] 1° 𝔊^{ed} La Aeth Arm Bo } ואם MT𝔐; אם MT^{MSS} 𝔐^{MSS} 𝔖 𝔗

The OG, this time with all Greek manuscripts in agreement, had αλλα as a good and free translation of the meaning of (ו)אם in its context.

Lev 26:15 [προστα]/γμασι μου } κριμασιν μου 𝔊[ed] La Aeth Arm Bo; משפטי MT𝔪

The OG three times uses προσταγμα for משפט in Leviticus (see 18:26, 19:37, and later in this chapter, 26:46), but it also uses κριμα five times for משפט in Leviticus (including verses 15 and 43 in this chapter, but note κριμα for חק in verse 46). For θ′ and α′, however, κριμα became the recensional lexeme for משפט, whereas προσταγμα became the recensional lexeme for חק or פקוד. Thus, if one of the variants should be recensional, it would be κριμασιν.

(a) If 𝔊[ed] is original, then the scroll simply presents the substitution of a synonym, intentional or not. (b) If the scroll is original, then 𝔊[ed] could also be simply a synonym, or it could be a secondary, routine recensional lexical revision toward the MT.

Lev 26:15 α[λλα ωστε?] } ωστε (2°) 𝔊[ed] = (ל(הפרכם MT𝔪; και ωστε 392 Aeth; και 44 75 Arm

This final reading is too uncertain to bear the weight of any solid argument or conclusion.

The Hebrew *Vorlage* Behind the Greek Translation

Having studied the variant readings preserved by 4QLXXLev[a] and suggested two possible vantage points from which to understand their interrelationship, it is tempting to draw a conclusion concerning which approach commends itself as more cogent. But first some explicit reflection on the character of the Hebrew text lying behind the Greek variants may help provide a more informed conclusion.

It is gratifying to note that a sophisticated, up-to-date understanding of the Hebrew *Vorlage* for the Septuagint has reached wide international scope. The parade example is Emanuel Tov's justly celebrated monograph, *The Text-Critical Use of the Septuagint in Biblical Research,*[8] but numerous others come to mind, only a few of which can be mentioned here. Anneli Aejmelaeus, in an article which offers both judicious breadth and specialized focus on the text of Exodus, concludes:

8. E. Tov, *The Text-Critical Use of the Septuagint in Biblical Research* (Jerusalem Biblical Studies 3; Jerusalem: Simor, 1981).

> All in all, the scholar who wishes to attribute deliberate changes, harmonizations, completion of details and new accents to the translator is under the obligation to prove [that] thesis with weighty arguments and also to show why the divergences cannot have originated with the *Vorlage.* That the translator *may* have manipulated his original does not mean that he necessarily did so. All that is known of the translation techniques employed in the Septuagint points firmly enough in the opposite direction.[9]

Julio Trebolle, in a series of books and articles concentrating on Samuel-Kings, has demonstrated repeatedly that a Hebrew text divergent from the Masoretic *textus receptus* both explains the translation of the OG and at times provides a superior Hebrew text.[10] Sharon Pace Jeansonne has provided analogous demonstrations for the book of Daniel, showing that the claim of "Theological *Tendenz*" on the part of the Greek translator cannot be maintained.[11]

In 1980 Zaki Aly and Ludwig Koenen published an edition of P. Fouad 266, and in the introduction Koenen says:

> the appearance of the new rolls was hailed by R. Hanhart [in *OLZ* 73 (1978) 39-46, esp. 40] as the beginning of a new era of studies in the text of the *Septuagint.* P. Fouad 266, indeed, shows that already in the middle of the first century B.C. the text of the Greek *Genesis* and *Deuteronomy* was basically steady, though the results of continuous attempts to bring the Greek text into closer accord with the Hebrew are clearly recognizable. Therefore, agreements between the new papyri and the Masoretic text against the majority of the best manuscripts of the later tradition do not necessarily establish what may be regarded as the original text of the Septuagint, but may very well result from later assimilations. Textual criticism of the same type as is known from the Christian era and is particularly connected with the name of Origen had already begun in the first century B.C., if not even earlier. This should be of no surprise. As soon as

9. A. Aejmelaeus, "What Can We Know about the Hebrew *Vorlage* of the Septuagint?" *ZAW* 99 (1987) 58-89, esp. 71.

10. See, most recently, J. Trebolle Barrera, *Centena in libros Samuelis et Regum: Variantes textuales y composición literaria en los libros de Samuel y Reyes* (Madrid: Consejo Superior de Investigaciones Científicas, 1989); idem, "Redaction, Recension, and Midrash in the Books of Kings," *BIOSCS* 15 (1982) 12-35; and idem, "From the 'Old Latin' through the 'Old Greek' to the 'Old Hebrew' (2 Kings 10:23-35)," *Textus* 11 (1984) 17-36.

11. S. Pace Jeansonne, *The Old Greek Translation of Daniel 7–12* (CBQMS 19; Washington, D.C.: Catholic Biblical Association, 1988); see also S. Pace, "The Stratigraphy of the Text of Daniel and the Question of Theological *Tendenz* in the Old Greek," *BIOSCS* 17 (1984) 15-35.

> an authoritative Greek translation existed, attempts must have started to improve it and to eliminate discrepancies between the Greek and the Hebrew.[12]

It is from this perspective — that Greek texts must be evaluated in light of the possibility that they represent a faithful translation of an ancient Hebrew text at variance with the Masoretic *textus receptus* — that I propose a reassessment of the value of the variants of the LXX manuscripts from Qumran.

I have high respect for John Wevers's work, both because he has produced eleven volumes on the Greek text of the Pentateuch,[13] and because as a personal friend I know what a learned and indefatigable worker he is. But on this one point it seems that a review of the evidence is in order, since (1) 4QLXXLev[a] is a pre-Christian witness three or four centuries earlier than our other Greek witnesses to Leviticus, (2) none of its variants are "errors" but are intelligible alternate readings, yet (3) none of its readings are selected as representing the OG.

Wevers, of course, is aware of the possibility of an alternate Hebrew parent text as the basis of the Old Greek of Leviticus:

> A Masoretic text of the entire Hebrew canon is available, and though it is not the exact form of the text which the translators rendered into Greek, it is an invaluable guide to it. The editor usually knows the parent text which was being translated and this serves as a reliable guide for eliminating various scribal errors from the Greek text tradition.[14]

Thus the question becomes whether and when an alternate Hebrew is considered the source of specific variants. As an example let us consider three instances concerning which preposition among attested variants is to be selected as the OG. In the *Text History of the Greek Leviticus,* Wevers says, "Prepositions occasionally create problems, though the critical text can often be determined by reading the Hebrew text."[15] First, in discussing Lev 24:8 (παρα vs. ενωπιον), he says, "The lectio difficilior which renders the MT liter-

12. Z. Aly with L. Koenen, *Three Rolls of the Early Septuagint: Genesis and Deuteronomy* (Papyrologische Texte und Abhandlungen 27; Bonn: R. Habelt, 1980) 1-2.

13. In addition to the five critical editions of the Greek Genesis–Deuteronomy and the five companion text-history volumes, see his recent *Notes on the Greek Text of Exodus* (SBLSCS 30; Atlanta: Scholars Press, 1990).

14. J. W. Wevers, "II. Die Methode," in *Das Göttinger Septuaginta-Unternehmen* (Göttingen: Vandenhoeck & Ruprecht, 1977) 18.

15. J. W. Wevers, *Text History of the Greek Leviticus* (Göttingen: Vandenhoeck & Ruprecht, 1986) 76.

ally is here to be preferred."[16] In this instance I do not disagree with the choice of παρα but rather pause at the reason adduced; παρα may render the MT (מאת) literally, but does that mean that παρα is necessarily the OG rather than a secondary revision of the OG back toward proto-MT? More importantly, when using the criterion "determined by reading the Hebrew text," is *the* Hebrew text presumed to be the MT?

For a second instance, at Lev 1:15 (προς 1° vs. επι),[17] again I do not disagree but rather stress that in such cases, just as it is necessary to check the meaning involved, so too is it equally necessary to consider whether an inadvertent אל vs. על variant in the *Vorlage* lies at the root of the Greek variant. The אל vs. על confusion of laryngeals is frequent in the text transmitted in the MT,[18] as it is in the ancient manuscripts from Qumran.[19]

For the third instance I do disagree. At Deut 31:5 the MT has the frequent promise, ונתנם יהוה לפניכם ("The Lord will give [your enemies] into your power"). There are three Greek variants: ενωπιον υμων, υμιν, and εις τας χειρας υμων, and Wevers selects και παρεδωκεν αυτους κυριος <u>ενωπιον υμων</u> as the OG translation. In his *Text History of the Greek Deuteronomy,* after discussing another locus where the decision on the originality of υμιν was difficult, Wevers says:

> Much simpler to decide is the case of υμιν in 31:5 where for Deut ενωπιον υμων, [Vaticanus and other witnesses] read υμιν. The verb modified is παρεδωκεν. The difficult παρεδωκεν . . . ενωπιον υμων, which is a literal equivalent to the MT, was smoothed out by the change. The same kind of simplification took place in [the hexaplaric and other witnesses] where εις τας χειρας υμων was substituted for ενωπιον υμων.[20]

Thus, ενωπιον υμων is viewed as original, and υμιν and εις τας χειρας υμων the results of smoothing and simplification.

Here there is evidence for the alternate choice. Hellenophiles who usually wear a slight wince when reading some of the Greek found in the Septua-

16. *Text History of the Greek Leviticus,* 77.

17. Ibid.

18. Note also, e.g., the מתאב error in the MT (for מתעב) in Amos 6:8 discussed under Lev 26:11 above.

19. At 2 Sam 14:30 the MT and 4QSam^c each make this same error in different words within a single line; see E. Ulrich, "4QSam^c: A Fragmentary Manuscript of 2 Samuel 14–15 from the Scribe of the *Serek Hay-yahad* (1QS)," *BASOR* 235 (1979) 1-25, esp. pp. 3, 7, 14 (2 Sam 14:30; 15:3 [column II, lines 12, 24]).

20. J. W. Wevers, *Text History of the Greek Deuteronomy* (Göttingen: Vandenhoeck & Ruprecht, 1978) 127.

gint do not wince noticeably more at παρεδωκεν . . . ενωπιον υμων than at numerous other parts of the translation. It is hard to escape the suspicion that Wevers presumes that the לפניכם found in the MT was the reading that the OG translator saw in the Hebrew copy being translated. The same sentence, however, occurs elsewhere in Deuteronomy, and at one occurrence (Deut 7:23) where the MT has לפניך and 4QpaleoDeut^{r} also has לפניך, another Deuteronomy scroll has בידך. These may be viewed as synonymous variants. When one seeks the OG translation, one finds only εις τας χειρας σου (without relevant variant) in the manuscript tradition. I would maintain that probability rests on בידך as the Hebrew word in the text (or at least in the mind) of the OG translator at that point, and that the OG translator translated faithfully. We do not need the Qumran evidence, however, for the ⅏ had already taught us this lesson: in Deut 2:36 where the MT has (. . . נתן) לפנינו, the OG has εις τας χειρας ημων (without relevant variant), and the ⅏ has בידנו — quite probably the word encountered in the Hebrew text used by the OG translator.

Such examples are frequent and widespread, a small sampling of which follows:

Exod 1:5	4QExod^{b}	חמש ושבעים נפש
	MT	שבעים נפש
	𝔊	ψυχαι . . . πεντε και εβδομηκοντα
		75/70 people
Lev 3:1	4QLev^{b}	קרבנו ליהוה
(cf. 2:12, 14)	MT	קרבנו
	𝔊	το δωρον αυτου τω κυριω
		his offering (+ to the Lord)
2 Sam 10:6	4QSam^{a}	[וא]ישטוב (= error)
Jos. *Ant.* 7.121	MT	ואיש טוב
	𝔊	και Ειστωβ (Ιστοβον Josephus)
		the men of Tob
2 Sam 7:23	4QSam^{a}	ואהלים (= error)
[*om* 1 Chr 17:21]	MT	ואלהיו
	𝔊	και σκηνωματα
		tents/its gods

Isa 23:1-2	4QIsa[a]	[2]למוׄדמוׄ
	MT	לָמוֹ: [2]דֹּמּוּ
	𝔊	[2]τινι ομοιοι γεγονασιν
		(= [2]למי דמו)
		[2]*Who are they like . . . ?*
		/ to them.[2] Be still!
Dan 8:3	4QDan[b]	[איל א]חׄד גׄדול
	MT θ′	איל אחד
	𝔊	κριον ενα μεγαν
		a (+ great) ram
Dan 8:4	4QDan[a]	W, E, N, S
	MT θ′	W, N, S
	𝔊	E, N, W, S (E, W, N, S 967)
		West, East, North, South

The conclusion to be drawn is that there was a wide variety of Hebrew texts available and in use when the OG translation of the various books was made and for several centuries during the early transmission of the OG. One must treat the elasticity of the Hebrew text with caution, to be sure, but one also must not underrate the variation in the Hebrew text abundantly demonstrated by the Qumran manuscripts and the versions. To underrate it will cause distortion in the understanding of the LXX and the forces behind its translation and transmission.

The Variant Readings of 4QLXXNum

With those general reflections on the Hebrew *Vorlage* of the LXX, we can now turn to 4QLXXNum. There are seventeen variants in 4QLXXNum, thirteen of which are unique, only four finding support in other Greek manuscripts.[21] Again, only one — where 𝔊[B] has an obvious error and 4QLXXNum has strong support from the manuscript tradition — is accepted in the Göttingen critical edition as an attestation of the OG. Some of the variants in 4QLXXNum are of minor significance, some remain ambiguous. The value of 4QLXXNum as a witness to the OG will hinge primarily on four variants (viewing the fourfold occurrence of αρτηρ- vs. αναφορ- as one variant).

21. See "The Greek Manuscripts," 80-81.

Num 3:40 αριθμησον] επισκεψαι 𝔊^ed; פקד MT𝔐

Five factors point with varying degrees of strength to αριθμησον as the OG.

(1) Lagarde had discovered the general, but not universal, rule of thumb that if two variants occur in the manuscript tradition, both correct and acceptable, one in literal agreement with the MT and the other more free, then the freer rendering is (other things being equal) to be selected as the OG and the literal rendering is to be seen as secondary revision toward the MT (see points 3 and 4 below).

(2) No evidence surfaces to question Αριθμοι as the original Greek title of the book, and the title surely derives from occurrences of the word in the text.[22]

(3) επισκεπτεσθαι became the standard recensional equivalent for פקד, while αριθμειν was used for מנה. Thus, where פקד occurs in the Hebrew with επισκεπτεσθαι/αριθμειν in the Greek witnesses, if recensional revision is at work, αριθμειν is probably the OG and επισκεπτεσθαι the recensional revision.[23]

(4) Consider the way translators and revisers work. If the translator sees פקד in the Hebrew of Numbers and is translating fresh, both επισκεπτεσθαι (as a literal translation) and αριθμειν (as a freer, contextual translation, suggested by the title and content of the book plus occurrences as early as 1:2b) are options, as are other possible words. If a reviser sees פקד in proto-MT and is revising the OG back toward that Hebrew text, one might (as θ′ and α′ certainly would) change αριθμειν to επισκεπτεσθαι; there would be no reason to change επισκεπτεσθαι to αριθμειν on the basis of the Hebrew. If one is copying the Greek text from another Greek text without reference to the Hebrew, one might change επισκεπτεσθαι to αριθμειν for contextual meaning. Thus, αριθμειν is due either to the original translation stage or to the later Greek transmission stage, but it is not due to the recensional stage.

(5) Finally, 2 Sam 24:1-9 narrating David's census has both αριθμειν and επισκεπτεσθαι. Insofar as this passage falls in a section usually considered recensional, the most logical explanation would be that the occurrences of both αριθμειν and επισκεπτεσθαι together represent the OG unrevised in that

22. H. B. Swete (*An Introduction to the Old Testament in Greek* [rev. ed. by R. R. Ottley; New York: Ktav, 1968] 214-15) considers the Greek titles "probably of Alexandrian origin and pre-Christian in use" and notes that some of them are used in Philo and the NT.

23. This is not, of course, a decisive argument, for a principle of the recensionists was to choose one of the several OG precedents and standardize it as the recensional equivalent. But it is nonetheless an argument.

passage, and that this in turn argues in favor of αριθμειν in 4QLXXNum as the OG revised in 𝔊[B].

Num 4:6	[α]ρτηρας] αναφορεις 𝔊[ed]; + αυτης *O f* Arab Syh; + *ab ea* Bo; בדיו MT𝔴
Num 4:8	αρτηρας] αναφορεις 𝔊[ed]; בדיו MT𝔴
Num 4:11	αρτη[ρας]] αναφορεις 𝔊[ed]; בדיו MT𝔴
Num 4:12	αρτηρος] αναφορεις 𝔊[ed]; המוט MT𝔴

It will be clearest to quote Wevers's exposition:

> Characteristic of the [4QLXXNum] revision is the substitution of αρτηρας for (τοὺς) ἀναφορεῖς. The word occurs four times in this fragmentary text, three times for בדים (4:6, 8, 11) and once for מוט (4:12). . . .
>
> In each case the reference in MT is to the staves by which the ark was to be carried. Apparently the reviser felt that ἀναφορεύς was an agent noun, i.e. a "carrier" rather than the means of carrying; in fact, in v. 12 the [𝔊[ed]] text could easily be interpreted as referring to the bearers instead of the carrying staves. . . . I suspect that the use of αρτηρ to designate staves for carrying the ark instead of ἀναφορεύς is meant to avoid possible confusion in meaning for ἀναφορεύς as an agent rather than an instrument for carrying.
>
> . . . [In] the case of αρτηρ, . . . this variant seems to be rooted in the desire to clarify the Greek text. It is not the kind of variant which is more Hebraic than [the OG] as would be expected from the so-called καίγε recension; rather it is a variant clarifying a Hebraic kind of Greek by a more idiomatic text.[24]

To my mind the opposite conclusion seems more persuasive, though neither Wevers nor I can offer much more to support our views on this pair of variants. I would simply note three points. (1) Although sporadic revision certainly occurred in the interests of clearer Greek in specific cases, Symmachus is our only ancient example of systematic recension for clearer Greek, and even he retains a large measure of Hebrew recensional material. (2) More importantly, αναφορευς is clearly used as a recensional substitute: Aquila uses it but never αρτηρ for בד. (3) The argument Wevers gives (Greek idiomatic clarity) is usually an argument used to demonstrate the OG translation in contrast to more wooden recensional revision.

24. Wevers, "An Early Revision," 236*-38*. In the last paragraph Wevers is talking about the επισκεπτεσθαι/αριθμειν variant and says: "As in the case of αρτηρ, so this variant [επισκεπτεσθαι/αριθμειν]. . . ." But he is making the same point about the two variants.

Num 4:7 υ[α]κινθι/[νον] = תכלת MT𝔪 } ολοπορφυρον 𝔊^{ed}

υακινθος means "dark blue" and usually translates תכלת. ολοπορφυρος means "dark red/purple" and usually translates ארגמן. The adjective here refers to the cloth (ιματιον) spread over the table of the bread of the presence. Although in the previous two variants there was no reason to suspect an alternate Hebrew text, here it is a question of the Hebrew *Vorlage*. The Hebrew text from which the OG was translated could have had either תכלת or ארגמן. But, since the Greek always translates the other colors throughout this passage mechanically and faithfully, I would maintain that the OG translator correctly translated whichever Hebrew word (he thought) lay before him. The alternate Greek text would have to be a mistake or an early revision toward an alternate Hebrew text. It is impossible to decide with the evidence available.

Num 4:14 τα σπ[ονδεια] = המזרקת MT𝔪 (קות- 𝔪) } τον καλυπτηρα 𝔊^{ed}

τα σπονδεια means "cups"; τον καλυπτηρα is simply an error. The issue is whether the error was made by the OG translator and was later corrected in 4QLXXNum toward the correct Hebrew, or whether the correct OG is faithfully represented by 4QLXXNum and became distorted (as in 𝔊^{ed}) later in the transmission stage. It appears impossible to decide between these possibilities on the strength of the evidence available.

Conclusion

As we argued above, it is essential to consider the possibilities for the Hebrew original that the OG was attempting to translate. Often it is, but often it is not, identical with the Masoretic *textus receptus*. Now that we have studied the variants of 4QLXXLev^{a} and several of the more important ones in 4QLXXNum, it is appropriate to reappraise their value as witnesses to the OG.

4QLXXLev^{a} displays fifteen variants from the text of 𝔊^{ed} (plus a sixteenth where it and 𝔊^{ed} both represent the OG in a variant from MT𝔪) — fifteen variants in twenty-eight less-than-half-extant lines of manuscript! But none of these variants is an error. All are sensible readings, constituting an alternate text or translation. Is Kahle correct that prior to the LXX translation there were divergent Greek targumim? No. These variants are embedded in a text that shows 75 percent agreement with 𝔊^{ed}. Thus 4QLXXLev^{a} and 𝔊^{ed} are two representatives of the same translation, one or both of which has developed a total of fifteen changes. Some or all could be isolated changes in either text. One or other text (but presumably not both) could display a pattern of revision, most commonly sought as recensional revision of the OG back to the emergingly dominant proto-MT.

On closer inspection, we note that of the fifteen variants, seven are unique and three others are attested by only one or two manuscripts. All the readings in 4QLXXLev^a can be seen as adequate, free ways of translating the MT or possibly as more literal translations of a slightly variant Hebrew text.

Despite the fact that this manuscript comes from the late second or the early first century B.C.E. — three or four centuries earlier than our next earliest witnesses — not one of its readings is accepted for the Göttingen critical text. Rather, for every variant the reading that agrees with the MT is chosen. My assumption is that Wevers's selection is partly based on the weight of the manuscript tradition (not a bad argument!). But I think all would agree that at many points our manuscript tradition does not take us all the way back to the OG translation. I am not certain, but I propose that 4QLXXLev^a penetrates further behind our oldest witnesses, especially with εθνος (Lev 26:12) and plausibly with τον ξυλινον καρπον (Lev 26:4), the πολεμος clause in its correct place (Lev 26:6^{fin}), and βδελυξομαι (Lev 26:11).

If we seek a comprehensive pattern for the majority of readings in 4QLXXLev^a vis-à-vis the Göttingen edition — either seeing the Göttingen edition as an accurate translation (the OG) of the proto-MT and 4QLXXLev^a as secondary (simplification, smoothing, error, etc.), or seeing the Qumran text as an acceptably free translation (the OG) of the proto-MT or a more literal translation of a slightly variant *Vorlage* and the text in the Göttingen edition as a revision toward the proto-MT — I think the latter has stronger probability on its side. In short, predominantly through the first part of this essay, the (b)-pattern seems more consistent.

4QLXXNum displays four crucial variants from the text of $\mathfrak{G}^{ed}$. The analysis of the first two indicated my preference for interpreting the Qumran text as the OG and the readings in $\mathfrak{G}^{ed}$ as recensional (partly because επισκεπτεσθαι and αναφορευς are documentably recensional substitutes). The evidence available for the remaining two variants is admittedly insufficient. But the reading of $\mathfrak{G}^{ed}$ is clearly an error in the fourth and apparently an error in the third, while the much older witness presents the correct readings in both. The cumulative evidence suggests that 4QLXXNum, just as 4QLXXLev^a above, presents the superior witness to the Old Greek translation.

CHAPTER 10

Josephus's Biblical Text for the Books of Samuel

Inquiry concerning the biblical text used as a source by Josephus for his monumental history, *The Jewish Antiquities*, can be doubly illuminating. It can shed light on the state of the biblical text in the first century C.E., and it can shed light on Josephus's method as a late first-century historian.

Josephus probably used scrolls of the Scriptures that were copied in the first two-thirds of the first century of our era or perhaps even somewhat earlier. Shortly after the First Jewish Revolt against Rome and the destruction of the Temple in 70 C.E., he left for Rome with some copies of "sacred books" (*Life* 417-18). Thus, the more that is known about the specific biblical texts that Josephus used, the more we know about the specific form, or one of the specific forms, of the biblical text circulating in Judaea during the late Second Temple period and during the formative stages of the literatures of the New Testament and the Mishnah. Similarly, the more we can determine about Josephus's biblical source, the more we can understand of his methods as a historiographer.[1]

1. See Harold W. Attridge, "Josephus and His Works," in *Jewish Writings of the Second Temple Period* (ed. Michael E. Stone; Compendia Rerum Iudaicarum ad Novum Testamentum, section 2, vol. 3; Assen: Van Gorcum, 1984) 185-232; idem, "Jewish Historiography," in *Early Judaism and Its Modern Interpreters* (ed. R. A. Kraft and G. W. E. Nickelsburg; Atlanta: Scholars Press, 1986) 311-43; L. H. Feldman, "Flavius Josephus Revisited: The Man, His Writings, and His Significance," *ANRW* II.21.2 (ed. H. Temporini and W. Haase; Berlin: de Gruyter, 1984) 763-862; idem, "Josephus' Portrait of Saul," *HUCA* 53 (1982) 45-99; idem, "Josephus as a Biblical Interpreter: The *'Aqedah*," *JQR* 75 (1985) 212-52.

The emphasis in this study, however, will be on the biblical text used by Josephus.

The scope of this study will be limited to the books of 1-2 Samuel.[2] In Septuagintal studies it is now common knowledge that the text type of one book is not necessarily that of another book and in fact is not necessarily the same within all parts of one book.[3] For books of the Masoretic Bible the same is true, though less attention is paid to this point. The biblical scrolls discovered in the area of the Dead Sea, dated to ca. 225 B.C.E. to 68 C.E., provide documentation for a measured variety in the texts of the different books. We should presume that, since the biblical books were copied on discrete scrolls, and since the text type of one scroll was not necessarily the same as that of another scroll, the relationship of Josephus's historical narrative to "the biblical text" will vary from book to book. Thus, for each biblical book, that relationship must be analyzed in detail. Since for this present study we will be concerned with the books of Samuel,[4] our results may well hold true for other books but should first be tested.

2. Even more specifically, the research behind the present analysis was focused for consistency of results on those portions of the text of 1-2 Samuel where 4QSam[a] was extant and where one or more of the biblical texts (Q, MT, G, $C^{MT,G}$) disagreed with another. Over two hundred such readings were isolated, and the text of Josephus was compared with each of these. In order to balance the somewhat random character of that selection of readings, the analysis also included the continuous text of a complete chapter, 2 Samuel 6. For this detailed analysis of the scroll and Josephus's relationship to it, see E. Ulrich, *The Qumran Text of Samuel and Josephus* (HSM 19; Missoula, Mont.: Scholars Press, 1978).

3. H. St. J. Thackeray (*The Septuagint and Jewish Worship* [London, 1921] 9-28) discerned the following divisions in the Greek text of Samuel-Kings: α (= 1 Samuel), ββ (= 2 Sam 1:1–11:1), γγ (= 1 Kgs 2:12–21:29), βγ (= 2 Sam 11:2–2 Kgs 2:11), γδ (= 1 Kgs 22:1–2 Kgs 25:30). He assigned α, ββ, γγ to one "translator" and βγ, γδ to a second "translator." D. Barthélemy (*Les devanciers d'Aquila* [VTSup 10; Leiden: Brill, 1963] 34-41) refined Thackeray's results, showing that the second grouping was not due to another "translator" but to a recensionist, i.e., a reviser of the first translation bringing it into greater conformity with the Masoretic Text, in word order, length of text, and choice of lexemes. Thus the majority of the Greek texts of Samuel represents the Old Greek for part of the narrative and the "Proto-Theodotionic" recension for the remainder.

4. The specific texts used for comparison in this analysis are, for Josephus, the Loeb edition checked against Niese's edition; for the Hebrew Bible, the extensive fragments of the Qumran scroll 4QSam[a] (to be published by F. M. Cross in *Discoveries in the Judaean Desert;* provisionally see Cross, "A New Qumran Biblical Fragment Related to the Original Hebrew Underlying the Septuagint," *BASOR* 132 [1953] 15-26; and Ulrich, *Qumran*) and the Masoretic text of both Samuel and Chronicles as in *Biblia Hebraica Stuttgartensia;* for the Septuagint, the text and apparatus as in the Cambridge Septuagint, edited by Brooke, McLean, and Thackeray; and for the Vetus Latina, Fischer's revised edition of OL 115 (see B. Fischer with E. Ulrich and J. E. Sanderson, "Palimpsestus Vindobonensis: A Revised

The Content of Josephus's Bible

Josephus preserves narrative material that is or was "biblical" but that no longer appears in our contemporary Bibles. That is, when the text of Josephus is compared with contemporary Bibles, either vernacular translations or even the Hebrew or Greek text in critical editions, there are words, phrases, ideas, and even an entire passage that prima facie could seem classifiable as "nonbiblical" and that indeed have been noted by some scholars as "nonbiblical."[5] They were, however, biblical for Josephus, and he had actually derived them from a "biblical text."

4QSam^{a} (Q) gives us a new vantage point on this question. It is a biblical scroll of the books of Samuel representing a text type at variance with the Masoretic *textus receptus* (MT) for Samuel.[6] It is interesting to compare Q and MT, and at the points of divergence to see with which text Josephus (J) agrees. Such a comparison highlights at least four readings in which the biblical scroll used by J agrees with Q against MT, but no readings emerge in which J agrees with MT against Q. The Septuagint (G) should also be compared,[7] since Josephus composed the *Antiquities* in Greek and since it has been claimed that Josephus's predominant biblical source was the Septuagint.[8] The four readings in which Josephus's biblical text differed from the *textus receptus* follow.

Edition of L 115 for Samuel-Kings," *BIOSCS* 16 [1983] 13-87; republished in B. Fischer, *Beiträge zur Geschichte der lateinischen Bibeltexte* [Vetus Latina: Aus der Geschichte der lateinischen Bibel 12; Freiburg: Herder, 1986] 308-438), Sabatier's collection, and the critical apparatus of the Cambridge Septuagint.

5. See, e.g., Marcus in the Loeb edition, vol. 5, p. 201 note c; pp. 330-31 note a; p. 425 note c; p. 433 note a; and passim.

6. For Samuel the Targum (T) and Peshitta (S) regularly agree with MT.

7. The Old Latin (OL), translated from early but somewhat developed forms of the Septuagint, is an important witness to the early Greek text before it suffered many of the intentional and unintentional variants exhibited in our extant manuscripts; see E. Ulrich, "The Old Latin Translation of the LXX and the Hebrew Scrolls from Qumran," in *The Hebrew and Greek Texts of Samuel: 1980 Proceedings IOSCS — Vienna* (ed. E. Tov; Jerusalem: Academon, 1980) 121-65; idem, "Characteristics and Limitations of the Old Latin Translation of the Septuagint," in *La Septuaginta en la investigación contemporánea (V Congreso de la IOSCS)* (Textos y estudios "Cardenal Cisneros" 34; ed. N. Fernández Marcos; Madrid: Instituto "Arias Montano," 1985) 67-80; and J. Trebolle, "Redaction, Recension, and Midrash in the Books of Kings," *BIOSCS* 15 (1982) 12-35; idem, "From the 'Old Latin' through the 'Old Greek' to the 'Old Hebrew' (2 Kings 10:23-25)," *Textus* 11 (1984) 17-36.

8. A. Mez, *Die Bibel des Josephus untersucht für Buch V-VII der Archäologie* (Basel: Jaeger und Kober, 1895) 79-84; Thackeray, *Josephus: The Man and the Historian* (New York: Ktav, 1967) 81; Ulrich, *Qumran*, 223-59.

1 Sam 11:1^{init} *Ant.* 6.68-69

Q [ונ]חׄש מלך בני עׄמון הוא לחץ את בני גד ואת בני ראובן בחזקה
ונקר להם כ[ול] \ [ע]יׄן ימין . . . בעׄ[בר \ הירדן] . . .
ויהי כמו חדש ויעל נחש העמוני ויחן על יביש [גלעד] . . .

MT ויהי כמחריש: [11:1]ויעל נחש העמוני ויחן על יבש גלעד

G Καὶ ἐγενήθη ὡς μετὰ μῆνα καὶ ἀνέβη Ναὰς ὁ Ἀμμανείτης καὶ παρεμβάλλει ἐπὶ Ιαβις Γαλααδ·

J Μηνὶ δ' ὕστερον . . . Ναάσην . . . τὸν τῶν Ἀμμανιτῶν βασιλέα· οὗτος γὰρ πολλὰ κακὰ τοὺς πέραν τοῦ Ἰορδάνου ποταμοῦ κατῳκημένους τῶν Ἰουδαίων διατίθησι . . . ἰσχύι μὲν καὶ βίᾳ . . . τοὺς δεξιοὺς ὀφθαλμοὺς ἐξέκοπτεν.

4QSam^{a} and Josephus share this extended passage absent from all other surviving biblical texts of Samuel.[9]

1 Sam 1:22 *Ant.* 5.347

Q	[ונת]תׄיהו נזיר עד עולם
MT T S	om
G OL	om
J	ἀνατιθεῖσα τῷ θεῷ προφήτην

The epithet *nazir* applied to Samuel is a plus in 4QSam^{a} attested in no other extant biblical manuscript, though reflected in Josephus. Josephus never uses ναζιραῖος for an individual, since his audience would not know the term; instead, he uses the more general term *prophet,* as he does, for example, in his description of the *nazir* Samson (*Ant.* 5.285).[10]

9. The line ויהי — יביש [גלעד] in 4QSam^{a} is written supralinearly *(prima manu).* For discussion of the passage, see (F. M. Cross's) note on 1 Sam 11:1 in *The New American Bible;* Cross, "The Evolution of a Theory of Local Texts," in *Qumran and the History of the Biblical Text* (ed. F. M. Cross and S. Talmon; Cambridge, Mass.: Harvard University Press, 1975) 306-15, esp. 315; Ulrich, *Qumran,* 166-70; Cross, "The Ammonite Oppression of the Tribes of Gad and Reuben: Missing Verses from I Samuel 11 Found in 4QSamuel^{a}," in Tov, ed., *The Hebrew and Greek Texts of Samuel,* 105-19. See further T. L. Eves, "One Ammonite Invasion or Two? I Sam 10:27–11:2 in the Light of 4QSam^{a}," *WTJ* 44 (1982) 308-26; D. Barthélemy, ed., *Critique textuelle de l'Ancien Testament 1: Josué, Juges, Ruth, Samuel, Rois, Chroniques, Esdras, Néhémie, Esther* (OBO 50.1; Fribourg: Editions Universitaires; Göttingen: Vandenhoeck & Ruprecht, 1982) 166-72; and A. Rofé, "The Acts of Nahash according to 4QSam^{a}," *IEJ* 32 (1982) 129-33.

10. See Cross, "A New Qumran Biblical Fragment," 18-19; Ulrich, *Qumran,* 165-66; cf. also 39-40.

1 Sam 28:1^{fin} *Ant.* 6.325
Q למ]לחמה יזרעאל
M om
G om
J εἰς τὸν πόλεμον εἰς Ῥεγάν (or Ρελαν)[11]

Here 4QSam^a probably has an addition, reflected by Josephus, but indirectly through the medium of a Greek *Vorlage.*[12]

2 Sam 11:3^{fin} (1 Chr 20:1 om) *Ant.* 7.131
Q [אוריה החתי נ]ושא כלי יואב
MT T S אוריה החת
G Οὐρείου τοῦ Χετταίου
J τὸν Ἰωάβου μὲν ὁπλοφόρον . . . Οὐρίαν

Josephus refers to Uriah as Joab's armor-bearer, and 4QSam^a is the only preserved biblical manuscript from which he could have derived that detail, here or elsewhere.[13]

Conclusion: There are at least four instances in which Josephus shows dependence on the contents of a biblical text at variance with all current Bibles. Since the content of his Bible was not necessarily identical with that of ours, Josephus should be studied to see if elements of his narrative that appear to be "nonbiblical" may occasionally point to a variant biblical text.

11. The following variants occur in the Josephan manuscripts: Ρεγαν RE; Ριγαν O; Ρεγγαν MSP; *Rella* Lat. On the accuracy of the Latin text of Josephus, see Franz Blatt, ed., *The Latin Josephus* (Copenhagen, 1985) 25. On the discovery of this reading, see Cross, "The History of the Biblical Text in the Light of Discoveries in the Judaean Desert," *HTR* 57 (1964) 293.

12. See Ulrich, *Qumran,* 171-72: The Greek text used by Josephus "must have had approximately ΕΙΣ (ΤΟΝ) ΠΟΛΕΜΟΝ ΕΙΣΡ(Α)ΕΛ. . . . Josephus saw and reproduced Λ (and not Γ), for Λ is solidly in the text tradition. The double (Λ and Γ) text-tradition is not explainable if Γ was original. . . . Josephus himself . . . did not recognize that in his *Vorlage* Jezreel was meant (though something quite similar was present), because he habitually (VIII, 346, 355, 407; IX, 105; etc.) identifies it for his foreign readers by appending 'πόλις' to it, whereas here he does not append 'πόλις.' Thus the 4Q text type had יזרעאל correctly, G frequently errs on the name . . . , and Josephus' *Vorlage* contained a form quite close to ΙΕΣΡΑΕΛ but already corrupt. That 'corruption already in the *Vorlage* of J' is a specifically Greek language corruption: -יזר > ΙΕΖΡ- (or ΙΕΣΡ-) > ΕΙΣ Ρ-."

13. See the text of The New American Bible at 2 Sam 11:3; Ulrich, *Qumran,* 173.

The Text Type of Josephus's Bible

The previous section showed that, at least for the books of Samuel, Josephus's biblical text was somewhat different from our *textus receptus* represented in the Masoretic text, though it did agree with another biblical manuscript. This section will address the question of whether we can determine which particular text type Josephus used.

If the text of Josephus for his narrative of the content of 1-2 Samuel is compared with known biblical texts, such as MT, the Targum (T), the Greek of Samuel (G), and the Masoretic and Greek of Chronicles ($C^{MT,G}$) as well as with the new biblical manuscript discovered in 1952, 4QSam[a], one can get a reasonably clear picture of the type of text Josephus used as his source for the Samuel portion of the *Antiquities.* That clarity will not extend to all the individual readings, that is, we should not hope to know all the details of the precise manuscript which Josephus used, but it should reveal the general text type used.

Text Types in Samuel

Q and MT clearly and distinctly display variant text types for 1-2 Samuel. The differences between them are multiple and complex, however, and here it is possible to offer only a rough summary.[14] Q and MT are sufficiently close to consider it plausible that they both ultimately derived from a single textual tradition (which may have developed, or preserved, some very ancient variants). But at one early point, or through the course of time in an early period, an ancestor of MT suffered a number of haplographies that were never corrected in the MT tradition.[15] The remainder of the textual witnesses continued to preserve the text now lost in MT, and the Old Greek (OG) version was

14. For fuller description, see F. M. Cross, "History of the Biblical Text," 281-99; Ulrich, *Qumran,* 194-207, 220-21, 257, and passim; and for helpful critique of the latter, E. Tov, "The Textual Affiliations of 4QSam[a]," *JSOT* 14 (1979) 37-53; idem, "Determining the Relationship between the Qumran Scrolls and the LXX: Some Methodological Issues," in Tov, ed., *The Hebrew and Greek Texts of Samuel,* 45-67; idem, *The Text-Critical Use of the Septuagint in Biblical Research* (Jerusalem: Simor, 1981) 260-71; idem, "A Modern Textual Outlook Based on the Qumran Scrolls," *HUCA* 53 (1982) 11-27.

15. For a partially similar, partially different, assessment see Barthélemy, ed., *Critique textuelle,* e.g., 270 (2 Sam 14:30); and S. Pisano, *Additions or Omissions in the Books of Samuel: The Significant Pluses and Minuses in the Massoretic, LXX, and Qumran Texts* (Freibourg: Universitätsverlag; Göttingen: Vandenhoeck & Ruprecht, 1984) 283-85 and passim.

translated from a Hebrew text that also preserved those readings. Through the course of time, all witnesses developed in unique ways: through errors and other unintentional changes, and through deliberate changes such as expansions (some in MT, more in Q, others in G), omissions, and alterations for various reasons. Q is a longer text than MT for two reasons: (1) MT suffered a considerable number of losses of text, and (2) Q exhibits more secondary expansions or additions than MT, though MT also exhibits some other expansions. If one seeks the "preferable" text, one would follow Q and OG for the first category but MT and OG for the second. Thus it emerges that Q is a longer text than MT for the two reasons just mentioned and that the OG translation (as opposed to simply the text of Vaticanus as printed in the Cambridge edition) agrees much more with the Q tradition than with the MT tradition.

Furthermore, comparison of the parallels in Chronicles with Q and MT of Samuel shows that C^{MT} also used as a source a text of Samuel significantly closer to Q than to MT.[16] Since C^{MT} demonstrates greater dependence upon the Q text type than upon the MT text type, and since the OG shows close and frequent affiliation with Q against MT, we must draw the conclusion that Q was not just some aberrant manuscript deviant from the widespread norm that was MT, but rather that it represented a text type influential in Judah during the fourth century B.C.E. (Chronicles), perhaps in Egypt around the end of the third century (the Old Greek translation), and again in Judah during the early (4QSam^{c}) and middle (4QSam^{a}) parts of the first century B.C.E. and the early centuries C.E. (the early, developed Greek texts used by Josephus and revised by Proto-Theodotion and Aquila).[17]

Thus, the evidence indicates that prior to the turn of the era MT was not the norm, not *the* text of Samuel, but rather that the text type exhibited in Q was, at least judging from the witnesses preserved, more influential.

Josephus's Affiliation with the Text Types

Josephus agrees in general with the Q G C tradition rather than the MT T G^{R} tradition.[18] Adam Mez in 1895 had already demonstrated that J used G^{L}, not

16. Cross, "History of the Biblical Text," 293; Ulrich, *Qumran,* 151-64, 193-221.

17. Cross, "History of the Biblical Text," 296.

18. Cross, "History of the Biblical Text," 292-97; Ulrich, *Qumran,* 220-21. Within the Greek manuscript tradition, the following symbols are used: G^{B} = codex Vaticanus, G^{L} = the (Proto-) Lucianic text, and G^{R} = a later recension (of the Proto-Theodotion or καίγε type) bringing the earlier Greek text into conformity with MT.

MT or G^B.[19] A. Rahlfs attempted to counter the results of Mez,[20] but fresh analysis[21] sparked by the discovery of 4QSam^a substantiated Mez's hypothesis in general, yielding four (or possibly five) readings in which J = Q alone ≠ MT G^(R?), already seen in the first section of this chapter. In thirty-four further readings, Josephus showed agreement with Q G against MT, and in five more agreed with Q C against MT G. The results demonstrate that Josephus shows no dependence on MT specifically.[22]

Here we have space to present only a few examples to illustrate Josephus's dependence on the Q text type as opposed to that of MT.

2 Sam 8:7^fin	(1 Chron 18:7) *Ant.* 7.104-5
Q	ירוש]ל̇[י]ם̊ גם [ ]א̇ותם [לקח . . . ב]ע̊ל̇ותו אל יר̊[ושלים] בימי רחבעם . . .
MT T S C^MT,G	ירושלם:
G OL	εἰς Ἰερουσαλήμ· καὶ ἔλαβεν αὐτὰ Σουσακεὶμ . . . ἐν τῷ ἀναβῆναι αὐτὸν εἰς Ἰερουσαλὴμ ἐν ἡμέραις Ῥοβοὰμ . . .
J	εἰς Ἰεροσόλυμα· ἃς ὕστερον . . . Σούσακος στρατεύσας ἐπὶ . . . Ῥοβόαμον ἔλαβε . . .

Josephus agrees with Q G OL against MT C for a plus in the Q G tradition (or possibly a haplography in MT); see Ulrich, *The Qumran Text of Samuel and Josephus*, 45-48.

2 Sam 13:21	*Ant.* 7.173
Q	[ולוא עצב את רוח אמנון בנו כי אה]בו כי בכור[ו הוא]
MT T S	om
G OL	καὶ οὐκ ἐλύπησεν τὸ πνεῦμα Ἀμνὼν τοῦ υἱοῦ αὐτοῦ, ὅτι ἠγάπα αὐτόν, ὅτι πρωτότοκος αὐτοῦ ἦν
J	φιλῶν δὲ τὸν Ἀμνῶνα σφόδρα, πρεσβύτατος γὰρ ἦν αὐτῷ υἱός, μὴ λυπεῖν αὐτὸν ἠναγκάζετο

Josephus agrees with Q G OL against MT (haplography in MT: **ולא ולא**); see Ulrich, *Qumran*, 84-85.

19. Mez, *Die Bibel*, 80.

20. A. Rahlfs, *Lucians Rezension der Königsbücher: Septuaginta-Studien III* (2d ed.; Göttingen: Vandenhoeck & Ruprecht, 1911) 83-92.

21. Ulrich, *Qumran*, 22-27.

22. Ulrich, *Qumran*, 190-91.

2 Sam 13:27^{fin}	*Ant.* 7.174
Q	[ויעש אבשלום משתה כמשתה ה]מׄ[ל]
MT T S	om
G OL	καὶ ἐποίησεν Ἀβεσσαλὼμ πότον κατὰ τὸν πότον τοῦ βασιλέως
J	ἐφ' ἑστίασιν

Josephus agrees with Q G OL against MT (haplography in MT המלך המלך); see Ulrich, *Qumran,* 85.

2 Sam 24:17	1 Chron 21:17	*Ant.* 7.328
Q	[וא]נׄכי הרעה הׄרׄעתי	
MT T S	ואנכי העויתי	
G^{L} OL	καὶ ἐγώ ὁ ποιμήν ἐκακοποίησα	
G^{Btext}	ἠδίκησα	
$G^{Bmargin}$	καὶ ἐγώ εἰμι ὁ ποιμήν	
G^{MSS}	καὶ ἐγώ εἰμι (om Ax) ὁ ποιμὴν ἐκακοποίησα (καὶ ἠδίκησα a_2)	
C^{MT}	והרע הרעותי	
C^{G}	κακοποιῶν ἐκακοποίησα	
J	αὐτὸς εἴη κολασθῆναι δίκαιος ὁ ποιμήν	

4QSam^{a} probably has the original reading; G^{L} represents the OG; ἐγώ εἰμι for אנכי shows that the G^{MSS} are influenced by a later recension. Josephus agrees with Q G OL against MT G^{R} and against $C^{MT,G}$; see Ulrich, *Qumran,* 86-87.

2 Sam 6:2	1 Chron 13:6	*Ant.* 7.78
Q	בעלה היא קרׄ[ת יערים]	
MT T S	מבעלי	
G	ἀπὸ τῶν ἀρχόντων . . . ἐν ἀναβάσει	
C^{MT}	בעלתה אל קרית יערים	
C^{G}	εἰς πόλιν Δαυειδ	
C^{L}	εἰς Καριαθιαρειμ	
J	εἰς καριαθιάριμα	

Josephus agrees with Q $C^{MT,L}$ against MT G C^{G} for a plus in Q (doublet in G); see Ulrich, *Qumran,* 179, 194, 230.

Conclusion: The first section displayed differences in the content of Josephus's biblical text compared with our current Bibles, and this second section has illuminated the cause of those differences: the affiliation of Josephus's biblical text with the text type found in 4QSam^{a} and/or in the Septuagint, rather than with the text type found in the Masoretic text.

The Language of Josephus's Bible

This section will address the question of whether we can determine the language — Hebrew, Aramaic, Greek, or a combination — in which Josephus's biblical text of Samuel was written. Since Josephus was writing his extensive history in Greek and since the Bible was one of the main sources, it stands to reason that his logical choice for a source text would be a Bible in Greek. A. Mez already in 1895, and H. St. J. Thackeray in 1927, had claimed that for the books of Samuel Josephus used primarily a Greek text.[23]

Josephus's Use of a Bible in the Greek Language

We have already seen one example (in the first section: "Jezreel" = 1 Sam 28:1; *Ant.* 6.325) in which Josephus displays an error that betrays that he was using a Bible in the Greek language; he must have seen the *Greek* error, ΕΙΣΡ-, already in his source, because if it had been some recognizable form of "Jezreel," he would have added πόλις, and the Josephan manuscript tradition would display variants on "Jezreel," not on "Rela." It is important to note here that, as far as extant manuscripts can show, Josephus agrees with the *Hebrew* text 4QSam^{a} alone; but his reading clearly demonstrates that he is dependent upon a *Greek* medium, a Greek text that had erred in interpreting a detail once found in a Greek manuscript but now lost from the manuscript tradition. A few further examples must suffice to illustrate Josephus's dependence on a Bible in the Greek, as opposed to Hebrew or Aramaic, language.

23. Mez, *Die Bibel*, 79-84. H. St. J. Thackeray, "Note on the Evidence of Josephus," in *The Old Testament in Greek* (ed. A. E. Brooke, N. McLean, and H. St. J. Thackeray; vol. 2.1; Cambridge: Cambridge University Press, 1927) ix: "With the books of Samuel (more strictly from I S. viii onwards), Josephus becomes a witness of first-rate importance for the text of the Greek Bible. Throughout the Octateuch he appears to have been mainly dependent for his Biblical matter upon a Semitic source, whether Hebrew or Aramaic (a Targum), and there has so far been little evidence of his use of the Alexandrian version. Throughout the later historical books, on the other hand, his main source is a Greek Bible containing a text closely allied to that of the 'Lucianic' group of MSS. . . . Besides this Greek Bible the historian still apparently employs a Semitic text as a collateral source. His use of a two-fold text renders his evidence somewhat uncertain. Instances where he agrees with the Masoretic text against all known Greek readings have been neglected in the apparatus to this volume, as presumably derived from his Semitic source."

1 Sam 25:3	*Ant.* 6.296
Q	וחאיש כלבי
MT	והוא כלבו (qerê כלבי)
G	καὶ ὁ ἄνθρωπος κυνικός
J	κυνικῆς ἀσκήσεως

The Greek apparently did not recognize the gentilic "Calebite" and translated the root כלב "dog-like." Josephus erroneously interprets κυνικός as meaning a Cynic (!), his interpretation clearly based on a Greek text (see Ulrich, *Qumran*, 79, 184).

2 Sam 6:13	1 Chron 15:26	*Ant.* 7.85
Q	[om?]	
MT	ששה צעדים	
G	ἑπτὰ χοροί	
C[MT,G]	om	
J	ἑπτὰ δὲ χορῶν	

Josephus clearly based not only his content, found only in the Septuagint, but also his diction on the Greek words in the Septuagint (see Ulrich, *Qumran*, 182, 235).

2 Sam 10:6	1 Chron 19:6-7	*Ant.* 7.121
Q	[ומן ארם] . . . [וא]ישטוב	
MT	. . . ואת ארם . . . ואיש טוב	
G	τὸν Σύρον (G[L]; τὴν Συρίαν G[B]) . . . καὶ τὸν (G[L]; om τὸν G[B]) Εἰστώβ	
C[MT,G]	ומן ארם . . . (om ואיש טוב)	
J	πρὸς Σύρον τὸν τῶν Μεσοποταμιτῶν βασιλέα . . . καὶ . . . Ἴστοβον ὄνομα	

The text tradition of 4QSam[a] and of the *Vorlage* of G contained [וא]ישטוב without word division, G erroneously interprets it as a proper name, and C[MT,G] lack it. Josephus, following G, accordingly treats it as a proper name. He makes a second, parallel error, interpreting Σύρος as king of the Mesopotamians! Josephus's *Vorlage* must have had the Greek masculine: Josephus could not have mistaken ארם for a person, named him Σύρος, and considered him to be "king of the Mesopotamians"! Thus, again for this pair of readings Josephus's *Vorlage* must have been in Greek (see Ulrich, *Qumran*, 152-56, 184).

This selection from a larger number of examples suffices to demonstrate that at times Josephus used a Bible in the Greek language, producing readings that would be implausible or impossible had he consulted a Hebrew Bible. But did he at other times use a supplementary Hebrew or Aramaic Bible? Does not the set of readings in which Josephus agrees with 4QSam^a alone, where no Greek text contains the material reflected by Josephus, substantiate the hypothesis that Josephus used a supplementary Hebrew Bible?

When the evidence is viewed comprehensively, we find, first, that the "Jezreel" reading shows that Josephus used a Greek text — a Greek medium linked intimately with the 4QSam^a tradition — which is no longer extant but which in his day contained the detail now extant only in 4QSam^a.[24] Second, there are eleven readings in which Josephus shows dependence upon G rather than 4QSam^a,[25] again because he is using a Greek Bible. And third, when the books of Samuel are studied systematically in comparison with the text of Josephus, it becomes quite clear that "for all the portions of the Samuel text for which 4QSam^a is extant, J shows no dependence on MT specifically or on a *Vorlage* in the Hebrew language."[26]

Contrary Evidence

Nonetheless, we find that in the notes to the Loeb edition Thackeray and Marcus indicate points in Josephus's recasting of the Samuel narrative where they allege that he is dependent upon a Hebrew or Aramaic source in contrast to a Greek source. We have seen, however, that Thackeray's conclusion with regard to the division of the Greek text of Samuel was generally accurate but required correction.[27] So also here his conclusion with regard to the language of Josephus's text of Samuel is generally accurate but requires correction. The results of my 1978 study confirmed the general hypothesis that Josephus used a Greek source continuously and predominantly. I went further, however, and examined all the evidence marshaled by Mez, Rahlfs, Thackeray, and Marcus that in their judgment indicated a Hebrew or Aramaic source. For the parts of 1-2 Samuel for which 4QSam^a is extant, not a single one of their arguments for a Hebrew or Aramaic source — primary or supplementary — turned out to be persuasive.

24. There are other examples where material that was originally in the ancient Greek text has demonstrably been excised in secondary recensional activity aimed at making the Greek text conform to the Masoretic *Hebraica veritas;* see, e.g., Ulrich, *Qumran,* 142.

25. Ulrich, *Qumran,* 181-83, 191.

26. Ulrich, *Qumran,* 191.

27. See note 3.

Mez listed, for the parts where 4QSam[a] is extant, only one instance in which he discussed the possibility of specifically Hebrew influence on Josephus,[28] but he himself thought that that possibility deserved "kräftiges Misstrauen."[29]

Rahlfs discussed five of Mez's readings for which 4QSam[a] is extant, but for three of them he agreed that Josephus's source was a Greek text. Of the other two, 4QSam[a] shows that Mez was correct and Rahlfs incorrect. For the first, Rahlfs had claimed that Josephus had derived his reading from Chronicles, not from Samuel; but now 4QSam[a] provides us with a text of Samuel (from which text type Chronicles derived the details in question) containing those details; moreover, close inspection shows that Josephus must have gotten one of the details from a text necessarily in the Greek language. For the second reading as well, Josephus does err, but his error demonstrates dependence on a preexisting error in a specifically Greek source.[30] Thus, Mez and Rahlfs agree that in general Josephus is using a Greek text, and none of their suspicions of a supplementary Hebrew source survives scrutiny.

Thackeray and Marcus at thirty-four places in the notes to the Loeb edition draw conclusions concerning the *Vorlage* employed by Josephus, for portions of Samuel where 4QSam[a] is extant. Of these, twenty-six agree that Josephus's *Vorlage* was in Greek, and five more, upon fuller consideration, also support that hypothesis. The remaining three are quite ambiguous: two involve proper names, the first resting on a dubious choice among the variant spellings in the manuscripts,[31] and the second involving the single difference between נ and כ in Hebrew manuscripts, both forms of which are reflected in Greek manuscripts especially in Chronicles.[32] The last of the three suspicions of a Hebrew or Aramaic source is due simply to failure to understand Josephus's style of paraphrasing his source, whether that source be biblical or nonbiblical, and whether it be in Greek, Hebrew, or Aramaic.[33]

Thus, all agree that Josephus's main biblical source was a Greek Bible; but with regard to the question whether he used additional manuscripts in

28. Mez, *Die Bibel,* p. 64 #XXXIV = 1 Sam 6:1 = *Ant.* 6.18.

29. Mez, *Die Bibel,* 57, 64.

30. For full discussion see Ulrich, *Qumran,* 25-26, 171-72, 250-52.

31. Ulrich, *Qumran,* 81, 188. Caution is warranted concerning proper names; Blatt, editor of *The Latin Josephus,* observed that in the Latin text of Josephus "Biblical names were given the form they had in the Vulgate" (p. 25), and thus the forms of names found there are witnesses to the Vulgate but not reliable witnesses to the original text of Josephus.

32. Ulrich, *Qumran,* 209, 213.

33. Ulrich, *Qumran,* 254.

Hebrew or Aramaic as a supplementary source, when all the specific instances are examined for which Hebrew or Aramaic influence has been claimed, not one single example proves clear and persuasive.

Since 1978, only three scholars, to my knowledge, have taken issue with this conclusion. First, Jonas Greenfield, though agreeing that Josephus's "closeness to the 4QSam^a text is clear," has argued that "the assumption that Josephus had no recourse to a Hebrew text seems to me to remain unproven. I find the viewpoint of Sebastian Brock . . . that Josephus made use of both the Greek and the Hebrew more logical, even if it is only an inference."[34]

Second, Louis Feldman has argued that it "seems hard to believe that [Josephus] would have stopped consulting the Hebrew text so suddenly,[35] especially since he must have heard in the synagogue portions from the historical and prophetical books in the form of *haftaroth*, the reading of which dates from at least the first century."[36]

Third, T. Muraoka, also acknowledging "Josephus' Greek source,"[37] nonetheless pleads for more caution, finding at least one case where he concludes that "Josephus is evidently not dependent on the Greek, but if anything, is aware of one plausible interpretation of the Hebrew text."[38]

In response to Professors Greenfield and Feldman I would say that it may be logical to assume that Josephus used a Hebrew Bible as a supplementary source, but that assumption (1) is an assumption, (2) is based on unrevised findings from early in this century, prior to the significant reorientation of our textual knowledge by the discovery of the Qumran manuscripts, and (3) as yet lacks justification by a demonstration of evidence. I agree that the assumption is logical, and it was not my initial intention to set out to prove that Josephus was exempt from dependence upon a Hebrew manuscript; on the contrary, I was attempting to demonstrate his close relationship with the Hebrew manuscript 4QSam^a. The conclusion, however, emerged from reexamination of the evidence: it happened to turn out that for the portions of 1-2 Samuel where 4QSam^a is extant none of the readings used by earlier scholars to found the hypothesis of a supplementary Hebrew or Aramaic

34. Jonas C. Greenfield, review of *The Qumran Text of Samuel and Josephus,* by Eugene C. Ulrich, Jr., *JNES* 42 (1983) 67-68.

35. Feldman is referring to Thackeray's view that Josephus had primarily used a Hebrew source for the Octateuch; see note 23.

36. Feldman, "Flavius Josephus Revisited," 800.

37. T. Muraoka, "The Greek Text of 2 Samuel 11 in the Lucianic Manuscripts," *Abr-Nahrain* 20 (1981-82) 37-59, esp. 51. I wish to thank Professor Feldman for reminding me of this article, which Professor Muraoka had kindly sent me several years ago.

38. Muraoka, "The Greek Text of 2 Samuel 11," 57.

manuscript actually demonstrated that he did so. Thus, the assumption is logical, but it is also unproven. It seems questionable to rest with a general refusal to accept detailed conclusions, when those conclusions are based on detailed analysis of over two hundred readings, without providing evidence to the contrary.[39]

I have suggested an alternate assumption, equally logical, equally unproven.[40] I can also imagine the possibility that, for portions of 1-2 Samuel not extant in 4QSam^a, one might find evidence of Hebrew influence that could withstand the counterclaim that the readings involved — like the readings illuminated by 4QSam^a — are dependent upon a Greek manuscript of the 4QSam^a tradition no longer extant.

In response to Professor Muraoka, I would like to commend his carefully detailed research on which his conclusions rest. As I also attempted to do, he has provided a general model for the kind of research needed to extend our knowledge of Josephus's biblical text to the remainder of the books of Samuel and to the other books of the Bible.

At only one point, however, does a negative conclusion of his overlap with extant data from 4QSam^a: 2 Sam 11:3 (the last example listed in the first section of this chapter). I should present his exact argument, since others may wish to compare the arguments in detail:

> Cf. Ulrich, *Qumran Text,* p. 173, where the addition in a 4Q Hebrew fragment at the end of the verse [3] of *nwś' kly yw'b* (= Josephus) is discussed. *Pace* Ulrich, the phrase can be more easily a later addition than a case of deliberate omission. See also Ulrich's discussion of *OL* at this point: Ulrich, "The Old Latin translation . . . ," 126f. Given the appalling mode of publication of 4Q Hebrew materials, one cannot be sure that this "unscriptural detail" is to be considered to be part of verse 3, as Ulrich thinks. This does not appear to be the case in Josephus, though he adds the detail on the first mention of Uriah (*JA* 7.131). Finally, it must be pointed out that there is

39. In a private communication, Professor Feldman recently indicated that it would be appropriate to mention that he has revised his view.

40. Ulrich, *Qumran,* 223-24: "There are, admittedly, Josephan readings which cannot be accounted for, but this is true of every biblical manuscript and of every extended series of quotations from the Bible. In addition to the explanations of the human margin of error due to Josephus and of the vicissitudes of the bimillennial transmission of his text, otherwise unaccountable readings can be explained in part as marginal annotations made by Josephus himself in his Greek Bible intermittently during the decade and more which he spent composing the *Antiquities.* What scholar's much-used source book is not replete with corrections, additions, recordings of private judgments, etc., made throughout the years he or she has labored over the material?"

some doubt as to whether Josephus' source read οπλοφορος or αιρων σκευη, the latter rendition corresponding to Heb. *nośe' kelim* and sometimes replaced by him by οπλοφορος (I Ki. xvi 21, xxxi 4), for Josephus (*JA* 7.132) reads παρεκοιμήθη τῷ βασιλεῖ σὺν τοῖς ἄλλοις ὁπλοφόροις, which is parallel to vs. 9 κοιμᾶται . . . μετὰ πάντων τῶν παίδων (Heb. *'abdê*) τοῦ κυρίου αὐτοῦ.[41]

(1) Concerning the "addition" vs. "omission," I am puzzled because I do explicitly call the phrase a "plus" and an "explanatory gloss" (Ulrich, *Qumran,* 173) and judge that the MT is "the preferable, unexpanded text" to which 4QSam[a] and Josephus "add" (Ulrich, "Old Latin" [see my note 7 above], 126-27). His idea of "deliberate omission" may derive from my admittedly deductive explanation that *if* the phrase was present in Josephus's Greek source, it was subsequently "excised" (Ulrich, *Qumran,* 173), because it no longer appears in any Greek biblical manuscripts. There are fairly clear examples of material excised from the Greek text because it did not correspond with the MT. Thus, concerning the "addition" we seem to be in agreement, and concerning the "omission" my conditional deductive argument remains true. The "problem" that "there is no Greek witness to support Josephus" is not "especially acute" (Muraoka, "The Greek Text," 57) in light of the other specifically Greek testimony adduced throughout 1-2 Samuel, unless one were to contend that it is legitimate to demand that the specific manuscript used by Josephus be actually present in one of our modern museums for collation in our critical editions.

(2) That this scriptural detail is part of verse 3 is virtually certain. My dissertation was explicitly not an edition, but an analysis, of 4QSam[a]; but scholars may be confident of my reading in this individual case, confirmed by Professors F. M. Cross, P. W. Skehan *(New American Bible),* and P. K. McCarter (Anchor Bible Commentary).

(3) Josephus adds the "armor-bearer" detail when he first mentions Uriah's name (*Ant.* 7.171), just as 4QSam[a] does. Once one understands Josephus's characteristic manner of composing his narratives, there is no reason at all to doubt that Josephus's biblical text had this detail at the end of verse 3. Nor is there a more likely place for it to occur.

(4) If Professor Muraoka refers to doubt concerning which of the two different possibilities, οπλοφορος vs. αιρων σκευη, was in Josephus's text, the answer does not matter because, as he says, the latter is "sometimes replaced by [Josephus] by οπλοφορος." If he refers to doubt as to whether some other

41. Muraoka, "The Greek Text of 2 Samuel 11," 40-41.

term (e.g., *ʿebed,* as he suggests from verse 9) — as opposed to either of the two equivalent possibilities, οπλοφορος or αιρων σκευη — was in the source, that seems implausible, especially in light of [נ]ושא כלי in 4QSam[a]. But in that unlikely event, he would then concur more closely with my thesis that Josephus used a Greek Bible; for if *ʿebed* were in Josephus's *Hebrew* Bible, there would have been no source other than a Greek (or Aramaic) Bible for the more specific οπλοφορος.

Finally, Professor Muraoka also concludes, discussing 2 Sam 11:8, that "Josephus is evidently not dependent on the Greek, but if anything, is aware of one plausible interpretation of the Hebrew text."[42] He is referring to the difficult מַשְׂאַת/ἄρσις/τῶν παρεστηκότων. But 4QSam[a] is not extant for this word, nor does Muraoka sort out the complex stratigraphy of the recensional layers, but merely refers to the undifferentiated "*L* text." Thus, we do not know what his source had, regardless of whether that source were in Hebrew or Greek.

Conclusion: For the books of Samuel the scholarly consensus that Josephus continuously and predominantly used a Greek Bible as the source for his narrative in *The Jewish Antiquities* is fully corroborated. The older view that he also used a supplementary Hebrew or Aramaic Bible is logical but, at least for those portions where the added control of 4QSam[a] is available, lacks evidence produced to support it.

Conclusion

From a study of Josephus's recasting of the narrative of the books of Samuel in *The Jewish Antiquities* compared with the major text of Samuel from Qumran, the Masoretic text of Samuel and Chronicles, and the Greek versions, we can sketch a fairly clear picture of the biblical text which he employed. He used a text intimately related to 4QSam[a]. His text was a biblical text in a tradition not aberrant but apparently more widely influential in the Second Temple period than that of the MT. It was a text of Samuel, not of Chronicles, though similarities in Chronicles indicate that the Chronicler also used as his source a text closer to 4QSam[a] than to the MT.

Josephus's biblical text was in the Greek, not Hebrew or Aramaic, language. Some scholars continue to hold that he used a Hebrew or Aramaic Bible as a supplementary source; this is a logical but unproven hypothesis which developed in an earlier period before we had wide documentation of

42. Muraoka, "The Greek Text of 2 Samuel 11," 57.

Hebrew biblical manuscripts clearly at variance with the MT. Occasionally, especially in errors — where textual affiliation is often most easy to detect — he betrays that he is using a form of the text tradition very closely allied to the 4QSam^a text tradition, but in the Greek language (the "proto-Lucianic text"). For the most part, the readings of his Greek Bible are still preserved in our Greek manuscript tradition, but it is an ancient text tradition a number of whose valuable readings succumbed to the knife of revisionists. These latter, part of a current whose culmination is well known in the recensions of (Proto-) Theodotion and Aquila, were intent upon bringing the old "Septuagint" into conformity with the *Hebraica veritas,* which they equated with the rabbinic Bible destined to be guarded by the Masoretes and thus to be handed down as our *textus receptus.* Our closest glimpse of Josephus's biblical text for the books of Samuel comes through critical synoptic scrutiny of 4QSam^a and the ancient Greek manuscript tradition.

CHAPTER 11

Origen's Old Testament Text: The Transmission History of the Septuagint to the Third Century C.E.

Origen is still commemorated eighteen hundred years after his birth, and one of the many reasons is the Hexapla that he composed — his monumental work striving toward exactness in the text of the Old Testament Scriptures.[1] As Charles Bigg has noted, Origen was perhaps "the first who distinctly saw that for the theologian, whatever may be [the] immediate object, controversy, edification, or doctrine, the prime necessity is a sound text."[2] Though Origen may have been the first Christian, he was not, as Bigg suggested, "the first" to

1. That is, the Jewish translation of their Scriptures into Greek, the Septuagint, which the early Christian church accepted. "Old Testament" is used predominantly in this article insofar as it reflects Origen's position and denotes the wider canon of Scripture. For the most recent comprehensive study of the Septuagint, see S. Jellicoe, *The Septuagint and Modern Study* (Oxford: Clarendon, 1968); this supplements, rather than replaces, the still valuable 1902 work by H. B. Swete, *An Introduction to the Old Testament in Greek* (rev. by R. R. Ottley; New York: Ktav, 1968). For a highly useful study concerning the relationship of the Septuagint to the Hebrew Bible and the use of it in OT textual criticism, see E. Tov, *The Text-Critical Use of the Septuagint in Biblical Research* (Jerusalem Biblical Studies 3; Jerusalem: Simor, 1981). For bibliography on the Septuagint, see S. P. Brock, C. T. Fritsch, and S. Jellicoe, eds., *A Classified Bibliography of the Septuagint* (ALGHJ 6; Leiden: Brill, 1973); for subsequent bibliography, see the "Record of Work" in the annual *Bulletin of the International Organization for Septuagint and Cognate Studies.*

2. Cited by Jellicoe (*Septuagint,* 101) from *The Origins of Christianity,* ed. T. B. Strong (Oxford: Clarendon, 1909) 423.

see this, for he clearly followed and built on the work of a long line of Jewish textual scholars.[3] Bigg's statement, however, does point in the right direction: in order to understand Origen correctly, just as it is necessary to know his historical context, his educational and philosophical context, and his religious and theological context, so too is it necessary — since Origen and his works were so thoroughly rooted in the Bible — to know the character, the evolving character, of the biblical text that he used.

The purpose of this study is to provide a focus on the nature of the Old Testament text used by Origen. What would the Old Testament text, the Septuagint, have looked like in Origen's day? What was the character of the text that Origen would have picked up and begun to use when he started reading, praying over, preaching from, and writing commentaries on the Old Testament text?

That question necessarily requires a diachronic perspective, for the biblical text that Origen used was the product of a historical process. But this is a complex undertaking, if for no other reason than that Origen himself significantly changed the shape of that text. Origen primarily used the Septuagint, and what later theologians, such as Eusebius, Jerome, or Pamphilus, would think of as the Septuagint text looked noticeably different from the Septuagint text that Origen first took in hand. We should presume, for example, that the Septuagint text of Jeremiah, or Psalms, or Daniel cited by Origen early in his career would read differently from the Septuagint text cited by him late in his career, because he devoted a substantial amount of time to reediting that Septuagint text.

Thus, understanding the character of Origen's Old Testament text means understanding the origins and developments that formed it. Indeed, there are several more complicating factors, each of which needs its trajectory carefully charted. The first concerns the transmission of the text during the century or two after Origen. The oldest extensive manuscripts of the Septuagint that are extant are dated in the fourth century, at least a century after Origen, so we cannot always be certain that our Septuagint text corresponds to that of his day (either in its pre-Origenic or post-Origenic form).

The second complicating factor concerns the transmission of the text during the centuries before Origen. Numerous changes and numerous types of change, both intentional and unintentional, buffeted the Septuagint on its

3. Not only did Origen fill his Hexapla columns with the content of the recensions of Aquila and Theodotion, but his methods were similar to theirs; see D. Barthélemy, *Les devanciers d'Aquila* (VTSup 10; Leiden: Brill, 1963); and K. G. O'Connell, "Greek Versions (Minor)," in *The Interpreter's Dictionary of the Bible*, Supplementary Volume (Nashville: Abingdon, 1976) 377-81.

journey from Jewish Alexandria in the third and second centuries B.C.E. to Christian circles in Egypt and Palestine in the third century of the common Jewish and Christian era.

A third complicating factor, only rarely suspected[4] prior to the discovery of the Qumran scrolls, is the shape of the Hebrew text of which the Septuagint was a translation. For a number of books the variation in the Hebrew text[5] was as significant as that in the Greek text between the second century B.C.E. and the late first century C.E.

Thus, my goal is to study some aspects of the text of the Greek Old Testament and of Origen's use of it. But since that text was an evolving text, we must first consider its origins and character, secondly its early transmission history, and then thirdly some aspects of Origen, his Hexapla, and his use of the Septuagint text.

4. P. Lagarde (*Anmerkungen zur griechischen Übersetzung der Proverbien* [Leipzig, 1863] 3) had already formed and elaborated the principle, summarized by Jellicoe (*Septuagint,* 6): "In a choice between alternative readings preference is to be given . . . to one which represents a Hebrew original other than MT." It is regrettable that many modern scholars, in religious loyalty to the MT, have failed to pay sufficient attention to this empirical principle, especially since it has been amply confirmed by the Qumran textual evidence.

5. Cf., e.g., S. R. Driver, *Notes on the Hebrew Text and the Topography of the Books of Samuel* (2d ed.; Oxford: Clarendon, 1913); F. M. Cross, "The Evolution of a Theory of Local Texts," in *1972 Proceedings: IOSCS and Pseudepigrapha* (ed. R. A. Kraft; Missoula, Mont.: Scholars Press, 1972) 108-26; Barthélemy, *Les devanciers d'Aquila;* idem, "Origène et le texte de l'Ancien Testament," in *Epektasis: Mélanges patristiques offerts au Cardinal Jean Daniélou* (Paris: Beauchesne, 1972) 247-61, esp. 252, reprinted in D. Barthélemy, *Études d'histoire du texte de l'Ancien Testament* (OBO 21; Fribourg: Éditions Universitaires, 1978) 203-17; S. Talmon, "The Textual Study of the Bible — A New Outlook," in *Qumran and the History of the Biblical Text* (ed. F. M. Cross and S. Talmon; Cambridge, Mass.: Harvard University Press, 1975) 321-400; E. Tov, "The Literary History of the Book of Jeremiah in the Light of Its Textual History," in *Empirical Models for Biblical Criticism* (ed. J. Tigay; Philadelphia: University of Pennsylvania Press, 1985) 211-37; J. Trebolle, "Redaction, Recension, and Midrash in the Books of Kings," *BIOSCS* 15 (1984) 12-35; E. Ulrich, *The Qumran Text of Samuel and Josephus* (HSM 19; Missoula, Mont.: Scholars Press, 1978); idem, "Characteristics and Limitations of the Old Latin Translation of the Septuagint," in *La Septuaginta en la investigación contemporánea (V Congreso de la IOSCS)* (Textos y Estudios "Cardenal Cisneros" 34; ed. N. Fernández Marcos; Madrid: Instituto "Arias Montano" C.S.I.C., 1985) 67-80. This last article is now reprinted below as Chapter 14 of this volume.

The Origins and Character of the Old Greek Text

Definitions

At the outset it is important to sort out the various entities for which we use the term "Septuagint" and to clarify our terms for them. There is no fully acceptable definition or consistent usage for the term "Septuagint."[6] The term originally designated the pristine translation of the Torah (only the first five books of the Hebrew Bible) by the seventy *(septuaginta)* or seventy-two elders commissioned to go from Jerusalem to Alexandria for that purpose — but all this as narrated in the *Letter of Aristeas*. But the *Letter of Aristeas* is legendary in content and, though epistolary in form, is really "a propaganda work."[7] Thus, historically, we cannot document any seventy-two elders who were the original translators of the Torah nor, *a fortiori*, of the entire Hebrew Bible. But the term "Septuagint" in its strictest usage refers only to the Pentateuch and only to the original Greek translation of it.

By extension, however, it legitimately[8] designates the original Greek translation of the entire Old Testament, including both the books later accepted as the Hebrew Bible and the apocryphal or deuterocanonical books. But it is excessive elasticity when the term is stretched further to mean "the Greek Old Testament," that is, any Greek form of the OT without regard to specific Greek textual tradition.

More accurate terms would be:

- *the Old Greek* for the original, single, or singly-influential, translation of each different book (many writers now use "the Old Greek" as a term preferable to "Septuagint," since "the Old Greek" is not necessarily confined to the Pentateuch, and since it clearly distinguishes from later forms of the Greek text);[9]

6. Swete, *Introduction*, 9-10; Kraft in E. Tov and R. A. Kraft, "Septuagint," in *The Interpreter's Dictionary of the Bible*, Supplementary Volume (Nashville: Abingdon, 1976) 807-15, esp. 811.

7. Jellicoe, *Septuagint*, 30; cf. P. Kahle, *The Cairo Geniza*, (2d ed.; Oxford: Blackwell, 1959) 211; and J. W. Wevers, "An Apologia for Septuagint Studies," *BIOSCS* 18 (1985) 16-38, esp. 16-19.

8. Justin is probably the first Christian to use the term (*Dialogue with Trypho* 68.7) in extant material, and his context shows that the term is already being used in a way that includes Isaiah and extends to the whole OT; see Jellicoe, *Septuagint*, 41-42; cf. Swete, *Introduction*, p. 9, n. 1.

9. See E. Tov and R. A. Kraft, "Septuagint."

- *the early Greek text(s)* for the gradually evolving forms that developed from that original translation;
- *the early recensions* of Proto-Theodotion (and perhaps Theodotion), Aquila, Symmachus, and possibly of others ("Quinta," etc.);[10]
- *the hexaplaric recension* for the text that Origen produced in his fifth column, "o′" (= "LXX"="70"); and
- *the Lucianic recension* for the fourth-century Antiochene recension of certain books.[11]

The ideal object of the quest for many Septuagintalists is "the text as it left the hand of the [original] translator," or even the Hebrew text behind the LXX.[12] But the practical object of the quest, that sought by the Göttingen critical editions, is the oldest recoverable text of each book, and this would be called "the Old Greek."[13]

This leads us to the final, and for the study of Origen and other ancient writers a very important, distinction: the distinction between the text of the Old Greek as the original Jewish translation of the Hebrew Scriptures, and the text of the Greek Old Testament as the living Bible of the ongoing church during the early Christian centuries. The former signals the translation's importance as a witness, in fact one of the most important witnesses, to the early Hebrew text. The latter signals the text's importance as the living Scriptures of the developing church. These are two different foci, the Greek Old Testament at two different points in its history, serving two different historical-theological purposes.

The two foci can be clearly exemplified by the works of Emanuel Tov and Marguerite Harl. Tov's book is entitled *The Text-Critical Use of the Septuagint in Biblical Research,*[14] and his aim is to understand the LXX and to use retroversion of it, wherever and insofar as possible, as a witness to a form of the Hebrew text — a witness that predates extensive Hebrew manuscript documentation of the Old Testament. Thus, he studies the LXX to see how it can help us get further and more reliably back to earlier or superior forms of the Hebrew Bible. Harl's project of a French translation of the LXX focuses on the use of Scripture in the early church and envisions that

10. See Barthélemy, *Les devanciers;* O'Connell, "Greek Versions (Minor)."

11. See n. 31 below. The "Proto-Lucianic" text tradition may belong to the second or third category above.

12. See Jellicoe's first and last pages (*Septuagint,* 1, 359).

13. See Kraft, "Septuagint," 811.

14. See n. 1 above.

> la Septante sera prise pour elle-même, non pas comme une traduction mais comme *un texte* au sens plein du terme: le texte de la Bible du Judaïsme hellénistique et de l'Eglise ancienne, le texte tel qu'il fut lu par des lecteurs qui n'avaient aucunement recours à l'original hébreu pour tenter de le comprendre, un texte qui s'explique à l'intérieur du système linguistique grec de son époque.[15]

From the perspective of Origen, both foci are necessary, for one of his goals was to restore "the translation of the Seventy," and another was to explain and expound the scriptural text of his church. Therefore, we must look at the original Septuagint, and the developed text that Origen used, and thus the intervening evolutionary process that produced the text he used.

Septuagint Origins: The Data from Early Manuscripts and Quotations

Rather than beginning with the *Letter of Aristeas,* which is legendary material, I think that it is preferable to begin with Septuagintal manuscript evidence and with quotations of the Septuagint by ancient authors. The evidence usually cited is the following:[16]

- Demetrius the Hellenist quoted the Greek Genesis in the late third century B.C.E.
- Eupolemos, a Hellenistic Jewish historian of the mid-second century B.C.E., based a part of his narrative on the Greek Chronicles.[17]
- The Prologue of Ben Sira, written shortly after 132 B.C.E., refers to "the law . . . , the prophecies, and the rest of the books" that had been translated.

15. M. Harl, "Projet d'une traduction de la Septante en français," *BIOSCS* 13 (1980) 7-8. Professor Harl is aware of the difficulties: "Un premier travail est d'établir le catalogue de ces difficultés, de les étudier, de proposer des solutions. Il faudra notamment décider quelle tradition textuelle de la Septante on choisira de traduire, faute de pouvoir rendre compte de la pluralité des états textuels" (p. 8).

16. See, e.g., Swete, *Introduction,* 369-80, and Jellicoe, *Septuagint,* 237-39. With all the advances in LXX research over the past decades, however, this evidence should be closely restudied; see, e.g., the following note.

17. See the caution already expressed by J. A. Montgomery (*A Critical and Exegetical Commentary on the Book of Daniel* [ICC; Edinburgh: Clark, 1927] 38): "On rather scanty evidence, that the Jewish historian Eupolemus, *c.* 150 B.C. (text given by Swete, *Int.,* 370 = Eus., *Praep.,* ix, 31) knew G of 2 Ch. $12^{12ff.}$, Torrey holds, p. 82, that the OGr. tr. of Ch.-Ezr.-Neh. (containing 2 Esd.) existed by the middle of the 2d cent."

- The John Rylands Library of Manchester has small papyrus scraps of the Greek Deuteronomy, dated (by C. H. Roberts) to the second century B.C.E.
- Papyrus Fouad 266, also containing small portions of Deuteronomy, comes from the late second or early first century B.C.E.
- Qumran has yielded five early Greek manuscripts of Genesis-Deuteronomy: 4QLXXLev[a] (late second century B.C.E.), 7QLXXExod (ca. 100 B.C.E.), 4QLXXLev[b] and 4QLXXNum (probably first century B.C.E. or the opening years of the first century C.E.), and 4QLXXDeut,[18] in addition to the Greek Minor Prophets scroll and a fragment of the Letter of Jeremiah.
- Papyrus 967 is a manuscript from the early third century C.E. containing portions of Ezekiel, Daniel, and Esther.[19] For Daniel, this manuscript displays a "pre-hexaplaric" text, that is, a text which is a developed form of the Old Greek, such as Origen would have used as a basis for the "o'" column, but which shows no admixture of elements from the Hexapla. In this case, 967 is for the most part very close to what Origen listed as the "o'" text of Daniel (and clearly at variance with the Theodotionic text, which became universally used and displaced the older "o'" text); but it does not yet have the demonstrably Origenian hexaplaric changes and additions taken from the Theodotionic text that are now found in the single extant Greek witness to Origen's revised "o'" text, MS 88.

The conclusions indicated by the evidence from manuscripts and citations are that the Torah was translated by the late third century B.C.E. and probably by ca. 250, that the Former Prophets were translated before the middle of the second century B.C.E. and probably by ca. 200 because they would have been translated prior to Chronicles, which was circulating by the mid-second cen-

18. See C. H. Roberts, quoted in Kahle, *The Cairo Geniza,* 223; and E. Ulrich, "The Greek Manuscripts of the Pentateuch from Qumrân, Including Newly-Identified Fragments of Deuteronomy (4QLXXDeut)," in *De Septuaginta: Studies in Honour of John William Wevers on His Sixty-Fifth Birthday* (ed. A. Pietersma and C. Cox; Mississauga, Ont.: Benben, 1984) 71-82. The derivative date in Jellicoe, *Septuagint,* 276, should read: ". . . assigned to the late second [not "the late first"] century B.C. or the early first A.D." I should stress that the palaeographically assigned dates quoted above for the Greek manuscripts at Qumran are rough and preliminary and need more thorough analysis.

19. For bibliographic information on the several volumes, see S. Pace, "The Stratigraphy of the Text of Daniel and the Question of Theological *Tendenz* in the Old Greek," *BIOSCS* 17 (1984) 15-35, esp. pp. 18-19 and n. 9; see also now S. Pace Jeansonne, *The Old Greek Translation of Daniel 7–12* (CBQMS 19; Washington, D.C.: Catholic Biblical Association, 1988) 11.

tury B.C.E. The Latter Prophets would very likely have been translated at the same time as the Former Prophets, and of the Writings many books would very likely have been translated about the same time as Chronicles.

Septuagint Origins: Hypotheses

The *Letter of Aristeas* purports to be a letter written in the mid-third century B.C.E., sent by Aristeas to his brother Philocrates, describing the events surrounding the original translation of the Hebrew Torah into Greek for the Ptolemaic king's library. It was taken at face value as historical as early as Philo, and continued to be taken as such by Josephus, early church writers such as Jerome, and others all through the centuries until 1705. The question of LXX origins was considered answered, indeed narrated in detail, by the *Letter of Aristeas.* Sidney Jellicoe traces the transmission history[20] of the *Letter,* including the steady embellishment as it went from hand to hand, all connected with the inspired and authoritative character of the LXX as the Greek form of God's word to Israel.

But in 1705 Humphrey Hody studied the letter and declared it legendary. John W. Wevers has recently presented a current view concerning it, again emphasizing that it is legendary in character, and that "it would be methodologically sound not to accept anything stated in the *Letter* that cannot be substantiated elsewhere."[21]

Since late in the nineteenth century, Paul de Lagarde's theory of LXX origins has held sway, except for a brief period when the influential figure Paul Kahle propounded a diametrically opposed theory. Lagarde thought that the widespread variation in our extant manuscripts led us back to three major recensions of the Greek text, differentiated geographically, and that behind those three recensions one could arrive at a single translation of the Hebrew Bible into Greek.

Kahle, in contrast, thought that the Septuagint arose as did the targumim — from a plethora of individually produced partial translations that, after a period of multiplication, were supplanted by a single translation now endorsed by rabbinic decision as being authoritative. In 1915 he claimed that the letter, though fictionally set in the third century B.C.E., was actually written as propaganda to assure the outcome for one side of a con-

20. Jellicoe, *Septuagint,* 38-47.

21. J. W. Wevers, "An Apologia for Septuagint Studies," *BIOSCS* 18 (1985) 16-38, esp. 17.

flict over the authority of competing Greek texts in the late second century B.C.E.[22]

Thus, Lagarde saw an original single translation gradually branching out both chronologically and geographically, whereas Kahle saw many targumim being displaced by a single standard translation. Lagarde's view, however, appears confirmed by nearly a century of multifaceted research by a wide spectrum of Septuagintal specialists and by the data available from the Qumran and other very early manuscripts, whereas Kahle's view finds no support in detailed research by Septuagintalists.[23]

There remain two schools of thought on the degree of intentional fidelity in the Old Greek translations: one, that the translators generally intended and attempted to render in the Greek language what they perceived to be said in the Hebrew original; the other, that the translators viewed themselves as in a certain measure free to adapt the original meaning to conform with contemporary historical knowledge or theological *Tendenz.* Though the case differs from book to book, I think that in general the former describes the situation more accurately.[24]

Summary

The Old Greek of the Pentateuch was translated starting near the mid-third century B.C.E., the last of the books (e.g., Daniel) being translated probably by the late second or early first century B.C.E. Thus the Old Greek of the Pentateuch antedated Origen by about 450-500 years and the latest of the books by about 300 years.

The earliest, nearly complete codices of the Greek Bible date from the fourth (Vaticanus) and fifth (Alexandrinus and Sinaiticus) centuries C.E., a

22. P. Kahle, "Untersuchungen zur Geschichte des Pentateuchtextes," in *Theologische Studien und Kritiken* 88 (Gotha, 1915) 399-439, esp. 410-26; idem, *The Cairo Geniza,* 212.

23. Cf. Jellicoe, *Septuagint,* 61-63.

24. Contrast, e.g., J. Trebolle, "Redaction, Recension, and Midrash in the Books of Kings," *BIOSCS* 15 (1982) 12-35, and A. van der Kooij, "A Short Commentary on Some Verses of the Old Greek of Isaiah 23," *BIOSCS* 15 (1982) 36-50. For an example of disproof of the *Tendenz* hypothesis, see S. Pace in *BIOSCS* 17 (1984) 15-35. It should be noted that the issue is not whether the translation is "literal" or "free"; we find both literal and free styles of translation in both "faithful" and "interpretative" translations. The question is: do the translators attempt to reproduce in Greek the meaning they find already in the text, or do they feel free to change the original meaning in light of new or current ideas, whether literary, historical, cultural, or theological, or whether private or communal.

century or two after Origen. But fragmentary manuscripts are preserved as far back as the second century B.C.E., and quotations by Hellenistic Jewish authors apparently document the Greek Genesis as far back as the late third century B.C.E.

Lagarde's view that the present variation in LXX manuscripts is traceable back through three ancient recensions to a single original translation receives confirmation by nearly a century of multifaceted research by a wide spectrum of Septuagintal specialists and by the data available from the Qumran and other very early manuscripts.

For each biblical book there seems to have been an original translation from the Hebrew into Greek. The translations, however, display differing translation techniques, and thus each book's translation should be presumed to derive from a different translator.

Though it is often not done, one must carefully consider the relationship of the Old Greek translation to its Hebrew *Vorlage*. Not infrequently, differences from the MT either in individual words or phrases or even in the form of the larger book (e.g., Jeremiah[25]) are due not to theological *Tendenz* but to faithful translation from a different Hebrew parent text.

Thus, as far as we can tell, originally the Old Greek would have been a collection of papyrus or leather scrolls, each normally containing one biblical book, each apparently translated by a different translator, and all (or many) attempting to reproduce in Greek the intended meaning of the Hebrew text (Masoretic, Qumran, or other) from which it had been translated.

The Transmission of the Early Greek Text up to the Hexapla

The collection of scrolls produced from the mid-third to the early first centuries B.C.E., containing the original Greek translations from varying Hebrew texts of the Scriptures, traversed a somewhat complex history of transmission, knowledge of which is essential for understanding the work of Origen — a history partially chartable, mostly lost in the darkness of the past.

We do not, and Origen did not, have extant for any book what anyone would consider the original form of that translation. All manuscripts display a considerable amount of textual development — certainly unintentional changes, such as the well-known panoply of errors, but also intentional changes, such as clarifications, revisions, doublets, and harmonizations.

Moreover, for some books, we no longer have even the changed, cor-

25. See Tov, "The Literary History."

rupted, and developed copies of the Old Greek. In these cases all of our extant manuscript evidence is traceable only to a later recension that either by chance or by conscious decision supplanted the original Greek. The book of Daniel furnishes an example in that this loss and supplanting was complete, except for one manuscript, MS 88, the single extant Greek witness to Origen's "o′" text.[26]

With regard to the Hebrew *Vorlage* or parent text, the transmission history becomes simplified: the evidence suggests that there were no variant Hebrew manuscripts generating further Greek variants due specifically to correction toward Hebrew readings at variance with the MT after approximately the beginning of the second century C.E. The Hebrew scrolls found at Murabbaʿat, dated prior to 135 C.E., conform very closely to the MT and indicate that the rabbinic Bible was already standardized both in general contents and in consonantal text by the second Jewish revolt.

A number of additional sources help illuminate parts of the transmission history of the early Greek text. Study of sources such as the Vetus Latina,[27] quotations of the Hebrew Bible or the Septuagint in the New Testament and in Jewish and Christian authors in antiquity, and ancient biblical manuscripts provides us with windows on the past, enabling us to glimpse what the early Greek text looked like in certain places and specific points in time.

Regarding the *devanciers d'Aquila,* as Dominique Barthélemy terms them, the predecessors of Aquila, we should not take the hexaplaric order as a chronological indicator. The text that circulated under the label "Theodotion" can more accurately be labeled "Proto-Theodotion"; that is, the main systematic revision which characterizes that text was done around the turn of the era, early enough to influence possibly Philo, the New Testament authors, and Justin.[28]

For Proto-Theodotion, Aquila, and Symmachus, it is important to stress

26. See the description of Papyrus 967 above.

27. See E. Ulrich, "The Old Latin Translation of the LXX and the Hebrew Scrolls from Qumran," in *1980 Proceedings IOSCS — Vienna: The Hebrew and Greek Texts of Samuel* (ed. E. Tov; Jerusalem: Academon, 1980) 121-65, reprinted in the present volume as Chapter 13. See also J. Trebolle, "From the 'Old Latin' through the 'Old Greek' to the 'Old Hebrew' (2 Kings 10:23-25)," *Textus* 11 (1984) 17-36.

28. See P. Katz, *Philo's Bible: The Aberrant Text of Bible Quotations in Some Philonic Writings and Its Place in the Textual History of the Greek Bible* (Cambridge: Cambridge University Press, 1950) 12, 102-3, 114-21; Jellicoe, *Septuagint,* 83-94; and P. Katz, "Justin's Old Testament Quotations and the Greek Dodekapropheten Scroll," *Studia Patristica* 1/1 (Berlin, 1957) 343-53.

that these were not new translations from the Hebrew but recensions, that is, systematic revisions, of earlier Greek texts. For Proto-Theodotion, the Old Greek (but already in developed form) was used as the basic text, and it was revised according to definite principles. The principles operative in the Proto-Theodotionic recension involved bringing the early Greek text into much closer conformity with the rabbinic Hebrew text (the consonantal text that would later become the vocalized "Masoretic" Text). This conformity embraced both quantitative and qualitative aspects. Quantitatively, material in the Greek not found in the rabbinic Bible was excised, and material in the Hebrew not matched by the Greek was filled in. Qualitatively, there was insistence on much greater, much more literal, fidelity to the details of the Hebrew text: lexically, Greek roots were matched much more consistently and mechanically with Hebrew roots, even if some violence was done to meaning; and the syntax of the Greek, already awash with semiticisms, was forced into even greater conformity to the syntax of the Hebrew, even if some syntactic violence occurred.

Aquila's recension was based on Proto-Theodotion but carried the systematic revision of Proto-Theodotion to even further levels of mechanical conformity toward the rabbinic text of the second century C.E. Aquila's recension is so systematic that Joseph Reider and Nigel Turner were able to compile *An Index to Aquila*,[29] which gives the Greek equivalents used by Aquila for the Hebrew roots in the biblical text.

Symmachus, about whom little is known,[30] produced a recension also based on Proto-Theodotion but aimed at good Greek style. Variants in which "the Three" (α′ σ′ θ′) agree against the Old Greek usually signal words revised in the Proto-Theodotionic recension and adopted but not further revised by Aquila and Symmachus.

Thus, the task of tracing the transmission of the Greek Old Testament during the early rabbinic and early church period is a multifaceted task, because that text differed for each century and for each geographical region.[31]

29. J. Reider and N. Turner, *An Index to Aquila* (VTSup 12; Leiden: Brill, 1966). Since 1968 a series of dissertations [see n. 32 below] have also been produced, exploring and charting the recensional developments of the Proto-Theodotion, or *Kaige*, recension.

30. See Jellicoe, *Septuagint*, 94-99.

31. Cf. H. Dörrie, "Zur Geschichte der Septuaginta im Jahrhundert Konstantins," *ZNW* 39 (1940) 57-110. P. A. de Lagarde (ed., *Librorum Veteris Testamenti Canonicorum Pars Prior Graece* [Göttingen, 1883]) attempted but failed to determine the Lucianic text of fourth-century Antioch. N. Fernández Marcos has recently contributed to this endeavor through *Theodoreti Cyrensis Quaestiones in Octateuchum: editio critica* (Textos y Estudios "Cardenal Cisneros" 17; ed. N. Fernández Marcos and A. Sáenz-Badillos; Madrid: Instituto "Arias Montano" C.S.I.C., 1979); idem, *Theodoreti Cyrensis Quaestiones in Reges et*

Book by book, we are learning the detailed characteristics of the Old Greek, the developments within the early Greek texts, and the characteristics of the subsequent recensions.[32]

Finally, to envision the "Septuagint" text that would have been available to Origen in the early third century one can study Codex Vaticanus or Papyrus 967. Both are codices containing all or many of the biblical books, inscribed in uncial script, with a text that is pre-hexaplaric. Both have numerous errors, and both display expansions clearly attributable to the vulnerabilities inherent in the process of transmission history. The "Septuagint" text, in varying forms, was the text used in the churches; the texts of Aquila, Symmachus, Theodotion, and others (such as "Quinta" and "Sexta"), mostly known to be Jewish and more closely based on the Hebrew, would also have been available by then.

Some Aspects of Origen and His Hexapla

So Origen began with the ordinary, somewhat corrupted, somewhat developed, koine Greek text of his day (called "the Translation of the Seventy" or simply "Septuaginta"), and he produced a text that was neither the original Old Greek translation nor the purified, inspired "Translation of the Seventy."

I would now like to bring a Septuagintalist's eye to focus on three aspects of Origen and his work: whether Origen knew Hebrew; whether the Hexapla contained a column with Hebrew characters; and an evaluation of Origen's hexaplaric labors as a contribution to the history of the Greek Bible.

Origen's Knowledge of Hebrew

Origen's alleged knowledge or use of Hebrew centers on three areas: (1) his Hebrew tutor(s), (2) references to "the Hebrew" in his writings, and (3) the

---

Paralipomena: editio critica (Textos y Estudios "Cardenal Cisneros" 32; ed. N. Fernández Marcos and J. R. Busto Saiz; Madrid: Instituto "Arias Montano" C.S.I.C., 1984). The same chronological and geographical diversity obtains for the Old Latin; cf. Ulrich, "Characteristics," 68-70, 80.

32. In addition to the Göttingen LXX editions by R. Hanhart, J. W. Wevers, and J. Ziegler, for recent monographs dealing with Exodus (O'Connell, Sanderson), Joshua (Greenspoon), Judges (Bodine), Samuel (Ulrich), Kings (Shenkel, Trebolle), Isaiah (van der Kooij), Jeremiah (Tov), and Daniel (Schmitt, Pace Jeansonne), see the annual bibliographic "Record of Work" in *BIOSCS*.

first column of the Hexapla. Let me begin by stating what would be a minimalist position on these three points:

(1) Perhaps Origen knew no Hebrew or very little Hebrew, so little that it was virtually nonfunctioning. (2) When Origen speaks of "the Hebrew," the basis of his knowledge is the Greek versions of Aquila, Symmachus, and Theodotion, that is, the Hebrew indirectly, as witnessed by literal Greek renditions, not the Hebrew text itself in Hebrew script.[33] (3) The extant hexaplaric manuscript fragments contain no Hebrew column, perhaps because there never was a "first" column containing the Hebrew characters.[34] One is hard-pressed to move beyond this minimalist position, but let us see what can be established or plausibly conjectured.

(1) Eusebius says that Origen took great pains to learn Hebrew and had copies of the Jewish Scriptures in the Hebrew script.[35] Jerome makes a similar assertion.[36] Now this may be attributed to the panegyric style of Eusebius and Jerome. But just because they are waxing eloquent about their hero does not mean that what they say is false; it simply means that we cannot *ipso dicto* consider the statements accurate without further verification. On the one hand, it is quite possible that Origen learned some Hebrew both from "his second teacher in Scripture . . . , the unnamed 'Hebrew,' son of a rabbi, earlier converted to Christianity in Palestine,"[37] and later from learned Jews through direct conversation or debate. On the other hand, this possibility remains nebulous; we can determine only whether he knew Hebrew and how much he knew through his actual uses of it in specific writings.

(2) To what specifically is Origen referring in his commentaries, homilies, and other writings when he speaks of "the Hebrew" or when he relates the Christian "Old Testament" to "the Hebrew"? I have not found any loci where Origen uses Hebrew[38] in such a way that he is free of possible dependence on a Greek intermediary, such as Aquila or the Greek transcription of the Hebrew,[39] or possible dependence on well-known early Christian tradi-

33. Barthélemy, "Origène," 254; Pierre Nautin, *Origène: Sa vie et son œuvre* (Christianisme Antique 1; Paris: Beauchesne, 1977) 337.

34. Nautin, *Origène,* 303, 312, 337, and passim.

35. *Historia Ecclesiastica* 6.16.1; see also Swete, *Introduction,* 59.

36. *De Viris Illustribus* 54; see also Swete, *Introduction,* 59.

37. C. Kannengiesser, unpublished notes for the Christianity and Judaism in Antiquity seminar, University of Notre Dame, 1985-86, p. 2. See Nautin, *Origène,* 347 and 417, where he refers implicitly to Origen's autobiographical note in the *Letter to Africanus* 11.

38. Also Barthélemy ("Origène," 254) says that Origen "se comporte toujours comme s'il ignorait l'hébreu."

39. Cf. Nautin, *Origène,* 337.

tion, such as the discussion of Isaiah 7:14 by Justin, Irenaeus, Tertullian, and others.[40]

On the contrary, Origen can be seen referring to the Hebrew at least once[41] where his argument founders because the Hebrew of the Masoretic *textus receptus* is other than he says; and it seems unlikely that we may appeal to a Hebrew different from the Masoretic, because the context demands precisely the word found in the MT.[42] The passage under discussion is Isaiah 7:14, and the Hebrew quoted is *Aalma* [= עלמה], which of course does occur in Isaiah 7:14. Origen argues that the word *Aalma* here means "virgin" and not simply "young woman." For support, he appeals to Deut 22:23-26, a legal text in which the point centers specifically on a virgin. Origen says that "the word Aalma, which the Septuagint translated by 'parthenos' (virgin) and others [i.e., Aquila and Theodotion] by 'neanis' (young woman), also occurs, so they say, in Deuteronomy applied to a virgin,"[43] and he proceeds to quote the full text of Deuteronomy. Immediately, one suspects that Origen's qualifier "so they say" indicates that he is getting his argument secondhand. And yet, one would think that such an indefatigable scholar as Origen on such a much-argued point as the virgin mother of Christ would certainly have checked the passage in Hebrew if he could have. Had he done so, he would have seen that *Aalma* does not occur in that passage, but rather *na'ărā[h]* ("youth") and the required *bĕtûlāh* ("virgin"). But it is the presupposition here, not specifically Origen's knowledge of Hebrew, that emerges as problematic: Origen was not sufficiently indefatigable — at least not at this point. For even if Origen knew no Hebrew — had he, as presupposed, made the effort to consult even the Greek transliteration — he would have found that his argument from Deuteronomy was baseless. Thus, even this argument where he errs with regard to the Hebrew does not prove that he did not know Hebrew, but rather that he simply did not check his sources, in Hebrew or in Greek transliteration.

In sum, one could conjecture from the evidence and the lack of it that Origen may possibly have learned some Hebrew at some time, but that his lack of display of that knowledge quite probably points to at most a modicum of acquired Hebrew, and that his Hebrew was virtually nonfunctioning.

40. Cf. Barthélemy, "Origène," 250.

41. *Contra Celsum* 1.34. I am grateful to Jeffrey Oschwald for pointing out this example to me.

42. A quick check of the unpublished scrolls from Qumran Cave 4 finds that, as for the published manuscripts from the other caves, Deut 22:23-26 is not preserved. But even if it were, one would not expect that it would display עלמה as a variant, since בתולה is necessary for the legal point made therein.

43. *Contra Celsum* 1.34.

(3) If Origen's knowledge of the Hebrew language is in serious doubt, that would seem to lend support to the position of Pierre Nautin and cast serious doubt as well on whether Origen's Hexapla contained a "first" column in the Hebrew script, and to this we now turn.

A Hebrew Column in the Hexapla?

Did the Hexapla have a column written in the Hebrew script? It is with regard to the Hebrew column of the Hexapla that the minimalist position stated above, echoing Nautin,[44] seems too minimal to me. The Mercati fragments of the "Hexapla," the Ambrosian palimpsest O 39 sup.,[45] contain no Hebrew column, nor do the other hexaplaric remains.[46] Does this prove, however, that there never was a "first" column that contained the Hebrew characters? Barthélemy, having published his article prior to Nautin's book, assumes with the majority of scholars that there was a Hebrew column.[47] My colleague John Wright[48] is convinced by Nautin, but I am not.

Beginning with the data, we note that the ninth- or tenth-century Mercati manuscript has as its initial column the transliteration of the Hebrew in Greek characters, followed by Aquila, Symmachus, the "o′," and a fifth column, customarily labeled "Theodotion" but in Psalms probably Quinta. The side margins are preserved, and it appears certain that there was no column with Hebrew characters prior to the transliteration column in this manuscript. Similarly, the other three synoptic fragments with excerpts of the Hexapla (the marginal notes in Ambrosian codex B 106, the Cambridge frag-

44. Nautin, *Origène,* 303, 312, 337, and passim.

45. Giovanni Mercati, ed., *Psalterii Hexapli Reliquiae . . . ,* Pars Prima: *Codex Rescriptus Bybliothecae Ambrosianae O 39 sup. phototypice expressus et transcriptus* (Vatican City, 1958). See also B. M. Metzger, *Manuscripts of the Greek Bible: An Introduction to Greek Palaeography* (New York: Oxford University, 1981) plate 30 and pp. 108-9; and E. Würthwein, *The Text of the Old Testament* (Grand Rapids: Eerdmans, 1979) plate 34 and pp. 188-89. For fuller discussion see Jellicoe, *Septuagint,* 130-33.

46. See Nautin, *Origène,* 303-9. F. Field (ed., *Origenis Hexaplorum quae supersunt sive veterum interpretum Graecorum in totum Vetus Testamentum fragmenta* [2 vols.; Oxford, 1875] 1:XIV-XV) lists some examples that contain a Hebrew column, but he does not give the source, and thus it is difficult to ascertain whether there are in fact remains of the Hexapla that preserve the Hebrew column.

47. Barthélemy, "Origène," 255.

48. J. Wright, "Origen in the Scholar's Den: A Rationale for the Hexapla," in *Origen of Alexandria: His World and His Legacy* (ed. C. Kannengiesser and W. L. Petersen; Notre Dame: University of Notre Dame Press, 1988) 48-62.

ment from the Cairo Geniza, and the Vatican codex Barberinus 549)[49] contain no column in the Hebrew script.

Starting from a different angle, it appears that the Greek transliteration column was clearly an element of the original Hexapla. It, with or without the Hebrew first column, is the key to the vertical format of the Hexapla. It is implausible that the Greek transliteration would have been added later by Origen or added to Origen's work between the third and eighth centuries had it not been there from the start. The question is whether Origen also had a column with the Hebrew text in Hebrew characters preceding the transliteration.

Nautin bases his assertion that there was no column in the Hebrew script on the format of the four preserved hexaplaric fragments and a critique of the description given by Eusebius.[50] But, turning first to Eusebius, Nautin's critique does not disprove Eusebius. Nautin admits that Eusebius had seen the Hexapla,[51] and quotes Eusebius's statement that Origen had learned the Hebrew language and had acquired personal copies of the Jewish scriptures in Hebrew characters.[52] The statement that Origen had learned the Hebrew language may well be eulogizing praise, founded or unfounded; but the statement about copies of the Hebrew scriptures sounds more like a statement of fact, a description of something Eusebius had seen in the library at Caesarea.

Nautin says that Eusebius "manifestly wants to give a complete description but makes no mention of a column containing Hebrew characters" (p. 314); thus, he concludes, there existed no such column.

Now Nautin is correct that in this passage Eusebius does not explicitly state that there was a column with Hebrew characters as the first column of the Hexapla. He is also probably correct that τῆς Ἑβραίων σημειώσεως means the Greek transliteration. But though he makes the curious remark (causing

49. See Nautin, *Origène,* 303-9.

50. Nautin, *Origène,* 303-9 (Hexaplaric fragments) and 311-16 (Eusebius). Nautin begins his chapter on the Hexapla (303) with a description that omits this column. He prepares his reader: "On observera qu'il n'existe pas de colonne contenant l'hébreu en caractères hébraïques, ce qui concorde tout à fait, nous le verrons, avec le témoignage d'Eusèbe" (305). And after his discussion of Eusebius (311-16) he discounts Epiphanius's testimony: "Mais il est contredit par celui d'Eusèbe . . . , qui mentionne une seule colonne d'hébreu, celle de la translittération" (320).

51. "Eusèbe a regardé les synopses qu'il trouvait dans la bibliothèque de Césarée" (Nautin, *Origène,* 312), and "Eusèbe avait une connaissance directe de la synopse" (ibid., 320).

52. Nautin, *Origène,* 312: ". . . qu'il acquit personnellement les Écritures protopyes conservées chez les Juifs et écrites avec les charactères hébreux eux-mêmes . . ."; Eusebius, *Historia Ecclesiastica* 6.16.1: πρωτοτύπους αὐτοῖς Ἑβραῖων στοιχείοις γραφάς ("the original writings in actual Hebrew characters").

one to wonder what presupposition lies behind) that the LXX comes only in the third rank among the four Greek versions (p. 305), he fails to bring to our attention that Eusebius does not describe the columns in order but is content to mention the LXX in one phrase but the versions of Aquila, Symmachus, and Theodotion together in a separate phrase. Nor does he bring to our attention that Eusebius mentions τῆς Ἑβραίων σημειώσεως after, not before, the other Greek versions.

In my view, just as Eusebius spoke of the LXX and "the Three" in one natural way of speaking, but not in a precise order of description, so he began this passage by speaking of Origen's Hebrew Bible "in Hebrew characters" and immediately continued describing — without having precisely stated that the Hebrew was inscribed in the first column — the other elements of the Hexapla. Eusebius is patently not giving the type of precise description required to support the weight of Nautin's conclusion. Put another way: why is it possible to conclude that, since Eusebius makes no explicit mention of a column containing Hebrew characters, there therefore existed no such column, if one is not prepared to say that, since Eusebius explicitly mentions the LXX in one phrase but the versions of Aquila, Symmachus, and Theodotion together in a separate phrase, the columns of the Hexapla were therefore precisely in the order he described?

Nautin's well-intentioned cross-examination appears more rigorous than Eusebius's words were meant to bear. At the level of concepts, Nautin has elaborated one provocative, perhaps possible reconstruction of the Hexapla. But at the level of judgment, he has not at all proved that the traditional (ancient and modern) reconstruction is incorrect, nor has he proven that his is correct; each of his conclusions still needs to be tested.

Turning now to Nautin's assessment of the Mercati manuscript, before considering his judgment it is important to state explicitly, as Nautin does not in his opening treatment of the manuscript, that the Mercati manuscript is not *the* Hexapla but a *ninth- or tenth-century copy* of excerpts from the Hexapla. In fact, our earliest fragments of the Hexapla date only from the eighth century, five hundred years after Origen. We should expect there to have been very few Christians after Origen and before the date of the four surviving fragments of the Hexapla who could have transcribed the Hebrew column,[53] and it would be extremely unlikely that for each instance of copying during those five hundred years there was someone who both knew Hebrew and saw a need to preserve the Hebrew column.

53. Jerome was one of the few Christian authors after Origen and before the twelfth century who studied Hebrew.

Furthermore, I am not at all sure that all four fragments support Nautin's conclusion. The twelfth-century (or later) marginal notes in the Ambrosian codex B 106 list five columns (the Greek transliteration, then presumably Aquila, Symmachus, the Septuagint, and Theodotion or Quinta); but prior to the Greek transliteration column there are four points arranged, according to Nautin, in a diamond shape. Mercati wondered whether these points would not have been put in place of the Hebrew letters, but Nautin says that "This supposition has no foundation since Eusebius himself did not find the column in Hebrew characters . . . and furthermore [the Mercati fragment] does not have it. These four points can have no other function than to mark the beginning of the citation or to signal the use of Hebrew words."[54]

However, Nautin's argument does not hold up. Against the three parts of his statement: first, I have argued above that Nautin has not proved that Eusebius did not see a Hebrew column in the Hexapla; secondly, the absence of the Hebrew column in the ninth- or tenth-century Mercati copy does not prove that the third-century Hexapla did not have a Hebrew column; and thirdly, the scribe's four points do, I would agree, signal the use of Hebrew words; but I would assume that these signaled Hebrew words were in the Hebrew script from the first column, where in fact the points are properly placed. In contrast, Nautin, if his argument is to be consistent, apparently assumes that these "Hebrew words" are the Greek transliteration in what is traditionally considered the "second" column. This point, however, must remain unresolved until it can be determined, from other usage in the manuscript or elsewhere, whether the four points substitute for words in the Hebrew script, seen, not copied, but their presence marked, or whether they simply indicate that the following words that were copied are foreign words, though written in Greek script.

Thus, for Nautin's denial of the Hebrew column on the basis of the manuscript evidence, I question his data on one of the four manuscripts, and I think that the five-hundred-year hiatus between Origen and the preserved fragments neutralizes his evidence, for one would not expect Christians either to have been able, or to have always wanted, to copy the column with the Hebrew script. Nautin has argued the case for one possible reconstruction of the Hexapla, but in my view he has not proved that the traditional reconstruction is wrong, and I still find myself holding the traditional understanding.

It may well be that none of the four fragments are really copies of "the Hexapla" but simply excerpts, or copies of excerpts, from the Hexapla. Three of the four are from the Psalms, and the citation in Vatican codex Barberinus

54. Nautin, *Origène,* 306-7, n. 5.

549 is a citation of one verse excerpted from the Hexapla ("'Εκ τῶν ἑξάπλων") — only a citation from Hosea 11:1, in connection, as it itself says, with Matthew's quotation of it in his infancy narrative. The Hosea usage is clearly Christian, and the Psalms usage may very well have been. Thus, a minimalist interpretation here would be that the Greek columns of the Hexapla of Psalms were copied and used, and excerpts were occasionally made from a copy of the Hexapla for Christian exegetical purposes.

Be that as is it may, from a larger perspective the point of the Hebrew column may be of little consequence, if Origen did not know or use the Hebrew. I think that, whether Origen's Hexapla contained a Hebrew column or not, the transliteration column arose earlier as a column in parallel with a column containing the Hebrew characters. Origen borrowed and placed in his Hexapla either the Hebrew text and the transcription (the traditional view) or simply the transcription (Nautin's view). It is quite conceivable that Origen borrowed a Jewish source that already had in parallel columns the Hebrew, a Greek transliteration, and Aquila's exactly corresponding version — and possibly even Symmachus's version as well for intelligibility or elegant style.

The picture which emerges is that Origen was confronted with manuscripts of the Greek Bible used by the church which disagreed with each other, and that he was confronted by argumentation (live or literary) with Jews whose Bible differed significantly from that of the church, and he had enough balance to understand that the Hebrew had a certain priority. So he took "the Hebrew" (probably in Hebrew script and also in Greek transliteration, possibly only the latter), Aquila, Symmachus, Theodotion, and whatever other *ekdoseis* were available plus the "Septuagint" in forms then current in Alexandria or Palestine, and had his copyists and calligraphers (probably including Hebrew) compile a work that he in his extant writings does not, but that Eusebius does, call "the Hexapla." In its fifth column he produced "the hexaplaric recension," a revised edition of the "Septuagint," with the quantitative changes marked by the Aristarchian symbols, with the qualitative changes including transposed word order not marked, and ineluctably with some copyists' errors.

Origen's Achievement

Finally, what evaluation do we render concerning Origen's Hexapla in relation to the transmission history of the Greek Bible? From Driver[55] to

55. Driver, "Notes," xliii.

Barthélemy, the judgment has been negative. Barthélemy even uses the word "catastrophique" and notes that, for us to arrive at the original Old Greek, "il nous faut commencer par purifier le texte de la Septante de toute contamination hexaplaire. . . ."[56]

The key to the problem engendered by the Hexapla is that by Origen's time the rabbinic Hebrew Bible had been standardized and there was a general assumption that it was the *Hebraica Veritas.* Origen assumed that the single Hebrew text type used by his contemporaries was identical to that from which the Septuagint had been translated. Deviations of the Greek from the Hebrew were considered problems or infidelities in the Greek. It is precisely in Origen's carrying out of his objective that he obscured and lost the most: in his changing the Greek "back" toward agreement with the rabbinic text, he lost, sometimes forever, many superior readings and many attestations to variant traditions.

Nautin and Trigg[57] think that Origen should not be blamed. They rather blame his followers who did not maintain his critical standards. But here again, I must disagree. Origen deserves high marks for industry, good intentions, and perhaps the highest standards conceivable and achievable in his era. But he did not achieve the *"incorrupta et inmaculata septuaginta interpretum translatio,"* as claimed by Jerome.[58] Neither did he achieve the original Old Greek translation, in the sense of the goal of the modern text critic; on the contrary, he moved farther away. Nor did he produce a text that would long stand as a purified text for the Eastern churches (in his sense of conforming to the Hebrew). Nor did he even have the luck to bequeath a very useful tool for the modern scholar — in that it is scarcely preserved, and what is preserved is confusedly preserved.

What is the difference between the hexaplaric Septuagint and the Septuagint that we use today? The Göttingen critical editions, and even Rahlfs's hand edition, have attempted to purify the text of any hexaplaric influence, and the Cambridge Septuagint chooses Vaticanus as its diplomatic text precisely because it is largely pre-hexaplaric. Is this "purification" good and desirable? The textual critic, attempting to drive further back toward earlier and "superior" forms of the Hebrew biblical text, would assent. One seeking the Bible of the early church may perhaps start by dissenting but would soon have to agree that Origen moved the Bible away from the form that the

56. Barthélemy, "Origène," 247.

57. Nautin, *Origène,* 359-61; J. W. Trigg, *Origen: The Bible and Philosophy in the Third-century Church* (Atlanta: John Knox, 1983) 85.

58. *Epistula* 106.2.2, in *Sancti Eusebii Hieronymi Epistulae* II (CSEL 55; ed. I. Hilberg; Vienna, 1912) 248-49.

church had previously known and produced yet another form of the varying Septuagint manuscript tradition — a form that, soon afterward at the hand of Lucian, spawned future diffusion in the transmission history.

On the positive side, Origen was the pioneer of biblical textual criticism for the Christian tradition. He also pioneered the path of integration of critical scholarship with theology and spirituality. He did achieve the removal of a number of mistakes from the text, and he brought the Christian text into greater conformity with the rabbinic Hebrew text of the third century, so that dialogue continued to be possible. A principal achievement was that he bolstered Christian confidence in the soundness of the Greek Old Testament, and this should be reckoned a significant milestone in the Christian use of the Hebrew Bible.[59]

59. This final idea and a significant amount of clarification throughout this paper I owe to the insightful discussion of Jeffrey Oschwald.

CHAPTER 12

The Relevance of the Dead Sea Scrolls for Hexaplaric Studies

The Hexapla is a rich testament to the textual diversity of the Hebrew Bible and its Greek forms in the second and third centuries C.E. Origen, in order to produce a reliable basis for disputation,[1] but with high dividends for text-critical purposes, attempted to bring the Greek text of his day into conformity with the Hebrew text. His noble purpose, however, produced results that proved as problematic as they were rewarding. The variant Greek traditions were not aberrant paraphrases in need of correction back toward the Hebrew, but faithful translations of variant Hebrew texts that were unknown to Origen. That is, Origen began with the incorrect assumption of a single Hebrew form of the biblical text, with the result that most who used his work, instead of being led closer to the original "Translation of the Seventy," with every step in this regard were led farther away from the text that was his goal.[2]

Despite those unfortunate ramifications, the Hexapla was the largest

1. See S. Brock, "Origen's Aims as a Textual Critic of the Old Testament," in *Papers Presented to the Fifth International Conference on Patristic Studies Held in Oxford 1967* (ed. F. L. Cross; Studia Patristica 10; Texte und Untersuchungen 102; Berlin: Akademie Verlag, 1970) 215-18, reprinted in *Studies in the Septuagint: Origins, Recensions, and Interpretation* (ed. S. Jellicoe and H. M. Orlinsky; New York: Ktav, 1974) 343-46.

2. D. Barthélemy judges Origen's results on the transmission history of the Greek Bible to be "catastrophique"; see his "Origène et le texte de l'Ancien Testament," in *Epektasis: Mélanges patristiques offerts au Cardinal Jean Daniélou* (Paris: Beauchesne, 1972) 247-61, reprinted in D. Barthélemy, *Études d'histoire du texte de l'Ancien Testament* (OBO 21; Fribourg: Éditions Universitaires, 1978) 203-17.

single repository in antiquity documenting the history of the biblical text over five hundred years. It was the convergence of hundreds of years of diverse currents in the history of the biblical text, and, of course, itself became the beginning of another era of diverse currents of the same.[3]

The reason for the Hexapla was that the multiplicity of texts and text traditions proved problematic for one espousing the principle that, because the text was inspired, there must be a single text of the Bible. But one of the main forces causing the major "cross currents" or "textual confusion" that prompted the Hexapla was unknown to Origen, and it has been unseen generally until the middle of this century: that the text of the Hebrew Scriptures was not uniform but pluriform during the late Second Temple period, during the rise of Christianity, perhaps as late as the second Jewish revolt (132-35 C.E.), and possibly later. Some of the tools that show this, principally the Samaritan Pentateuch (SP) and the Old Greek (OG), lay within easy reach of scholars through the centuries but were not generally understood in this context. However, the scrolls from Qumran and other sites along the Dead Sea paint the picture with exciting clarity. They are crucial for understanding the textual pluriformity in the Hebrew biblical text as well as the textual diversity, disturbance, and confusion in the Greek transmission history. Moreover, their witness simply confirms the picture of the nature and history of the Hebrew and Greek text taught by the SP and OG. The scrolls are essential, therefore, for understanding and working on the Hexapla.

These new Hebrew biblical manuscripts provide us with a greater understanding both with regard to the specific text forms of the individual books and with regard to the extent and classification of the collection of the books at the end of the Second Temple period.[4] Here, however, we will focus on the specific text forms of the individual books and their relevance for the study of the Hexapla.

Numerous readings scattered throughout the Hexapla are the result of

3. Jerome, in *Praefatio Hieronymi in Librum Paralipomenon,* would later lament the multiplicity of text forms resulting in the geographical *trifaria varietate* (*Patrologia Latina,* 28.1324B-1325A).

4. On the scrolls and the biblical canon, see E. Ulrich, "The Bible in the Making: The Scriptures at Qumran," in *The Community of the Renewed Covenant: The Notre Dame Symposium on the Dead Sea Scrolls* (ed. E. Ulrich and J. VanderKam; Notre Dame: University of Notre Dame Press, 1994) 77-93, now reprinted as Chapter 2 in this volume; idem, "The Canonical Process, Textual Criticism, and Latter Stages in the Composition of the Bible," in *Sha'arei Talmon: Studies in the Bible, Qumran, and the Ancient Near East Presented to Shemaryahu Talmon* (ed. M. Fishbane and E. Tov with W. W. Fields; Winona Lake, Ind.: Eisenbrauns, 1992) 267-91, reprinted as Chapter 4 in this volume.

textual turbulence. One helpful way to begin to clarify the text of the Hebrew Bible is to distinguish between three fundamentally different types of variation in manuscripts and textual traditions. First, differences in orthography (i.e., different legitimate ways to spell the same word), whether Hebrew or Greek, usually do not affect meaning and are, or can be, independent of manuscript interrelationships that can be traced by textual variants. Second, the textual variants within a single manuscript are commonly unrelated to each other; that is, one variant in a manuscript may be an inadvertent error, another a scribal clarification, the next a harmonization, and so forth. Third, in contradistinction to this random fluctuation, the pattern of variants in some texts proves to be an intentional and systematic production of a revised form of the text. This tripartite division of types of variation is well known and accepted in Septuagint studies.

Orthography

For our present purposes we need not dwell on this category. Usually, orthographic differences are irrelevant for tracing the interrelationships between texts until they are at a more developed stage. It may be useful to point out that in the Cambridge Septuagint editions orthographic differences in the majuscules are separated and placed in the first apparatus.

Individual Variants

The main apparatus in *BHS* and in the Göttingen and Cambridge Septuagint editions would be examples of the common category for textual variants, the one into which variants usually fall unless proven otherwise. With respect to the Hexapla, its structural arrangement in narrow columns of parallel vertical text is conducive to focusing on individual variants. But the huge size of the Hexapla and the small amount of biblical text on any single page makes it more difficult to contemplate variant editions or to analyze the textual character of a book or a column.

Variant Literary Editions

Some of the most important new findings are in the area of variant editions of biblical texts, whether of entire books or of circumscribed passages. In

Septuagint studies it has long been axiomatic that close study of the textual character of each book is an essential basis for solid results in one's analysis. Knowledge of the textual character of each book in its Hebrew stages is equally important, although that point is seldom expressed and perhaps seldom considered. Emanuel Tov correctly points out that the Qumran texts have "taught us no longer to posit MT at the center of our textual thinking."[5] It is not that the Masoretic Text has decreased in value or respect. Rather, we can see it more clearly, we can see beyond it to a variety of Hebrew texts in antiquity, and we can see that it faithfully reflects an ancient collection of disparate texts of the individual biblical books. But, just like the Septuagint, the Masoretic Text is not homogeneous; the textual character and quality of the various books within the Masoretic collection change from book to book. And, since the textual character and quality of each book within the Septuagint collection also changes, energy should be focused on identifying the textual character of the book in the Masoretic collection and that of the corresponding book in the Septuagint collection. We should not *presume* that the OG of any particular book was translated from the Masoretic form of that book. Once we begin with a neutral question regarding the character of the Hebrew text of a particular book that the OG was attempting to translate, we can gain clearer focus on the nature of the Greek text whose transmission we are trying to chart through the Hexapla.

Variant Literary Editions in the Hebrew Scrolls

The following textual survey for a broad selection of the biblical books may prove to be of service as a background to Hexapla studies.

Genesis. The text of Genesis appears mostly to have stabilized prior to all of the extant manuscript witnesses, so that all witnesses exhibit generally a single textual tradition, except for the chronological sections of Genesis 5 and 11, which may show intentionally variant schemata in MT, SP, and OG.[6]

Exodus. The MT and the OG contain presumably an earlier, shorter edition of most of Exodus, whereas 4QpaleoExod^{m} displays a later, harmonized edition that in turn was similar to the one that had been used as the

5. E. Tov, "Hebrew Biblical Manuscripts from the Judaean Desert: Their Contribution to Textual Criticism," *JJS* 39 (1988) 5-37, esp. 7.

6. R. S. Hendel, "Toward a Critical Text of Genesis: Method and Results," lecture at the annual meeting of the Society of Biblical Literature, Chicago, November 20, 1994.

basis of the SP.[7] It is probable that these two variant editions were both in use by Jews of the late Second Temple period, just as the following pair of editions were. For Exodus 35–40, MT and OG have different editions of those chapters, and here 4QpaleoExod^{m}, SP, and MT share the same tradition against OG, suggesting that OG may represent an earlier form of the tabernacle tradition.

Numbers. MT and SP bear witness to different editions of Numbers, with patterns similar to those in Exodus; OG mainly agrees with MT, but sometimes with SP.[8]

Joshua. It is not certain, but it is quite probable that 4QJosh^{a} contained an edition of the text of Joshua with claim to an earlier sequence of narrative components than that preserved in MT and the transmitted LXX. According to this understanding of 4QJosh^{a}, Joshua built the first altar in the newly entered promised land at Gilgal immediately after crossing the Jordan (prior to Joshua 5), and not later, in the odd detour into unprotected territory, as the MT (Josh 8:30-35) and the transmitted LXX (Josh 9:3-8) narrate. Josephus (*Ant.* 5.1.4 §20) supports the sequence of the 4QJosh^{a} narrative.[9]

Kingdoms. The case for Samuel as a whole remains unclear, but MT and LXX may present intentionally variant editions in 1 Samuel 1, and they clearly do in 1 Samuel 17–18.[10] Whether it can be judged a variant edition or

7. For the edition of 4QpaleoExod^{m}, see P. W. Skehan, E. Ulrich, and J. E. Sanderson, *Qumran Cave 4, IV: Palaeo-Hebrew and Greek Biblical Manuscripts* (DJD 9; Oxford: Clarendon, 1992) 53-130. For an analysis, see J. E. Sanderson, *An Exodus Scroll from Qumran: 4QpaleoExod^{m} and the Samaritan Tradition* (HSS 30; Atlanta: Scholars Press, 1986).

8. For the edition of 4QNum^{b}, see N. Jastram, "4QNum^{b}," in E. Ulrich et al., *Qumran Cave 4, VII: Genesis to Numbers* (DJD 12; Oxford: Clarendon, 1994); for analysis, see N. Jastram, "The Book of Numbers from Qumrân, Cave IV (4QNum^{b})" (Dissertation, Harvard University, 1990).

9. For the edition of 4QJosh^{a} and an analysis, see E. Ulrich, "4QJoshua^{a}," in *Qumran Cave 4, IX: Deuteronomy, Joshua, Judges, Kings* (DJD 14; Oxford: Clarendon, 1996) 143-52; idem, "4QJoshua^{a} and Joshua's First Altar in the Promised Land," in *New Qumran Texts and Studies: Proceedings of the First Meeting of the International Organization for Qumran Studies, Paris 1992* (ed. G. J. Brooke with F. García Martinez; STDJ 15; Leiden: Brill, 1994) 89-104 and plates 4-6.

10. For 1 Samuel 1, see Stanley D. Walters, "Hannah and Anna: The Greek and Hebrew Texts of 1 Samuel 1," *JBL* 107 (1988) 385-412. For 1 Samuel 17–18, see esp. the contributions of E. Tov and J. Lust in D. Barthélemy, D. W. Gooding, J. Lust, and E. Tov, *The Story of David and Goliath: Textual and Literary Criticism: Papers of a Joint Research Venture* (OBO 73; Fribourg: Editions Universitaires; Göttingen: Vandenhoeck & Ruprecht, 1986).

not, 4QSam^{a} displays a text tradition that was used by the OG translator of Samuel, by the Chronicler, and by Josephus, in sharp contrast with MT, which was not the *Vorlage* of the OG nor used as their source by the Chronicler or Josephus.[11]

For the books of Kings, Julio Trebolle Barrera has demonstrated variant literary editions of selected parts, sometimes utilizing the Old Latin for clues to the OG, which mediated forms of the Hebrew narratives now lost.[12] In addition, Zipora Talshir has recently retrieved "the lost Hebrew story" behind the Greek narrative in 3 Kingdoms 12:24a-z, highlighting another variant edition in the biblical text.[13]

Psalms. Although there is still no consensus on this point, most indicators point toward a pair of variant editions of the biblical Psalter in the late Second Temple period. 11QPs^{a}, followed by 11QPs^{b} and possibly 4QPs^{e}, displays an expanded and somewhat differently arranged series of psalms.[14] The preserved LXX (not necessarily the OG) of Psalms mostly follows the MT arrangement, although it does, in agreement with 11QPs^{a}, include Psalm 151 at the end. Interestingly, there is no Psalms manuscript from Qumran, and only one from Masada (MasPs^{b}), "whose order *unambiguously* supports the Received Psalter against the 11QPs^{a} arrangement."[15]

Jeremiah. Ever since Frank Moore Cross's identification of 4QJer^{b} as parallel to the *Vorlage* of the OG of Jeremiah, and Emanuel Tov's analysis and

11. See F. M. Cross, "A New Qumrân Biblical Fragment Related to the Original Hebrew Underlying the Septuagint," *BASOR* 132 (1953) 15-26; idem, "The History of the Biblical Text in Light of Discoveries in the Judaean Desert," in *Qumran and the History of the Biblical Text* (ed. F. M. Cross and S. Talmon; Cambridge: Harvard University Press, 1975) 177-95; E. Ulrich, *The Qumran Text of Samuel and Josephus* (HSM 19; Missoula, Mont.: Scholars Press, 1978).

12. For Trebolle Barrera's method, see his "Redaction, Recension, and Midrash in the Books of Kings," *BIOSCS* 15 (1982) 12-35 and "From the 'Old Latin' through the 'Old Greek' to the 'Old Hebrew' (2 Kings 10:23-35)," *Textus* 11 (1984) 17-36. For the edition of 4QKings and an analysis, see his "A Preliminary Edition of 4QKings (4Q54)," in *The Madrid Qumran Congress: Proceedings of the International Congress on the Dead Sea Scrolls, Madrid 18-21 March, 1991* (2 vols.; ed. J. Trebolle Barrera and L. Vegas Montaner; STDJ 11; Leiden: Brill; Madrid: Editorial Complutense, 1992) 1:229-46.

13. See Zipora Talshir, *The Alternative Story of the Division of the Kingdom: 3 Kingdoms 12:24a-z* (Jerusalem: Simor, 1993) esp. 278-79.

14. For the edition of 11QPs^{a}, see J. Sanders, *The Psalms Scroll of Qumrân Cave 11 (11QPs^{a})* (DJD 4; Oxford: Clarendon, 1965). For an analysis of the 4Q Psalms texts and the issues, see P. W. Flint, "The Psalters at Qumran and the Book of Psalms" (Dissertation, University of Notre Dame, 1993), now published as *The Dead Sea Psalms Scrolls and the Book of Psalms* (STDJ 17; Leiden: Brill, 1997).

15. Flint, "Psalters," 147.

contrast of the OG and MT forms of the text of Jeremiah, the two variant editions of that book are well known.[16]

Daniel. Although the Greek tradition preserves both variant literary editions of Daniel, the OG translation and the recensional text marked θ′, rarely is the connection made that there must have been (at least) two Semitic editions of the text. The shorter Semitic edition is preserved in MT and in the Qumran manuscripts, and the longer Semitic edition is reflected first in the text that the OG translated and later in the text toward which the recensionist revised the OG.[17] The texts of Daniel provide an example of the threefold distinction discussed above: 4QDan[a] consistently agrees with MT (against 4QDan[b]) in orthography, but 4QDan[a] agrees with 4QDan[b] (against MT) in individual textual variants. All three, however, appear to agree in the earlier, shorter edition against the longer edition of the OG and θ′ traditions.[18]

From this selective and compressed summary of the evidence provided by the Hebrew biblical scrolls from the Judaean Desert, the importance of identifying the nature of the Hebrew text behind any Greek text is manifest.

16. See F. M. Cross, *The Ancient Library of Qumran and Modern Biblical Studies* (rev. ed.; Grand Rapids: Baker, 1980) 186-87. For the edition of 4QJer[b], see E. Tov, "Three Fragments of Jeremiah from Qumran Cave 4," *RevQ* 15 (1992) 531-41; for the variant editions of the book, see E. Tov, "Some Aspects of the Textual and Literary History of the Book of Jeremiah," in *Le livre de Jérémie: Le prophète et son milieu, les oracles et leur transmission* (ed. P.-M. Bogaert; BETL 54; Leuven: Leuven University Press, 1981) 145-67.

17. For editions of 4QDan[a,b,c], see E. Ulrich, "Daniel Manuscripts from Qumran. Part 1: A Preliminary Edition of 4QDan[a]," *BASOR* 268 (1987) 17-37; idem, "Daniel Manuscripts from Qumran. Part 2: Preliminary Editions of 4QDan[b] and 4QDan[c]," *BASOR* 274 (1989) 3-26. For analyses of the OG and Theodotion, see S. Pace Jeansonne, *The Old Greek Translation of Daniel 7–12* (CBQMS 19; Washington, D.C.: Catholic Biblical Association, 1988); D. O. Wenthe, "The Old Greek Translation of Daniel 1–6" (Dissertation, University of Notre Dame, 1991); McLay, "Translation Technique and Textual Studies in the Old Greek and Theodotion Versions of Daniel" (Dissertation, University of Durham, 1994).

18. See E. Ulrich, "Orthography and Text in 4QDan[a] and 4QDan[b] and in the Received Masoretic Text," in *Of Scribes and Scrolls: Studies on the Hebrew Bible, Intertestamental Judaism, and Christian Origins Presented to John Strugnell on the Occasion of His Sixtieth Birthday* (ed. H. W. Attridge, J. J. Collins, and T. H. Tobin; College Theology Society Resources in Religion 5; Lanham, Md.: University Press of America, 1990) 29-42, reprinted as Chapter 8 in this volume.

The Greek Scrolls

The Greek manuscripts from the Judaean Desert are also bountifully instructive. They provide documentary evidence for the presence in first-century Palestine of both Septuagintal and recensional texts.

For example, pap7QLXXExod, 4QLXXLev^{a}, pap4QLXXLev^{b}, and 4QLXXNum show us texts that are unquestionably in the OG tradition, although they have noteworthy variants from the principal uncials and the general manuscript tradition.[19] By contrast, the Greek Minor Prophets scroll (8ḤevXII gr) attests the recension commonly referred to as Proto-Theodotion or καιγε.[20] Working through this Greek scroll and the substantial analyses by Barthélemy and Tov is fundamental for anyone doing Hexaplaric studies.

With regard to the Septuagintal texts, they urge a conversion in our thinking analogous to that demanded by the variant Hebrew texts. When comparing the variants between the traditional LXX manuscripts and the LXX scrolls, one must ask which text form is closer to the original (or primarily influential) Greek translation? It is instructive, if perhaps unfair, to ask the question again this way: which witness presents an earlier or more original text, the second- and first-century-B.C.E. Qumran manuscripts, or the fourth- and fifth-century-C.E. Vaticanus and Alexandrinus, or the medieval minuscules? This is admittedly an unfair way of putting the question, since age is not necessarily determinative of quality; but age should be seriously considered, and in this case, I think, may lead in the right direction. This is not the place for a full discussion of this issue, but the question should be raised.[21]

When making decisions in Hexaplaric work, one needs three-dimensional vision for "the LXX." Is "𝔊" or "𝔊^{ed}" or "the LXX" or even "the OG" really the original *translation* (absolutely or by influence) from a Hebrew

19. For editions of the 4QLXX manuscripts, see P. W. Skehan, E. Ulrich, and J. E. Sanderson, *Qumran Cave 4, IV: Palaeo-Hebrew and Greek Biblical Manuscripts* (DJD 9; Oxford: Clarendon, 1992); for pap7QLXXExod, see M. Baillet, J. T. Milik, and R. de Vaux, *Les 'Petites Grottes' de Qumrân. 1: Texte. 2: Planches* (DJD 3; Oxford: Clarendon, 1962) 142-43 with plate 30.

20. E. Tov with R. A. Kraft, *The Greek Minor Prophets Scroll from Naḥal Ḥever (8ḤevXIIgr)* (The Seiyâl Collection 1; DJD 8; Oxford: Clarendon, 1990); preliminary publication: D. Barthélemy, *Les devanciers d'Aquila* (VTSup 10; Leiden: Brill, 1963) 163-78.

21. John W. Wevers has put us all in his debt with his Göttingen critical editions of the Greek Pentateuch. I trust that he will receive as a tribute to his achievements my article "The Septuagint Manuscripts from Qumran: A Reappraisal of Their Value," in *Septuagint, Scrolls, and Cognate Writings* (ed. G. J. Brooke and B. Lindars; SBLSCS 33; Atlanta: Scholars Press, 1992) 49-80, reprinted as Chapter 9 in this volume.

text into Greek? Sometimes yes, sometimes no; and often from word to word we cannot know. But we must consider that the text is frequently what I have sometimes designated "G_2." That is, it is a developed form of the OG, partly corrupted, partly developed by expansions and clarifications. A small percentage of these developments are due to influence by Hebrew texts, but most are inner-Greek. When judging between the variants of the Greek scrolls and the LXX manuscript tradition, we are usually attempting to determine which reading is the OG and which is G_2.

The Greek scrolls as well as the Hebrew scrolls are fragmentary, and the remains of the Hexapla are fragmentary, and so the problem is compounded. Despite the fragmentary nature of the witnesses, sufficient work has been done on both the Hebrew and the Greek biblical scrolls from the Judaean Desert to make available a reasonably clear picture of the state and development of the biblical texts in antiquity. That picture is more than sufficiently clear to be of significant service to Hexaplaric studies. Yet a stronger statement is necessary: it is perilous to navigate the broad and varied seas that constitute the Hexapla, its contents, and the forces that formed it without knowing the map of the textual winds and currents that the scrolls from the Judaean Desert have brought to light for us. With the new evidence from the Dead Sea Scrolls and the newly refined criteria developed during the past half century of scholarship for both the Hebrew and the Greek forms of the biblical text, there can be substantial, new advances in the study of the Hexapla.

CHAPTER 13

The Old Latin Translation of the LXX and the Hebrew Scrolls from Qumran

The Problem

The character of the Vetus Latina (= L)[1] and its various forms was beyond critical control in the days of Jerome and Augustine,[2] did not yield to Sabatier's gi-

1. The sigla used in this article are, with some exceptions, in general conformity with those used in *Biblia Hebraica Stuttgartensia,* the Brooke-McLean edition of the Septuagint, and my edition of 4QSam^c in *BASOR* 235 (1979) 1-25, but several sigla and abbreviations require specific mention. See below and on pages 234, 237-38.

M	the Masoretic text as in *Biblia Hebraica Stuttgartensia,* ed. P. A. H. de Boer
G	the Greek Version or the majority of Greek uncials and minuscules (for individual manuscripts, cf. Brooke-McLean)
G^L	early or late elements in the text of the Lucianic recension (MSS boc_2e_2)
G^O	the text of Origen's recension
G^R	the "Palestinian" or "*kaige*" recension (see Barthélemy, *Les devanciers d'Aquila*), which revised the Old Greek toward greater conformity with M; the majority of G manuscripts in 2 Samuel 11–24 reflect this recension
OG	the Old Greek translation

I wish to thank Profs. John Wevers and Emanuel Tov, for the invitation to contribute this study; Prof. Frank Moore Cross, for the opportunity to work on the scrolls; P. Bonafatius Fischer and Drs. Frede and Thiele of the Vetus Latina Institut in Beuron, for their friendly and efficient help, for the microfilms of their collection entrusted to the Notre Dame library, and especially for making the Fischer edition of L^{115} available. I wish also to thank Scholars Press, for permission to quote extensively from my book *The Qumran Text of Samuel and Josephus;* the staff of Notre Dame's Medieval Institute, for the use of their microfilms; and Ms. Carolyn Cross, for her competent and elegant metamorphosis of my scribbles.

gantic efforts,[3] and still in our day eludes a critical consensus among scholars.[4] Even if its character is determined for one book,[5] it varies, like the Septuagint, from book to book and may not be presumed to exhibit that same character in another book.[6] The books of Samuel specifically have not yet been blessed with complete collations and trustworthy critical editions such as those from the Vetus Latina Institut at Beuron and the Septuaginta Unternehmen at Göttingen. The only person to attempt a full-length study of the Old Latin within the books of Samuel was Henry Voogd in a 1947 dissertation.[7] He noted that "the history of the Old Latin manuscript fragments is quite obscure" and lamented "the present uncertainty and obscurity" regarding the Old Latin prior to his day, attributing it, with a large degree of accuracy, to the confusion concerning the various forms of the Greek text upon which L was dependent.[8]

L the Old Latin; note esp. L^f = Fischer's corrected edition of L^b
Ambr Ambrose's citation of L, quoted from Sabatier (see note 13, below)
V the Latin Vulgate, critical ed. of Samuel by the Benedictine Monks of the Abbey S. Hieronymi, Rome, 1944
S the Peshitta, Leiden critical edition, ed. P. A. H. de Boer, or the Ambrosian codex, ed. Ceriani
J Josephus, *Jewish Antiquities*, ed. B. Niese
QTSJ textual analysis of $4QSam^a$: Ulrich, *The Qumran Text of Samuel and Josephus*
Edn, Photo, Trscr, Comm, Affil: preliminary edition of $4QSam^c$ with photographs, transcription, commentary, and textual affiliation in *BASOR* 235 (1979) 1-25.
** readings partially or totally reconstructed in L or $4QSam^{a,c}$

2. Cf. H. A. A. Kennedy, "Latin Versions, The Old," in Hastings' *Dictionary of the Bible* (Edinburgh: Clark, 1923) 3:48; Sidney Jellicoe, *The Septuagint and Modern Study* (Oxford: Clarendon, 1968) 249-50; and B. J. Roberts, *The Old Testament Text and Versions* (Cardiff: University of Wales, 1951) 238.

3. Cf. Kennedy, "Latin Versions," 53b; Roberts, *Old Testament Text and Versions,* 237-38; and Henry Voogd, "A Critical and Comparative Study of the Old Latin Texts of the First Book of Samuel" (Dissertation, Princeton Theological Seminary, 1947) 4.

4. Cf. S. R. Driver, *Notes on the Hebrew Text . . . of Samuel,* 2d ed. (Oxford, 1913) liii; Kennedy, "Latin Versions," 48 and passim; Jellicoe, *Septuagint and Modern Study,* 249-51; F. Stummer, *Einführung in die lateinische Bibel* (Paderborn, 1928) 50-56; and Voogd, "Critical and Comparative Study," 9-13.

5. See, for example, B. Fischer's edition, *Vetus Latina,* Band 2: *Genesis* (Freiburg: Herder, 1954); J. Schildenberger, *Die altlateinischen Texte des Proverbienbuches.* I: *Die alte afrikanische Textgestalt* (Texte und Arbeiten 32/3; Beuron, 1941); and P. W. Skehan, "Notes on the Latin Text of the Book of Wisdom," *CBQ* 4 (1942) 230-43.

6. Cf. A. V. Billen, *The Old Latin Texts of the Heptateuch* (Cambridge, 1927) 7, 13; Kennedy, "Latin Versions," 48.

7. See note 3; see also Driver, *Notes on the Hebrew Text,* lxxvi-lxxx.

8. Voogd, "Critical and Comparative Study," 111, 1, 19, 13. Cf. also Driver, *Notes on the Hebrew Text,* lxxvi-lxxx; and Kennedy, "Latin Versions," 49, 58, 61.

Voogd's investigation covered only 1 Samuel, and, though significant advances have been achieved with respect to the Greek text of Samuel,[9] it is not yet clear to the present writer how solid are the "definite results" that Voogd achieved.[10]

Accordingly, in light of the lack of consensus concerning the Old Latin and the lack of concentrated study on the Old Latin of Samuel,[11] it is necessary to state at the outset that the present study is preliminary and partial. It is simply an attempt to contribute a limited amount of new evidence and to draw appropriately limited and tentative conclusions. It would require the labor of at least a decade to achieve such a comprehensive control of all the aspects of the problem that one could construct reliable groundbreaking conclusions.

The first purpose of this study, then, is to provide for the section 2 Samuel 11–24 the readings in which extant fragments of Old Latin manuscripts intersect with preserved variants on the fragments of the first and third scrolls of Samuel from Qumran (4QSam^a and 4QSam^c). That is, this study includes only the section[12] 2 Samuel 11–24, not 1 Samuel 1–2 Samuel 10. It includes only L manuscript readings, not quotations cited by the Fathers.[13] It includes only 4QSam^a and 4QSam^c, not 4QSam^b, since the latter survives only in fragments of 1 Samuel. It includes only readings that are actually preserved both in the L manuscripts and on the leather of the scrolls — with but

9. See the works of Mez, Rahlfs, Thackeray, Barthélemy, Cross, Johnson, Brock, Shenkel, Tov, and Ulrich. For summaries and bibliographic details, see E. Tov, "The State of the Question: Problems and Proposed Solutions," in *1972 Proceedings: IOSCS and Pseudepigrapha*, ed. R. Kraft (Missoula, Mont.: Scholars Press, 1972) 3-15, and Ulrich, *QTSJ*, 22-37. For a judicious and masterful incorporation of Septuagintal evidence into a commentary, see P. Kyle McCarter, *I Samuel* (Anchor Bible; Garden City, N.Y.: Doubleday, 1980).

10. Voogd, "Critical and Comparative Study," 200. Jellicoe does not mention Voogd but in 1968 considers the Old Latin variety "still an open question" (*Septuagint and Modern Study*, 249).

11. In 1927 Billen stated that "very little literature so far exists on the Old Latin version especially of the Old Testament" (*Old Latin Texts of the Heptateuch*, 6), and in 1968 Jellicoe noted: "In general very little of importance in the study of the Old Latin versions has been achieved during the present century" (*Septuagint and Modern Study*, 250).

12. For the choice of this section, see H. St. J. Thackeray, *The Septuagint and Jewish Worship* (Schweich Lectures; London, 1921) 9-28, 114-115; D. Barthélemy, *Les devanciers d'Aquila* (VTSup 10; Leiden: Brill, 1963); and *QTSJ*. I envision a second study, which will complete the comparison of L with the Qumran manuscripts for 1 Samuel 1–2 Samuel 10.

13. Cf. Voogd, "Critical and Comparative Study," 4-5, 14-15, 19-107, 200-202; and Roberts, *Old Testament Text and Versions*, 238-39. The one exception is Ambrose at 2 Sam 12:16 and 15:2, because (1) he is already quoted in *Comm;* (2) at 12:16 his agreement with L^V confirms his validity; and (3) at 15:2 no other L manuscripts are extant, and it is not so much the exact wording as the aspect of the verbs that is important.

few exceptions: a few readings where L or 4QSam, though partially or even fully reconstructed, are either virtually certain or highly probable; these will always be explicitly noted so that the reader may judge them accordingly.[14] It includes, finally, only readings where L intersects with a disagreement between 4QSam^{a,c} and either the Masoretic Hebrew (= M) or the main Greek text traditions (Vaticanus = G^{B}; Lucianic = G^{L}).

The second purpose of this study is to examine (1) what new light the scrolls shed on the nature of L; (2) whether, how, and how frequently L provides a witness to the original or early Greek text, especially where no extant G manuscripts still preserve the reading;[15] and (3) the textual affiliations of the various L manuscripts.

The investigation will proceed by listing, in the next section of the essay, the manuscripts extant for the Vetus Latina of 1-2 Samuel; in the third section, the readings of 4QSam^{a} in contrast with MGL plus an assessment of the significance of those readings; and then, in the fourth section, the readings of 4QSam^{c} in contrast with MGL plus an assessment of their significance. The study will then end, in the fifth section, with conclusions warranted by the study of these texts.

Vetus Latina Manuscripts for 1-2 Samuel

The evidence of L for 1-2 Samuel comes from two sources, manuscripts and patristic citations. Here we are dealing only with the manuscript evidence, which for Samuel is quite circumscribed. Apart from the collection of fragmentary readings compiled by Sabatier (L^{S}), there are only Old Latin glosses in the margins for Spanish Bibles (L$^{91\text{-}96}$) and the fragmentary remains of a few Old Latin manuscripts (L$^{115\text{-}117}$). For full descriptions, see Fischer's list in *Vetus Latina* 1: *Verzeichnis der Sigel* (1949) 17-18; Brooke-McLean, *The Old Testament in Greek,* vol. 2, part 1, p. vii; Kennedy, "Latin Versions, The Old," *HDB* 3.50; and Würthwein, *The Text of the Old Testament,* 88-90. Since these

14. Reconstructed readings will be marked with a double asterisk (**) when tabulated or when referred to in the discussions of significance or the conclusion.

15. Cf. Kennedy, "Latin Versions," 62a; and Roberts, *Old Testament Text and Versions,* 241, 245-46. Walter Bodine, *The Greek Text of Judges: Recensional Developments* (HSM 23; Missoula, Mont.: Scholars Press, 1980) p. 32, n. 5, finds that the "L in Judges is often the surest guide to the earliest form of the OG." He quotes Burkitt's observation (*The Rules of Tyconius,* cvii) that the L text cited by Tyconius "may preserve genuine readings independent of all our Greek MSS," and lists both Billen's and his own (*Greek Text of Judges,* 32, n. 5; 135-36) investigations of Judges as confirmation of that hypothesis.

lists are all, with the exception of Brooke-McLean, composite lists and there is no separate list for Samuel that is complete and up-to-date, the following list of Old Latin manuscript witnesses for Samuel is provided:[16]

L^{S}	Sabatier's collection of various L readings plus patristic quotations from manuscripts at Corbey and S. Germain. Published by Sabatier. Fragments of 1-2 Samuel, passim.
L^{91}	Léon, S. Isidoro, Codex Gothicus Legionensis. L glosses in the margin of a Vulgate codex, copied 960.[17] Fragmentary glosses throughout 1-2 Samuel.
L^{92}	Léon, S. Isidoro 1.3. Legionensis 2. A copy of L^{91}, copied 1162.
L^{93} (= L^{v})	Rome, Biblioteca Apostolica Vaticana, codex Vatic. lat. 4859. A copy of L^{91}, copied 1587. Published by Vercellone.
L^{94}	Escorial, Biblioteca de S. Lorenzo 54.V.35. L glosses inserted by Hernando del Castillo in 1577 from (among others) a now-lost tenth-century (?) Bible of Valvarnera Abbey into the margin of a Vulgate incunabulum (Venice, 1478). Published by M. Revilla (see *Verzeichnis*), Weber.
L^{95}	Madrid, Academia de Ia Historia 2-3. Twelfth century.
L^{96}	Calahorra, Catedral. First volume of a Vulgate Bible containing L glosses, copied 1138.
L115 (= $L^{f,b}$)	Naples, Biblioteca Nazionale, codex lat. 1 (formerly Vindobonensis 17). Palimpsestus Vindobonensis, fifth century. Publisherd by J. von Eichenfeld and S. Endlicher (1835), Belsheim (1885); the Belsheim transcription (L^{b} in Brooke-McLean) is inaccurate, and B. Fischer (L^{f}) prepared in 1942 a corrected transcription (unpublished).[18] See now *BIOSCS* 16 (1983) 13-87. Contains: 1 Sam 1:14–2:15; 3:10–4:18; 6:3-17; 9:21–10:7; 10:16–11:13; 14:12-34; 2 Sam 4:10–5:25; 10:13–11:19; 13:13–14:3(4); 17:12–18:9.
L^{116} (= $L^{q,m}$)	Berlin, Preussische Staatsbibliothek, Th. lat. fol. 485; + Quedlinburg, Archiv der Oberpfarre St. Servatii. Fragmenta Quedlinburgensia et Magdeburgensia, fifth century. Published by Weissbrodt (1887), Degering & Boeckler (1932). Contains: (L^{q}): 1 Sam 9:1-8; 15:10-18; (L^{m}): 2 Sam 2:29–3:5.

16. The author would appreciate notification of any L manuscripts of 1-2 Samuel not listed here. For bibliographic details of the publications, see the first section of the bibliography.

17. Not copied in 690, as stated in E. Würthwein, *The Text of the Old Testament* (trans. E. F. Rhodes; Grand Rapids: Eerdmans, 1979) 89.

18. Cf. Fischer, "Lukian-Lesarten in der Vetus Latina der vier Königsbücher," *Studia Anselmiana* 27-28 (1951) 170, n. 1.

L^{117} (= L^{h}) Vienna, Nationalbibliothek, two folios marked 15479 (Suppl. 2868). Fragmenta Vindobonensia, two folios that had earlier been glued to old covers of books, late seventh or early eighth century.[19] Published by Haupt. Contains: 2 Sam 10:18–11:17; 14:17-30.

L^{e} Einsiedeln, MS 2. Part of the L text of the Song of Hannah is written, *prima manu,* in the margin; it is almost identical with Codex Gothicus Legionensis; copied 1420. Published by Berger. Contains 1 Sam 2:3-10c.

L^{gl} Vat. Palat. 135, tenth century. Published by de Bruyne. Contains readings from 1 Sam 1:1, 18; 2:5, 13, 36; 9:24; 10:12; 14:26; 17:49; 20:3, 34; 21:5, 13; 23:5; 2 Sam 8:2; 17:3; 20:18; 23:20.

L^{j} A fragment from Julius Toletanus reproduced by Vercellone, p. 441, and included by Brooke-McLean (cf. B-M, p. vii). Contains 2 Sam 24:11-16.

L^{R} Verona, Biblioteca Capitolare, Codex Veronensis, Greek–Old Latin Psalter plus some canticles, sixth century. Published by Bianchini. Contains 1 Sam 2:1-10.

The manuscripts that intersect with the surviving fragments of 4QSam^{a,c} are: L^{93} (= L^{v}), L^{115} (= L^{b}), L^{117} (= L^{h}), and L^{s}. All four are collated in Brooke-McLean. The readings from L^{s} cited in the present study are quoted directly from Sabatier's collection. The readings of $L^{93,117}$ are taken primarily from the microfilms of the Vetus Latina Institut cards from Beuron. The readings from L^{115} are taken from a photocopy of Fischer's transcription (L^{f}); substantial variants in L^{b} will be inserted for comparison with the published edition of L^{b}, but orthographic variants in L^{b} will not be noted. In the present study the sigla with letters ($L^{f,h,s,v}$) will be used, since the author worked from others' editions, not from the manuscripts themselves, and since this is still the common practice. Eventually, when Vetus Latina scholarship for the Old Testament reaches a sufficient plateau, a standard set of sigla should be adopted in conformity with the Beuron and Göttingen editions.

4QSam^{a} and the Old Latin for 2 Samuel 11–24

A rough edition of 4QSam^{a} illuminated over two hundred instances of disagreement[20] among the three text traditions, 4QSam^{a}, M, and G. Old Latin

19. My understanding of Haupt (p. 5) differs from that of Fischer (*Verzeichnis der Sigel,* p. 18, §117) and Würthwein (*Text of the Old Testament,* 90).

20. Ulrich, *QTSJ,* summarized in "4QSam^{a} and Septuagintal Research," *BIOSCS* 8

manuscript fragments are extant for a sufficiently large number of these disagreements to raise hopes that we could gain a sharper focus on the character of the L texts by testing their textual affiliation. Here, then, we will list the readings for 2 Samuel 11–24 in which L manuscripts intersect with those disagreements.

Readings

a1. 2 Sam 11:3^fin^

4QSam^a^	]אוריה החתי נ[ושא כלי יואב
MTS	אוריה החתי׃
G	Ουρειου του Χετταιου;
L^f^	uri cetthei
L^h^	Urie Cetthei.
V	Uriae Hetthei
J 7.131	τον Ιωαβου μεν οπλοφορον . . . Ουριαν

4QSam^a^ and Josephus alone in this striking agreement add the note that Uriah was Joab's armor bearer (see Ulrich, *The Qumran Text of Samuel and Josephus* [hereafter *QTSJ*], 173; and contrast 2 Sam 23:39 with 23:37b). L^fh^ follow the preferable, unexpanded text.

L^fh^ = M G ≠ 4QSam^a^ J.

a2. 2 Sam 11:4

4QSam^a^	ותבוא אליו
M(TS)	ותבוא אליו
G	και εισηλθεν προς αυτην (-τον s*[vid])
G^cx^	και ηλθε προς αυτον
L^f^	Et intrauit at eam
L^h^	et [intra]uit ad illam
V	quae cum ingressa esset ad illum

The Hebrew text is probably to be preferred (cf. 13:11b, in contrast to *QTSJ*, 145). G offers a (probably inner-Greek) *lectio facilior*, followed by L^fh^, but G^O^ V correct to M.

L^fh^ = G ≠ 4QSam^a^ M G^O^ V.

(1975) 24-39. See also now the clarifying critique of E. Tov, "The Textual Affiliations of 4QSam^a^," *JSOT* 14 (1979) 37-53.

a3,4. 2 Sam 11:4

4QSam^a	מתקדשת ותב̊[וא]	
MT	מתקדשת מטמאתה ותשב	
S	*sḥt mn kpsh*	*whpkt twb w'zlt*
G	αγιαζομενη απο ακαθαρσιας αυτης	και απεστρεψεν
G^L	ην λελουμενη εξ αφεδρου αυτης	και απηλθεν
a′	απολελουμενη (-νην j) jz	
L^f	lota erat post purgationem	^{5}et intrauit
L^h	[	] ^{5}et intrauit
L^v	erat dimissa (abluta L^{v2}) excelso loco	[ ]
V	sanctificata est ab inmunditia sua	^{5}et reversa est

See *QTSJ*, 137. 4QSam^a lacks מטמאתה, and the word immediately following מתקדשת is very probably ותבוא: one-third of the base line of *bet* is visible; it cannot possibly be *šin* or any other letter except a too-shallow *kap*.

It cannot be decided confidently whether מטמאתה is a plus in M being tacitly understood in 4QSam^a, whether it was lost (by haplography?) in the 4QSam^a tradition, or whether the entire circumstantial clause is a secondary addition. The later laws in Lev 15:19-33 use different vocabulary. Methodologically, we shall consider preferable the *lectio brevior* (4QSam^a).

Similarly, though we expect ותשב, ותבוא appears original, because the refinement to ותשב is natural while the reverse is not, and because the verb can be seen as the beginning of verse 5 rather than the conclusion of verse 4 (cf. L^{fh} V; 4QSam^a? G^L?). Again, the Peshitta is conflate; because its final form is closely dependent upon M, certain preferable variants may be considered to reflect a non-M substratum. *whpkt twb* = ותשב, whereas *w'zlt* = ותבא.

G^L (λελουμενη, -ηλθεν) appears to represent the Old Greek (OG). For all three G^B words (αγιαζεσθαι, ακαθαρσια, and αποστρεφειν)[21] are the standard and the Aquilan (despite the marginal readings of jz) correspondents to M, while the early witnesses, 4QSam^a (ותבוא) and L *(lota, abluta,* and esp. *dimissa)* argue against simply late Lucianic revision. απερχεσθαι = הלך normally, but = בוא in 1 Sam 25:5 and 2 Sam 3:24 (A; εισ- B); it never corresponds to שוב in Samuel or Kings (though it does in other books).

The strange reading *dimissa excelso loco* in one of Vercellone's variants results from a pair of errors, both dependent upon G^L: *dimissa* = λελ<u>υ</u>μενη,[22]

21. Cf. Bodine, *Greek Text of Judges,* 54-56 and 64-66, nn. 85-110, where επιστρεφω is listed as the preferred *kaige* correspondent for שוב.

22. I wish to thank Prof. John Strugnell for the insight concerning *dimissa.* Cf. also Driver, *Notes on the Hebrew Text,* 289n. A note on the Beuron card "at excelso loco undenam exsculpsit?" piques me to suggest εξ αφ εδρου.

and *ex/celso loco* is an interpretation of εξ αφ / εδρου (seat, throne, lofty position) instead of εξ αφεδρου (sitting apart, menstrual period). V is corrected back to MG^R.

a3. **מטמאתה**

$L^f = M\ G^{LR}\ S\ V \neq 4QSam^a$;

$L^v = G^L \neq M\ G^R\ S\ V \neq 4QSam^a$.

a4. **ותבוא**

$L^{fh} = 4QSam^a(vid)\ G^L(?)\ S_1(?) \neq M\ G^R\ S_2\ V$.

a5. 2 Sam 11:5

$4QSam^a$	**אנוכי הרה**
M T S	**הרה אנכו**
G	Εγω ειμι εν γαστρι εχω
G^L	Συνειληφα εγω
L^{fh}	concepi ego
V	concepi

See Barthélemy, *Les devanciers,* 69-78; Kevin C. O'Connell, *The Theodotionic Revision of the Book of Exodus* (HSM 3; Cambridge, Mass.: Harvard University Press, 1972) 19-22, 281; Bodine, *The Greek Text of Judges,* 15-16; and *QTSJ,* 87-88. For the apparent affiliation of these synonymous variants,

$$L^{fh} = M\ G^L \neq 4QSam^a\ G.$$

a6. 2 Sam 11:7fin

$4QSam^a$	[המלחמ]ה̇ ו̊י̊[אמ]ר̊	
MTS	**המלחמ** [8]**ויאמר**	
G	του πολεμου	και ειπεν
$G^{L,71}$ A	ο πολεμος και ειπεν υγιαινει	και ειπεν
G^z	του πολεμου και ειπεν εις ειρηνην	και ειπεν
G^a2	του πολεμου και ειπεν Ουριας παντες εις ειρηνην	και ειπεν
L^f	belli et dixit urias omnes rectae sunt. et dixit	
L^h	po..lo et respon..... omnia .....te s... .. dixit	
V	bellum. et dixit	
J7.132	λεγοντος δε παντα κατα νουν αυτοις	

See *QTSJ,* 187-88. $4QSam^a$ appears to agree with MGV. G^L and the G minuscules z, a_2, 71, plus L^{fh} A and Josephus, all include the answer to the question, which is probably original, for this narrative normally includes the responses to questions, commands, and reports (11:3, 6, 10-11, 11-12).

For the shorter M text, Cross suggests a common haplography: ולשלום המלחמה <ויאמר לשלום> ויאמר — note that לשלום already occurs three times in the last six words of the question, and see L^{h} below and G^{s,v}, each of which betrays a similar haplography here. G^{L} exhibits the Old Greek correspondent for לשלום, G^{B} the recensional correspondent (cf. Barthélemy, *Les devanciers,* 106; and *Comm* at col. I, line 2 [14:8]); and it is interesting that witnesses to the recensional text (esp. a$_{2}$, which is usually the closest congener to G^{B} in Samuel) preserve the και ειπεν (Ουριας παντες) εις ειρηνην. L^{f} most closely follows a$_{2}$; L^{h} is now haplographic but originally followed G^{L}, a$_{2}$:

> L^{h} et po[pu]lo et<bello et> respon[dit] omnia [rec]te s[unt].
> G^{L} και ει υγιαινει ο λαος και ει υγιαινει ο πολεμος και ειπεν υγιαινει.

L^{fh} = G^{L} J ≠ 4QSam^{a}(vid) M G^{R} V.

a7. 2 Sam 12:14

4QSam^{a}	א̊ת̇ ד̊בר יהוה
M	את איבי יהוה
T	דסנאי עמא דיוי
S	*lb'ldbbwhy dmry'*
Gα′σ′ο′	τους εχθρους κυριου
G^{L}	εν τοις υπεναντιοις/τον Κυριον (trp o)
θ′G^{MN}	τοις εναντιοις Κυριου.
G^{c}	τω Κυριω
L^{v}	contrarios Domini
V	inimicos Domini
C	verbum Domini

All texts here (except G^{c}) display a euphemistic insertion. Only C agrees with 4QSam^{a}. L^{v} most closely agrees with G^{L} S, G V with M. For this expansion,

L^{v} = G^{L} S (M G^{BO} V) ≠ G^{c} ≠ 4QSam^{a} C ≠ T.

a8. 2 Sam 12:16

4QSam^{a}	[וב]א̊ ו̇ישכב בשק ארצה	
M	ובא ולן ושכב ארצה	
T	ועל ובת ושכיב על ארעא	
S	*wbt bh wdmk '1 'r''*	
G^{B}	και εισηλθεν και ηυλισθη	επι της γης
G^{A}	και εισηλθεν και ηυλισθη και εκοιμηθη	επι της γης

G^L	και εισελθων		εκαθευδεν εν σακκω επι την γην
G^{MN}	και εισηλθεν (και ηυλισθη)		εν σακκω επι της γης
L^v		] et dormivit in cilicio [	
Ambr		et in cilicio jacuit	
V	et ingressus seorsum	iacuit	super terram
J 7.154	πεσων επι σακκου κατα γης εκειτο		

See *QTSJ*, 100-101. 4QSam[a] apparently expands with **בשק**, M with **ולן**. The early G^L followed 4QSam[a], while αυλιζειν and κοιμαν are the G^R correspondents of **לון** and **שכב** (see *QTSJ*, 100-101 and 58; Bodine, *The Greek Text of Judges*, 52-53). L^v Ambr and J reflect G^L.

L^v = 4QSam[a] G^L Ambr J ≠ M G^{RO} V.

a9. 2 Sam 13:3

4QSam[a]	**[י]הונתן**
MTS	**יונדב**
GACE	Ιωναδαβ
G^L S^j	Ιωναθαν
L^f	*deest* here; Ionathab (at 13:32), Ionadab (at 13:35, 36)
V	Ionadab
J 7.164	Ιωναθη

4QSam[a] G^L J attest Jonathan, M G V Jonadab (cf. Cross, *HTR* 57 [1964] 294; and *QTSJ*, 105-6). L^f is lacking at 13:3, but has *Ionathab* at 13:32 and *Ionadab* at 13:35, 36. G^{B*} and its close congener a_2 have -δαμ; at 13:32 G^N has -δαβ over an erasure that originally could have read -θαν, though this is conjecture. Adam Mez, however, in *Die Bibel des Josephus* (Basel, 1895), p. 44, lists Ιωναθαμ as his reading of G^B; I have presumed that this is an error, but it deserves firsthand checking. At any rate, L^f remains ambiguous; one can only conjecture that L may originally have contained *Ionathan* but was gradually corrected back toward the dominant MG tradition.

L^f (Ionath-) = 4QSam[a] G^L J ≠ M G V;
L^f(-ab) = M G V ≠ 4QSam[a] G^L J.

a10. 2 Sam 13:21

4QSam[a] **[והמלך דויד] שמע אתֺ [כול]**]
[הדברים. . . מאד ולוא עצב את רוח אמנון בנו כי אה]בו כי בכור[ו]
[הוא]

MTS והמלך דוד שמע את כל
הדברים האלה ויחר לו מאד

G και ηκουσεν (post Δαυειδ G^L) ο βασιλευς Δαυειδ
παντας τους λογους τουτους και εθυμωθη (ηθυμησεν G^L) σφοδρα
και ουκ ελυπησεν το πνευμα Αμνων του υιου αυτου
οτι ηγαπα αυτον οτι πρωτοτοκος αυτου ην.

L^f Et rex dauit audiuit
omnia uerba haec et defecit (deficit L^b) animo ualde
et noluit contristare spiritum hammon fili sui
quia amabat eum prior (prae L^b) enim natus erat ei.

L^s [ ]
et noluit contristare spiritum Amnon filii sui,
quoniam diligebat eum, quia primogenitus erat ei.

L^v [
] et iratus factus est valde,
et non contristavit spiritum Ammon filii sui,
quoniam amabat eum, quoniam primogenitus erat ei.

V cum autem audisset rex David verba haec contristatus est valde.

J 7.173 τοις μεν πεπραγμενοις ηχθετο, φιλων δε τον Αμνωνα σφοδρα,
πρεσβυτατος γαρ ην αυτω υιος, μη λυπειν αυτον ηναγκαζετο.

4QSam[a] preserves a noticeably longer but original text (Wellhausen), lost in M through haplography (ולא . . . ולא, Cross). L^{fsv} contain the reading in slightly variant forms. L^f follows G^L especially in the opening clause but also with *defecit animo,* which reflects (as does ηχθετο of J; cf. *QTSJ,* 84-85) the mitigated ηθυμησεν of G^L, whereas *iratus* of L^v reflects εθυμωθη of GM[4QSam[a]]. For this original reading, lost in M,

$$L^{fsv} = \text{4QSam}^a \text{ G J} \neq \text{M V.}$$

a11. 2 Sam 13:24[fin]

4QSam[a]	אל עבדו
MTS	עם עבדך
G	μετα του δουλου σου
G^L	προς τον δουλον αυτου
L^fV	at seruum suum
J 7.174	προς αυτον

See *QTSJ,* 106, and *Comm* at II.3 (14:22). Both the preposition and the suffix in M are superior, עבדך being standard courtly usage. J, as frequently, appears to reflect G^L 4QSam^a. In a pair of inferior variants, even followed by V,

$$L^f = 4QSam^a\ G^L\ V\ (J) \neq M\ G.$$

a12. 2 Sam 13:27^{fin}

4QSam^a	[ ]אׄת אמנון ואתׄ [כול] בני המלך
	[ויעש אבשלום משתה כמשתה ה]מׄ[ל] [28וי]צׄוׄ אבשלום את נעריו לאמור
MTS	את אמנון ואת כל בני המל֞ך
	28ויצו אבשלום את נעריו לאמר
G	τον Αμνων και παντας τους υιους του βασιλεως
	και εποιησεν Αβεσσαλωμ ποτον κατα τον ποτον του βασιλεως
L^f	Ammon et omnes filios regis
	et fecit Abessalon epulum magnum secundum epulum regis.
L^s	[ ] Feceratque Absalom convivium quasi convivium regis.
V	Amnon et universos filios regis.
J 7.174	. . . προς αυτον εφ εστιασιν.

See *QTSJ*, 85. 4QSam^a, followed by G L^{fs} J, preserves an original fuller reading lost by parablepsis (המלך 1°⁀2°) in M, thus not appearing in TSV.

$$L^{fs} = 4QSam^a\ G\ J \neq M\ V.$$

a13. 2 Sam 13:31^{fin}

4QSam^a	בגדיו (*sic;* not [בג]דיו as in *BHS* note)
M	בגדים
TS	לבושיהון
G	τα ιματια αυτων
G^L	τα ιματια
L^fV	uestimenta sua

4QSam^a and M both err, 4QSam^a being attracted to that same form earlier in the verse, M omitting the *he* of the suffix (ם<ה>י–; cf. 2 Sam 1:2, (11); 3:31; and the first half of this verse!). The suffix is customarily used when בגד is in construction with קרע in Samuel. GTS (and maybe V) are based on a real or presumed correct reading in the M tradition. G^L may be either polished classical Greek or late, hexaplaric fidelity to M; cf. 2 Sam 1:11, where G adds the tacitly understood διερρηξαν τα ιματια αυτων, but where G^{OL} alone omit these words found in G but not in M. V appears to follow L^b; this is possible, though it could also reflect a correct variant in the M tradition, or sense.

$$L^b = G\ T\ S\ V \neq 4QSam^a \neq M\ G^L.$$

a14. 2 Sam 13:32a

4QSam^a	[את כול] \ הׄנׄעׄרים כול בני המלׄ[ך]
MT	את כל הנערים בני המלך
S	*dklhwn bny mlk'*
G	παντα τα παιδαρια τους υιους του βασιλεως
G^L	παντα τα παιδαρια οι υιοι του βασιλεως
cxE	παντας τους υιους αυτου (του βασ. E)
uA	παντες οι υιοι του βασιλεως
a_2	παντα τα παιδαρια του βασιλεως
L^fV	omnes pueri fili regis

The *BHS* note listing הנערים כול for כל הנערים is imprecise. Rather, S $G^{u(cx)}$ A E (reflecting כל בני המלך) plus a_2 (omitting בני) suggest a doublet, incorporated fully into 4QSam^a, but smoothed in M G. L^f follows G^L, which in turn is dependent on M.

L^f = M G^L (G^B) V ≠ 4QSam^a ≠ S $G^{u(cx)}$.

a15. 2 Sam 13:32b

4QSam^a	[\ היה [מיום] עׄ[נ]תׄו
M	היתה שומה מיום ענתו
T	הות כמינא מיומא דעני
S	*sym' hwt . . . mn ywm' dṣʿr*
G	ην κειμενος απο της ημερας ης εταπεινωσεν
G^L	ην . . . αφ ης ημερας εταπεινωσεν
α'σ'	ην . . . απο της ημερας ("α'σ' . . . parum probabiliter" — Field)
L^f	est . . . ex (a L^b) qua die humiliauit (-uerit L^b)
V	erat positus ex die qua oppressit

See *QTSJ*, 103. 4QSam^a has space for only one four-letter word. מיום is essential, while שומה appears dubious, though Wellhausen and Driver both presume שומה, or some similar form, to be original. κειμενος (except for its masculine gender) is an exact translation of שומה. G^L construes this whole clause differently from G^{BAMN}. The latter (= G^R?) closely follow M. G^L, mirrored by L^f, appears, from the little Qumran evidence, to be based on 4QSam^a. Against the presumed addition of שומה in M,

L^f = 4QSam^a(vid) G^L ≠ M S G^R V.

a16. 2 Sam 13:37

4QSam^a	[גשור בׄאׄ]רץ
MTS	גשור
G	Γεσσειρ (-δσουρ BA) εις γην (την Bo*) Χαλλαμα (Μαχαδ BA)
L^f	Gessir (-ssur L^b) in terra Maacha (Hacma L^b)
L^v	Gessur Callam
V	Gessur
J 7.180	Γεσσουραν . . . χωρας

4QSam^a probably expands here, followed by Gomn and L^{fv}. V T S follow the preferable short text of M. Though Josephus adds χωρας, it does not appear to reflect this plus, because χαλλαμα is absent; but neither would his silence prove that his *Vorlage* lacked it. In this expansion,

$$L^{fv} = 4QSam^a\ G \neq M\ V.$$

a17. 2 Sam 13:39

4QSam^a	[רו]ח המלך
M	ותכל דוד המלך
T	וחמידת נפשא דדויד מלכא
S	*w'ḥmy mlk' dwyd*
G^B A	και εκοπασεν ο βασιλευς Δαυειδ
G^A E	και εκοπασεν Δαυειδ ο βασιλευς
G^{LMN} C	και εκοπασεν το πν̄α του βασιλεως (+ Δαυειδ G^L)
L^f	Et requietus est iratus regis
L^v	Et proposuit rex
V	Cessavitque David rex
J 7.181	τα της οργης . . . λελωφηκει

See *QTSJ,* 106-7. 4QSam^a preserves the original Hebrew, and G^{LMN} preserve the faithful Old Greek, though G^L later includes the expansion Δαυειδ. M has the *lectio facilior* and *ad sensum* corruption רוח > דוד (signaled by the preceding fem. ותכל). G^{BA} V follow the error in M. L^f follows the early, correct G^L (without the later Δαυειδ), though it has suffered a two-stage error: first, ETREQUIETUSESTSPIRITUSREGIS (from OG = G^L) suffered haplography (E<u>STSP</u>IRITUS > E<u>ST</u>IRITUS), and then IRITUS was "corrected" to IRATUS. L^v is apparently a rendering *ad sensum,* dependent upon G^{BA}. J depends upon the correct reading in G^L and ultimately upon the 4QSam^a tradition.

$$L^f = 4QSam^a(T)\ G^{LMN}\ J \neq M\ G^{BA}\ V \neq L^v;$$
$$L^v = (M\ G^{BA}) \neq 4QSam^a\ G^L \neq L^f.$$

a18. 2 Sam 14:19

4QSam^a TS	[והוא שם] \ בפי אמתך
4QSam^c	ו֯הוא֯[ה] שם בפי \ [אמתכה]
M	והוא שם בפי שפחתך
G	και αυτος εθετο εν τω στοματι της δουλης σου
L^h	et ipse posuit ancillae tuae
V	et ipse posuit in os ancillae tuae

Though L^h can make sense as it stands, very likely it simply errs, omitting *in os* through parablepsis: *in⁀ancillae.* Nonetheless, as the texts stand for this omission in L^h,

L^h ≠ 4QSam^{a,c} M G V.

a19. 2 Sam 15:2

4QSam^a	על יד הדרך
M	על יד דרך השער
T	על כיבש אורח תרעא
S	*ʿl gnb trʿʾ dmlkʾ*
G	ανα χειρα της οδου της πυλης
G^L	επι της οδου της πυλης
Ambr	ante portam in via
V	iuxta introitum portae

See *QTSJ*, 139, for the textual affiliations; and cf. 18:4. Ambrose reflects an L reading (see note 13 above, and Sabatier, p. 540a, note on 15:1) that could depend on M or on either form of the Greek, but not on 4QSam^a.

Ambr M G ≠ 4QSam^a ≠ V.

a20. 2 Sam 15:2

4QSam^a	וה[יה]
M	ויהי
G	και εγενετο
G^{Lnz}	και ην (εγινετο nz)
Ambr	(et si)
V	et
J 7.195	παρεγινετο

See *Comm* at II.21^{sup}-III.3 (15:1-6) and *QTSJ*, 107. 4QSam^a, followed by G^L J, preserves the correct reading. Ambrose, whose text continues with the imperfect form *accedebat* (cf. a21 immediately following), reflects 4QSam[a] G^L.

$$\text{Ambr} = \text{4QSam}^a\ G^L\ J \neq M\ G.$$

a21. 2 Sam 15:2

4QSam[a]	וקרא לו אבשל[ום \ [
MT	ויקרא אבשלום אליו
S	*qr' hw' lh 'bšlwm lwth*
G	και εβοησεν προς αυτον Αβεσσελωμ
G^{Acx}	και εβοησεν (εβοα cx) Αβεσσαλωμ προς αυτον
G^L	και εκαλει αυτον Αβεσσαλωμ
Ambr	accedebat ad eum
V	vocabat Absalom ad se
J 7.195	(παρεγινετο . . .) ομιλων

See *Comm* at II.22 (15:2) and *QTSJ*, 107. Ambrose interestingly reflects a variant interpretation best explained at the Hebrew stage: *accedebat* = קרה\א ("to approach, meet"). There are no extant Greek variants recorded in Brooke-McLean that would serve as a medium for L-Ambr. Several possible explanations emerge: (1) L was translated directly from the Hebrew; (2) L was translated from a Greek text (with *ηντα, *παρεγινετο, or something similar) that has been superseded by the dominant G tradition; (3) some G manuscript had a double rendering of ויקרא (εκαλει plus *ηντα/*παρεγινετο), the latter excised in subsequent revision toward M (cf. *QTSJ*, 142); or (4) Ambrose is narrating the sense of the story, not citing an L manuscript. παρεγινετο in J describes Absalom's approaching the palace, not the plaintiffs; but J does not explicitly mention the latter, whereas he does occasionally use the words of his *Vorlage* in a slightly changed context (see *QTSJ*, chaps. VII and VIII).

Lexically, Ambrose appears dependent upon 4QSam[a] (M), not upon any Greek source (except possibly J's source). For tense, Ambrose agrees with 4QSam[a] G^{Lcx} V. Combined, for this unique reading,

$$\text{Ambr} = \text{4QSam}^a \neq M \neq C^{BOL}\ V.$$

a22. 2 Sam 15:2

4QSam[a]	[וענה האיש] ואמר
4QSam[c]	וענה [האיש ואמר]
MTS	ויאמר

G^{BMN}	και ειπεν
G^{L}	και απεκρινατο ο ανηρ και ελεγεν
G^{O} AE	και ειπεν (ελεγεν cxA-edE[vid]) ο ανηρ
Ambr	Respondebat ille
V	qui respondens aiebat
S^{j}	dicebat

See *Comm* at II.23 (15:2) and readings a20, 21 above. Ambrose reflects the expansion and the proper tense/aspect in 4QSam[a,c] G^{L} V.

Ambr = 4QSam[a,c](vid) G^{L} V ≠ M G.

a23. 2 Sam 15:6

4QSam[a]	ו֯[גנ]ב
M	ויגנב
G	και ιδιοποιειτο
L^{v}	et sua faciebat
V	et sollicitabat
J 7.195	κατεσκευαζε

A tracing sketched over 4QSam[a] favors the shorter ו[גנ]ב, though ו[יגנ]ב is possible. However, the other three preserved verb forms of 4QSam[a] in 15:1-6 are converted perfects (a20, 21, 22) in contrast to M. In this preferable reading where M errs slightly,

L^{v} = 4QSam[a](vid) G V J ≠ M.

a24. 2 Sam 18:3

4QSam[a]	[ויאמר] העם [ל]א֯ תצא
MT	ויאמר העם לא תצא
G	και ειπαν Ουκ εξελευση
G^{L}	και ειπεν ο λαος Ουκ εξελευση
L^{f}	et dixit populus non exies in pugnam
V	et respondit populus non exibis

See *QTSJ*, 114. G is the Old Greek reflecting the original Hebrew reading, העם being an unnecessary expansion (cf. 18:2). Only the Lucianic manuscripts add ο λαος, and it is echoed in L^{f}, which further expands with the explanatory plus *in pugnam.* If L^{f} is the/a Vetus Latina translation, then G^{L} is a proto-Lucianic plus based on the Hebrew (probably the 4QSam[a] tradition). A less likely possibility, without evidence, is that the late Lucianic text included a hexaplaric plus based on M and that L^f was later brought into conformity with a Lucianic manuscript. At any rate, for the expansion *populus,*

$$L^f = 4QSam^a \text{ M } G^L \text{ V} \neq G(OG).$$

a25. 2 Sam 18:3

$4QSam^a$	[לא ישים לנו לב . . . לא י]שׂ[י]ם לנו לב
MT	לא ישימו אלינו לב . . . לא ישימו אלינו לב
G	ου θησουσιν εφ ημας καρδιαν . . . ου θησουσιν εφ ημας καρδιαν
G^L	ου στησεται εν ημιν καρδια . . . ου θησουσιν εις ημας καρδιαν
L^f	non stabit in nobis cor nostrum . . . non occident nobiscum
V	non magnopere ad eos de nobis pertinebit . . . non satis curabunt

See *QTSJ,* 107-8, and the preceding reading. The text history of this verse is a nightmare, though a number of problems have yielded to analysis. $4QSam^a$ preserves for the problematic section only]°[ ]ם לנו לב. The doubtful trace of a letter looks most like the bottom central stroke of *sin* or *qop;* possibly there was a small letter between it and the clear final *mem.* Thus, ישים, ישם, יושם, יקום, יקם, יוקם are all possible, in approximately that order of descending probability, palaeographically and semantically. The text of M is essentially sound, except for עתה, which should be אתה (cf. *BHS* note b). G follows M closely. G^L agrees with G for the second clause, but its first clause stands out startlingly from all other traditions except $4QSam^a$ and L^f. That first clause does not translate the intended meaning of $4QSam^a$ or M, but, not understanding the Hebrew idiom, it does present an exact translation of another possible interpretation of the $4QSam^a$ text. (I do not argue this here, but, since the first and second clauses are identical in all Hebrew and Greek traditions except G^L, it is possible that the second clause was lost by haplography from the early G^L text, just as it was from G manuscripts $acgxa_2$ and from S E, then was restored with the reading taken from the G text.) At any rate, L^f obviously follows G^L:

G	και ειπαν	Ουκ εξελευση	
G^L	και ειπεν ο λαος	Ουκ εξελευση	
L^f	et dixit populus	non exies	in pugnam (explanatory plus)

G	οτι εαν φυγη	φυγωμεν, ου θησουσιν εφ ημας καρδιαν
G^L	οτι εαν θυγοντες	φυγωμεν, ου στησεται εν ημιν καρδια
L^f	quia si fugientes	fugerimus non stabit in nobis cor nostrum

G	και εαν αποθανωμεν το ημισυ ημων, ου θησουσιν εφ ημας καρδιαν
G^L	και εαν αποθανωμεν το ημισυ ημων, ου θησουσιν εις ημας καρδιαν
L^f	et si mortui fuerimus dimidiam partem nostram non occident nobiscum

(L^f divides differently, interpreting ημισυ not as subject of αποθ', but as object of a real or presumed θνησκουσιν: "and if *we* die, they will not kill a half part of our [army] along with *us*.")

G	οτι συ [= אתה]	ως ημεις	δεκα χιλιαδες
G^L	οτι και νυν [= עתה] αφαιρεθησεται	εξ ημων . . .	δεκα χιλιασιν
L^f	et nunc separentur	de nobis	x mil

(G^L follows the erroneous Hebrew with νυν, misreads כמנו as ממנו and thus inserts αφαιρεθησεται [though this could have happened at the Hebrew stage], and inserts η γη (εν) after/before εξ ημων [probably a dittographic mistake for ημων]. L^f follows G^L in the first two errors.)

In sum, though 4QSam^a is extant for only the second clause, and though G^L now agrees with M G for the second clause, the first clause in G^L reflects the 4QSam^a second clause (and presumably the first), and L^f is derived from G^L, displaying an error *(occident)* which shows dependence on the Greek, not Hebrew, language. Thus, though 4QSam^a is extant for only a small part of this reading, it appears that for this series of variants and errors,

$$L^f = \text{4QSam}^a\text{(vid) } G^L \neq \text{M G V.}$$

a26. 2 Sam 18:6

4QSam^a	[ה]שדה̇
MT	השדה
G	εις το δρυμον
G^L	εις το πεδιον
L^f V	in campum
J 7.236	εν πεδιω

G (or its *Vorlage*) simply errs, attracted to δρυμω (יער) later in the verse. For this correct reading,

$$L^f = \text{4QSam}^a \text{ M } G^L \text{ V J} \neq \text{G.}$$

a27. 2 Sam 18:9

4QSam^a [ ] והוא֯
MTS ואבשלום רכב
G και Αβεσσαλωη επιβεβηκως
G^L και αυτος επιβεβηκως
L^f et ascendit [
V sedens

4QSam^a preserves the original reading, with the customary Hebrew style for a circumstantial clause. M makes the subject more explicit, with the unnecessary repetition of the name (four words earlier). G^L literally follows 4QSam^a as G^R does M. L^f, as V indicates, is ambiguous, though it is more likely that it reflects 4QSam^a G^L.

L^f is ambiguous.

a28. 2 Sam 19:8(7)

4QSam^a Seb [נש]בׄע֯[ת]י֯ כי אׄםׄ אי[נך יוצא]
MT נשבעתי כי אינך יוצא
S *ymyt d'n l' npq 'nt*
G ομωσα (-σαν G^N) οτι ει μη εκπορευση σημερον
G^L ομωμοκασιν οτι ει μη συ εξελευση εις απαντησιν του λαου
L^s iurauerunt [
L^v iuraverunt, quia si non tu prodieris hodie in obviam huic omni populo
V iuro . . . quod si non exieris
J 7.256 τημερον, αν επιμενης . . . , τον λαον

See *QTSJ*, 86. The main reading under consideration is the frail, simple (haplographic) omission of אם in M, but followed by T.

The immediate context, however, illuminates the nature of L. Note (1) that for *iuraverunt*, L^{sv} = G^L ≠ 4QSam^a(vid) M G V; (2) that G^L adds συ, and L^v echoes it, pleonastically for both; (3) that G adds σημερον (om G^L), influencing both J and L^v; and (4) that G^L adds εις . . . λαου, and L^v records it in fuller form (while λαον in J may depend on the plus or may depend on the context). In (1, 2, 4) L^v depends on G^L alone; the plus in (3) looks like a conflation from G, but it is early (J) and may have been lost in G^L. In all these, except (3), L^v depends on G^L in disagreement with M and G. In all four, L^v agrees with G^L against V.

Preserving, with 4QSam^{a} the correct text, against the omission in M,

L^{V} = 4QSam^{a} S G V J $\neq$ M T.

a29. 2 Sam 22:33 // Ps 18(17):33

4QSam^{a}	מאזרני
MTS	מעוזי
G	ο κραταιων με
G^{L}	ο περιτιθεις μοι
L^{V}	[ ] accingit [ ]
V	qui accingit me
Ps-M	המאזרני
Ps-G	ο περιζωννυων με

Cf. *NAB; BHS,* note 33a. L^{V} follows the early G^{L} text, which depends upon the original reading preserved in 4QSam^{a} and Ps. T S G (= G^{R}) follow the inferior variant in M, though V echoes L^{V}.

L^{V} = 4QSam^{a} G^{L} V (Ps-MG) $\neq$ M G^{R}.

a30, 31. 2 Sam 23:1

4QSam^{a}	[ ] \ הגבר הקי̊ם אל
M	ונאם הגבר הקם על
T	ואימר גברא דמרבא למלכו
S	*'mr gbr' d'qym nyr'*
G	και πιστος ανηρ ον ανεστησεν Κυριος επι
G^{L}	πιστος ανηρ ον ανεστησεν ο θεος
L^{V}	fidelis vir quem suscitavit Deus
V	dixit vir cui constitutum est de

See F. M. Cross, *Canaanite Myth and Hebrew Epic,* 234-37; *QTSJ,* 113-14; *NAB.* הקם אל was the original consonantal text. 4QSam^{a} preserved this in correct *plene* form. The Old Greek interpreted its *Vorlage* as having נאמן and הק(י)ם אל. M confused the laryngeal. S interpreted this error one way (*nyr'* = yoke = עֹל), whereas G^{R} (after adding και = M) interpreted the error another way, adding επι. L^{V} agrees exactly with the erroneous and correct elements of G^{L}, while V reverts to the contrasting correct and erroneous elements of M. Though L^{V} is obviously dependent upon G^{L}, for the two preserved correct readings in 4QSam^{a},

a30. הקים,
L[v] = 4QSam[a] (M?) G T S ≠ (M?) V;
a31. על,
L[v] = 4QSam[a] G^L ≠ M G^R S V.

a32-35. 2 Sam 23:3

4QSam[a]	[משל] \ בׄאדם [צדי]קׄ משל [יראת אלוהים]
M	מושל באדם צדיק מושל יראת אלהים
T	דשליט בבני אנשא קושטא. . . וישליט בדחלתא דיוי
S	*dšlyṭ b'nš' zdyq' dšlyṭ bdḥl' d'lh'*
G	Παραβοληη ειπον Εν ανθρωπω πως κραταιωσητε φοβον θεου (χριστου B)
G^L	αρξον εν αν̅ο̅ις δικαιως αρχε φοβω θεου
L[v]	parabolam dic hominibus iuste incipit in timore Domini
V	dominator hominum iustus dominator in timore Dei.

See F. M. Cross, *Canaanite Myth and Hebrew Epic,* 234-37; *NAB; QTSJ,* 114. 4QSam[a] preserves, with משל 2° and presumably with משל 1°, the original reading. The G and G^L renderings παραβοληη ειπον and αρξον must both derive directly from the Hebrew: aorist imperatives for two senses of the verb משל. One is original, the other is apparently a revision based on the Hebrew. αρξον is the correct interpretation, whereas παραβολη is the standard correspondent that the Old Greek, Aquila, and presumably G^R use for משל, "proverb." Εν ανθρωποις (not -πω) is the correct rendering of באדם. Correct also are δικαιως and αρχε (now present imperative); there is much manuscript variation on κραταιωσητε, which must have begun as a singular imperative or subjunctive variant of αρχε based on the Hebrew (cf. Prov. 16:32; 17:2). That variation plus -ωπω πως (cf. αν̅ο̅ις δικαιως) suggests inner-Greek confusion, resulting in the pious example of tropological (cf. esp. G^B) interpretation in G.

L[v] reflects the G rendering of the first verb but then the G^L rendering of the remainder, including misunderstanding αρχε(ι) as "begins" instead of "rules." This error demonstrates dependence on the Greek language specifically. L[v] thus either displays dependence on a mixture of Greek texts (the more economical explanation) or preserves a fossilized stage in the history of the text, which would have developed thus: (1) The original Hebrew as preserved in 4QSam[a]. (2) The Old Greek translation as preserved in G^L. (3) An interpretative revision based on the Hebrew: *παραβοληη ειπον εν ανθρωποις δικαιως αρχε. . . . It is at this stage that L[v] was translated. (4) The Hebrew-based variant *κραταιωσ-. (5) The M interpretation, influencing T S and eventually V. (6) An inner-Greek confusion in the dominant text, resulting in the spiritual interpretation in the present G text.

In summary, L^v depends upon the Greek text(s) in specifically the Greek language. Either it was directly translated from the G^L text but over αρξον (which it probably misunderstood) chose the interpretatively more attractive variant παραβολην ειπον, or it was directly translated from a Greek text at a medial stage of the textual development. Whichever be the case, for the individual readings,

a32. **משל** 1°,
L^v = (4QSam^a) G ≠ G^L ≠ M V;
a33. **באדם**,
L^v = 4QSam^a M G^L (V) ≠ G;
a34. **צדיק**;
L^v = 4QSam^a M G^L (V) ≠ G;
a35. **משל** 2°,
L^v = (4QSam^a) G^L ≠ G ≠ M V.

a36. 2 Sam 24:17//1 Chr 21:17

4QSam^a	[וא]נׄכי הרעׄה הׄרׄעתי
MT	**ואנכי העויתי**
S	*w'rgzt*
G	και εγω ειμι (om Ax) ο ποιμην εκακοποιησα (και ηδικησα a_2)
B(txt)	ηδικησα
B^{ab}(mg)	και εγω ειμι ο ποιμην
G^L	και εγω ο ποιμην εκακοποιησα
L^s	pastor . . . et ego male feci
V	ego inique egi
Chr-M	**והרע הרעותי**
Chr-G	κακοποιων εκακοποιησα
J 7.328	αυτος ειη κολασθηναι δικαιος ο ποιμην

See *NAB;* Shenkel, *HTR* 62 (1969) 81; *QTSJ,* 86. 4QSam^a probably preserves the original text (cf. the antithetical **ואלה הצאן**, which follows immediately). Chr-M seems to present **הרע** as *Hip'il* inf. abs., and Chr-G certainly understands it thus. εγω ειμι = the G^R correspondent for **אנכי**; κακοποιειν = **רעע**, and αδικειν = **עוה**. Thus, G^L represents the Old Greek here. M T S V omit "shepherd," but the Old Greek, all subsequent Greek traditions (except G^{B*}, which suffered post-G^R haplography, εγω ειμι 1°⌒2°, thus suggesting that it did not have ποιμην), plus A C E and Josephus all have ποιμην.

Ambrose himself (see note in Sabatier) has several renderings, including *ego pastor male (malum) feci.* Ambrose also quotes from "Vict. Tun." (presumably Victor, Bishop of Tunnunna), and this is the reading that the text of L^s has: *ego pastor peccavi, et ego male feci: grex autem hic. . . .* Three of Chrysostom's six citations of this passage also display that order: ο ποιμην ημαρτον και εγω (+ ο ποιμην 2/6) εκακοποιησα. Since it is only in the Hebrew play on words that the position of הרעה is significant, it is understandable that L, or a Greek tradition before it, may have placed *pastor* earlier (note similarly the changed order of *grex/hic*). At any rate, G^L L^s Chr J include this original reading from 4QSam^a, now lost from M G^R.

L^s = 4QSam^a G^L J (Chr-M) ≠ M (G^{B*}) V ≠ Chr-G.

Significance of the 4QSam^a-L Readings

L^f (= L^{115}): Palimpsestus Vindobonensis

L^f offers seventeen readings for comparison. It is extant for nineteen readings in which 4QSam^a, M, or G disagree, but in two of those it is ambiguous (a9, 27). 4QSam^a is reconstructed in seven readings, L^f in two readings (marked with **).

	4QSam^a	M	G^L	G
a1	/	=	=	=
a2	/	/	=	=
a3	/	=	=	=
a4	=**	/	(=)	/
a5	/	=	=	/
a6	/**	/	=	/
a9**	ambiguous			
a10	=	/	=	(=)
a11	=	/	=	/
a12	=**	/	=	=
a13	/	/	/	=
a14	/	=	=	(=)
a15	=**	/	=	/
a16	=**	/	(=)	/
a17**	=**	/	=	/
a24	=	=	=	/
a25	=**	/	=	/
a26	=	=	=	/
a27	ambiguous			

[The symbol = denotes agreement with L; / denotes disagreement; (=) denotes agreement though L probably depends on another reading.]

Of the seventeen reasonably clear readings, L^f agrees with G^L sixteen times. The disagreement is in a13, where G preserves the correct Old Greek reading, while G^L makes a minor classical, inadvertent, or hexaplaric omission, which

L would automatically supply (as does V against M). On the other hand, two of the agreements (a4, 16) are complicated. In a4, L^f agrees with the partially reconstructed reading of 4QSam^a, supported by S in the non-M element of its doublet. One might conjecture that the Old Greek had *εισηλθεν, which was subsequently revised to απη- for conformity with M or sense. In a16, the correct, Old Greek reading is MAAXA. This was transcribed correctly by L^f, slightly corrupted by G^{BA}, and substantially corrupted by G^L. We may note here that L^v reflects the corrupt form in G^L.

In sharp contrast to these sixteen agreements with G^L, L^f agrees with 4QSam^a in only ten of the seventeen readings, with M six times, and with G eight times, in two of which (a10, 14) L^f is really dependent upon G^L.

There are only three readings in which L^f agrees with a single tradition against the other traditions (a4, 6, 13). The first and third have just been discussed. In a6, L^f agrees with G^L, z, a_2, 71 and Josephus (z and a_2 showing signs that G^R may have had the fuller reading).

Statistically, it is evident that L^f is most closely affiliated with the G^L text. This, of course, is the general conclusion that most studies for Samuel have formed. But we may go further. L^f actually reflects the Old Greek in most readings where the Old Greek can be determined. It reflects the Old Greek in preferable readings, expansions, errors, and freedom from omissions.

L^f reflects the Old Greek in many preferable readings (a1, 4?, 5?, 6, 10, 12, 13, 15, 16, 17, 26), all but three of which are preserved in G^L (a4, 13, 16 — discussed above). It shows that twice the Old Greek has been lost, once through revision (a4) and once through corruption (a16). It also shows that, though G^L in this section is an impressive witness to the Old Greek, in three instances G^L displays later development (a4, 13, 16). L^f itself has erred once in these preferable readings (a17), but this is an inner-Latin corruption that demonstrates original dependence on the correct Old Greek preserved in G^L.

Similarly in its four expansions, L^f reflects the Old Greek three times (a3, 14, 16 — the first two of which are G^L, the last, G^B) and a G^L expansion once (a24). As is true for the Old Greek, L^f exhibits no omissions; and indeed for all three omissions by M it retains, with the Old Greek, the original text (a6, 10, 12).

In its four errors, L^f twice translates correctly, accurately reflecting errors in the Old Greek (a2, 11 — the first in both G and G^L, the second specifically in G^L). Once it is guilty of an inner-Latin copyist's error, where again the original Latin had correctly translated the correct Old Greek (a17). In its complex fourth error (a25), L^f first correctly translates an erroneous interpretation in G^L *(non stabit . . .)* then continues with an error *(occident)* at a point where the G^L text appears to be secondary; this last suspicion is strengthened earlier in the verse (cf. a24), where L^f follows not the Old Greek but the expanded G^L text.

Concerning the language of its *Vorlage,* L^f appears dependent specifically upon the Greek language in the two translations *defecit animo* and *occident* (a10, 25; cf. also *QTSJ,* no. 55 on pp. 210, 218, and no. 71 on pp. 233, 234). There are no hints that it was translated directly from the Hebrew language.

Thus, L^f is most closely affiliated with the G^L text, which is predominantly the Old Greek but a slightly revised, slightly corrupted, form of the Old Greek.

L^h (L^{117}): Fragmenta Vindobonensia

L^h is extant for only six readings:

	4QSam^a	M	G^L	G		4QSam^a	M	G^L	G
a1	/	=	=	=	a5	/	=	=	/
a2	/	/	=	=	a6**	/**	/	=	/
a4	=**	/	(=)	/	a18	/	/	/	/

The first five readings show the same textual affiliation as L^f, whereas the last is apparently an idiosyncratic omission, a simple parablepsis. Of those five readings in common with L^f, there are only two significant differences between the Latin texts (a2, 6).

L^s: The Sabatier Collection

L^s, Sabatier's collection of Vetus Latina readings from manuscripts and patristic citations, still requires critical sorting, but its readings are nonetheless presented here with that caveat. Sabatier provides two manuscript readings and six readings from Ambrose, the last of which is from "Vict. Tun."[23] as well as from Ambrose:

23. "Vict. Tun." presumably is Victor, Bishop of Tunnunna, who died after 566 C.E. (*Vetus Latina Verzeichnis* [1963] 479). Questions, of course, are raised by the apparent anomaly of his text being quoted by Ambrose.

	4QSam^a	M	G^L	G	
a8	=	/	=	/	Ambr (Sabatier, pp. 536-37, n. 16)
a10	=	/	=	=	MSS Germ 7, Corb 1, 3 (mg), Germ 9 (expuncta)
a12	=	/	=	=	MSS Germ 7, Corb 3 (mg), Germ 9 (expuncta)
a19	/	=	=	=	Ambr
a20	=	/	=	/	Ambr
a21	=	(=)	/	/	Ambr
a22	(=)	(/)	(=)	/	Ambr
a36	=	/	=	=	Vict. Tun. (apud Ambr), Ambr

The two manuscript readings (a10, 12) record L translations of the common G text, which is based upon the 4QSam^a tradition in contrast to long haplographies in M. The first reading is also documented by L^{fv}, the second by L^f. These readings vary significantly from each other, but there is as yet insufficient material to determine whether they are separate translations or are recensionally related.

The six Ambrose (and Vict. Tun.) readings require little caution for our purposes. They probably reflect L in general. L^v is extant for only one of them (a8), but it is in agreement with it: an expansion in the Old Greek or proto-Lucianic text, based on 4QSam^a. In another (a19), its two nouns interpret the two nouns in the common Greek and M. In three other readings from the same verse (a20-22), Ambr reflects the correct reading with 4QSam^a G^L J against MG, with two exceptions: first, *accedebat* (a21) indicates a variant interpretation specifically of the Hebrew; this could have taken place at the Greek translational or revisional stage, rather than at the Old Latin stage, but no evidence is forthcoming to support that possibility. Secondly, *respondebat* (a22) need not represent απεκρινατο exactly (om ελεγεν), but it probably does (note V). Finally, we can be confident that *pastor* (a36) reflects L as dependent upon the Old Greek and ultimately upon 4QSam^a. Josephus supports the Ambrose readings in three out of the six instances (a8, 20, 36), vaguely paraphrasing the other three (a19, 21, 22), but never showing signs of disagreement. This support is confirmed by his agreement with the two manuscript readings as well.

Two points should be stressed. First, the two manuscript readings agree with 4QSam^a G^L G against M, while the six Ambr readings agree with 4QSam^a G^L four (and probably five) times, while agreeing with M only once (or possibly twice) and with G only twice (both because OG, in common with G^L). Secondly, Ambrose once (a21) seems to be dependent directly upon the Hebrew. Especially since this is the unique clear instance of such dependence (to which a possible instance in a5 may be added) among the thirty-six readings reviewed, it is important to recall the analogous startling fact that Josephus preserves five unique readings in his narrative of 1-2 Samuel undocumented in biblical manuscripts — until the discovery of 4QSam^a. The point at issue here is that one might immediately conclude that Josephus is dependent upon a Hebrew manuscript in the 4QSam^a tradition. But analysis of those five readings (*QTSJ*, 165-73, 190) demonstrates that for three of them Josephus betrays dependence on a *Vorlage* specifically in the Greek language as his medium. Nor is there any evidence to doubt that the same is true for the other two readings; we simply do not have sufficiently differentiated readings to determine the language for them.

Thus, the proper way to describe the Ambrose agreement is that Ambrose reflects an interpretation based directly on the Hebrew. We simply lack evidence to determine whether that interpretation was made at the Latin stage (the Vetus Latina translation or even Ambrose) or at the Greek stage, upon which L Ambr are dependent but which is no longer extant. The Josephus analogy and the dominant scholarly conclusions thus far would suggest the latter.

L^v (= L^{93}): The Vercellone Glosses

Burkitt (*The Old Latin and the Itala*, 9-10) doubts the reliability of the L$^{(91),93}$ readings published by Vercellone: "it is by no means certain that this interesting document does not represent readings extracted and translated from some Greek codex, so that it may have no connection with the Old Latin properly so called." Voogd (pp. 110-11) notes, however, that Vercellone was convinced of "the Old Latin character of these marginal readings," and adds his own judgment "that the marginal notes possess genuineness as Old Latin evidence." They are included in this study as plausible evidence, until the writer can verify them more precisely.

L^v offers fifteen readings for comparison:

	4QSam^a	M	G^L	G		4QSam^a	M	G^L	G
a3	/	/	=	/	a29	=	/	=	/
a7	/	(=)	=	(=)	a30	=	=	=	=
a8	=	/	=	/	a31	=	/	=	/
a10	=	/	(=)	=	a32	(=)**	/	/	=
a16	(=)**	/	=	/	a33	=	=	=	/
a17	/**	(=)	/	(=)	a34	=**	=	=	/
a23	=**	/	=	=	a35	/	/	=	/
a28	=	/	=	=					

Again L^V predominantly agrees with G^L: twelve (+1) out of fifteen times, whereas it agrees with G only five (+2) times, with 4QSam^a nine (+2) times, and with M only three (+2) times. L^V preserves eight preferable readings (a10, 23, 28-31, 33, 34), three expansions (a7, 8, 16), no omissions, and six errors (a3^{bis}, 16, 17, 32, 35) — all of which, with the exception of the errors a17 and 32, simply reflect the preferable readings, expansions, lack of omissions, and errors in G^L. In a17 it presents a unique, independent reading, but that is probably due to the fact that it does not have the preferable G^L text but the erroneous G^B text. The other non-G^L error (a32) will be discussed immediately below.

Of the unique agreements, three or probably four are with G^L (a3, 16, 35, and probably a7); only one is not with G^L: the error in a32 is patently dependent upon the erroneous interpretation by G^B of the 4QSam^a reading. It is difficult to determine whether G^B is the Old Greek or rather a more spiritually enticing interpretation based at an early point upon the Hebrew.

At times it is difficult to isolate the Old Greek with confidence, but L^V probably reflects the Old Greek in nine or ten instances (a3, 10?, 23, 28-31, 33-35), though twice it errs while reflecting the correct Old Greek (a3, 35). Once it reflects a later, corrupt form of G (a16) and once a corrupt form (a17), which is possibly a later development in the Greek text; but this displays a pattern similar to that of a32, and more evidence is needed before deciding whether in a17, 32 the G^L readings are corrections of the Old Greek (G^B) or whether the G^B readings are corruptions of the Old Greek (G^L).

There are no hints that L^V derives directly from a Hebrew source; the manuscript does show, however, dependence on a *Vorlage* specifically in the Greek language in five instances (a3^{bis}, 16, 23 [*sua faciebat* for ιδιοποιειτο], 35 [*incipit*]).

4QSam^c and the Old Latin for 2 Samuel 14–15

The L manuscripts extant for the portions of Samuel preserved in the third Samuel scroll from Qumran are: L^h (2 Sam 14:17-30), L^s (14:26, 27, 30; 15:1-5), and L^V (fragments from 14:7-30 and 15:4, 6, 12). Since the edition of 4QSam^c is published in *BASOR* 235 (1979) 1-25, the L readings for 4QSam^c can be more briefly listed here, and the reader may consult the edition with its photographs, transcriptions, commentary, and analysis of textual affiliations (hereafter *Edn, Photo, Trscr, Comm, Affil*), as appropriate.

The qualitative assessment of the readings will be abbreviated as follows:

pref.	original or preferable reading
inf.	inferior or secondary reading
var.	admissible, inferior, or synonymous variant
add.	addition, expansion
om.	omission, loss
err.	error
sens.	*ad sensum* change

Readings

c1. 2 Sam 14:7 (col. I, line 1)

L^v: (et extinguetur) titio [ ] (pref.)
= 4QSam^c G^L(OG) S (pref.) ≠ M $G^{(R)}$ V (var.)

See *Comm.* This passive verb plus nominative construction undoubtedly reflects the passive verb plus nominative construction of G^L: και σβεσθησεται ο σπινθηρ.

c2. 2 Sam 14:11 (I.6)

L^v: ut non auferas (sens. var.)
= G^L S-ap-Barh (sens. var.) ≠ 4QSam^c M G(OG) V (pref.).

c3. 2 Sam 14:18 (I.16-17 // 4QSam^a

L^h: (Et respondit rex) mulieri (et dixit) (var. 1°)
= 4QSam^c 4QSam^a(vid) (var. 1°) ≠ M $G^{(R?)}$ V (var. 2°)

See *Comm.* This could simply be a synonymous variant among the frequent formulaic options. Or it could be conjectured, partially on the basis of the G^L variant τη γυναικι (προς την γυναικα G^B), that the Old Greek originally read *και απεκριθη ο βασιλευς τη γυναικι και ειπεν, and that the last two pairs of words were revisionally transposed to conform with M G^R.

c4. 2 Sam 14:19 (I.20; cf. a18 above)

L^h: posuit (om. *in os*)
≠ 4QSam^{c,a} M G(OG) V (pref.).

c5. 2 Sam 14:20 (I.22)

L^h: (sciat) omnia (add.)
= M $G^{(R)}$ V (add.) ≠ $4QSam^c$ G^L (pref.). See *Comm.*

c6. 2 Sam 14:21 (I.23)

L^h: uade et a[dduc] (2 add.)
= G^L (2 add.) ≠ G^B (pref.) ≠ $4QSam^c$ G^O (V?) (3 add.) ≠ M (2 add.).

c7, 8. 2 Sam 14:22 (II.2)

L^h: scio (c7: sens. var.; c8: om. ο δουλος σου)
= G^{Lcx} (sens. var.) ≠ $4QSam^c$ M G(OG?) V (pref.)
≠$4QSam^c$ M G(OG) V (pref.)

After following the change to first person in G^L, L^h omitted the now superfluous subject.

c9. 2 Sam 14:22^{fin} (II.3)

L^h: (secundum ue[rbum]) serui tui (fecisti m[ise] ricordiam) (pref.)
= $4QSam^c$ G^d(OG?) T^{ed} V (pref.) ≠ M G T^{MSS} S (inf. var.)

ʿbdk is the correct court usage (see *Comm*). M errs here through synesis, though earlier in the verse (cf. c8) it reads correctly. G, possibly through recension, agrees with M, as do T^{MSS} S. G^d may preserve the Old Greek reading. L^h, though slightly paraphrastic, depends upon $4QSam^c$ (OG?). V is possibly the result of Jerome's consciously critical selection of L over M G.

c10. 2 Sam 14:23 (II.3)

L^h: Et sur[rexit] Joab (pref.)
= M G(OG) V (pref.) ≠ $4QSam^c$ (om: idiosyncratic parablepsis)

c11. 2 Sam 14:25 (II.5)

L^h: erat [por]ro Abessalon (pref.)
= $4QSam^c$ (pref.) ≠ M G V (err.)

$4QSam^c$ preserves the original reading, the M variant being due to earlier palaeographic confusion (see *Photo*) and subsequent smoothing. The Old Greek may no longer be extant, but see G^d. *Porro* = *gm* exactly, and the order and syntax of L appear closer to 4QSam^{c} than to M, but the correspondence is not exact.

c12. 2 Sam 14:26 (II.8)

L^{hsv}: centum (siclorum) (pref.)
= G^{L} (OG: pref.) ≠ 4QSam^{c} M G$^{(R)}$ V J 7.189 (var.)

c13. 2 Sam 14:27 (II.9)

L^{h}: Thamar (pref.); [L^{v}: Moacha (err.)]
L^{h} = 4QSam^{c} M G(OG) V (pref) ≠ L^{v} G^{L} (err.)

c14. 2 Sam 14:27 (II.9)

L^{v}: et (haec) (add.)
= 4QSam^{c} G^{L} S (add.) ≠ M G (pref.) ≠ V (om.)

c15. 2 Sam 14:27^{fin} (II.9)

L^{hsv}; Thamar's marriage (add.)
= G J 7.190 (add.) ≠ 4QSam^{c} M V (pref)

c16. 2 Sam 14:29^{init} (II.10)

L^{h}: (misit) om Abessalon (om.?)
= V ≠ 4QSam^{c} M G (pref.?)

This is possibly the original short text in L^{h}. But it is also possibly a stylistic omission, since Abessalon occurs as subject in 14:28, which L^{h} syntactically connects as a subordinate clause to 14:29:

> [28]Et cum biennium esset, quod sederet Abessalon in Hierusalem faciem regis non uidens, [29]misit ad Joab. . . .

c17. 2 Sam 14:29 (II.11)

L^{h}: (misit iterum) om *'lyw* 2° (pref.)
= M G^{de}2(OG?) V^{ed} (pref.) ≠ 4QSam^{c} G V^{mss} (add.)

c18. 2 Sam 14:30 (II.12)

L^{h}: (dixit) + Abessalon (add.)
= G$^{LMN(BA)}$ S (add.) ≠ 4QSam^{c} M T V (pref.)

Because of the different placement of Abessalom in the G traditions, the expansion was probably not in the Old Greek; L^h follows G^L.

c19. 2 Sam 14:30 (II.12)

L^h: (pars est Joab) in agro iuxta nos (var.)
= G^L (η μερις) η εχομενη ημων εν αγρω (του Ιωαβ) (var.)
= G^{vB} (ημερις του Ιωαβ [τ.Ι. post αγρω G^B]) εν αγρω εχομενα μου (var.)
≠ על י[די] 4QSam^c (pref.) ≠ אל ידי M (err.).

Though the word order shifts in the Greek witnesses, *in agro* shows dependence upon the Greek, and *nos* specifically upon G^L.

c20. 2 Sam 14:30 (II.13)

L^h: Et illi obaudienter praeceptis domini sui congregauerunt segetem Joab posita in confinio agri illorum.

L^h is strongly interpretative and grammatically problematic here: where "the servants burned the field" in 4QSam^c M G, in L^h "they, obediently to their master's commands, gathered Joab's crop placed (?) on the border of their (?) field" (*posita* agrees with no antecedent, and *illorum* should not refer to Absalom's servants [*sui!*]). Josephus (*Ant.* 7.191) also mollifies the action, saying that they burned the field next to Joab's. Finally, rabbinic tradition, similarly troubled by the action, says that "Absalom's sons died before him as a punishment for having set fire to Joab's field."[24]

This reading provides no positive evidence for textual affiliation, but it is instructive for understanding the character of the L translation.

c21. 2 Sam 14:30^{fin} (II.14-15)

L^{hsv}: include the servants' report to Joab (pref.)
= 4QSam^c G (pref) ≠ M (om.)

c22, 23. 2 Sam 15:1 (II.21^{sup})

Ambr: Abessalon fecit sibi (c22: pref. order; c23: var. tense/aspect)
= 4QSam^c (pref. order) ≠ M G V (var.)
= M G V (var. aspect) ≠ 4QSam^c (pref. aspect)

24. Cf. Marcus's reference to Ginzberg in note *d* in the Loeb edition of Josephus, *Jewish Antiquities*, vol. 5, pp. 490-91.

c24. 2 Sam 15:2 (II.23)

Ambr: Respondebat ille (add.)
= 4QSam^c 4QSam^a(vid) G^L(OG?) V (add.) ≠ M G (pref.)

c25. 2 Sam 15:12 (III.12)

L^v: (et) erat (cogitatio firma) (pref.)
= 4QSam^c(vid) G^L(OG) (pref.) ≠ M G V (err.)

Significance of the 4QSam^c-L Readings

L^h (L^{117}): Fragmenta Vindobonensia

	4QSam^c	M	G^L	G		4QSam^c	M	G^L	G
c3	=**	/	/	/	c12	/	/	=	/
c4	/	/	/	/	c13	=	=	/	=
c5	/**	=	/	=	c15	/	/	=	=
c6**	/	/	=	/	c16	/	/	/	/
c7	/	/	=	/	c17	/	=		/
c8	/	/	(=)	/	c18	/	/	=	(=)
c9	=	/	/	/	c19	/**	/	=	(=)
c10**	/	=	=	=	c20	/	/	/	/
c11**	=	/	/	/	c21	=	/	=	=

For the 4QSam^a readings, the primary textual affiliation of L^h was with G^L: four (and a possible fifth) agreements out of six with G^L, where the sixth was a simple omission unique to L^h.

For the 4QSam^c readings, L^h disagrees with all four traditions in three readings: a simple parableptic omission (c4), a stylistic omission (c16), and a distinctive, independent interpretation where Josephus and rabbinic tradition also mollify the report (c20).

Of the remaining fifteen readings that provide comparisons, L^h agrees with G^L nine times (technically, c8 is a disagreement; but the L^h omission is possible [indeed advisable] only because L^h followed G^L alone in the previous word [c7]). G^L preserves the Old Greek in five of these nine readings (c8, 10, 12, 15, 21), G^L shows a secondary reading three times (c6, 7, 18), and once there is a problem with identifying the Old Greek (c19).

L^h agrees with the majority G tradition in five readings, plus two other technical agreements where it really depends on G^L (c18, 19). Of these, G preserves the Old Greek four times (c10, 13, 15, 21) and shows one secondary reading (c5).

L^h displays six unique agreements with G^L (c6, 7, 8, 12, 18, 19 [*nos*]), none with G, three with 4QSam^c (c3, 9, 11), and one with M (c17). The unique agreement with M is simply the preferable reading, which rejects the expansion *'lyw* 2°, where the Greek manuscripts e_2 (Lucianic) and d agree with M L^h V^{ed}. Of the three unique agreements with 4QSam^c, one is simply a synonymous variant (c3), and the remaining two again display the preferable text (c9, 11). Uncannily, the peculiar and abbreviating manuscript G^d agrees with 4QSam^c L^h for c9, and for c11, though it shows severe confusion with entire lines displaced, it displays the reconstructed 4QSam^c text (see *Comm* at II.5 [14:25]). G^d deserves special study, for one of the ancestors of this manuscript provides the Greek readings that bridge the Latin with the Hebrew in three of the four instances where L^h shows agreement with 4QSam^c or M in contrast with the G^L and dominant G traditions.

The only hint at dependence upon a *Vorlage* in specifically the Hebrew language or specifically the Greek language is in c19, where *pars . . . in agro* patently reflects the Greek η μερις . . . εν αγρω, not the simple *ḥlqt* of M.

Thus, as was the situation for the 4QSam^a readings, so also here, L^h predominantly follows G^L. L^h follows the Old Greek, as often found in G^L but occasionally in G as opposed to G^L (c13), and it possibly follows the Old Greek (cf. G^d) where both G and G^L have together conformed to M (c3, 9, 11) or to the 4QSam^c tradition (c17). But it displays a slightly developed Greek text, again usually following G^L, but once showing a minor expansion found in G but not G^L (c5).

L^s: Sabatier Collection

	4QSam^c	M	G^L	G	
c12	/	/	=	/	S. Paulin
c15	/	/	=	=	Corb. 13, Germ. 9 (deleta), Germ. 11 (mg)
c21	=	/	=	=	Corb. 13, Corb 1 and 3 (mg), Germ. 7 and 9
c22	=	/	/	/	Ambr
c23	/	=	=	=	Ambr
c24	=	/	=	/	Ambr

With the exception of the reading divided as c22, 23, we may confidently treat this list of readings as genuinely being or reflecting the Old Latin. The readings in c15, 21 are from manuscripts, the citation by S. Paulin (c12) agrees with both L^h and L^v, and the Ambrose reading in c24 is attested in $4QSam^c$, $4QSam^a$(vid), G^L (= OG?), and V.

L^s follows G^L in all readings except c22, which refers specifically to word order (a minor transposition), while it does agree with G^L in content and tense/aspect (c23). One of these readings is a unique agreement with G^L (c12), and all are Old Greek (with the possible exception of c22, 23). In contrast, L^s agrees with G only three times (all OG in common with G^L: c15, 21, 23), with $4QSam^c$ three times (c21, 24, plus the unique agreement on word order in c22), and with M only once, where it also agrees with G^L, G, and V (c23).

In these readings collected by Sabatier, L clearly depends on the Old Greek as preserved in G^L.

L^v (= L^{93}): The Vercellone Glosses

	$4QSam^c$	M	G^L	G
c1**	=**	/	=	/
c2	/	/	=	/
c12	/	/	=	/
c13	/	/	=	/
c14	=	/	=	/
c15	/	/	=	=
c21	=	/	=	=
c25	=**	/	=	/

L^v agrees with G^L in all eight readings, uniquely so in three (c2, 12, 13). It agrees with G only twice, both Old Greek in common with G^L (c15, 21). It agrees with $4QSam^c$ four times (c1, 14, 21, 25), and with M never.

L^v follows G^L as it preserves the Old Greek in five of the readings (c1, 12, 15, 21, 25) and shows secondary developments in three: a smoothing of the narrative for sense (c2), an error in a proper name (c13), and a minor addition of a conjunction (c14).

No clues are given which would betray the specific language of its *Vorlage.*

For the $4QSam^a$ readings, L^v had predominantly reflected the G^L text, which was mainly the Old Greek but in a developed form. Though it sporadically displayed dependence upon an error in the G^B text tradition, it mainly followed the preferable readings, expansions, lack of omissions, and errors in G^L. For these $4QSam^c$ readings, it displays with striking clarity its dependence on the G^L text, which is a slightly developed form of the Old Greek translation.

Conclusion

This has been primarily a study presenting and analyzing new data. For a number of reasons, large-scale hypotheses or conclusions would be premature. First, the general field of Old Latin studies for the Old Testament is not well developed. Again, this particular study has had to be confined to fragments of the Qumran and Latin texts covering only one-quarter of the text of Samuel. Furthermore, it is obviously important to study the Latin manuscripts as documents with their own character and integrity. Fischer's corrected edition of L^{115}, for example, transforms the impression of its character gained from Belsheim's edition.

Significant results, nonetheless, have emerged from the analysis of the witnesses to the Old Latin of Samuel in the new light dawning from the Qumran scrolls.

L proves to be a reasonably faithful and controllable witness to the Old Greek, which in turn is not infrequently a witness superior to the Masoretic text for the ancient text of Samuel. L, however, is not Old Greek in its "pure form," but is reflective of numerous early developments in the Greek text, including conscious revisions, expansions, alternate interpretations, and errors; and it has its share of similar developments beyond its parent text.

The scrolls help us to understand errors in the Latin text (e.g., a17); the Old Latin helps us reconstruct the fragmentary scrolls (e.g., a4, *Edn*, pp. 21-22), and the Old Latin occasionally preserves the Old Greek when the latter is no longer extant in surviving Greek manuscripts (e.g., a4?, 16).

The frequency of the pattern L = 4QSam^{a,c} $G^L \neq$ M G and the infrequency of the pattern L = M G $\neq$ 4QSam^{a,c} G^L again confirm the general hypothesis according to which this study has been structured and conducted, namely, the theory of the textual history of Samuel conceived by Barthélemy, developed by Cross, and tested in *QTSJ* and elsewhere: the Old Greek and some of its early developments, including conscious revisions, are based predominantly on the text tradition shared by 4QSam^{a,c} as opposed to the Masoretic text, whereas the majority Greek text for 2 Samuel 11–24 displays a text that in its basic stratum was the same but that underwent subsequent recension toward conformity with the ascendant Masoretic text.

But the fundamental importance of the Old Latin, once again demonstrated by this study, is that it often takes us back with controllable reliability to the text of Samuel as it was when the Greek was first translated from the Hebrew, ca. 200 B.C.E. And in a book for which the Masoretic text so often errs, a valuable resource is thus available in the witness of the Old Latin.

Bibliography

Editions of Texts

Belsheim, J. *Palimpsestus Vindobonensis.* Christianiae, 1885.
Berger, S. *Notice sur quelques textes latines inédites de l'Ancien Testament.* Paris, 1893.
Bianchini, G. "Psalterium duplex cum Canticis." *Vindiciae Canonicarum Scripturarum.* Rome, 1740.
Brooke, A. E., N. McLean, and H. St. J. Thackeray, eds. *The Old Testament in Greek According to the Text of Codex Vaticanus . . . , with a Critical Apparatus. . . .* Volume 2, Part 1. Cambridge, 1927.
de Bruyne, D. "Fragments d'anciennes versions latines tirés d'un glossaire biblique." *Archivum Latinitatis Medii Aevi* 3, 113-20. Paris, 1927.
Degering, H., and A. Boeckler. *Die Quedlinburger Italafragmente.* Berlin, 1932.
Dold, A. *Das älteste Liturgiebuch der lateinischen Kirche.* Texte und Arbeiten 26/8. Beuron, 1936.
Fischer, B. Unpublished edition of Palimpsestus Vindobonensis, correcting the misreadings of Belsheim. Beuron, 1942.
Haupt, P. *Veteris versionis antehieronymianae libri II Regum sive Samuelis fragmenta Vindobonensia.* Vienna, 1877.
Sabatier, P. *Bibliorum sacrorum latinae versiones antiquae seu vetus italica et ceterae quaecumque in codicibus manuscriptis et antiquorum libris reperiri potuerunt.* Reims, 1739-49; Paris, 1751.
Vercellone, C. *Variae lectiones Vulgatae Latinae Bibliorum editionis.* 2 vols. Rome, 1860 and 1864.
Vetus Latina. Microfilms of the typed cards collected by 1952 in the Vetus Latina Institut, Beuron, Germany, with manuscript and patristic evidence for the Old Latin, including L^{93} (Vercellone), L^{115} (Belsheim, plus some corrections; von Eichenfeld and Endlicher), L^{117} (Haupt). Medieval Institute Library, University of Notre Dame, Indiana.
Weber, R. *Les anciennes versions latines du deuxième liure des Paralipomènes.* Collectanea Biblica Latina 8. Rome, 1945.

Studies

Barthélemy, Dominique. *Études d'histoire du texte de l'Ancien Testament.* Fribourg: Editions Universitaires; Göttingen: Vandenhoeck & Ruprecht, 1978.
Billen, A. V. *The Old Latin Texts of the Heptateuch.* Cambridge, 1927.
Bodine, Walter R. *The Greek Text of Judges: Recensional Developments.* HSM 23. Missoula, Mont.: Scholars Press, 1980.
———. "*Kaige* and Other Recensional Developments in the Greek Text of Judges." *BIOSCS* 13 (1980).
de Boer, P. A. H. "Confirmatum est cor meum: Remarks on the Old Latin Text of the Song of Hannah." *Oudtestamentische Studiën* 13 (1963) 173-95.

———. "Once Again the Old Latin Text of Hannah's Song." *Oudtestamentische Studiën* 14 (1965) 206-13.

La Bonnardière, A. M. *Biblia Augustiniana.* II, *Livres historiques.* Paris, 1960.

———. "Les livres de Samuel et des Rois, les livres de Chroniques et d'Esdras dans l'oeuvre de Saint Augustin." *Revue des Etudes Augustiniennes* 2 (1956) 335-63.

Brock, S. P. "The Recensions of the Septuagint Version of I Samuel." Dissertation, Oxford University, 1966.

Burkitt, F. C. *The Old Latin and the Itala.* Texts and Studies 4, part 3. Cambridge, 1896.

———. "The Old Latin Heptateuch." *JTS* 29 (1928) 140-46.

———. *The Rules of Tyconius.* Texts and Studies 3, part 1. Cambridge, 1894.

Cantera Ortiz de Urbina, J. "Origin, familias y fuentes de la Vetus Latina." *Sefarad* 22 (1962) 296-311.

———. "Puntos de contacto de la Vetus Latina con la recensión de Luciano y con otras recensiones griegas." *Sefarad* 25 (1965) 69-72.

Cross, F. M. "The History of the Biblical Text in the Light of Discoveries in the Judaean Desert." *HTR* 57 (1964) 281-99.

———. "A New Qumran Biblical Fragment Related to the Original Hebrew Underlying the Septuagint." *BASOR* 132 (1953) 15-26.

———. "The Oldest Manuscripts from Qumran." *JBL* 74 (1955) 147-72.

von Dobschütz, E. "A Collection of Old Latin Bible Quotations: Somnium Neronis." *JTS* 16 (1915) 1-27.

Dold, A. "Ein altlateinisches Zitat aus dem Canticum Annae in einer der Vita des hl. Evurtius entnommenen Oration." *Libri* 2 (1952) 50-54.

———. "Honorificatus est rex Israel: Eine Bedeutungsvolle Übersetzung von 2 Sam. vi:20 aus der altlateinischen Bibel." *Benediktinische Monatschrift* [Beuron] 22 (1946) 292-95.

Driver, S. R. *Notes on the Hebrew Text and the Topography of the Books of Samuel.* 2d ed. Oxford, 1913

Fischer, B. "Lukian-Lesarten in der Vetus Latina der vier Königsbücher." *Studia Anselmiana* 27-28 (1951) 169-77.

Harrington, Daniel. "Text and Biblical Text in Pseudo-Philo's 'Liber Antiquitatum Biblicarum.'" Dissertation, Harvard University, 1969.

Haupert, R. S. "The Relation of Codex Vaticanus and the Lucianic Text in the Books of Kings from the Viewpoint of the Old Latin and the Ethiopic Versions." Dissertation, Philadelphia, 1930.

Kennedy, H. A. A. "Latin Versions, The Old," in Hastings' *Dictionary of the Bible,* vol. 3, 47-62. Edinburgh: Clark, 1923.

de Lagarde, P. A. *Probe einer neuer Ausgabe der lateinischen Übersetzungen des AT.* Göttingen, 1885.

Méchineau, L. "Latines, versions de la Bible." In *Dictionnaire de la Bible,* vol. 4, 97-123.

Metzger, Bruce. *Chapters in the History of New Testament Textual Criticism.* Leiden: Brill, 1963.

———. "Lucian and the Lucianic Recension of the Greek Bible." *NTS* 8 (1962) 189-203.

———. *The Text of the New Testament.* 2d ed. New York: Oxford University Press, 1968.

Orlinsky, H. M. "The Septuagint as Holy Writ and the Philosophy of the Translators." *HUCA* 46 (1975) 89-114.

Peebles, B. M. "Bible. IV, Texts and Versions. 13. Latin Versions." In *New Catholic Encyclopedia,* vol. 2, 436-39. New York: McGraw-Hill, 1967.

Pietersma, Albert. *Chester Beatty Biblical Papyri IV and V: A New Edition with Text-Critical Analysis.* American Studies in Papyrology 16. Toronto: Samuel Stevens Hakkert, 1977.

Rahlfs, A. *Lucians Rezension der Königsbücher.* Septuaginta Studien 3. Göttingen, 1911.

Roberts, Bleddyn J. *The Old Testament Text and Versions.* Cardiff: University of Wales, 1951.

Skehan, Patrick W. "The Biblical Scrolls from Qumran and the Text of the Old Testament." *BA* 28 (1965) 87-100.

———. "Notes on the Latin Text of the Book of Wisdom." *CBQ* 4 (1942) 230-43. Reprinted in *Studies in Israelite Poetry and Wisdom,* 137-48. CBQMS 1. Washington, D.C.: Catholic Biblical Association, 1971.

———. "The Qumran Manuscripts and Textual Criticism." In Supplements to *Vetus Testamentum,* vol. 4, 148-60. Leiden: Brill, 1957.

———. "Texts and Versions." In *Jerome Biblical Commentary,* ed. R. Brown et al., vol. 2, 561-80. Engelwood Cliffs, N.J.: Prentice-Hall, 1968.

Stummer, F. *Einführung in die lateinische Bibel.* Paderborn, 1928.

Swete, Henry B. *An Introduction to the Old Testament in Greek.* Rev. ed. R. R. Ottley. New York, 1968.

Talmon, Shemaryahu. "The Old Testament Text." In *Cambridge History of the Bible,* ed. P. R. Ackroyd and C. F. Evans, vol. 1, 159-99. Cambridge University Press, 1970. Reprinted in *Qumran and the History of the Biblical Text,* ed. F. M. Cross and S. Talmon, 1-41. Cambridge, Mass.: Harvard University Press, 1975.

———. "The Textual Study of the Bible — A New Outlook." In *Qumran and the History of the Biblical Text,* ed. F. M. Cross and S. Talmon, 321-400. Cambridge, Mass.: Harvard University Press, 1975.

Thiele, W. "Lateinische altkirchliche Bibelübersetzungen." *Die Religion in Geschichte und Gegenwart,* vol. 1, 1196-97.

Thompson, Edward M. *A Handbook of Greek and Latin Palaeography.* London, 1901. Reprinted, Chicago: Ares Publishers, 1975.

Tov, Emanuel. "Lucian and Proto-Lucian — Toward a New Solution of the Problem." *RB* 79 (1972) 101-13.

———. "The State of the Question: Problems and Proposed Solutions." In *1972 Proceedings: IOSCS and Pseudepigrapha,* ed. R. Kraft, 3-15. Missoula, Mont.: Scholars Press, 1972.

———. "The Textual Affiliations of 4QSam^{a}." *JSOT* 14 (1979) 37-53.

Ulrich, E. C. "4QSam^{c}: A Fragmentary Manuscript of 2 Samuel 14–15 from the Scribe of the Serek Hay-yaḥad." *BASOR* 235 (1979) 1-25.

———. *The Qumran Text of Samuel and Josephus.* HSM 19. Missoula, Mont.: Scholars Press, 1978.

Voogd, Henry. "A Critical and Comparative Study of the Old Latin Texts of the First Book of Samuel." Dissertation, Princeton Theological Seminary, 1947.

Walters, Peter. *The Text of the Septuagint: Its Corruptions and Their Emendation.* Ed. D. W. Gooding. Cambridge, 1973.

Weber, R. "Les interpolations de Samuel dans les manuscrits de la Vulgata." In *Miscellanea G. Mercati,* vol. 1, 19-39. Rome, 1946.

Wellhausen, J. *Der text der Bücher Samuelis.* Göttingen, 1871.

Wevers, J. W. "The Attitude of the Greek Translator of Deuteronomy towards His Parent Text." In *Beiträge zur Alttestamentlichen Theologie: Festschrift für Walther Zimmerli,* ed. H. Donner, R. Hanhart, and R. Smend, 498-505. Göttingen, 1977.

———. "Text History and Text Criticism of the Septuagint." In *Congress Volume Göttingen 1977,* 392-402. VTSup 29. Leiden: Brill, 1978.

Würthwein, Ernst. *Der Text des alten Testaments: Eine Einführung in die Biblia Hebraica von Rudolph Kittel.* 4th ed. Stuttgart, 1973. English edition, *The Text of the Old Testament: An Introduction to the Biblia Hebraica.* Trans. E. Rhodes. Grand Rapids: Eerdmans, 1979.

Resources for the Old Latin

Brock, S., C. Fritsch, and S. Jellicoe. *A Classified Bibliography of the Septuagint,* 168-86. Leiden: Brill, 1973.

Eissfeldt, Otto. *The Old Testament: An Introduction,* §123, 716-17. Trans. P. Ackroyd. New York: Harper and Row, 1965.

Jellicoe, Sidney, *The Septuagint and Modern Study,* 370-400, esp. 373-74. Oxford: Clarendon, 1968.

Kennedy, H. A. A. "Latin Versions, The Old." In Hastings' *Dictionary of the Bible,* vol. 3, 47-62. Edinburgh: Clark, 1923.

The Old Testament in Greek According to the Text of Codex Vaticanus. Ed. A. E. Brooke and N. McLean. Cambridge, 1906-40. Prefatory Notes to the several volumes.

"Record of Work Published, in Hand, or Projected." Published annually in *BIOSCS,* 1967-.

Roberts, Bleddyn J. *The Old Testament Text and Versions,* 310-14. Cardiff: University of Wales, 1951.

Septuaginta: Vetus Testamentum Graecum . . . Gottingensis. Ed. R. Hanhart, W. Kappler, A. Rahlfs, J. W. Wevers, and J. Ziegler. Göttingen, 1931-.

Vetus Latina: Arbeitsberichte der Stiftung V. L. und Berichte des V. L. Instituts. Beuron, 1952-. Published annually.

Die Reste der altlateinischen Bibel nach Petrus Sabatier neu gesammelt und herausgegeben von der Erzabtei Beuron. Volume 1: *Verzeichnis der Sigel für Handschriften und Kirchenschriftsteller,* esp. 17-18. Freiburg, 1949. Volume 1, part 1: *Verzeichnis der Sigel für Kirchenschriftsteller.* 2d ed. Freiburg, 1963.

Voogd, Henry. "A Critical and Comparative Study of the Old Latin Texts of the First Book of Samuel," 204-10. Dissertation, Princeton Theological Seminary, 1947.

Würthwein, Ernst. *The Text of the Old Testament,* 88-90. Trans. E. Rhodes. Grand Rapids: Eerdmans, 1979.

CHAPTER 14

Characteristics and Limitations of the Old Latin Translation of the Septuagint

The purpose of this study is to explore in short compass some of the characteristics of the Old Latin (OL) translation of the Septuagint (LXX). More specifically, what features of the Septuagintal text can the Latin language accurately and distinctly reflect, and which features can it not? Further, insofar as practice diverges from theory, to what extent do individual OL translators accurately and distinctly reflect their Greek parent text? The framing of these questions displays thorough agreement with two theses posed by John Wevers:[1] that for use of any version for textual criticism one must have in mind as clearly as possible, first and theoretically, a comparative knowledge of the contrasting features of the two languages, and secondly and concretely, the peculiar characteristics of the particular translation or manuscript being

1. John W. Wevers, "The Use of Versions for Text Criticism: The Septuagint," in *La Septuaginta en la investigación contemporánea (V Congreso de la IOSCS)* (Textos y Estudios "Cardenal Cisneros" 34; ed. N. Fernández Marcos; Madrid: Instituto "Arias Montano" C.S.I.C., 1985) 15-24. See also his article "The Attitude of the Greek Translator of Deuteronomy towards His Parent Text," in *Beiträge zur Alttestamentlichen Theologie: Festschrift für Walther Zimmerli zum 70. Geburtstag* (ed. H. Donner, R. Hanhart, and R. Smend; Göttingen: Vandenhoeck & Ruprecht, 1977) 498-505, and his discussions under "The Critical Text," in *The Text History of the Greek Genesis;* idem, *The Text History of the Greek Numbers;* idem, *The Text History of the Greek Deuteronomy* (Göttingen: Vandenhoeck & Ruprecht, 1974-82).

I am grateful to the University of Notre Dame and the Andrew W. Mellon Foundation for providing the support which made this study possible.

used. Within the confines of this paper, only a few aspects of the topic will be able to be discussed.

Preliminary Observations

A number of observations and clarifications must be made immediately. First, theories and conclusions must rest upon data, and our data for the study of the OL version are very fragmentary. Neither do we have available an abundance of OL manuscripts covering complete books of the Bible,[2] nor do we have tools (such as critical editions or concordances)[3] comparable to those for the Hebrew and Greek Bibles, nor has there been a sustained, vigorous history of OL scholarship.[4]

Secondly, just as the Septuagint is not a unified translation consistent through all books, so too the character of the OL, as far as we can judge, varies from book to book. As for the Septuagint, so for the OL, we must analyze the manuscripts available to discover whether the surviving text form is likely to reflect the original translation or a later — developed or corrupted — form.

2. For a catalogue of OL manuscripts, see *Vetus Latina: Die Reste der altlateinischen Bibel nach Petrus Sabatier neu gesammelt und herausgegeben von der Erzabtei Beuron:* 1. *Verzeichnis der Sigel für Handschriften und Kirchenschriftsteller* (ed. B. Fischer; Freiburg: Herder, 1949).

3. The primary center for OL studies, including critical editions and basic research materials, is the Vetus Latina Institut at the abbey of Beuron, Germany. See also Martin R. P. McGuire, *Introduction to Mediaeval Latin Studies: A Syllabus and Bibliographical Guide* (Washington, D.C.: Catholic University of America Press, 1964); cf. esp. 27-33. The intention of my remarks throughout this paper is confined to Old Testament, not New Testament, studies.

4. It is difficult to name for the Old Testament more than a few Old Latin scholars in the twentieth century: at Beuron, A. Dold, B. Fischer, W. Thiele, I. Peri (the present Director, H. J. Frede, has been editing the Pauline epistles); elsewhere, A. Billen, P.-M. Bogaert, D. de Bruyne, F. C. Burkitt, P. Capelle, H. Degering, H. A. A. Kennedy, S. Lundström, M. Stenzel, F. Stummer, and R. Weber. For bibliographical details, see S. Brock, C. Fritsch, and S. Jellicoe, *A Classified Bibliography of the Septuagint* (Leiden: Brill, 1973), and E. Ulrich, "The Old Latin Translation of the LXX and the Hebrew Scrolls from Qumran," in *The Hebrew and Greek Texts of Samuel* (ed. E. Tov; Jerusalem: Academon, 1980) 121-65, esp. 157-65. This article is now reprinted as Chapter 13 of the present volume.

For editions of texts see B. Fischer, *Genesis* (*Vetus Latina* 2; Freiburg: Herder, 1951-54); W. Thiele, *Sapientia Salomonis* (*Vetus Latina* 11/1. Lfg. 1-5; Freiburg: Herder, 1977-81). See also P.-M. Bogaert's edition of Judith forthcoming from Beuron and the corrected edition of L 115 for Samuel-Kings, edited by B. Fischer with the collaboration of E. Ulrich and J. Sanderson, in "Palimpsestus Vindobonensis: A Revised Edition of L 115 for Samuel-Kings," *BIOSCS* 16 (1983) 13-87.

We must ask how a particular manuscript relates to other manuscripts of the same biblical book, and how it relates to its own text form in other biblical books (if the manuscript extends to other books).

Thirdly, the previous question presumes that we know whether there was a single original OL translation of "the LXX" or whether there were multiple separate translations of an individual book, of some books, or of all the books of the Bible, that is, whether all our manuscripts and all the quotations by early Latin writers are stemmatically related. For the book of Genesis and probably for the books of Samuel and Kings, Bonifatius Fischer thinks that the evidence indicates that there was a single original OL translation that underwent the development (corruption, revision, expansion, omission) attested in our extant witnesses.[5] But we are unsure whether this would hold true for other types of books such as Isaiah, Psalms, and Job. Linked with this is the whole question of the provenience of the OL — North Africa, or Italy, or both, or more?

Fourthly, the second and third questions require as a basis a critically sorted Greek text, and a critically sorted Latin text. We should not presume that in "the OL text" (i.e., in OL manuscripts or quotations) we have an original Latin translation of the "pure, original Old Greek text." An earlier study in which I probed the OL manuscripts extant for 2 Samuel 11–24 showed that the OL does not reflect the "OG [Old Greek] in its 'pure form', but is reflective of numerous early developments in the Greek text, including conscious revisions, expansions, alternate interpretations, and errors. . . ." That study also demonstrated that the OL "has its share of similar developments beyond its parent text."[6] That is, our OL witnesses already contain errors, revisions, expansions, and other features that are developments within the period of the textual transmission of the OL, subsequent to the translation process. Such further developments have no usefulness for the textual criticism of the OG.[7]

Fifthly, we must remember, both throughout this paper and throughout our study of the OL[8] version, that we are contrasting Vulgar Latin with Koine

5. Private communication.

6. Ulrich, "Old Latin," 156. The critical distinction between the OL and subsequent, secondarily revised or corrupted witnesses to the OL is clearly made and productively utilized by J. Trebolle in "Textos 'Kaige' en la *Vetus Latina* de Reyes (2 Re 10,25.28)," *RB* 89 (1982) 198-209.

7. An exception would be developments in the OL that were conscious revisions toward the Greek text of the day; those developments, if proved to be such, would be valuable witnesses and indices for the transmission history of the LXX.

8. To obviate ambiguity it should be stated explicitly that the term "Old Latin" in this paper refers to the *Vetus Latina* translation, the original translation(s) of the Septuagint into Latin; it will not be used to refer, as is common in classical studies, to the period in the history of the Latin language prior to the "classical" period.

Greek. In classical scholarship there have been comparative studies of Attic Greek and Classical Latin;[9] and in biblical scholarship we are accustomed to comparative studies of Hebrew and Koine Greek; but comparative studies of Koine Greek with Vulgar Latin are rare.[10] We need not dwell on the well-known chronological and geographical variations in the Hebrew and the Greek languages, but it may be helpful to consider briefly the many types of variation in the Latin of the OL translation.

Latin, as a living language, both possessed a substantial self-identity and was constantly subject to change. Geographically, as the Romans spread their empire radiating throughout the four points of the compass, they spread their language as well, so that, except for Greece and the Near East, the entire empire was Latinized by the fourth century C.E. Latin was sometimes substituted for or sometimes blended with the different native idioms, with varying degrees of purity or fusion in vocabulary, syntax, and pronunciation. As is common with languages, there were differences between the literary Latin of the upper classes and the common parlance of the lower classes; and the Latin spoken in the major metropolitan areas was different from that spoken in isolated rural areas. Finally, we are all aware of the large-scale, gradual development of the Latin language as a whole from the ancient classical language to the family of Romance languages, each displaying somewhat different blends of the original with the regional. Thus, one must take into account the many possibilities for types of variation in "the OL": it will vary in its types and degree of divergence from literary Latin depending not only upon the degree of mastery of literary Latin by the individual translator, but also upon the degree of mastery by subsequent copyists and upon the contingencies of whether the particular translation or manuscript derives from the second or the fourth century, from North Africa or Italy, and so forth.

This rather lengthy list of preliminary observations is necessary because we do not have a widespread and widely known tradition of OL scholarship. It is therefore important for textual criticism, before dealing with individual variants, to determine insofar as possible the nature or character of a particular manuscript and to determine whether the text displayed in that individual manuscript is a text which directly reflects the parent Greek text.

9. See esp. C. D. Buck, *Comparative Grammar of Greek and Latin* (Chicago: University of Chicago, 1933) and his bibliography on 364-67.

10. See, however, Sven Lundström, *Übersetzungstechnische Untersuchungen auf dem Gebiete der Christlichen Latinität* (Lund: Gleerup, 1955). B. Fischer's introduction to his edition of L 115 ("Palimpsestus Vindobonensis: A Revised Edition of L 115 for Samuel-Kings") discusses features of Vulgar Latin pertinent to that manuscript.

Relationship to the *Vorlage*

Since the ultimate purpose of OT textual criticism is to establish insofar as possible "the original Hebrew text,"[11] we must discuss one further point before proceeding to our main topic, a point which concerns the Hebrew text, though it has ramifications for the Greek and Latin translations.

The biblical texts discovered in the Judaean Desert from 1947 to 1956 have illuminated a feature of the transmission of the Hebrew text of the Bible previously undocumented: the Hebrew text enjoyed a certain controlled fluidity prior to the Rabbinic stabilization that eventuated in our Masoretic *textus receptus* (MT).[12] Thus, though the Hebrew Bible at the turn of the eras was substantially identical with the Hebrew Bible we possess in modern editions, it also contained considerable variation in its text forms, more in some books, less in others. Thus, we may not presume that our present MT contains the exact text from which the LXX was translated, nor that our codices or printed editions contain that original Greek translation. The OG translation of a given verse or book is, with virtual certainty in some instances, to be seen as a reflection, not of our present MT, but of a variant Hebrew text tradition, sometimes documentable, sometimes not.[13] The point relevant for our study of the OL would be that, since generally the OL is a translation of a developed form of the OG, and since the OG is a translation of a Hebrew text that may or may not be identical with our MT, we must try to establish what the Hebrew reading was that our Greek witnesses were attempting to translate, and we must try to establish what the Greek reading was that our OL witnesses were attempting to translate. The Hebrew reading in question may be

11. For a comprehensive discussion, see Emanuel Tov, *The Text-Critical Use of the Septuagint in Biblical Research* (Jerusalem: Simor, 1981).

12. See S. Talmon, "The Textual Study of the Bible — A New Outlook," in *Qumran and the History of the Biblical Text* (ed. F. M. Cross and S. Talmon; Cambridge, Mass.: Harvard University Press, 1975) 321-400, esp. 322-27.

13. Julio Trebolle has examined what he terms the *Vorlage versus Midrash* question for texts in Samuel and Kings — that is, whether variants in the LXX and the OL are to be seen as witnesses to a different Hebrew *Vorlage* or as intentionally divergent interpretations on the part of translators — and concludes: "Sin embargo, en términos generales y tratándose de Samuel-Reyes, puede afirmarse que en los casos de conflicto entre *Vorlage* y Targum o Historia y Midrás la balanza se inclina más a favor del supuesto de la existencia de un original hebreo subyacente a las variantes de LXX, y a favor, aunque con más cautela, del valor literario y del testimonio histórico de este tipo de texto palestino, testificado fundamentalmente por 4Q, LXX y Crónicas"; see J. Trebolle, "El estudio de 4Q Sam^a: Implicaciones exegéticas e históricas," *Est Bib* 39 (1981) 5-18, esp. 17-18. See also the discussion of *Vorlagen* by Tov, *The Text-Critical Use of the Septuagint.*

that of the MT or it may be extant in another ancient Hebrew text such as one of the Qumran texts, or it may be no longer extant or have never existed except in the erring mind of the Greek translator. The Greek reading in question may be that of our major codices, or in the text of our critical editions, or in the critical apparatus, or no longer extant, or only in the erring mind of the OL translator. The Latin reading in question may be the original OL reading, or a secondary corruption, interpretation, revision, and so forth.[14]

I think that this point is both sufficiently important and insufficiently widely accepted and incorporated that a couple of examples should be presented. (I should explicitly state at the outset that of course many variants do *not* signal a deviant *Vorlage*. We must balance the *Vorlage* issue with many other considerations. My point here is that sometimes what appear to be variants really are not so — they can be seen as faithful translations of a variant *Vorlage* — and that methodologically we should first consider as one factor the possibility of their accurately reflecting a variant *Vorlage*).

1. We may begin with an example in which an ancient, non-Masoretic, Hebrew text of Samuel (4QSam[a]) documents what we may consider with virtual certainty the *Vorlage* of the Septuagint (1 Sam. 1:23):[15]

4QSam[a]	יהו]ה היוצא מפיך
M	יהוה את דברו
G	κυριος (+ παν G[L]) το εξελθον εξ του στοματος σου
L 115, 93	*dominus* (+ *omne verbum* 93) *quod exiit de ore tuo.*[16]

The Latin text is a close, faithful translation of the Greek text, which is a close, faithful translation of its Hebrew *Vorlage* reflected by 4QSam[a]. Before the availability of the Hebrew manuscript evidence of the Qumran reading, most would have considered the Greek an incorrect translation of "the Hebrew," that is, of the Masoretic Text, though it would still have been clear that the Latin was translated from the Greek, not from the Hebrew. Now we are in a position to recognize that in this instance the Greek is a correct, faithful translation of its Hebrew *Vorlage*, which was simply not the Masoretic Text.

2. We may follow this example, in which the Hebrew *Vorlage* of the Septuagint is extant in a Hebrew manuscript at variance with the MT, with an example in which *no* Hebrew manuscript evidence is extant that documents ex-

14. See examples of these many diverse possibilities in Ulrich, "Old Latin."

15. See E. Ulrich, *The Qumran Text of Samuel and Josephus* (HSM 19; Missoula, Mont.: Scholars Press, 1978) 71.

16. The correct reading of L 115 is *tuo;* Beisheim had misread it as *eius*, and I quoted it as such in *Qumran*, 71, but Fischer's corrected edition has *tuo*.

actly the *Vorlage* of the Septuagint but where the Septuagint points toward the no-longer-extant Hebrew *Vorlage,* which again differs from the MT (1 Sam. 1:24):[17]

4QSam^{a}	ותעל אותו *(= Hipʿil)*
M	ותעלהו עמה *(= Hipʿil)*
G	και ανεβη μετ αυτου (= ותעל אִתּוֹ *Qal)*
L 115	*et ascendit cum eo.*

The Hebrew reading that best explains the various readings is ותעל אתו*. The Septuagint translator interpreted that Hebrew reading in one correct way. About a century later, the scribe of 4QSam^{a} (or sometime during that century an earlier scribe in that tradition) interpreted the Hebrew reading in another correct way by inserting the *mater lectionis.* The MT tradition preserved both possible interpretations, making each unambiguously clear, if conflated. Again, the Latin faithfully translates its Greek *Vorlage.* Thus, we do not have attested the precise Hebrew *Vorlage* of the Greek, but 4QSam^{a} clearly hints at it, and the Greek is most probably a faithful translation of that *Vorlage.*

There are many further examples, involving increasing complexity, that show the need for investigating the readings in the Greek *Vorlage* from which the OL was translated and especially the readings in the Hebrew *Vorlage* from which the Greek was translated, but space does not permit their inclusion here.[18]

A Comparison of Greek and Latin Grammar

Since we are interested not so much in describing the Latin language in itself or the Greek language in itself, but rather in describing their interrelationship especially with regard to the one practical question of biblical translation, we must necessarily confine our discussion to those features which figure most prominently in the translational contrast. Fortunately, since both Greek and Latin are closely related languages within the same Indo-European family, the ancient translation process was much simpler and our present task is much simpler than comparison of Greek with languages in other families, such as

17. See Ulrich, *Qumran,* 48-49, 71.

18. For examples, see Ulrich, *Qumran;* idem, "Old Latin"; idem, "4QSam^{c}": A Fragmentary Manuscript of 2 Samuel 14–15 from the Scribe of the *Serek Hay-yaḥad* (1QS)," *BASOR* 235 (1979) 1-25.

Greek with Hebrew or Syriac or Coptic. Latin is even considered by some as more closely related to Greek than Armenian is to Greek, insofar as Greek and Latin are both in the so-called "centum" division of the Indo-European languages, whereas Armenian is in the "satem" division.[19]

Grammar is traditionally divided into phonology, morphology, syntax, and lexicology or vocabulary. But it seems necessary to add one category beyond the strictly grammatical, namely what we may simply call style or translation technique. Style is difficult to define and can mean many things; but here we are referring to the individual, personal, particular way in which the translator characteristically chose among and utilized the range of the grammatical possibilities. We can use "style" to refer to what John Wevers has described: *"just how and from what points of view this translation was done by a particular translation."*[20]

Phonology deals with the sound system of the language, especially the functionally meaningful differences in sound. Here we shall not deal with phonology, because this aspect bears on our topic less than other aspects of grammar. We should simply mention certain features such as the *b/v* ambiguity (*ama*b*it* [future]/*ama*v*it* [perfect]) which has been noted by Professor Wevers,[21] and the transliteration of personal names, place names, and specific technical terms. More important than saying anything in particular about the use of phonological witness for textual variants is to say that, for witness to personal or place names, and so forth, it is very important to study how a translator or manuscript *characteristically* treats names and sounds.[22]

Morphology deals with the inflectional system of the language, especially the functionally meaningful differences in the forms of words. It is morphology that we shall principally discuss here, both because this is the most commonly developed aspect in most grammars and, more to the point, because, since the OL appears in general for many of the biblical books to be a fairly literal translation of the LXX, the morphological aspect seems to be the most fruitful area to explore for understanding the interrelationship between the OL and the LXX.

19. See Buck, *Comparative Grammar,* 1.

20. Wevers, "The Use of Versions," 20.

21. Ibid., 20.

22. See, e.g., R. J. H. Shutt, "Biblical Names and Their Meanings in Josephus' *Jewish Antiquities,* Books I and II, 1-200," *JSJ* 2 (1971) 167-82; and Franz Blatt, *The Latin Josephus* (Copenhagen, 1958), who notes that in the Latin translation of Josephus, the forms of proper names have been systematically changed to the spelling found in the Vulgate, thus nullifying their witness for the original Greek text of Josephus.

Syntax deals with the interrelationships between words, determining larger units of meaning in the language. Syntax we shall study on an *ad hoc* basis. It is a complex area, made more complex by what we have just referred to as "style." Insofar as we are forced to examine individual manuscripts of the OL and interrelate them with the LXX, the aspect of syntax can most economically be treated according to individually occurring significant examples, to illustrate the consistent character of the manuscripts and possible departures from that consistent character. Here, however, it may be noted that Latin is capable of the same barbarisms as Greek for literal translations of Hebraisms (2 Sam. 18:3)[23]:

M	כי אם נס ננוס לא ישימו אלינו לב
G^L	οτι εαν ψυγοντες ψυγωμεν ου θησουσιν εφ' ημας καρδιαν
L 115	*quia si fugientes fugerimus non stabit in nobis cor nostrum.*

Both the protasis and the apodosis in the Greek contain Hebraisms, and both, of course, make the Hellenophile wince; but the protasis is readily intelligible, and the apodosis (if one knows Hebrew, as the Greek translator did but the Latin translator probably did not) can be understood. The Latin translator followed the Greek protasis accurately, for the expression is intelligible (though we never find it in the rhetoric of Demosthenes or Isocrates!). The apodosis, however, overstrained this particular translator, though not the Latin language; he could have mechanically reproduced *non imponent super nos cor,* but he was one step too far removed from the Hebrew idiom and presumably felt the need to make the clause make sense. Thus, again, we point to the distinction between what the Latin language is able to reflect theoretically and what in practice the individual translator did reflect. But even more importantly we reiterate the principle that, before we can formulate a conclusion with confidence, the characteristics of the translation technique of the individual translator and manuscript must be studied as thoroughly as possible.

Lexicology deals with the semantic meanings of individual words, especially in their historical and contemporary use within context in literature or speech. Lexicology will be treated, just as syntax, only *ambulando.* Latin shares with Greek a large number of related lexical roots, and the two languages further share to a large extent their patterns of word formation. Consider, at the level of word formation, the following suffixes for noun formations:

23. See Ulrich, "Old Latin," 138-39.

-τηρ, -τωρ, fem. -τρια, -τρις	*tor,* fem. *-trix*
-ων	*-o, -io*
-μα	*-men, -mentum*
-τρον, -τηριον	*-trum, -torium*
-της	*-tas, -tia.*[24]

In addition, the genders for the nouns formed by those suffixes are identical in the two languages. Practically, however, at the level of individual words, the genders of many words have no interrelationship, for example, οικος (masc.), *domus* (fem.). Here it will be helpful to recall that some words were used differently in Vulgar Latin than in Classical Latin.[25]

The Verbal System

The verbal systems of the two languages are largely congruent, since they derive from the ancestral Indo-European language, but each also has its distinctive developments. Greek verbs are inflected for voice, mood, aspect/tense, number and person, and the same is true for Latin.

The ancestral language had two *voices,* an active and a medio-passive, represented in the Greek middle and the Latin deponent; there was no distinct passive voice.[26] Formally, however, Greek and Latin both developed passive systems. The Greek passive forms are identical with the middle forms except in the future and aorist, and thus they are a possible source of ambiguity for a Latin translator. The Latin deponent-passive

> represents a type which is unknown in Greek, Sanskrit, and most of the IE languages. . . . It is in origin a medio-passive of a different formal type from that [of Greek], though partly dependent upon the latter. . . . It is characterized by an *r*-element, which was combined partly with active, partly with middle forms.[27]

Thus, the voice possibilities are generally congruent for Greek and Latin, formally in their origin, and functionally in their development. The particular correspondence must be checked in each instance, but we often find fortunate congruencies such as the following in 1 Sam 1:19:

24. See Buck, *Comparative Grammar,* 346-47.

25. See the listing and discussion in Charles H. Grandgent, *An Introduction to Vulgar Latin* (Boston: Heath, 1907) 6-12.

26. Buck, *Comparative Grammar,* 237.

27. Ibid., 251.

M	ויזכרה ("and he remembered her")
G	και εμνησθη αυτης
L 115	*et rememoratus est eius.*

Greek is inflected for four *moods*, the indicative, the subjunctive, the optative, and the imperative. Latin is inflected for only three, the indicative, the subjunctive, and the imperative; the subjunctive and the optative were merged into the former. In the Greek of the Septuagint and the New Testament, however, the optative is rare, and so the inflection for mood in the two languages is for practical purposes congruent. Though morphologically the Latin language is able to reflect the Greek moods, it is necessary to check whether in practice a particular translator has done so (in the books of Samuel the translator appears to have followed the Greek moods generally, though there are both intentional and mistaken departures). In 1 Sam 1:23 we find the Latin subjunctive reflecting the Greek subjunctive:

G	εως αν απογαλακτιση αυτον
L 115	*donec tolleret eum a lacte,*

but in the previous verse the same Latin text has the subjunctive reflecting the Greek infinitive:

G	εως του αναβηναι το παιδαριον
L 115	*donec ascendat puer.*

Concerning *aspect* and *tense*, Professor Buck maintains that the tenses of the ancestral Indo-European

> served to denote differences in the "aspect" of the action, and to some extent also differences of time. It is the aspect of the action that was indicated by the different tense stems, while certain tenses of these tense stems denoted past time.[28]

The present stem denoted action going on or a state — the present tense for such action in present time, the imperfect tense for such action in past time. The aorist stem denoted punctiliar action, or the point of the beginning or end, or action without reference to its duration. The perfect stem denoted action completed or a present state resulting from past action. "There was probably," in Buck's view, "no distinctive future tense, future time being expressed

28. Ibid., 238.

by the present indicative, by the subjunctive, or by certain *s*-formations with desiderative and future force. . . ."[29] This point is strengthened by the lack of a distinctive future tense in Armenian, as Claude Cox has pointed out.[30]

In Buck's reconstruction, Greek retains these features of aspect and tense, though the Greek perfect used as a simple past tense was not uncommon in the Hellenistic period.[31] In Latin the aorist merged with the perfect, and all tenses except the imperfect/perfect distinction (distinguishing continuing from completed action in the past) became purely temporal. Each language developed both a future tense and the relative tenses of pluperfect and future perfect. Latin can thus reflect all the tenses of Greek, though it cannot distinguish between the Greek aorist and the Greek true perfect: ἀπέθανε "he died" and τέθνηκε "he is dead" would both be translated *mortuus est.* (Adverbs, however, could be added to differentiate: e.g., *tunc* or *ibi* could distinguish the simple, aorist past event; *nunc mortuus est* would distinguish the present, enduring result.) The historical present, which in biblical Greek occasionally occurs in narrative passages, appears not to occur in Latin (1 Sam 1:19):

M	וישכמו בבקר וישתחוו לפני יהוה
G	και ορθριζουσιν το πρωι και προσκυνουσιν τω κυριω
L 115	*et ante lucem surrexerunt et adoraverunt dominum.*

(Syntactically, we may note in passing that the Latin has transposed the order of the first clause, producing preferable Latin word order, and that it has used the accusative in the second clause for its transitive verb in contrast to the dative in Greek, which often follows compound verbs.)

In *number* and *person* the two languages pattern similarly, though the exception should be recalled that Greek, unlike Latin, employs a singular verb after a neuter plural subject.

Participles, like adjectives, are declined for gender, number, and case in both languages morphologically, and syntactically their patterns for usage are generally congruent. Greek participles in the middle voice must be compensated in Latin either with special lexical choices or added words, such as *sibi* or *se.*

The infinitive, originally a nominal formation, presents the same general complications for voice, due to the lack of the middle voice in Latin. Syn-

29. Ibid., 239.

30. Claude Cox, "The Use of the Armenian Version for the Textual Criticism of the Septuagint," in *La Septuaginta en la investigación contemporánea (V Congreso de la IOSCS)* (Textos y Estudios "Cardenal Cisneros" 34; ed. N. Fernández Marcos; Madrid: Instituto "Arias Montano" C.S.I.C., 1985) 30.

31. Buck, *Comparative Grammar,* 239-40.

tactically, its usage is generally similar in the two languages, though due to the possibility of articulation in Greek but not in Latin, the Latin translation sometimes loses the definiteness of the Greek.

The Nominal System

The nominal systems of the two languages are also largely congruent, so that most features of nouns, adjectives, and pronouns in Koine Greek can be accurately translated into Latin. That is, the Greek nominal system is inflected for gender, number, and case, by means of suffixes, and the same is true for Latin.

Gender is a grammatical, not biological, distinction, but both languages tend to follow biological gender when appropriate. As was mentioned above, some classes of nouns formed by suffixes share the same gender in the two languages, but there is no necessary interrelationship for the gender of individual words.

For *number*, the usage in the two languages is practically identical. Though Attic Greek inflects for three numbers (singular, dual, and plural), the dual is virtually nonexistent in Biblical Greek, thus eliminating that difference.

Greek lacks an ablative *case*, but since Latin has all of the cases of Greek, that particular difference becomes otiose. A problem of case, however, does arise due to the development of Vulgar Latin: in the general development from Classical Latin to the Romance languages, there was a gradual loss of case distinctions in Vulgar Latin. "By the end of the Vulgar Latin period the cases were generally reduced . . . to two, — a nominative and an accusative-ablative. . . ."[32] Now the OL (second to fourth centuries) falls into the middle of the Vulgar Latin period (roughly 200 B.C.E. to 600 C.E.),[33] so that the loss of case distinction was not advanced, but traces are clearly visible in L 115: *a faciem; de inimicum meum.* Ambiguity in cases can sometimes arise from morphologically undifferentiated forms, such as some nominative/vocative forms or genitive/dative forms (e.g., 2 Sam 14:19):[34]

G	και αυτος εθετο εν τω στοματι της δουλης σου
L 117	*et ipse posuit ancillae tuae*
V	*et ipse posuit in os ancillae tuae.*

32. Grandgent, *An Introduction,* 147-48.

33. Ibid., 4.

34. See Ulrich, "Old Latin," 135.

Since *ancillae tuae* could be dative, L 117 could present a correct clause; but the genitive case is more likely, *in os* probably having been omitted through parablepsis: *in⌒ancillae* (since the MT, 4QSam^a, and 4QSam^c all have *bpy*).

Articulation is perhaps the clearest systematic distinction in the usage of the nominal system between Greek and Latin. The definiteness or indefiniteness of the Greek noun is simply not signaled in Latin translation. Syntactically, due to the availability of articulation, Greek can decline "indeclinable" words such as infinitives and, more importantly, proper names transcribed without case endings from the Hebrew. Latin, just as Greek, can, but often does not, reflect the case of Semitic proper names by adding case endings; thus Greek can still distinguish, but Latin cannot: τῷ Δαυείδ becomes simply *Dauid*.

Adjectives agree in gender, number, and case with the nouns they modify in both languages. Pronouns are also declined for the three genders, the two numbers, and the four Greek and five Latin cases, plus vocative when appropriate. But though there is morphological congruity, practice may differ. For example, Greek and Latin both have reflexive and nonreflexive pronouns; but some LXX translators did not distinguish them, presumably because the Hebrew does not, whereas some OL translators did distinguish nevertheless. Thus, for example, in 1 Sam 10:25 the LXX has εκαστος εις τον τοπον αυτου, which L 115 translates *unusquisque in locum suum* (not *eius*).[35] But complicating the picture further is the gradual erosion of the distinction between the reflexive and the nonreflexive forms in Vulgar Latin; there was "great irregularity in the use of reflexives, especially possessives, *suus* being generally substituted for *eius*."[36]

Conclusion

There are many unexplored and unknown areas in the study of the Old Latin version, partly due to the fragmentary nature of the OL remains, partly due to the lack of a sustained history of scholarship. But we have been able to note some causes of the variation found in the OL tradition: that the character of the OL translation varies from book to book, that the OL witnesses vary depending upon century and region, and that the OL has its own complex transmission history requiring an attempt to establish the original Latin translation. We also saw the importance of determining the Hebrew *Vorlage* of the Greek translation as well as the Greek *Vorlage* of the Latin translation.

35. For the *Vorlage*, see Ulrich, *Qumran*, 77.

36. Grandgent, *An Introduction*, 34.

Characteristics and Limitations of the OL Translation of the LXX

Finally, on the conviction that it is essential, in order to use the OL version reliably for the textual criticism of the Septuagint and ultimately of the Old Testament, to understand the contrasting features of Greek and Latin, we attempted to sketch an overview of the comparative grammar of the two languages. Greek and Latin are comfortably close members of the family of Indo-European languages. Their verbal and nominal systems, their syntax, and to a significant extent their vocabulary and some processes of word formation are very closely related. But we also observed that, beyond the theoretical possibilities of the Latin language for reflecting the features of the Greek language, it is also important to study the customary style or translation technique of the particular translator, or, often more immediately for an individual OL manuscript, the particular character of that manuscript. At least for the books of Samuel, from which our examples were taken, the Old Latin translation of Samuel appears to be a reasonably literal, but not wooden, translation, attempting to mirror accurately and faithfully its parent text, a developed form of the Old Greek translation.

Acknowledgments

The author and publisher gratefully acknowledge permission to reprint the essays collected in this volume from the following sources:

"The Community of Israel and the Composition of the Scriptures." In *The Quest for Context and Meaning: Studies in Intertextuality in Honor of James A. Sanders,* edited by Craig A. Evans and Shemaryahu Talmon, 327-42. Leiden: Brill, 1997.

"The Bible in the Making: The Scriptures at Qumran." In *The Community of the Renewed Covenant: The Notre Dame Symposium on the Dead Sea Scrolls,* edited by Eugene Ulrich and James VanderKam, 77-93. Christianity and Judaism in Antiquity 10. Notre Dame: University of Notre Dame Press, 1994.

"Double Literary Editions of Biblical Narratives and Reflections on Determining the Form to Be Translated." In *Perspectives on the Hebrew Bible: Essays in Honor of Walter J. Harrelson,* edited by James L. Crenshaw, 101-16. Macon, Ga.: Mercer University Press, 1988.

"The Canonical Process, Textual Criticism, and Latter Stages in the Composition of the Bible." In *Sha'arei Talmon: Studies in the Bible, Qumran, and the Ancient Near East Presented to Shemaryahu Talmon,* edited by Michael Fishbane and Emanuel Tov with Weston W. Fields, 267-91. Winona Lake, Ind.: Eisenbrauns, 1992.

"Pluriformity in the Biblical Text, Text Groups, and Questions of Canon." In *The Madrid Qumran Congress: Proceedings of the International Congress on the Dead Sea Scrolls — Madrid, 18-21 March, 1991,* edited by Julio Trebolle Barrera and Luis Vegas Montaner, 1:23-41. Studies on the Texts of the Desert of Judah 11. Leiden: Brill; Madrid: Editorial Complutense, 1992.

"Multiple Literary Editions: Reflections Toward a Theory of the History of the Biblical Text." In *Current Research and Technological Developments on the Dead Sea*

Scrolls: Conference on the Texts from the Judean Desert, Jerusalem, 30 April 1995, edited by Donald W. Parry and Stephen D. Ricks, 78-105. Studies on the Texts of the Desert of Judah 20. Leiden: Brill, 1996.

"The Palaeo-Hebrew Biblical Manuscripts from Qumran Cave 4." In *Time to Prepare the Way in the Wilderness: Papers on the Qumran Scrolls by Fellows of the Institute for Advanced Studies of the Hebrew University, Jerusalem, 1989-1990*, edited by Devorah Dimant and Lawrence H. Schiffman, 103-29. Studies on the Texts of the Desert of Judah 16. Leiden: Brill, 1995.

"Orthography and Text in 4QDan^{a} and 4QDan^{b} and in the Received Masoretic Text." In *Of Scribes and Scrolls: Studies on the Hebrew Bible, Intertestamental Judaism, and Christian Origins Presented to John Stugnell on the Occasion of His Sixtieth Birthday*, edited by Harold W. Attridge, John J. Collins, and Thomas H. Tobin, 29-42. College Theological Society Resources in Religion 5. Lanham, Md.: University Press of America, 1990.

"The Septuagint Manuscripts from Qumran: A Reappraisal of Their Value." In *Septuagint, Scrolls, and Cognate Writings: Papers Presented to the International Symposium on the Septuagint and Its Relation to the Dead Sea Scrolls and Other Writings (Manchester, 1990)*, edited by George J. Brooke and Barnabas Lindars, 49-80. Septuagint and Cognate Studies 33. Atlanta: Scholars Press, 1992.

"Josephus's Biblical Text for the Book of Samuel." In *Josephus, the Bible, and History*, edited by Louis H. Feldman and Gohei Hata, 81-96. Detroit: Wayne State University Press, 1989.

"Origen's Old Testament Text: The Transmission History of the Septuagint to the Third Century C.E." In *Origen of Alexandria: His World and His Legacy*, edited by Charles Kannengiesser and William L. Petersen, 3-33. Christianity and Judaism in Antiquity 1. Notre Dame: University of Notre Dame Press, 1988.

"The Relevance of the Dead Sea Scrolls for Hexaplaric Studies." In *Origen's Hexapla and Fragments: Papers Presented at the Rich Seminar on the Hexapla, Oxford Centre for Hebrew and Jewish Studies, 25th July–3rd August 1994*, edited by Alison Salvesen, 401-7. Texte und Studium zum Antiken Judentum 58. Tübingen: Mohr Siebeck, 1998.

"The Old Latin Translation of the LXX and the Hebrew Scrolls from Qumran." In *The Hebrew and Greek Texts of Samuel*, edited by Emanuel Tov, 121-65. 1980 Proceedings IOSCS — Vienna. Jerusalem: Academon, 1980.

"Characteristics and Limitations of the Old Latin Translation of the Septuagint." In *La Septuaginta en la Investigación Contemporánea (V Congreso de la IOSCS)*, edited by Natalio Fernández Marcos, 66-70. Textos y Estudios "Cardenal Cisneros" 34. Madrid: Instituto "Arias Montano" C.S.I.C., 1985.

Index of Modern Authors

Aejmelaeus, A., 174, 175n.9
Albright, W. F., 126n.7, 144n.31, 148n.1, 150n.7
Allegro, J. M., 61n.30
Aly, Z., 175, 176n.12
Andersen, F. I., 88n.23
Attridge, H. W., 31n.49, 96n.44, 96n.45, 96n.46, 96n.47, 104n.5, 127n.10, 184n.1, 230n.17, 291

Baillet, M., 18n.1, 31n.49, 70n.57, 97n.48, 122n.3, 149n.2, 166, 166n.1, 231n.19
Barr, J., 54, 54n.10, 60n.28, 61, 61n.29
Barthélemy, D., 9n.14, 18n.1, 29n.41, 29n.42, 31n.49, 36, 36n.4, 37n.6, 38n.9, 42, 66n.45, 66n.46, 68n.54, 69n.57, 97n.48, 110n.18, 122n.3, 149n.2, 166n.1, 184n.2, 187n.9, 189n.15, 203n.3, 204n.5, 206n.10, 212, 215n.33, 215n.38, 216n.40, 217, 217n.47, 222, 222n.56, 224n.2, 228n.10, 231, 231n.20, 233, 235n.9, 235n.12, 241, 242, 243
Beckwith, R., 55n.11, 59n.23, 60n.27, 84n.11
Belsheim, J., 237
Benoit, P., 18n.1
Berger, S., 238, 271
Beyer, H. W., 55, 55n.13, 56n.14, 56n.15, 56n.16
Bianchini, C., 238
Bigg, C., 202, 203
Billen, A. V., 234n.6, 235n.11, 236n.15, 271, 276n.4
Black, M., 10n.21
Blatt, F., 188n.11, 196n.31, 282n.22
Blenkinsopp, J., 5n.5, 27n.29, 76n.72
Bloch, R., 62n.34
Bludau, A., 70, 70n.60
Bodine, W. R., 105, 214n.32, 236n.15, 240n.21, 241
Boeckler, A., 237
Bogaert, P.-M., 9n.14, 40n.14, 69n.55, 116n.33, 230n.16, 276n.4
Brock, S. P., 197, 202n.1, 224n.1, 235n.9, 276n.4
Brongers, H. A., 72n.63
Brooke, A. E., 184n.4, 193n.23, 233, 236, 237, 238, 249
Brooke, G. J., 10n.19, 27n.36, 104n.8, 228n.9, 231n.21
Brooks, R., 13n.26, 152n.10
Brown, R., 273
Bruce, F. F., 42n.17, 72n.63
Buck, C. D., 278n.9, 282n.19, 284n.24,

284n.26, 284n.27, 285, 285n.28, 286, 286n.29, 286n.31
Burkitt, F. C., 236n.15, 261, 276n.4
Burrows, M., 18n.1, 29n.42
Busto Saiz, J. R., 80n.1, 214n.31

Capelle, P., 276n.4
Childs, B. S., 53, 53n.5, 54n.9, 58, 58n.21, 59, 59n.24, 59n.25, 77n.76, 78n.76
Collins, J. J., 7n.10, 7n.11, 13n.26, 31n.49, 96n.44, 96n.45, 96n.46, 96n.47, 104n.5, 127n.10, 152n.10, 230n.17
Cook, S. A., 142n.26
Coote, R. B., 77n.73
Cox, C., 166n.1, 208n.18, 286, 286n.30
Crawford, S. W., 10n.20
Crenshaw, J. L., 33n.52, 63n.36, 146n.35
Cross, F. L., 224n.1
Cross, F. M., 5n.6, 9n.13, 10n.16, 10n.17, 10n.18, 10n.20, 18n.1, 27n.30, 28n.39, 29n.42, 29n.44, 47n.33, 51n.1, 62n.32, 66n.49, 81, 81n.3, 81n.4, 82, 83, 88n.22, 106n.13, 124n.5, 126n.7, 127, 132n.15, 142n.25, 143, 150n.7, 184n.4, 187n.9, 187n.10, 188n.11, 189n.14, 190n.16, 190n.17, 190n.18, 199, 204n.5, 229, 229n.11, 230n.16, 235n.9, 242, 243, 244, 254, 255, 279n.12
Crown, A. D., 132n.15

Davila, J. R., 9n.13, 25n.20, 94n.42
de Boer, P. A. H., 233
de Bruyne, D., 238, 276n.4
Degering. H., 237, 276n.4
de Jonge, M., 150n.3
de Lagarde, P. A., 180, 204n.4, 208n.18, 210, 211, 213n.31
del Castillo, H., 237
Delcor, M., 27n.35
Dimant, D., 82n.8, 88n.24, 110n.19, 122n.3
Diringer, D., 142n.26
Dold, A., 276n.4
Donner, H., 111n.23, 274, 275n.1
Dörrie, H., 213n.31
Driver, S. R., 66n.48, 204n.5, 221, 221n.55, 234n.4, 234n.7, 234n.8, 240n.22, 246
Duncan, J. A., 10n.20, 26n.25, 138

Eichenfeld, J. von, 237
Eichhorn, J. G., 54
Endlicher, S., 237
Eshel, E., 26n.25, 121n.1, 130n.14
Eves, T. L., 187n.9

Feldman, L. H., 184n.1, 197, 197n.35, 197n.36, 197n.37, 198n.39
Fernández Marcos, N., 80n.1, 185n.7, 204n.5, 213n.31, 214n.31, 275n.1, 286n.30
Fields, F., 217n.46
Fields, W. W., 9n.14, 24n.19, 89n.25, 108n.15, 146n.35, 225n.4, 290
Fischer, P. B., 185n.4, 185n.4, 233, 234n.5, 236, 237, 237n.18, 238, 238n.19, 276n.2, 276n.4, 277, 278n.10, 280n.16
Fishbane, M., 9n.14, 24n.19, 89n.25, 108n.15, 146n.35, 225n.4
Fitzmyer, J. A., 19n.1
Flint, P. W., 7n.10, 10n.21, 15, 16n.31, 29n.43, 30n.47, 30n.48, 115n.31, 229n.14, 229n.15
Forbes, A. D., 88n.23
Fraenkel, D., 166n.1
Frede, H. J., 276n.4
Freedman, D. N., 26n.23, 27n.30, 122n.3
Fritsch, C. T., 202n.1, 274, 276n.4
Fuller, R. E., 10n.17, 30n.45

García Martínez, F., 7n.10, 10n.19, 10n.20, 19n.1, 26n.23, 27n.36, 80n.1, 104n.8, 105n.12, 122n.3, 228n.7
Ginzberg, L., 266n.24
Golb, N., 9n.12, 143n.30
Gooding, D. W., 9n.14, 29n.41, 36, 36n.4, 37n.5, 37n.6, 38n.9, 42, 42n.18, 42n.19, 66n.45, 66n.46, 68n.54, 94, 94n.41, 110n.18, 228n.10
Gordon, R. P., 66n.48

Goshen-Gottstein, M., 46n.29
Grandgent, C. H., 284n.25, 287n.32, 287n.33, 288n.36
Gray, J., 105
Green, W. S., 62n.34
Greenfield, J. C., 197, 197n.34
Greenspoon, L., 214n.32
Greer, R. A., 62n.34

Haase, W., 184n.1
Hanhart, R., 166, 166n.1, 175, 214n.32, 275n.1
Harl, M., 46n.31, 206, 207n.15
Harrelson, W. J., 33n.52, 63n.36, 146n.35
Hart, D., 82, 82n.7
Hata, G., 291
Haupt, P., 238, 238n.19, 271
Hendel, R. S., 225n.6
Herr, M. D., 62n.34
Hilberg, I., 222n.58
Hody, H., 209
Hoffman, T. A., 53n.4
Holladay, W. L., 77n.73
Hurvitz, A., 26n.23

Isidoro, L. S., 237

Janzen, J. Gerald, 29n.44, 30n.47
Jastram, N., 9n.13, 10n.16, 26, 26n.24, 228n.8
Jeansonne, S. P. or Pace Jeansonne, S., 42n.17, 43, 43n.24, 70, 70n.60, 72n.63, 175, 175n.11, 208n.19, 210n.24, 214n.32, 230n.17
Jellicoe, S., 202n.1, 202n.2, 204n.4, 205n.7, 205n.8, 206n.11, 207n.16, 208n.18, 209, 209n.20, 210n.23, 212n.28, 213n.30, 217n.45, 224n.1, 234n.2, 234n.4, 235n.10, 235n.11, 276n.4
Johnson, A. R., 235n.9

Kahle, P., 182, 205n.7, 208n.18, 209, 210, 210n.22
Kaiser, O., 77n.73
Kannengiesser, C., 215n.37, 217n.48
Kapera, Z. I., 27n.36
Katz, P., 212n.28
Kennedy, H. A. A., 234n.2, 234n.3, 234n.4, 234n.8, 236, 236n.15, 276n.4
Klein, R., 66n.48
Knoppers, G., 5n.6
Koenen, L., 175, 176n.12
Kooij, A. van der, 28n.39, 210n.24, 214n.32
Kraft, R. A., 12n.25, 18n.1, 30n.46, 166n.1, 184n.1, 204n.5, 205n.6, 205n.9, 206n.11, 231n.20, 235n.9, 273
Kugel, J. L., 62n.34
Kutscher, E. Y., 111, 111n.24

La Bonnardière, A. M., 272
Leiman, S., 10n.21, 53, 54, 54n.7
Lindars, B., 169n.6, 231n.21
Lundström, S., 276n.4, 278n.10
Lust, J., 9n.14, 27n.33, 29n.41, 36, 36n.4, 37n.5, 37n.6, 39n.12, 42, 66n.45, 66n.46, 66n.47, 110n.18, 228n.10

Macuch, R., 130n.14
Malamat, A., 148n.1
Marcus, R., 186n.5, 195, 196, 266n.24
Mathews, K. A., 122n.3, 124n.4
Mazor, L., 10n.19, 105n.9
McCarter, P. K., 66n.48, 199, 235n.9
McGuire, M. R. P., 275n.3
McLay, T., 230n.17
McLean, M. D., 127, 127n.10, 130, 130n.13, 134, 134n.18, 137, 139, 139n.21, 139n.22, 140, 140n.28, 142, 142n.27, 143, 145, 184n.4
McLean, N., 193n.23, 233, 236, 237, 238, 249
Méchineau, L., 272
Mercati, G., 217, 217n.45, 219, 220
Metzger, B. M., 53n.6, 56n.16, 57, 57n.18, 58n.19, 217n.45
Meyers, C. L., 27n.30, 124n.4
Mez, A., 9n.15, 185n.8, 190, 191, 191n.19,

193, 193n.23, 195, 196, 196n.28, 196n.29, 235n.9, 243
Milgrom, J., 26n.23, 91n.30
Milik, J. T., 7n.10, 18n.1, 27n.36, 29n.42, 30n.47, 69n.57, 70n.57, 122n.3, 166n.1, 231n.19
Miller, C., 91n.31
Miller, M. P., 55n.12, 62n.34
Montgomery, J. A., 70, 70n.59, 71n.61, 207n.17
Morano Rodríguez, C., 80n.1
Morrow, F. J., Jr., 29n.42
Muilenburg, J., 29n.42
Muraoka, T., 197, 197n.37, 197n.38, 198, 199, 199n.41, 200, 200n.42

Nautin, P., 215n.33, 215n.34, 215n.37, 215n.39, 217, 217n.44, 217n.46, 218, 218n.49, 218n.50, 218n.51, 218n.52, 219, 220, 220n.54, 221, 222, 222n.57
Naveh, J., 88n.21, 126n.7, 142, 142n.28, 142n.29, 144n.31
Nelson, R. D., 35n.3, 63n.38
Neusner, J., 83n.9
Nickelsburg, G. W. E., 184n.1
Niese, B., 233n.
Noth, M., 5n.6

O'Connell, K. G., 203n.3, 206n.10, 214n.32, 241
O'Connor, M., 27n.30, 124n.4
Orlinsky, H. M., 166n.3, 224n.1, 273
Oschwald, J., 216n.41, 223n.59
Ottley, R. R., 21n.9, 90n.26, 180n.22, 202n.1

Parry, D. W., 16n.31
Paulin, S., 268
Peri, I., 276n.4
Petersen, W. L., 217n.48, 291
Pietersma, A., 166n.1, 208n.18, 273
Pisano, S., 189n.15
Puech, É., 7n.10, 122n.3

Qimron, E., 91n.30, 157n.18
Quast, U., 166n.1

Rahlfs, A., 165, 191, 191n.20, 195, 196, 222, 235n.9
Rappaport, U., 122n.3
Reider, J., 213, 213n.29
Rendtorff, R., 5n.5
Ricks, S. D., 16n.31
Roberts, B. J., 234n.2, 234n.3
Roberts, C. H., 208, 208n.18, 235n.13
Rofé, A., 106n.13, 187n.9
Röllig, W., 111n.23

Sabatier, P., 233, 234, 236, 237, 238, 248, 257, 259, 260, 269
Sáenz-Badillos, A., 80n.1, 213n.31
Sanders, J. A., 3, 3n.1, 10n.21, 11, 11n.23, 11n.24, 15, 16n.32, 18n.1, 24, 24n.18, 51, 51n.2, 73, 73n.64, 75, 75n.69, 75n.71, 229n.14
Sanderson, J. E., 9n.13, 10n.16, 19n.1, 25n.21, 26n.25, 39n.11, 39n.13, 47n.32, 64, 64n.39, 64n.42, 65n.43, 84n.10, 84n.12, 102n.3, 121n.1, 123, 128, 128n.12, 132n.15, 132n.16, 136, 136n.20, 185n.4, 214n.32, 228n.7, 231n.219, 276n.4
Schiffman, L. H., 82n.8, 83, 86n.16, 88n.24, 110n.19, 112n.25, 115, 115n.32, 116, 291
Schildenberger, J., 234n.5
Schmitt, A., 214n.32
Shenkel, J. D., 214n.32, 235n.9, 256
Shutt, R. J., 282n.22
Skehan, P. W., 9n.13, 10n.16, 10n.20, 16n.31, 19n.1, 25n.21, 26n.25, 27n.35, 29n.42, 30n.47, 38, 38n.10, 39n.11, 64, 64n.40, 64n.41, 84n.10, 102, 102n.3, 106n.13, 121, 121n.1, 122, 122n.2, 123, 124n.5, 128, 132n.15, 133n.17, 166, 166n.1, 199, 228n.7, 231n.19, 234n.5
Smalley, W. A., 10n.21
Smend, R., 274, 275n.1
Soggin, A., 105
Sperber, A., 130n.14

Stenzel, M., 276n.4
Stone, M. E., 184n.1
Strong, T. B., 202n.2
Strugnell, J., 31n.49, 91n.30, 96n.44, 96n.45, 96n.46, 96n.47, 104n.5, 127n.10, 148, 148n.1, 230n.17, 240n.22
Stummer, F., 234n.4, 276n.4
Sukenik, E. L., 18n.1, 29n.42
Sundberg, A. C., Jr., 55n.11, 84n.11
Swete, H. B., 21n.9, 90n.26, 180n.22, 202n.1, 205n.6, 205n.8, 207n.16, 207n.17, 215n.35, 215n.36

Tadmor, H., 106n.13
Talmon, S., 9n.14, 24n.19, 51, 60n.28, 61, 61n.31, 62, 62n.32, 62n.35, 81, 81n.3, 81n.4, 82, 83, 84, 85, 89n.25, 92, 92n.33, 92n.34, 92n.35, 93n.37, 107n.15, 108n.15, 124n.5, 132n.15, 146n.35, 187n.9, 204n.5, 225n.4, 229n.11, 279n.12
Talshir, Z., 229, 229n.13
Temporini, H., 184n.1
Thackeray, H. St. J., 184n.3, 184n.4, 185n.8, 193, 193n.23, 195, 196, 197n.35, 235n.9, 235n.12
Thenius, O., 66n.48
Thiele, W., 276n.4
Thomas, D. W., 169n.6
Thompson, E. M., 20n.4, 273
Thompson, W. G., 74n.65, 74n.66, 74n.67
Tigay, J. H., 29n.44, 40n.14, 69n.55, 204n.5
Tobin, T. H., 31n.49, 96n.44, 96n.45, 96n.46, 96n.47, 104n.5, 127n.10, 230n.17
Toletanus, J., 238
Torrey, C. C., 207n.17
Tov, E., 9n.13, 9n.14, 10n.17, 10n.20, 10n.22, 12n.25, 13, 13n.27, 14, 14n.28, 14n.29, 18n.1, 19n.1, 24n.19, 25n.23, 26n.23, 27n.36, 28n.39, 29n.41, 29n.44, 30n.46, 36, 36n.4, 37n.5, 37n.6, 40, 40n.14, 40n.15, 42, 43, 46n.28, 47n.34, 62, 62n.33, 65n.43, 66n.45, 66n.46, 69, 69n.55, 69n.56, 81, 81n.2, 81n.5, 82, 82n.8, 83, 85, 85n.15, 87, 87n.18, 87n.19, 89n.25, 99n.1, 104n.6, 108n.15, 109n.16, 110n.18, 111, 111n.20, 111n.21, 111n.22, 112, 114, 116n.33, 121n.1, 122n.3, 141n.24, 143n.33, 145, 145n.32, 146n.35, 166, 166n.1, 174, 174n.8, 185n.7, 187n.9, 189n.14, 202n.1, 204n.5, 205n.6, 205n.9, 206, 211n.25, 212n.27, 214n.32, 225n.4, 227, 227n.5, 228n.10, 229, 231, 231n.20, 235n.9, 239n.20, 273, 276n.4, 279n.11, 279n.13
Trebolle Barrera, J., 10n.20, 27n.27, 27n.28, 27n.32, 28n.39, 79n.1, 80n.1, 89n.25, 92n.36, 93n.38, 101n.2, 105n.12, 106, 106n.14, 175, 175n.10, 185n.7, 204n.5, 210n.24, 212n.27, 214n.32, 229, 229n.12, 230n.16, 277n.6, 279n.13
Trever, J. C., 18n.1, 29n.42, 117n.35, 149n.2
Trigg, J. W., 222, 222n.57
Turner, N., 213, 213n.29

Ulrich, E., 7n.9, 9n.13, 9n.14, 9n.15, 10n.16, 10n.17, 10n.18, 10n.19, 10n.20, 13n.26, 16n.31, 16n.32, 19n.2, 24n.19, 25n.21, 26n.25, 27n.29, 27n.31, 27n.36, 28n.36, 28n.37, 28n.39, 31n.49, 33n.52, 43n.21, 47n.33, 52n.3, 63n.36, 66n.49, 70n.57, 72n.62, 74n.65, 74n.66, 74n.67, 82n.6, 88n.23, 88n.24, 89n.25, 92n.36, 93n.38, 93n.39, 95n.43, 96n.43, 96n.44, 96n.45, 96n.46, 96n.47, 98n.50, 99n.1, 100n.1, 102n.3, 104n.5, 104n.7, 104n.8, 105n.11, 106n.13, 106n.14, 107n.15, 110n.19, 113n.36, 145n.34, 146n.35, 149n.2, 152n.10, 166n.1, 167n.4, 168n.5, 177n.19, 185n.2, 185n.4, 185n.4, 185n.7, 185n.8, 187n.9, 187n.10, 188n.12, 188n.13, 189n.14, 190n.16, 190n.18, 191, 191n.21, 191n.22, 192, 194, 195n.24, 195n.25, 195n.26, 196n.30, 196n.31, 196n.32, 196n.33, 198,

198n.40, 199, 208n.18, 212n.27, 214n.31, 214n.32, 225n.4, 228n.7, 228n.8, 228n.9, 229n.11, 230n.17, 231n.19, 235n.9, 237n.20, 239, 276n.4, 277n.6, 280n.14, 280n.15, 218n.17, 281n.18, 283n.23, 287n.34, 288n.34

VanderKam, J. C., 7n.9, 20n.6, 225n.4
Van Seters, J., 5n.5
Vaux, R. de, 18n.1, 70n.57, 122n.3, 166n.1, 231n.19,
Vegas Montaner, L., 27n.28, 80n.1, 106n.14, 229n.12
Vercellone, C., 237, 238, 261, 269
Vermes, G., 21n.12
Voogd, H., 234, 234n.3, 234n.4, 234n.8, 235, 235n.10, 235n.13, 261

Walters, S. D., 28, 29n.40, 37, 37n.7, 43, 66, 67, 67n.50, 67n.51, 228n.10,
Weber, R., 271, 274, 276n.4
Weinfeld, M., 106n.13
Weissbrodt, 237
Wellhausen, J., 66n.48, 105, 244, 246, 274
Wenthe, D. O., 31n.50, 41n.16, 70, 70n.60, 97n.49, 230n.17
Wevers, J. W., 166, 166n.1, 116n.2, 166n.3, 167, 173, 176, 176n.14, 176n.15, 177, 177n.16, 177n.17, 177n.20, 181, 181n.24, 183, 205n.7, 208n.18, 209, 209n.21, 214n.32, 231n.21, 275, 275n.1, 282, 282n.20, 282n.21
White, S. A., 26n.25, 138
Whitehead, E. E., 74n.65, 74n.66, 74n.67
Whitehead, J. D., 74n.65, 74n.66, 74n.67
Wilson, G. H., 54n.6, 54n.7
Woude, A. S. van der, 26n.23, 46n.28
Wright, D. P., 26n.23
Wright, G. E., 126n.7, 150n.7
Wright, J., 217, 217n.48
Würthwein, E., 217n.45, 236, 237n.17, 237n.19

Yadin, Y., 148n.1

Ziegler, J., 214n.32

Index of Ancient Literature

I. HEBREW BIBLE/OLD TESTAMENT

Genesis 9n.13, 10n.16, 19n.2, 21n.7, 25, 52, 94n.42, 101n.1, 101n.2, 123, 124, 125, 131, 133, 146, 175, 176n.12, 176n.13, 208, 211, 275n.1, 277

5 227
5:18-32 101n.2
6:14 131
11 227
11:10-32 101n.2
18:18 173
26:21-28 130
26:21 131
26:22 129
26:25 129
29:35 130
46:3 173

Exodus 9n.13, 10n.16, 13, 19n.2, 21n.7, 25, 26, 38, 38n.10, 39, 41, 42, 47, 49, 64, 64n.40, 65, 68, 76, 77, 93, 101, 101n.1, 102, 102n.3, 109, 113, 121n.1, 123, 124, 125, 127, 128, 129, 132, 132n.15, 135, 146, 166, 166n.1, 174, 176n.13, 208, 214n.32, 227, 228, 228n.8, 241

1–4 124
1:1-5 124
1:5 178
1:17 127
1:19 127
3:4 129
5:4 127
6:25 132
6:25–7:19 132n.15
6:26-29 134
7:4 134
7:9 127
7:18 135
7:21 127
8–12 124
8:14 127
9:4 135
9:23 127
9:28 127, 128
9:29 127
9:56 135
11:6 128
11:9 127
12:4 128
12:7 128
12:35, 36 135
14 124
16–20 124
16:2 128

16:7 128
16:30 128
16:33 134
17:1 127
17:21 127
18:21 128, 134
19:24 134
20 135
20:17 25n.22, 39, 64
22 124
23:11 128
25–28 124
25:18 128
25:19 128
25:20 128
26:35 129
27:12 129
30:1-10 129
32 38, 64
32:10-11 103
32:10-30 121n.1
35–39 102, 109
35–40 39, 65n.44, 228
36 124
37:16 132
40 124

Leviticus 9n.13, 10n.16, 19n.2, 25, 101n.1, 101n.2, 122n.3, 125, 166, 166n.1, 166n.2, 174, 176, 176n.13, 176n.15, 177, 177n.16, 208, 228n.8
1:15 177
2:12, 14 178
3:1 178
15:19-33 240
18:26 174
19:16 173
19:37 174
24:8 176
26:4 168, 169, 183
26:5 169, 170
26:6 171, 183
26:8 171
26:9 171
26:10 172
26:11 169, 172, 177, 177n.18, 183
26:12 168n.5, 172, 173, 183
26:13 173
26:14 173
26:15 173, 174
26:46 174
27:30 169

Numbers 9n.13, 10n.16, 19n.2, 26, 49, 101, 101n.1, 113, 125, 166, 166n.1, 166n.2, 176n.13, 180, 208, 228, 228n.8
1:2b 180
3:40 180
4:6 181
4:7 182
4:8 181
4:11 181
4:12 181
4:14 182
24:4 131

Deuteronomy 5, 10n.20, 19, 19n.2, 26, 26n.25, 27n.36, 28n.36, 39, 65, 101n.1, 101n.2, 117, 123, 137, 138, 166n.1, 175, 176n.12, 176n.13, 177, 178, 208, 208n.18, 216, 228n.9, 275n.1
2:36 178
7 136
7:23 178
9:20 102, 103
10–15 136
11 135
11:30 138
12:5 25n.22, 138
17 136
19–26 117
19 136
21 136
22–23 136
22:23-26 216, 216n.42
[22:6] 137
[23:14] 137
26:14-15 138

26:15 139
27 135
27:4 85n.14
28 136
28:12 168
28:19 138
29 136
30 136
31–34 136
31:5 177
32 26n.25, 136
32:1-43 26n.25
32:20 170
32:6 137

Joshua 5, 9n.15, 10, 10n.19, 10n.20, 14, 19n.2, 21, 27, 27n.36, 28n.36, 101n.1, 104, 105, 105n.9, 187n.9, 214n.32, 228, 228n.9
5 28, 228
8 28
8:30-35 [9:3-8] 105, 228
9:2 28
9:3-8 228
21 123
23:10 170

Judges 5, 9n.15, 10, 10n.20, 19n.2, 21, 27, 27n.36, 28n.36, 80n.1, 101n.1, 105, 105n.12, 106, 169n.6, 187n.9, 214n.32, 228n.9, 236n.15, 240n.21, 241, 243, 271
6:2-6 105
6:6 105
6:7-10 105
6:11-13 105
8:7 169
8:16 169

Ruth 27, 101n.1, 187n.9

1 Samuel 5, 9n.15, 14, 19n.2, 21, 28, 28n.39, 38, 38n.8, 39, 40, 41, 42, 43, 43n.21, 47, 49, 64, 65, 66n.49, 68, 68n.53, 71, 72, 76, 80n.1, 89n.25, 93, 101n.1, 111, 114n.28, 116, 145, 146, 175, 175n.10, 184, 185, 185n.2, 185n.3, 186, 186n.4, 186n.6, 186n.7, 187, 187n.9, 189, 189n.15, 190, 191, 193n.23, 195, 196, 197n.34, 198, 199, 200, 201, 204n.5, 212n.27, 214n.32, 228, 229, 229n.11, 234, 234n.3, 234n.4, 235, 236, 237, 240, 245, 261, 262, 270, 272, 274, 276n.4, 277, 278n.10, 279n.13, 280n.15, 285, 289
1 28, 37n.7, 67, 67n.50, 228, 228n.10
1:1, 18 238
1:19 284, 286
1:22 187
1–2 37, 38, 41, 66, 67, 68, 72, 77
1:14–2:15 237
1:23 280, 285
2:1-10 238
2:3-10 238
2:5, 13, 36 238
3:4-6, 8 67n.51
3:10–4:18 237
6:3-17 237
9:1-8 237
9:21–10:7 237
9:24 238
10 32
10:12 238
10:25 288
10:27–11:2 187n.9
11 32, 106n.13
11:1 187, 187n.9
14:12-34 237
14:26 238
15:10-18 23
17–18 9n.13, 29, 38, 41, 68, 72, 77, 110, 228, 228n.10, 110n.18
17:4 110
17:49 238
20:3, 34 238
21:5, 13 238
23:5 238
25:3 194

25:5 240
28:1 188, 193

2 Samuel 5, 9n.15, 14, 19n.2, 21, 28, 28n.39, 38, 38n.8, 39, 40, 41, 42, 43, 43n.21, 47, 49, 64, 65, 66n.49, 68, 68n.53, 71, 72, 76, 80n.1, 89n.25, 93, 101n.1, 111, 114n.28, 116, 145, 146, 175, 175n.10, 184, 185, 185n.2, 185n.3, 186, 186n.4, 186n.6, 186n.7, 187, 187n.9, 189, 189n.15, 190, 191, 193n.23, 195, 196, 197n.34, 198, 199, 200, 201, 204n.5, 212n.27, 214n.32, 228, 229, 229n.11, 234, 234n.3, 234n.4, 235, 236, 237, 240, 245, 261, 262, 276n.4, 277, 278n.10, 279n.13, 280n.15, 285, 289

1:1–11:1 185n.3
1:2 245
1:11 245
2:29–3:5 237
3:24 240
3:31 245
4:10–5:25 237
6 185n.2
6:2 192
6:13 194
7:23 178
8:2 238
8:7 191
10 235, 235n.13
10:6 178, 194
10:13–11:19 23
10:18–11:17 238
11 197n.37, 197n.38, 199n.41, 200n.42
11–24 233, 235, 239, 270, 277
11:2 185n.3
11:3 188, 188n.13, 198, 239
11:3, 6, 10-11, 11-12 241
11:4 239, 240
11:5 241
11:7 241
11:8 200
12:14 242
12:16 235n.13, 242
13:3 243
13:11b 239
13:13–14:3 237
13:21 191, 243
13:24 244
13:27 192, 245
13:31 245
13:32 243, 246
13:35, 36 243
13:37 247
13:39 247
14–15 28n.39, 47n.33, 88n.23, 104n.7, 145n.34, 177n.19, 262, 273, 281
14:7-30 262
14:7 263
14:8 242
14:11 263
14:17-30 238, 262
14:18 263
14:19 248, 263, 287
14:20 263
14:21 263
14:22 244, 263
14:23 263
14:25 263
14:26 263
14:26, 27, 30 262
14:27 263
14:29 265
14:30 177n.19, 265, 266
15:1 266
15:1-5 262
15:1-6 248, 250
15:2 235n.13, 248, 249, 250, 267
15:3 177n.19
15:4, 6, 12 262
15:6 250
15:12 267
17:3 238
17:12–18:9 237
18:2 250
18:3 250, 251
18:6 252
18:9 253

19:8(7) 253
20:18 238
22:33 254
23:1 254
23:1-7 116
23:3 255
23:20 238
23:37b 239
23:39 239
24:1-9 180
24:11-16 238
24:17 192, 256

1 Kings 5, 10n.20, 14, 19n.2, 21, 27, 27n.28, 27n.36, 28n.36, 38n.8, 68n.53, 80n.1, 89n.25, 101n.1, 175, 175n.10, 185n.3, 186n.4, 186n.7, 187n.9, 204n.5, 210n.24, 214n.32, 228n.9, 229, 240, 277, 278n.10, 279n.13
1:17 67n.51
2–12 80n.1
2:11 185n.3
2:12–21:29 185n.3
16:21 199
31:4 199

2 Kings 5, 9n.15, 10n.20, 14, 19n.2, 21, 27, 27n.28, 27n.36, 28n.36, 38n.8, 68n.53, 80n.1, 89n.25, 101n.1, 175, 175n.10, 185n.3, 186n.4, 186n.7, 187n.9, 204n.5, 210n.24, 214n.32, 228n.8, 229, 240, 277, 278n.10, 279n.13
10:23-35 80n.1, 175n.10

1 Chronicles 5, 27, 38n.8, 43n.22, 68n.53, 101n.1, 111, 145, 185n.4, 187n.9, 189, 190, 196, 200, 207, 207n.17, 208, 209, 279n.13
13:6 192
15:26 194
19:6-7 194
20:1 188
21:17 192, 256

2 Chronicles 27, 38n.8, 68n.53, 101n.1, 111, 145, 185n.4, 187n.9, 189, 190, 196, 200, 207, 207n.17, 208, 209, 279n.13

Ezra 27, 27n.29, 27n.31, 187n.9, 207n.17

Nehemiah 19, 27, 187n.9, 207n.17

Esther 14, 19, 26, 60, 187n.9, 208

Job 7, 27, 77, 123, 277
13:18-20, 23-27 139
13:24 140
13:26 140
13:27 140
14:13-18 139
14:14 140
14:15 140
14:16 140
14:17 140
38:23 170n.7

Psalms 7, 10, 10n.21, 19, 21, 22, 30, 30n.47, 60, 60n.28, 77, 91, 101n.1, 203, 217, 220, 221, 229, 229n.14, 277
18:33[17:33] 254
68:31[67:30] 170n.7
78:9[77:9] 170n.7
107:18[106:18] 172
134 117
136 116
146 116
146:1 116
149 116
150 30, 116

Proverbs 7, 15, 16, 16n.31, 27, 52, 77, 108

Qoheleth (Ecclesiastes) 27, 27n.29, 27n.31, 90, 115
9:18 170n.7

Song of Songs (Canticles) 10, 10n.22, 21, 60, 90, 115

Isaiah 6, 7, 8, 19, 21, 29, 52, 60, 61n.30, 77, 77n.73, 90, 92, 101n.1, 111, 116, 205n.8, 214n.32, 216, 277
1–12 77n.73
2:2-4 77
7:7 142
7:14 216
9–55 117
23 210n.24
23:1-2 179
23:1-14 29n.43
30:17 170

Jeremiah 6, 9n.14, 13, 14, 21, 29, 29n.44, 31, 38, 40, 40n.14, 41, 43, 49, 61n.30, 64, 69, 69n.55, 69n.56, 72, 76, 77, 83, 90, 93, 116, 116n.33, 146, 203, 204n.5, 208, 211, 214n.32, 229, 230, 230n.16
26:1 109n.16
27:1 [34:1] 109n.16
27:3, 12 109n.16
28:1 [34:2, 10; 35:1] 109n.16
33:8 111
46:27[26:27] 171
49:7-22 77

Lamentations 27
1:1-22 27n.30

Ezekiel 14, 21, 27, 27n.33, 60, 61n.30, 90, 208
3:1-3 23
34:26 168
34:27 173
37:26 171

Daniel 7, 7n.10, 7n.11, 9n.14, 14, 21, 22, 31, 31n.50, 38, 40, 41, 42, 43, 43n.23, 44, 47, 49, 60, 61, 61n.30, 64, 69, 70, 70n.58, 70n.59, 72, 72n.63, 73, 76, 77, 91, 92, 93, 95, 95n.43, 96, 96n.43, 97, 97n.49, 98, 104n.5, 149, 150, 152, 153, 153n.13, 162, 175, 175n.10, 203, 207n.17, 208, 208n.19, 210, 212, 214n.32, 230, 230n.17
1–12 71
1–6 31n.50, 41n.16, 70n.60, 97n.49, 230n.17
1–2 43, 71
1:1 153
1:1, 5 153
1:4 153
1:16-20 151
2:1 153
2:2 153
2:4 150, 153
2:5 153
2:9-11 151
2:19-33 150
2:19-49 151
2:20 154
2:22, 28 153
2:24 154
2:29, 30 153
2:30 154
2:32 153, 154
2:33-46 150
2:44 155
2:46 153
2:47 153
3 71
3:1-2 151
3:5 153
3:7 153
4–6 40, 41, 43, 49, 70, 71, 72, 77
4 71
4:8 41, 71
4:29-30 151
5–8 150
5 44, 71
5:1, 22, 29, 30 153
5:5-7 151
5:6 153, 154
5:7 153, 153n.12
5:7, 8, 12, 16, 17 160

5:8, 16, 17 153
5:10-12 41, 71
5:11 153
5:12-14 151
5:12 153, 153n.12, 156, 160, 161
5:13-16 41, 71
5:14-16 151
5:16 153
5:16-19 151
5:17 154, 155
5:17-23 41, 71
5:19-22 151
6 71, 151
6:8-22, 27-29 151
6:8, 25 153
6:9 156
6:11 156
6:13 153, 156
6:14 156
6:15 156
6:18 156
6:19 156
6:20 156
6:21 156
7–12 42, 43, 43n.24, 70n.60, 71, 175n.10, 208n.19, 230n.17
7:1 153
7:1-6, 11? 151
7:5-7 151
7:21 170n.7
7:25-28 151
7:26-28 151
8:1 150, 153
8:1-4 158
8:1-5 151, 157, 162n.27
8:1-8, 13-16 151
8:2 153
8:3 155, 157, 159, 179
8:3, 6 153
8:3, 6, 15 153
8:4 152n.11, 153, 154, 155, 157, 157n.17, 179
8:5 153, 154
8:7 156
8:8, 21 153
8:13 156
8:14 153, 156
8:15 156
9:2 153
9:12 153
9:21 153
9:23 153
9:27 153
10:1 153
10:3 153
10:3, 11, 19 153
10:7, 8 153
10:8, 16, 17 153
10:16-20 151
10:16 153
10:19 158n.18
11:6 153
11:10 153
11:13-16 151
11:15 153
11:16 153
11:16, 36 152n.11, 153
11:17 153
11:31 153
11:38 153
12:1 153
12:12 153

Hosea 61n.30, 114n.28, 146, 221
11:1 221

Joel
4:19 111

Amos 6, 77, 92, 116
6:8 169, 172, 177n.18
9:11-15 6
9:13 170

Obadiah
1–10 77

Jonah
1:14 111

Micah
4:1-4 77
7:4 56n.14

II. APOCRYPHA AND PSEUDEPIGRAPHA

Bel and the Dragon 70

1 Enoch 16, 19n.3, 22, 22n.17, 90

Epistle of Jeremiah 19n.3

2 Esdras 207n.17

Jubilees 16, 19n.3, 22, 60, 90
23:11 22n.17

Letter of Aristeas 205, 209

4 Maccabees 56n.14

Prayer of the Three Youths 70

Psalm 151 30, 116, 117, 229

Sirach/Ben Sira 16, 19n.3, 22, 90, 91, 148, 207

Susanna 70

Testament of Levi 150n.3

Testaments of the Twelve Patriarchs 150n.3

Tobit 16, 19n.3

III. DEAD SEA SCROLLS

CD *(Cairo Damascus Document)*
10:8-10 22n.17
16:3-4 22n.17

1Q3 (paleoLeviticus[a]) 122, 122n.3

1Q3 (paleoLeviticus[b]) 122, 122n.3

1Q3 (paleoNumbers) 122

1QIsa[a] (Isaiah[a]) 8, 18n.1, 20, 47, 118, 119, 141

1QpHab *(Pesher on Habakkuk)* 18n.1

1QS *(Community Rule)* 21, 28n.39, 47n.33, 88n.23, 104n.7, 112, 141, 142, 145n.34, 177n.19, 273, 281n.18
1:1-3 21n.12

1QH *(Thanksgiving Hymns)* 30

1Q71 (Daniel[a]) 31n.49, 69n.57, 97n.48, 149n.2, 150

1Q72 (Daniel[b]) 31n.49, 69n.57, 149n.2

2Q3 (Exodus[b]) 117, 118

2Q5 (paleoLeviticus) 122, 122n.3

2Q13 (Jeremiah) 40, 69

4Q1 (Genesis-Exodus[a]) 21n.7, 90, 25n.20, 125, 133

4Q2–4Q8, 4Q9–4Q10 (Gen[b-h, j-k]) 25n.20

4Q11 (paleoGen-Exod[l], *olim* paleoExod[l or n]) 21n.7, 90, 122, 124, 125, 126, 127, 127n.10, 128, 129, 132, 133, 134, 137, 141, 143, 144, 146

4Q12 (paleoGenesis[m]) 122, 130, 130n.13, 131, 141, 143, 144, 145, 146

4Q17 (Exod-Lev[f], *olim* 4QExod[f]) 21n.7, 143

4Q20 (Exodus[j]) 117, 118

4Q22 (paleoExod[m], *olim* 4QExod[a]) 9n.13, 10, 10n.16, 25, 25n.21, 38, 38n.10, 39, 39n.11, 40, 41, 42, 47, 48, 64, 64n.39, 64n.40, 64n.42, 65, 69, 71, 84, 84n.10, 84n.12, 102, 103, 109, 112, 121n.1, 122, 128, 128n.12, 129, 132, 133, 134, 134n.18, 135, 137, 141, 143, 144, 146, 178, 227, 228, 228n.7

4Q23 (Leviticus-Numbers[a]) 21n.7, 125

4Q24 (Leviticus[b]) 178

4Q25 (Leviticus[c]) 25n.23

4Q26 (Leviticus[d]) 26n.23, 141

4Q26b (Leviticus[g]) 117, 118

4Q27 (Numbers[b]) 9n.13, 10, 26, 26n.24, 228n.8

4Q28 (Deuteronomy[a]) 26n.25

4Q29 (Deuteronomy[c]) 26n.25

4Q31 (Deuteronomy[d]) 26n.25

4Q33 (Deuteronomy[f]) 26n.25

4Q34 (Deuteronomy[g]) 26n.25

4Q36 (Deuteronomy[i]) 26n.25

4Q37 (Deuteronomy[j]) 26n.26

4Q38 (Deuteronomy[k2]) 117, 118

4Q41 (Deuteronomy[n]) 26n.25, 26n.26

4Q45 (paleoDeuteronomy[r]) 122, 130, 136, 137, 138, 141, 143, 144, 146, 178

4Q46 (paleoDeut[s], *olim* 4QpaleoDeut[b]) 122, 136, 138, 139, 139n.21, 140, 142, 143, 144, 146

4Q47 (Joshua[a]) 10n.19, 27n.36, 28, 104, 104n.8, 105, 105n.11, 109, 228, 228n.9

4Q48 (Joshua[b]) 27n.36

4Q49 (Judges[a]) 10n.20, 27n.28, 80n.1, 105, 105n.12, 106, 109

4Q51 (Samuel[a]) 10, 10n.15, 28n.39, 43, 47, 47n.33, 66, 83, 104n.7, 106, 106n.13, 109, 110, 178, 185n.2, 185n.4, 186, 187, 187n.9, 188, 189, 189n.14, 190, 191, 192, 193, 194, 195, 196, 197, 198, 199, 200, 201, 229, 234n.1, 235, 236, 238, 238n.20, 239, 239n.20, 240, 241, 242, 243, 244, 245, 246, 247, 248, 249, 250, 251, 252, 253, 254, 255, 256, 257, 258, 259, 260, 261, 262, 263, 267, 269, 280, 281, 288

4Q52 (Samuel[b]) 28n.39, 47, 143, 235

4Q53 (Samuel[c]) 28n.39, 47, 47n.33, 88n.23, 112, 118, 119, 145, 145n.34, 177n.19, 190, 234n.1, 235, 236, 238, 248, 249, 250, 262, 263, 264, 265, 266, 267, 268, 269, 281n.18, 288

4Q54 (Kings) 27n.28, 229n.12

4Q55 (Isaiah[a]) 179

4Q57 (Isaiah[c]) 117, 118, 119, 145

4Q70 (Jeremiah[a]) 40, 43, 69, 143

4Q71 (Jeremiah[b]) 10, 29, 40, 43, 47, 69, 83, 229, 230n.16

4Q71a (Jeremiah[d]) 10, 69

4Q72 (Jeremiah[c]) 40, 43, 69

4Q73 (Ezekiel[a]) 27n.33

4Q74 (Ezekiel[b]) 27n.33

4Q76 (XII[a]) 143

4Q84 (Psalms[b]) 30n.47

4Q87 (Psalms[e]) 30

4Q101 (paleoJob[c], *olim* 4QpaleoJob[x]) 27n.34, 122, 130, 139, 140, 140n.23, 141, 143, 144, 146

4Q109 (Qohelet[a]) 27n.29, 143

4Q110 (Qohelet[b]) 27n.29

4Q112 (Daniel[a]) 31n.49, 70n.57, 88, 95, 96, 96n.43, 96n.44, 96n.46, 97, 98, 98n.50, 104n.5, 104n.7, 110n.19, 113n.26, 127n.11, 149n.2, 150, 150n.4, 150n.6, 151, 151n.8, 154, 154n.14, 155, 157, 157n.17, 158, 158n.18, 158n.19, 159, 159n.20, 159n.21, 160, 160n.23, 161, 162, 162n.27, 162n.28, 179, 230, 230n.17, 230n.18

4Q113 (Daniel[b]) 31n.49, 70n.57, 88, 95, 96, 96n.43, 96n.44, 96n.46, 97, 97n.48, 98, 98n.50, 104n.5, 104n.7, 127n.11, 145, 145n.34, 149n.2, 150, 150n.7, 151, 154, 155, 155n.15, 156, 157, 157n.17, 158, 158n.19, 159, 160, 160n.23, 160n.24, 161, 161n.26, 162, 162n.27, 162n.28, 179, 230, 230n.17, 230n.18

4Q114 (Daniel[c]) 31n.49, 70n.57, 96n.43, 145n.34, 149n.2, 230n.17

4Q115 (Daniel[d]) 70n.57, 141, 149n.2

4Q116 (Daniel[e]) 70n.57, 149n.2

4Q117 (Ezra) 27n.29

4Q118 (Chronicles) 27n.32

4Q119 (LXXLeviticus[a]) 165, 166, 166n.1, 167, 168, 169

4Q120 (papLXXLeviticus[b]) 165, 166, 208, 231

4Q121 (LXXNumbers) 165, 166, 166n.1, 167, 179, 181, 182, 183, 208, 231

4Q122 (LXXDeuteronomy) 165, 166, 166n.1, 208, 208n.18

4Q123 (paleoParaJoshua) 27, 122

4Q124 (paleoUnidentified) 122, 134

4Q125 (paleoUnidentified) 122

4Q126 (Unidentified gr) 165

4Q127 (papParaExodus gr) 165, 166, 166n.1

4Q171 (Psalms Pesher[a]) xvii, 22, 22n.15, 91n.29

4Q172? (Unidentified Pesher) 22, 22n.15, 91n.29

4Q173 (Psalms Pesher[b]) 22n.15, 91n.29

4Q174 (Florilegium) 21, 150
2:3 21n.13, 61n.30, 91n.27

4Q213 (Levi[a] ar) 150n.3

4Q242 (Prayer of Nabonidus) 7

4Q243-245 (pseudo-Daniel ar[a-c]) 7, 7n.10

4Q245(pseudo-Daniel[c]) 7n.10

4Q364 (Reworked Pentateuch[b]) 32n.51, 90

4Q365 (Reworked Pentateuch[c]) 32n.51, 90

4Q366 (Reworked Pentateuch[d]) 32n.51, 90

4Q367 (Reworked Pentateuch[e]) 32n.51, 90

4Q394–399 (MMT, *Halakhic Letter*) 22, 91

6Q1 (paleoGenesis) 122, 122n.3

6Q2 (paleoLeviticus) 122

6Q7 (papDaniel) 70n.57, 97n.48, 149n.2

7Q1 (papLXXExodus) 165, 166n.1, 208, 231, 231n.19

7Q2 (papEpistle of Jeremiah) 165, 166n.1

11Q1 (paleoLeviticus[a]) 122, 122n.3

11Q5 (Psalms[a]) 10n.21, 15, 18n.1, 22, 30, 115, 115n.31, 116, 117, 118, 119, 229, 229n.14
27:11 22n.16, 91n.29

8ḤevXII gr 12n.25, 18n.1, 125n.6, 166n.1, 231, 231n.20

Mur XII 125n.6

MasPs[b] 30, 229

IV. NEW TESTAMENT

Matthew
24:15 21n.14, 61n.30, 91n.27

Mark
13:14 21n.14, 61n.30, 91n.27

Luke
4:16-20 20
16:16, 29, 31 21n.11, 91
24:27 21n.11, 91
24:44 91

Acts
26:22 21n.11, 91
28:23 21n.11, 91

Galatians
6:16 56

2 Corinthians
6:16 173

V. HELLENISTIC JEWISH LITERATURE

Josephus, *Antiquities*
5 §20 28n.38, 105n.10, 228
5 §45-57 105n.10
5 §285 187
5 §347 187
6 §§68-69 187
6 §171 110n.17
6 §296 194
6 §325 188, 193

7 §78 192
7 §85 194
7 §§104-5 191
7 §121 194
7 §131 188, 198
7 §132 199
7 §171 199
7 §173 191
7 §174 192
7 §328 192
10 §§249, 266-67 61, 91n.27

Josephus, *Life*
§§417-418 184

VI. RABBINIC LITERATURE

Mishnah
Megilla 1:8 58
Megilla 2:1 58
Soperim 2:2 125
Yadayim 3:4 58
Yadayim 3:5 57
Yadayim 4:5 58
Yadayim 4:6 57

Babylonian Talmud
Baba Batra 14b 21n.10, 61, 61n.30, 90n.36, 91n.28, 123
Baba Batra 13b 125
Yoma 77a 61

Jerusalem Talmud
Megilla 1:9[8] 125

VII. CHRISTIAN LITERATURE

Eusebius
Historia Ecclesiastica 6.16.1 215n.35, 218n.52

Jerome
De Viris Illustribus 54 215n.36

Justin Martyr
Dialogue with Trypho 68.7 205n.8

Origen
Letter to Africanus 11 215n.37
Contra Celsum 1.34 216n.41, 216n.43